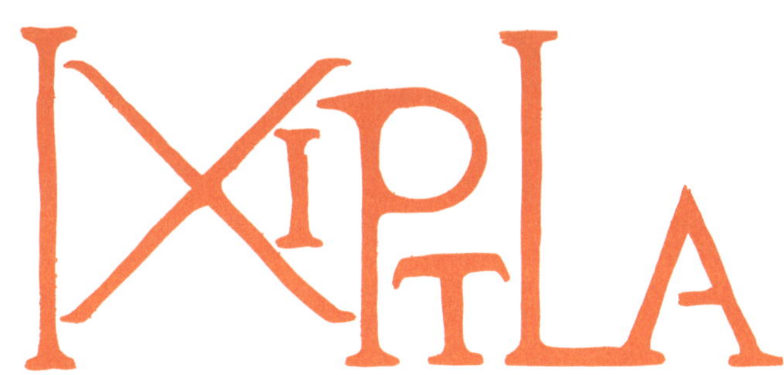

2023 VOLUME V

AMARANTUS

Ixiptla Volume V is published as part of the exhibition *Amarantus*, presented at:

MGKSiegen, Museum für Gegenwartskunst Siegen, Germany, January 29–August 8, 2021
Curated by Thomas Thiel

MUAC, Museo Universitario Arte Contemporáneo, Mexico City, Mexico, October 16, 2021–May 1, 2022
Curated by Catalina Lozano

Museo Artium, Vitoria-Gasteiz, Spain, November 5, 2021–March 13, 2022
Curated by Catalina Lozano

This publication was produced with the support of

MGKSiegen

and

Ministry of Culture and Science of the State of North Rhine-Westphalia

Published by:

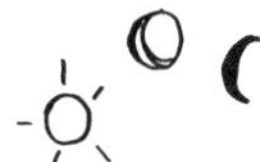

BOM
DIA
BOA
TARDE
BOA
NOITE

Rosa-Luxemburg-Strasse 17
10178 Berlin
Germany
www.bomdiabooks.de

ISBN 978-3-96436-046-5

The Deutsche Nationalbibliothek lists this publication in the Deutsche Nationalbiblio-graphie; detailed bibliographic data are available on the Internet at http://dnb.dnb.de

Ixiptla, Spring 2023, Vol. V, *Amarantus*

Editor: Mariana Castillo Deball
Contributors: Catalina Lozano, Tatiana Falcón, Barbara Mundy, Emiliano Monge, Isadora Hastings, Diana Magaloni, Hubert Matiúwàa, Yansnaya Elena, Jennifer Reynolds-Kaye
Design: Mariana Castillo Deball and Studio Manuel Raeder
Proofreading: Courtney Johnson
Edition: 800

Cover image: *She Bends to Catch a Feather of Herself, as She Falls*, 2022,
Custom handmade paper sheets, linocut unique prints
56×76 cm
Paper made by: Gangolf Ulbricht, Werkstatt für Papier, Berlin
Printing: Keystone Editions, Berlin

Image credits
Mariana Castillo Deball, p. 6, p. 10, p. 12–13. p. 16, p. 19, p. 78–79, p. 86–87, p. 88–89, p. 90–91, p. 112, p. 117, p. 130–131, p.132, p. 142, p. 196, p. 198–199, p. 204–207
© Staatsbibliothek zu Berlin, p. 8, p. 11
© Cooperación Comunitaria, p. 14, p. 126–127, p. 133, p.136–140
David Reiber Otálora, p.15
© Berlin Art Week 2022, Charlotte Landwehr p. 17
© Bristol Museums, Galleries & Archives/Bridgeman Images, p. 24, p. 30
Ramiro Chaves, p. 29, p. 31–39, p. 44–49, p. 52–58, p. 69–70, p. 119–120, p.144–149, p. 158–159, p. 166–168
Philipp Ottendörfer, p. 40–42, p. 44, p. 152–155
Documentation art, p. 43
Gunter Lepkowski, p. 45–49, p. 160–165
© Instituto Nacional de Antropología e Historia, INAH, Mexico, p. 60
Tatiana Falcón, p. 62
Luis Aguilar Marco, p. 63
© Newberry Library, Chicago, p. 82
Jean-Christophe Lett, p. 83
Estudio Michel Zabé, p. 84
© Benson Latin American Library, University of Texas at Austin, p. 85
Juan Esteban Fassio, p. 116
Manuel Raeder, p. 123
© Stiftung Humboldt Forum, p. 143
© Artium Museoa Quintas fotógrafos p. 150–151
Kristien Daem, p. 156–157
Robert Chase Heishman, p. 175, p. 179, p. 184
© The Trustees of the British Museum, Am, Maud, B72.35/Asset Number 1010457001., p. 200
© The Trustees of the British Museum, Am, Maud, B68.31/Asset Number 981818001., p. 201
© FAMSI, p. 203

Studio Castillo Deball
Remko Van der Auwera, Anna Szaflarski, David Reiber Otálora, Silvia Andrade

CONTENTS

7 *About the Book's Grid*
Mariana Castillo Deball, edited by Moosje M. Goosen

21 *The Only Way to Find a Larger Vision Is to Be Somewhere In Particular*
Catalina Lozano

30 IMAGES

58 *The Painter's Garden*
Tatiana Falcón, translated by Christopher Fraga

81 *Cartographic Presence in the Work of Mariana Castillo Deball*
Barbara Mundy

92 From *Tejer la Oscuridad / Weaving Darkness*
Emiliano Monge, translated by Jen Hofer

112 *Vùjá de: Beyond Books*
Mariana Castillo Deball, translated by Christopher Fraga

129 *The Double Life of the Azoyú Codex*
Mariana Castillo Deball & Isadora Hastings,
translated by Christopher Fraga

137 IMAGES

168 *The Identity of Images Past and Present*
Diana Magaloni, transcribed and edited by Aurora van Zoelen Cortés

177 *Mbo Xtá rídà Skin people*
Hubert Matiúwàa, translated by Elizabeth Anguamea

188 *A Dystopic Mesoamerica*
Yansnaya Elena, translated by Jen Hofer

194 *The Intermediaries in Between: Alfred Maudslay and Mariana Castillo Deball on Zoomorph P*
Jennifer Reynolds-Kaye

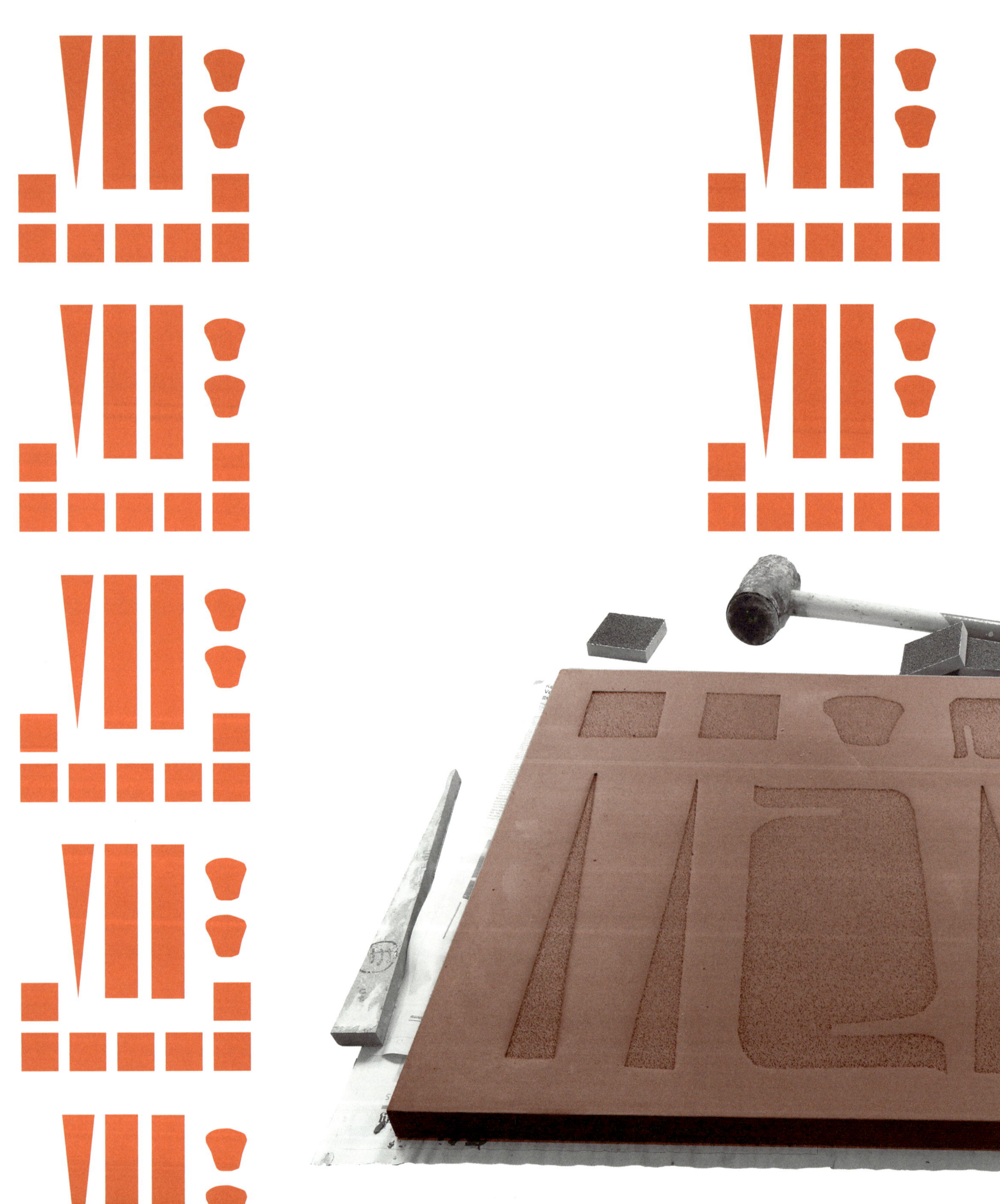

ABOUT THE BOOK'S GRID

MARIANA CASTILLO DEBALL

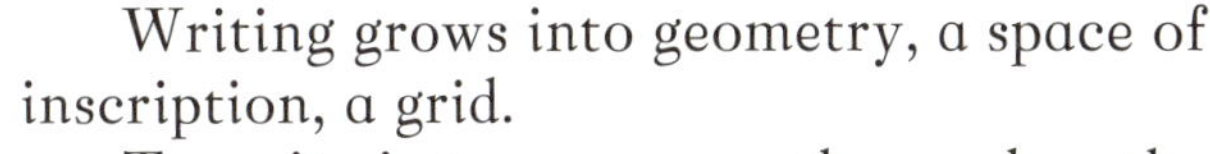

Writing grows into geometry, a space of inscription, a grid.

To write is to carve a path, as when the plowman cuts, lifts, and turns over soil, opening a furrow. The etymology of the word "page" has a rural origin: *pagine* in Latin refers to vines, planted next to each other and formed into a trellis, thus producing a grid, like columns of writing.

In early manuscripts, the letters were arranged without space between the words, which further suggests a surface strewn with letters.

Perhaps writing grew along with sedentary societies and agriculture, together with the delimitation of territories and the accounting of goods.

Writing as accounting is a material record of the control that the state establishes over its properties, inhabitants, and territories.

To grasp the word, to fix it in matter or matrix.

To carve it in wax, wood, clay, stone, paper, light.

A stone, a wall, a folded stripe, a scroll, a book.

The following text describes my relationship with a codex split between two territories. I have been living between these territories in recent years, often working with museum collections, following the stories of these *uncomfortable objects*. The Greek meaning of the word *amarantus* conveys the idea of a flower that never wilts. It is in a similar way that I understand the objects I follow, like flowers that never die, even when they live past and outside of their original context.

The *Códice Humboldt Fragmento 1 / Códice Azoyú Reverso 2* is a manuscript that records the tributes given from 1486 to 1522 by the kingdom of Tlachinollan, in the province of Tlapa, Guerrero, to the Mexica Empire. The codex ended up split between Mexico and Germany. One part, the *Códice Humboldt Fragmento 1* was taken to Europe by Alexander von Humboldt, who acquired it in Mexico City around **1803–1804**. This part is now at the National Library in Berlin. The other part, its homologue, the *Códice Azoyú Reverso 2*, was brought from the community of Azoyú in Guerrero to the library of the Museo Nacional de Antropología (MNA) in Mexico City in **1940**. Researchers have worked under the supposition that both fragments are pieces of a large indigenous pictorial codex whose original form would have contained at least **52** painted folios, measuring up to **15.5** meters in length.

Almost all the payments by the kingdom of Tlachinollan were made in gold—an abundant material in the region, even today—and in textiles. An envoy from the Mexica kingdom would come to collect the tribute four times a year. The codex includes records of what was paid, along with calendrical information, thus depicting the history of taxation between political powers. This has allowed the study of the tribute system of a province that had surrendered to the Triple Alliance, examining indigenous political economy on the eve of the Spanish Conquest.

The document's grid has five columns, and it is read from bottom to top, from right to left. The first two columns refer to the

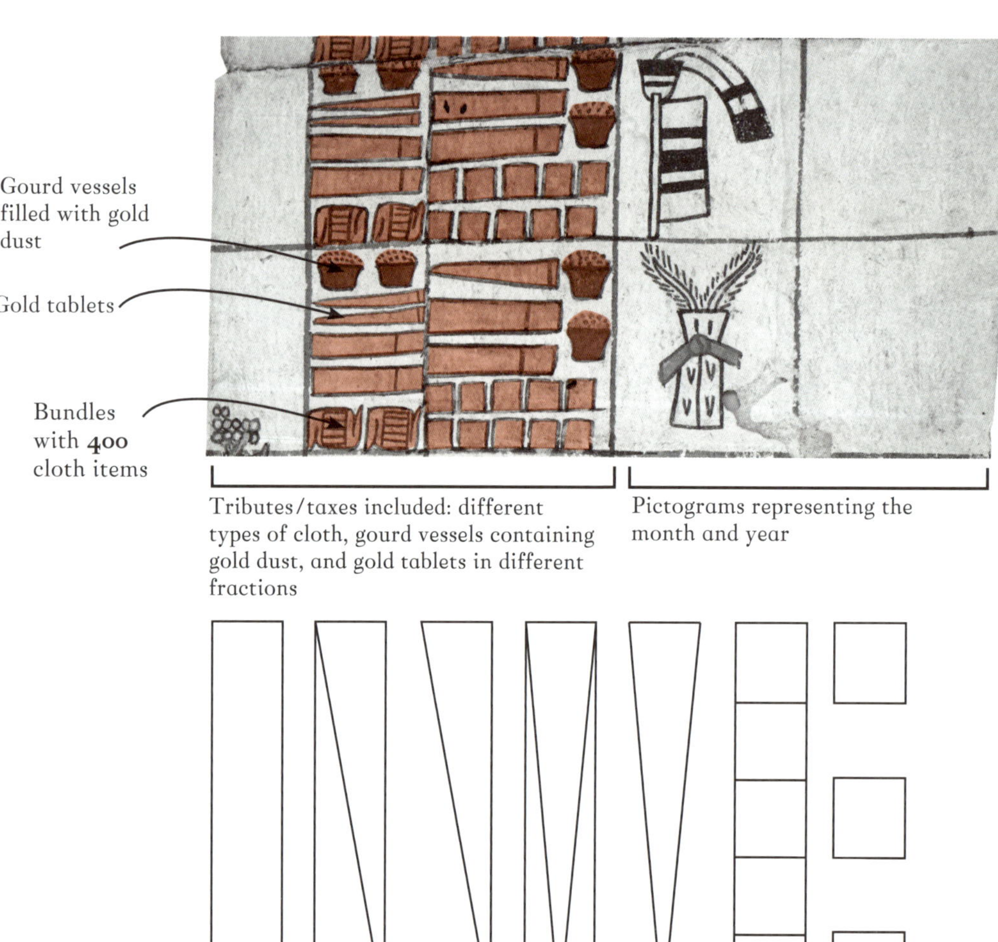

Folio **23**: Codex Humboldt Fragment **1** © Staatsbibliothek zu Berlin

The rectangular tablets are divided in fractions of triangles and squares, indicating the amount of gold payed in taxes.

calendrical information, and the remaining three columns depict the tribute. Gold is represented in fractions of geometrical shapes: squares, rectangles and triangles refer to divisions of golden sheets; gold dust is depicted with cups. Textiles are drawn with a symbol that also appears in other tribute codices.

I took this codex as a point of departure for a site-specific artwork, a ceramic mural for one of the Mesoamerican galleries of an ethnographic museum. As a reference I used the tributary registry's grid, transforming the codex, originally painted on amate paper, into fired clay. Mounted on the wall, the work became a skin for architecture.

This project kept me busy for the last eight years. It was always on my mind and in the making, but I didn't want to speak very much about it. I still prefer not to. It is the story of a project developed under frustrating circumstances, strange encounters, disappointments, and events that still feel stranger to me than fiction. I remain ambivalent about the whole process. Yet, I keep asking this question with curiosity: What can an artist do in an ethnographic museum? Can the artist leave a different mark, forge an alternative path, within the existing institutional grid established by the museum?

Imagine an open space, a square. When I entered this project I thought I entered a forum, a space where people gather to debate and exchange opinions. A space that, I also knew from the start, would be politically charged. The forum was a museum, an institution responsible for the ethnographic collections in Berlin, previously housed at the Ethnographic Museum in Dahlem. The collections stayed in Dahlem, while a new museum, a reconstruction of the earlier Berliner Schloss, was built on the location of the former Palast der Republik.

The forum is both the physical space and the people that assemble there. In Berlin, it is (it was) a building in the making, and a collective; a group of people I was in dialogue with over the years. During those years, I experienced several misunderstandings, and broken communications. I also experienced honest compromise and commitment. I experienced silences, meetings that never took place, and unspoken tensions. I thought that, by entering this forum, there would be space, a possibility for dialogue. I listened to the murmurs, the chatter, the voices that spoke in this forum, and I felt the hot breath of a beast on my neck. In some cases there was real interaction, but often it felt as if I was speaking in a hollow room, and the answers were echoes, distorted messages from those walls that were being built, walls that I saw rising slowly over the Berlin landscape.

Who takes responsibility for what is said in the forum; and what, or who, remains silent or unheard? Who is prepared or trained to enter the conversation? The museum was built on contradictions and voices that spoke, and still speak, in different tongues: the colonial past, the ethnographic collections, and the reconstruction of a royal castle, on top of the demolished Palast der Republik. It was an almost impossible endeavor to let the ethnographic collections speak, and to develop a novel way of display and dialogue with the people and places of origin, in an architecture that still represents colonial power.

Every forum has an architectural plan, and the museum took the blueprint of a fifteenth-century Schloss to organize the ethnographic collections. This new old building erased several layers of material history in order to re-erect an imperial palace in its former place. To create a forum modeled after a Schloss (literally, a lock) is a physical contradiction in terms. So now I no longer think of this place in terms of a forum.

In *The Construction of the Tower of Babel*, Juan Benet looks at the actual architecture

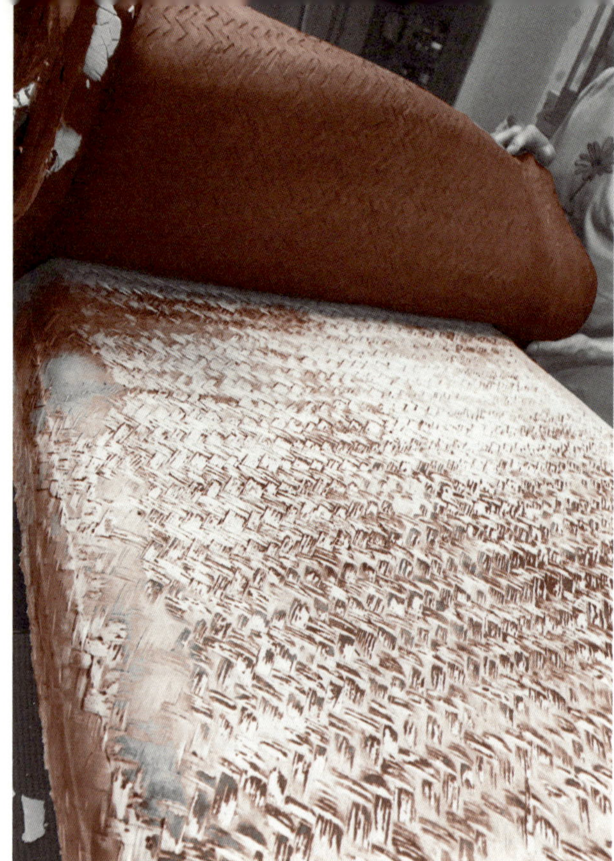

Petate benches fabrication process: the textured surface of a petate woven mat transferred into clay, in order to make a positive form out of plaster

of the Babel tower, as it was painted by Pieter Bruegel the Elder's 1563 painting *The Tower of Babel*—the first painting in European art history, he points out, to feature a building as a protagonist. Benet writes: "It is plain from Bruegel's painting that the abandonment of the tower's construction, caused by the jumble of languages the godhead has introduced to censure the profane enterprise, did not take place in a single day, and that even after a lack of understanding among its artisans had condemned it to failure, the work went on for a long time, perhaps even for a period as long as when linguistic unity had reigned."[1]

While the new building in Berlin was under construction, the institution kept changing its plans, its mission and purpose, and it was difficult to distinguish a clear direction. Berlin Babel is a kind of mirror double to the Babel tower, in the sense that in its case, its multiplicity of tongues were expected to inhabit one building, and through that architectural European encyclopedic gesture, amalgamate their voices—a project that is equally bound to fail—under the name of Alexander von Humboldt, a name that I have been avoiding throughout this text, in order to sidestep its power as a unifying symbol.

Benet draws an analogy between the tower and a warm-blooded body, envisioning society as an "amplified body (. . .) sharing the nature of man (. . .) but adopting the form of the first thing a man creates when he submits himself to its laws: a building."[2]

Babel means confusion, and now, when I think of this whole enterprise as a Babel construction, it is because I see it as an entity with political and cultural power that centralizes the energy of its interlocutors towards its own legitimation. I can describe my relation with this multi-tongued construction as one that leaves me tangled. For each tongue did speak differently, and corresponded to a different function. The architects, the museography team, the engineer, the logistics manager, the curator of the ethnographic collection, the friends of the museum, the director, and so on.

This is the list of characters.

And if I place them in a timeline, I see conflict, confusion, agreements, resolutions, silence. The main problem with Babel is that each of its multiple tongues is talking in a different direction, telling its own opinion. It wasn't always clear to me to whom—or to what—I was speaking.

1 Juan Benet, *The Construction of the Tower of Babel*, trans. Adrian Nathan West (Cambridge: Wakefield Press 2017), 36–37.

2 Benet, 12

ONE CODEX/TWO CODICES

I started working on the project in **2015**, by invitation from Viola König, who was the director of the Ethnographic Museum of Berlin in Dahlem at that time. When Viola König left the museum, I continued working in close collaboration with Maria Gaida, the curator of the Mesoamerican collections. In **2017** the project was cancelled without a clear explanation. It was argued that the piece no longer fit the plans of the new team that joined the institution. It seemed that my project was considered obsolete as it was part of the plans proposed by the former curatorial team. With the building still under construction, Babel cancelled the dialogue.

Through Isadora Hastings, I got acquainted with the poems and essays of Hubert Matiúwàa. His book of poems, *Skin People* (a selection of which is included in this publication), was a revelation to me, and it made me understand the inherent connection between the codex and the contemporary territory of Guerrero, Mexico. They share the same geopolitical grid.

Within the *Códice Humboldt Fragmento 1/ Códice Azoyú 2 Reverso*, the collection and delivery of the tribute is associated with four sacred holidays. Xipe Totec, the skin deity, is celebrated at the beginning of spring, in the calendar marker Tlacaxipehualiztli.

The original Xipe Totec ritual actually comes from the the Montaña de Guerrero,

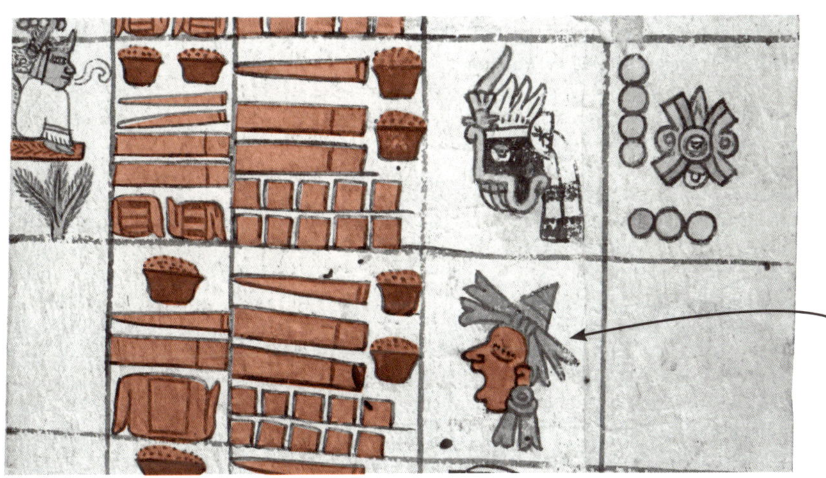

Calendar marker Tlacaxipehualiztli Folio **23**: Codex Humboldt Fragment 1 © Staatsbibliothek zu Berlin

Under these circumstances, with the project in Berlin canceled or on hold, I decided to realize the project elsewhere: in the Montaña de Guerrero, Mexico, in the vicinity of the region where the codex was written. I contacted the nonprofit organization Cooperación Comunitaria, with which I started working on the project in the province of Malinaltepec, Guerrero. For a deeper understanding of the project in Guerrero, please refer to the conversation with Isadora Hastings, founding member of Cooperación Comunitaria, included in this publication.

and it originates from the *mè'phàà* culture. Hubert Matiúwàa, who has been writing about and within the *mè'phàà* tongue, elaborates on the notion of skin people:

"The word *xtá*/skin is very important in *mè'phàà* culture, it is the ethical principle. The verb *estar/vivir* in Spanish, to be/to live, has the same root as *xtá* in its daily use. The word *xtá* is the foundation for naming and indicating the characteristics of the personality, it aligns being with acting: *Phú xtátsíska tàtá tsúkuè*/That man is a piece of lazy skin/ That man is very lazy."

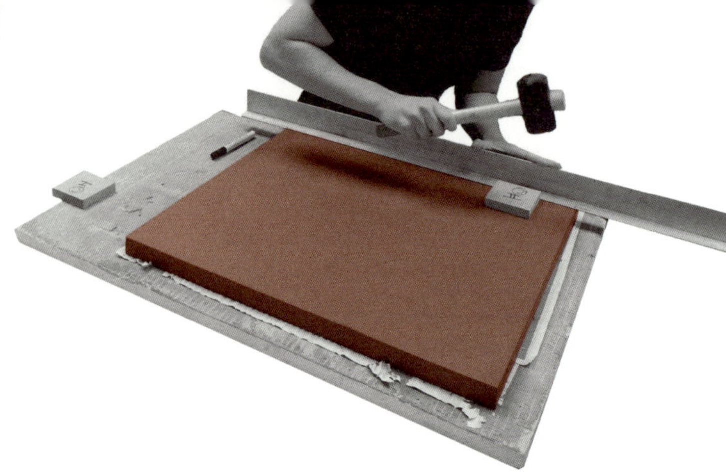

Process of embossing textured stamps into the clay tiles

The purpose of skin is to give cover to, and care for that of which it forms a part, like the relationship between flesh and skin. The root of the word *xtá*/skin is related to the words *xtáyaa*/stalk of a tree, *xtíya*/honeycomb/the clothing of water, *xtá ga'un*/ womb/skin that nourishes. All of these words relate to care: the stalk of the tree protects it from the open sky, the honeycomb protects the honey, the womb protects and nourishes the fetus. We, the *mè'phàà*, are the *mbo Xtá rídà*/skin people, this means we must care for the place where we live; we are the skin of the *numbaa*/earth-world.

In the Montaña de Guerrero, Mexico and in Sutiaba, Nicaragua, the *mè'phàà* defended this conception of life, first in the face of Náhuatl expansion, then in the face of Spanish colonization, and currently in the face of extraction by mining companies and territorial control by the criminal groups of the illegal drug trade."[3]

In **2019** I was contacted again by the museum in Berlin with a request to complete the artwork. In spite of all the frustrations caused over the years because of the many miscommunications with the Babel forum, I ended up accepting this renewed invitation, and the project materialized in both places, Berlin and Mexico—just as the original codex is now located in these two places.

The ceramic artwork in Berlin departs from the grid of the original codex. I worked on it based on digital reproductions and a printed facsimile that accompanies both fragments of the document in Mexico and in Berlin.[4] This facsimile also includes the gaps, the missing parts—lost, or, a more ideal scenario, still unfound. In my work I followed the sequence of the entire codex, including these sections that are presumed lost. The work ends with the start of the Spanish conquest, because there was a change of power, and the Mexicas did not turn up to collect the quarterly tribute.

I changed the materiality and scale of the codex, choosing fired clay as a material. I converted the painted symbols into clay writing. The clay tiles were cast in plaster molds. Once the clay achieved a leather consistency, stamps with the different symbols of the codex were imprinted on the surface. The symbols were cut out in wood and I added a textured surface made out of heavy grain sanding paper. This texture enhances the embossed stamp's relief.

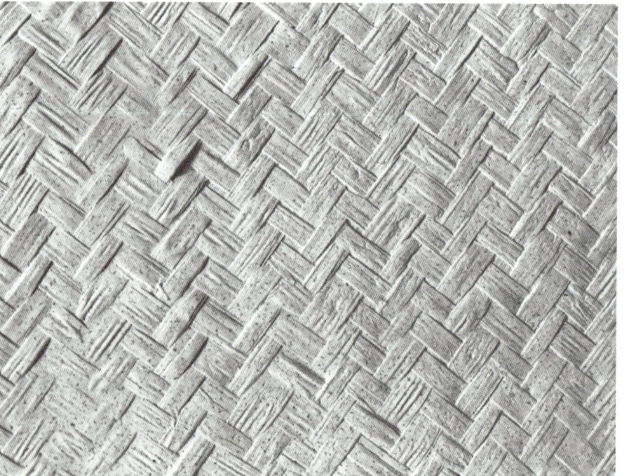

Petate benches

3 Hubert Matiúwàa, *Mbo Xtá rídà, Gente Piel, Skin People* (Chilpancingo de los Bravo, Guerrero: Gusanos de la memoria, Ícaro Ediciones, **2020**), **15–16**.

4 Gerardo Gutiérrez, Viola König, and Baltazar Brito, *Códice Humboldt Fragmento* ***1*** *Ms. amer.* ***2*** *y Códice Azoyú* ***2*** *Reverso, Nómina de tributos de Tlapa y su provincia al Imperio Mexicano* (México D.F., Berlin: CIESAS; Stiftung Preussischer Kulturbesitz, **2009**).

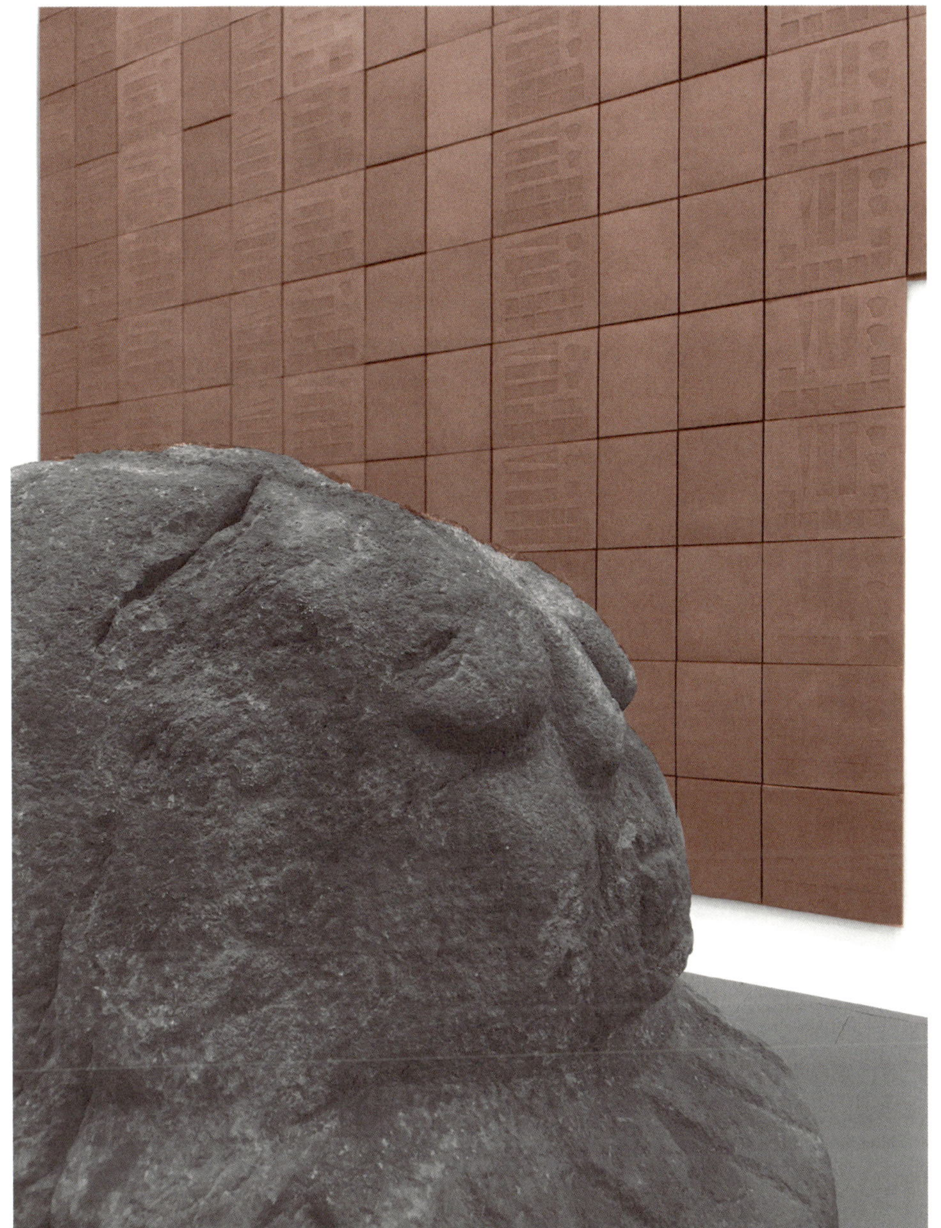

Back right: Mariana Castillo Deball, *Codex Azoyú 2/ Codex Humboldt Fragment 1 Reverso*, 2020, terracotta tile mural, 841 × 931 × 3 cm. Humboldt Forum, Berlin

Left front: Basalt sculpture in the form of a human figure. Regional style, 500 to 300 AC Guatemala, coastal lowlands. Collected by Adolf Bastian, acquired 1885, IV Ca 7196. Humboldt Forum, Berlin

Because each of the stamps is pressed by hand into the fresh clay surface, every single tile has its particular character. This adds to the natural behavior of clay, which still transforms in the drying and firing process, and makes each tile slightly different from the other, both in size and surface. The humble gestures of embossing and pressing are made by hand, but at the end the work is monumental in its dimensions and presence, covering a prominent wall. This list imprinted on clay speaks about time, material, and symbolic exchanges. Each of the 367 ceramic tiles that comprise the work were hung individually from the concrete wall, perforating its surface as a permeable grid.

This process of embossing and transferring surfaces from one material to another is also tangible in four sitting benches made to complement the ceramic mural. The codex painters, or *tlacuilos*, are often depicted sitting on a woven straw mat or petate. For the benches, I transferred the textured surface of a petate into clay, made a positive form out of plaster, afterward a silicone mold, and finally cast them in white concrete. These usually utilitarian objects, placed in the middle of the room so people can sit amidst the objects, are strange in their irregularity.

The exhibition room displays several volcanic stone monuments from Mesoamerica, and very present are the Cozumalhuapa stelas, originally from Guatemala. These stone monumental stelas show the scars of their extraction from the original site, the places where they were broken or cut out from the original buildings in order to be transported across the ocean, and to be exhibited inside a European museum.

Displayed on this new ground, I wanted to mirror the character of the volcanic stone into the floor, which is made with a dark gray color, integrating the room with the sediments and the materials of the pieces on display.

I conceived the ceramic mural, the black floor, and the petate benches as skin works that transfer the presence of a material and the hand that made it—a moment—from one materiality into another.

I think of the Babel Forum as a tribute building. For instance, the reconstructed facade of the former *Schloss* was done thanks to donors in exchange for prestige and presence in concrete and stone. Probably the most upsetting for me is to acknowledge that I also paid tribute to the beast; I waited and worked in silence for it, believing that, with my artistic practice, I could make a critical comment from within. The presence of my work echoes within Babel's walls. The grid, the structure, the fact that this work exists, all haunt me. Perhaps, in the fictional realm, I would undo my actions. But the fact is that, with the work, another material record is made.

In the Montaña de Guerrero, the work covers the outside facades of three buildings: the environmental hall at the UIEG, the community center in La Ciénaga, and the community center in Ojo de Agua, where it will further transform by the sun and other weather elements.

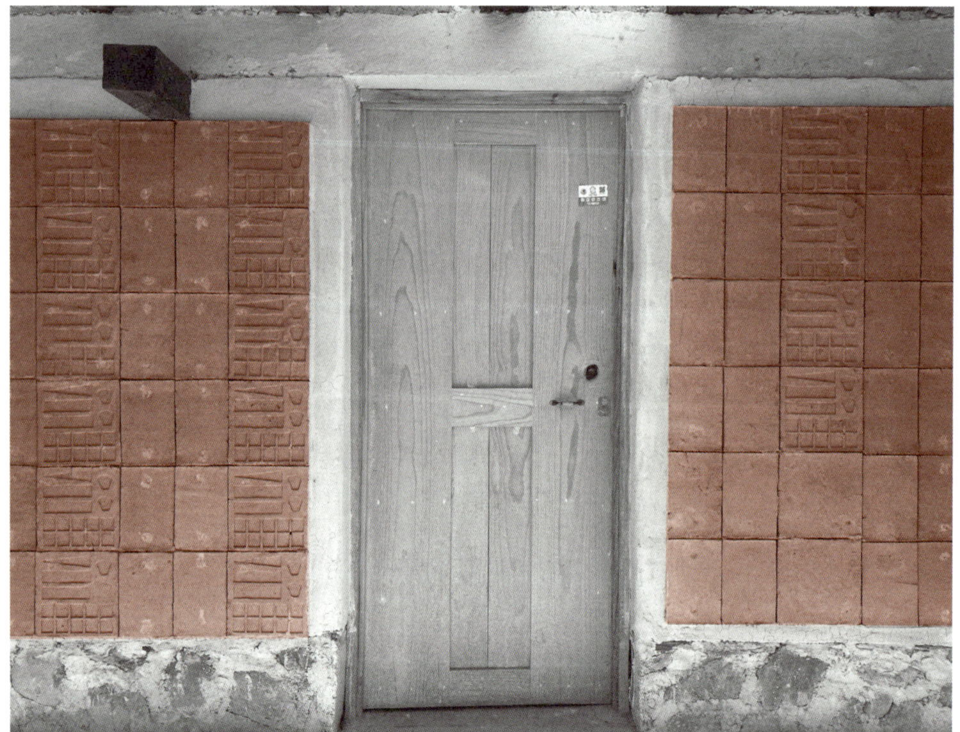

Codex Humboldt Fragment 1 / Codex Azoyú Reverso 2, **2020**, in Ojo de Agua, Malinaltepec, Guerrero, with Cooperación Comunitaria

AMARANTUS

Slave hands
Have meticulously worked
That little lump that you, remarkable
foreign consumer, suitably emperifoliated
while sitting in the open air,
throw to the bottom of the modern vessel
Slave hands
made possible that spill of saliva

Reinaldo Arenas

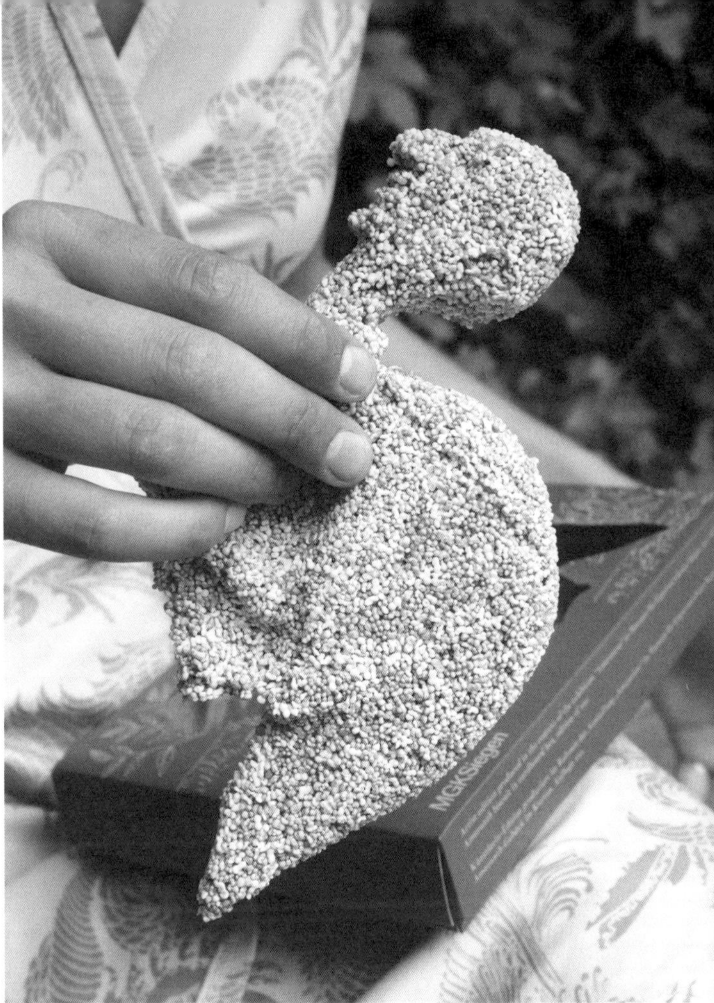

A chicken with a man's head, amaranth sweet

A chicken with a man's head, a dragon, a tiger and a lama escaped from the ornamental rim of the "Silver Baptismal Bowl of Siegen," becoming Amaranth figures. Freed from the cold metal surface, now they are soft, malleable, and edible.

The silver bowl was made in Peru around **1586**, and had travelled to Africa and Brazil in the context of economic exchange and the slave trade. It was brought to Europe by Johan Maurits, Prince of Nassau-Siegen, who in **1630** was appointed governor to Brazil by the Dutch West India Company. During his time as a governor, thousands of people were kidnapped from the west coast of Africa to Brazil. From there, goods such as sugar, Brazilwood, cochineal, coffee beans and tobacco were transported to Europe. In **1658**, Johan Maurits brought the silver bowl to the city of Siegen, as a gift for the Nikolaikirche.

In Greek, *amarantus* refers to an imaginary flower that never dies. Amaranth is also one of the most important foodstuffs in Mexico. Forbidden by the Spanish during colonial times due to its importance in indigenous ritualistic practices, the plant survived in subversive cultivation, and is still used to prepare *ixiptlahuan* or, *ixiptla*, anthropomorphic and zoomorphic figures that are ritually consumed. In Nahuatl *huautli*, the word for amaranth means "the smallest giver of life."

For the first iteration of the exhibition Amarantus in MGK Siegen, in **2021**, I made a series of amaranth sweets. Following the traditional recipe, I mixed amaranth seeds, called *huauhtli* in Nahautl, with brown sugar and, after kneading it into a dough, formed figures with it. I offered the sweets to the audience, who could eat them while listening to the story of the creatures that escaped the "Silver Baptismal Bowl of Siegen," becoming amaranth.

These soft edible sculptures that can be shared with a group of people while having a conversation opened up a space of hope, a way for me to continue working with and on ethnographic collections, and a kind of relationship I would like to create.

In the summer of 2022 I went to install the petate benches at the Babel Forum, and while I was walking around the collection display in the adjacent room, I saw a rattlesnake carved in volcanic stone, entangled on itself. This knotted snake, the caption reads,

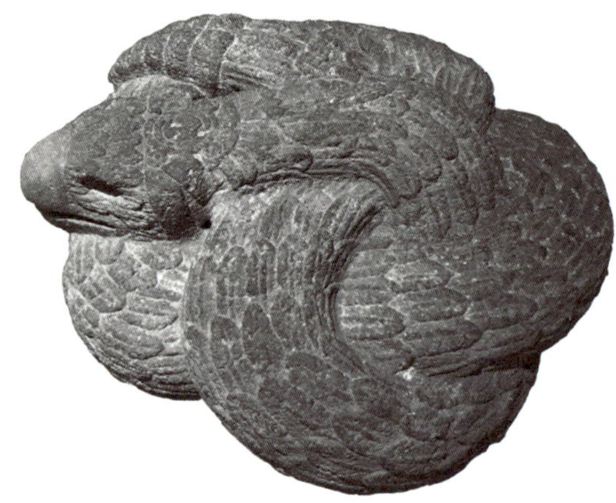

Cuauhcoatl, Aztec 1325–1521, stone sculpture, 80×80×25 cm, from Azcapotzalco, Mexico City

comes from the vicinity of Azcapotzalco, a borough of Mexico City.

In September 2022 I was invited by Paz Guevara to participate in *Crossings #2*, a day of sharing and actions initiated by Archive, Berlin.[5]

For this event, I made a small version of the Azcapotzalco knotted snake in clay, a negative silicone rubber mold, and cast it in a paste made from amaranth and brown sugar.

A series of sweet amaranth snakes resulted from this process, in different stages of completion. The substance is very difficult to handle, as the sugar needs to be at the right temperature before it caramelizes, but can hold together the amaranth grains. Some amaranth snakes were complete, while others came out of the mold already in a fragmented stage, similar to some objects at ethnographic museums.

During the performance, I shared the amaranth sweets with the attendees, and told them about the skin people as surface people. Surface as a sensitive skin, as an external organ that can feel, sweat, and react to the environment. Skin people produce soft objects such as the amaranth Ixiptlas.

That I shared with them and invited them to eat.

The event took place on Friday, September 16, 2022, which coincided with the official opening of the Berlin Babel Forum. After all those years I just couldn't go there; I didn't want to take part in its celebration. Instead, I shared the amaranth sweets in a different, social architecture, a soft one.

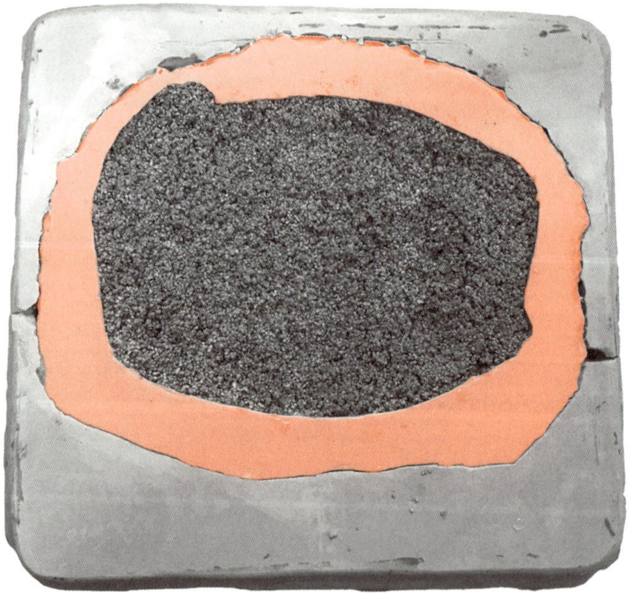

Small version of the Azcapotzalco knotted snake in clay, a negative silicone mold, and cast in a paste made from amaranth and brown sugar

5 *Crossings #2*. Friday, September 16, 2022, Archive, Berlin. Curated by Chiara Figone and Paz Guevara. With Aziza Ahmad, Ruth Buchanan, Mariana Castillo Deball, Gabriella Kolandra, Yaniya Lee, José Carlos Oscar, and Rebeca Pak.

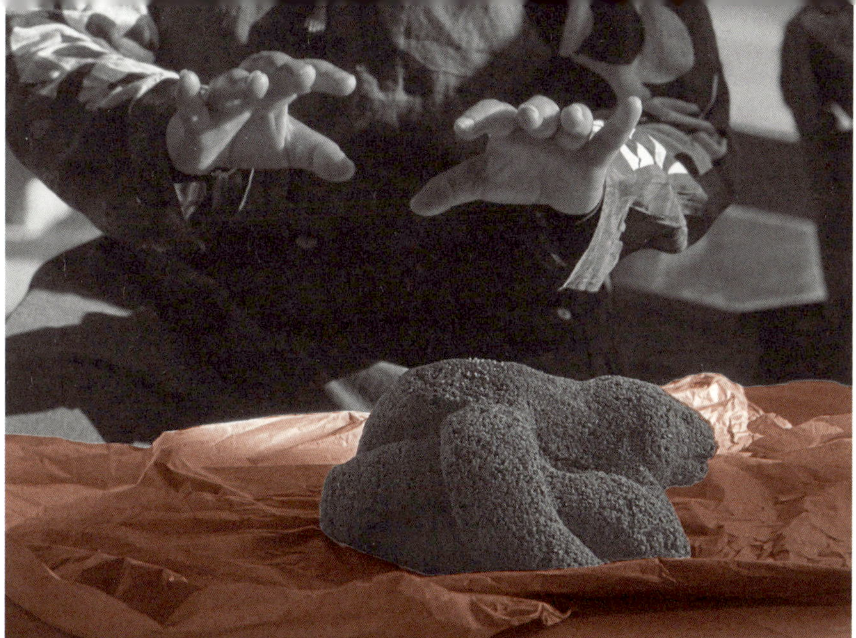

Crossings #2, *Amarantus Story and Eating Figures*, Friday, September **16**, **2022**, Archive, Berlin.

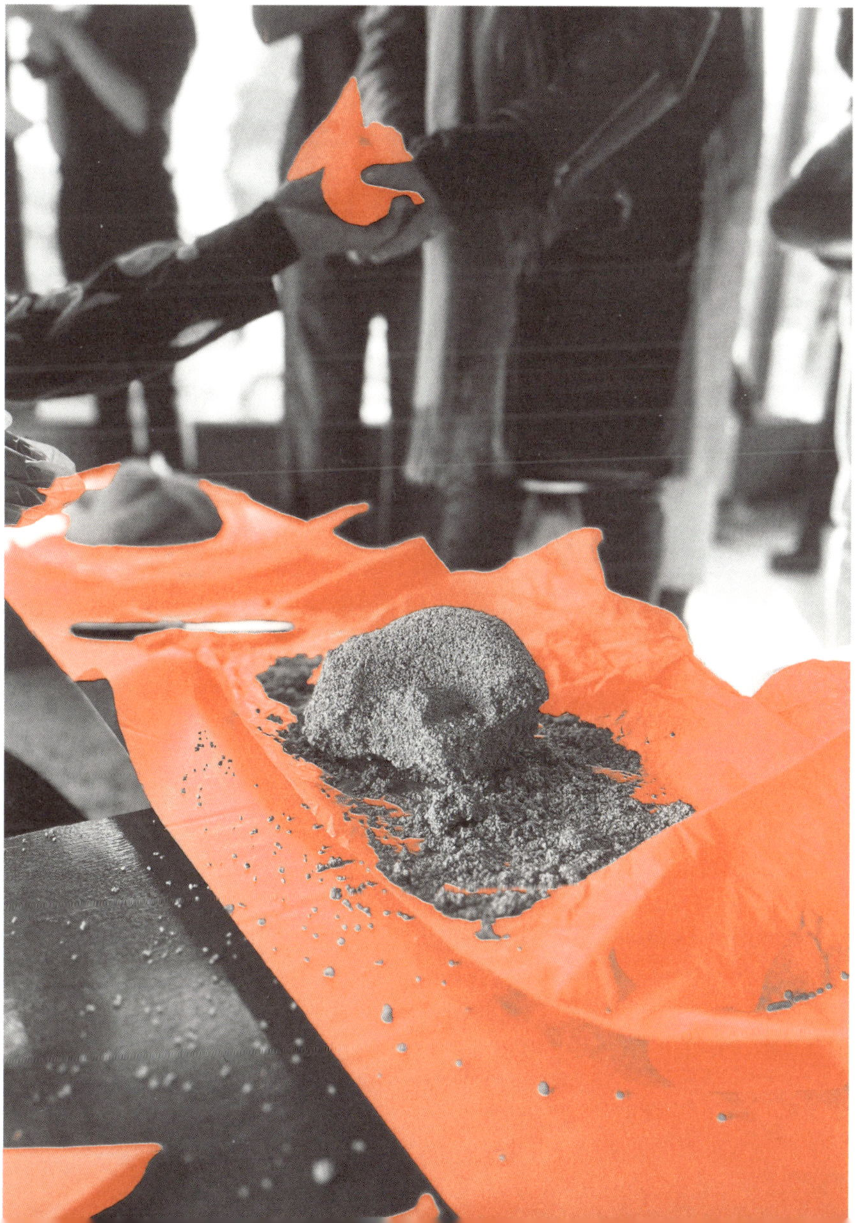

I am thinking about the body, and its relation to the format of a book, in proportion to the size of our open hands, and our open fingers flipping through the pages. Recently I learned to make paper from scratch, and I realized that the frames used to collect paper pulp to make paper sheets, are also related to body proportions, so that they can be carried by one person with both arms.

This is perhaps the beginning of the grid—the body.

This text has been written by hand on an A4 blank notebook, so the grid depends on my ability to write in a straight line. The first pages are very tight and ordered, but I realize that emotions unsteady my hand, change my writing.

I do not have an eraser, so I simply cross out certain parts, and make annotations for the future of this text, when it will be transcribed into my computer, by these very fingers. There, on the computer, all the words will suddenly have the potential to be replaced, reordered, and deleted, and the outcome of this text will be further dictated by the suggestions of digital dictionaries, thesauri, and search engines. The text in the computer exists in a parallel grid, the grid of infinite varieties and endless change. For this piece of writing, I did not want to have all these options from the start.

While writing this text I read the novel *Feral* by Gabriela Jauregui, which tells the story of four female friends. One of them, Eugenia, is an archaeologist who works near Teotihuacan, where she is excavating a tunnel in a community close to the main archaeological site. Every day she works on this narrow tunnel, assisted by a small robot that moves through the black hole taking pictures, so that the archaeologists can see if they should keep on excavating. In the tunnel, Eugenia finds hundreds of small objects, fragments of stone, bones and ceramics; often the shards disintegrate in the process of being excavated, and Eugenia gets nervous by all this ancient rubble falling down like stardust. Every day, she works from morning until late at night. Once she returns home, she makes notes in a field diary.

One of her diary entries reads: ". . . everything here calls me: the dust, the bones, the mud in pieces. Digging is a rather peculiar act and goes against all intuition and instinct. Our natural reflex is to bury. We are like a cross between ostriches and magpies. But what I do is the opposite. Marina, my favorite teacher, used to say that archaeology is the art of slow destruction. You destroy, codexing the very process of destruction, in order to find out what's underneath. But to find out, to preserve what you discover, you have to destroy what you discover. And to know what is that you destroy, you document its destruction. That's what I'm doing, documenting the destruction, maybe that's why I'm addressing you."[6]

Eugenia lives nearby with a local family, and she starts to attend community meetings concerning a mining company that is excavating without proper supervision. They are destroying the territory and the sacred sites. She is an outsider, an archaeologist, also excavating, but with a different purpose. She joins the inhabitants digging large holes in the middle of the night so the tractors of the mining company cannot access the field when they arrive in the early morning.

One day Eugenia is found dead inside of her excavation tunnel; it appears she has been murdered. Diana, Tunuen, and Saratoga, her close friends, travel to the site to speak with the family that hosted her, to collect her

6 Gabriela Jauregui, *Feral* (Ciudad de México: Editorial Sexto Piso, 2022), 44. Author's translation.

belongings and take care of her body. This group of friends forms the beginning of what becomes a larger community of women, taking care of each other, searching for their disappeared relatives, and trying to find fragments, bodies, and justice. Together they form a tissue, an organic mesh made out of solidarity, sweat, and tears.

"Below, we know that our archive is, first of all, a promise. The hand turned. It is also, after all, a dwelling, a task, a refuge. Our archive, which is also yours, is a wound and a possible antidote.

To make subjects of so many objects and codices we found, to weave their stories out of scraps, splinters, sawdust. We decided not to suppress or repress but to excavate, to open ourselves like uncovered mouths, to dilate ourselves, and to let their remains, traces, faces, speak through us."[7]

As Hubert Matiúwàa says in his introductory essay of *skin people*, the purpose of skin is to shelter, and care for that of which it forms a part, like the relationship between flesh and skin
paper and writing
fire and clay

In a fictional realm I imagine a body that breathes through skin
a protective layer that also picks up touch, temperature, light
the pores make a grid

I am interested in open architectures where breathing occurs.

7 Ibid. 26. Author's translation.

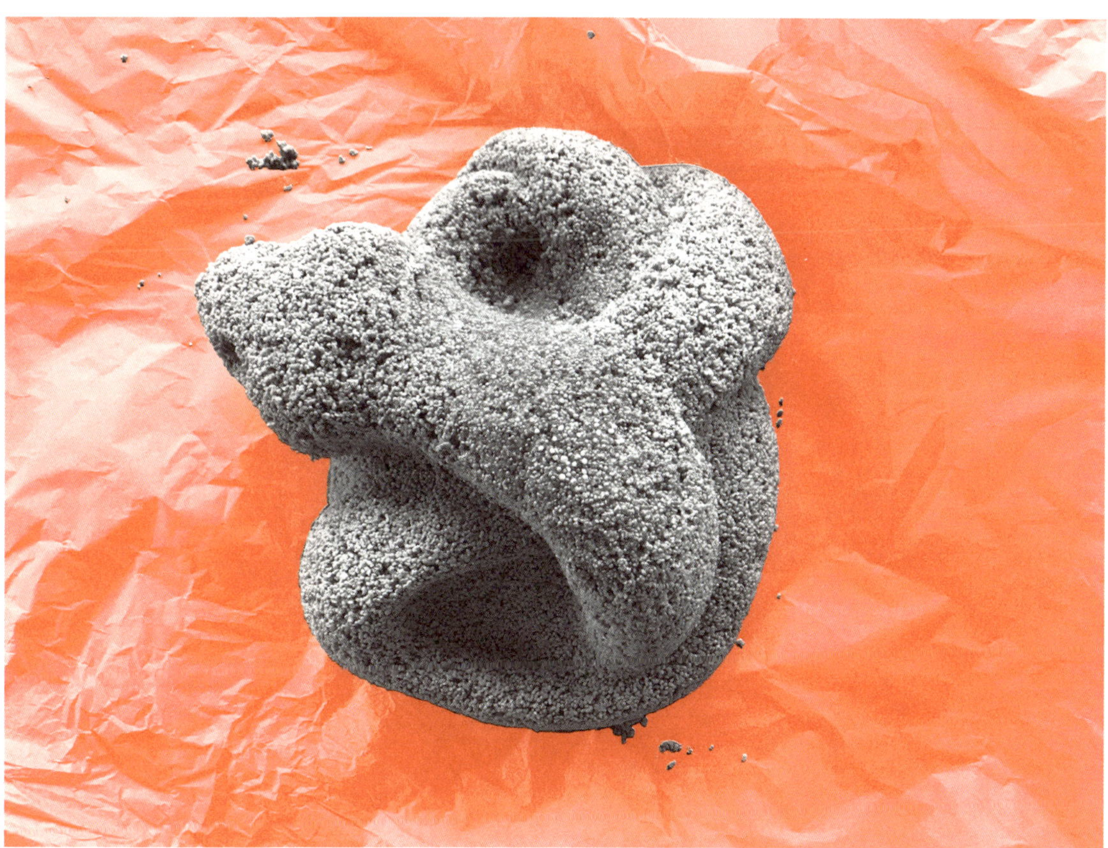

amaranth
edible figure
knotted snake

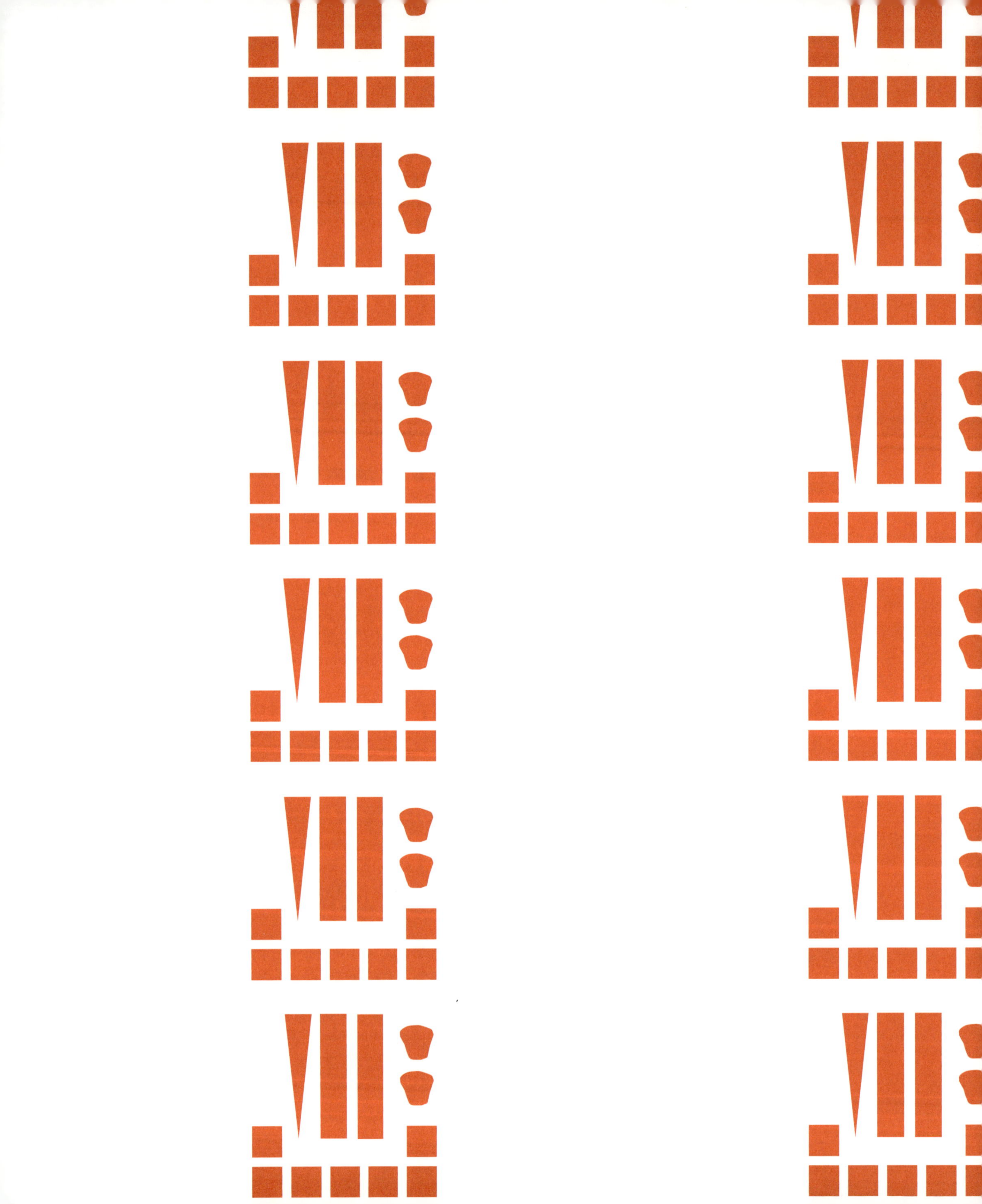

THE ONLY WAY TO FIND A LARGER VISION IS TO BE SOMEWHERE IN PARTICULAR*

CATALINA LOZANO

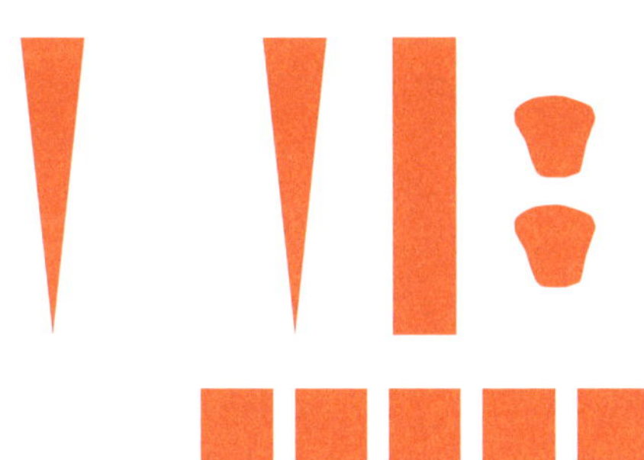

1.

My initial intention with this essay was to "excavate" the history of women who have practiced archaeology in Mexico; to dig down and, using the analogy of their own discipline, to uncover the ways in which their specific contributions have changed the course of the understanding of what we today call pre-Hispanic and Colonial Mexico. In the process I realized the importance of assuming the implications of considering the trade of archaeology from a feminist perspective,[1] but also to consider the role of women archaeologists as specific historical subjects.

Excavating is of course an efficacious and well known metaphor for historical research, detective-esque quests, and psychic revelations. It is indeed a field of knowledge that has developed methods for unearthing "material evidence" of the past, and in principle it allows us "to bring the edges of the formerly invisible into the field of human perception."[2] Archaeology, as a field of knowledge, is surrounded by a well established imagery in popular culture that supports an ideology of discovery strongly associated with colonial enterprises that remained largely unquestioned. In short, this is a masculinist, colonial imagery. We know as well that in this imagery, and outside of it too I believe, these objects sometimes come back as curses.

The idea of writing about women in archaeology comes from the intuition that, as with most professions, there must be a

* This title is taken from Donna Haraway, "Situated Knowledges: The Science Question in Feminism and the Privilege of Partial Perspective" in *Feminist Studies* 14, no. 3 (Autumn, 1988): 590.

1 I use the term "feminism" with an awareness that not all women's movements identify as such. I however aspire to include with the term all critiques of the modern, patriarchal episteme.

2 Matt Edgeworth, "The Clearing: Heidegger and Excavation," *Studio Michael Shanks* archeology lab blog, https://web.stanford.edu/group/archaeolog/cgi-bin/archaeolog/2006/09/01/the-clearing-heidegger-and-excavation/.

backlog in the historiography that acknowledges women's contributions. To a certain degree, it considers women who practiced archaeology from the late nineteenth century and into the twentieth as anomalous subjects in a microhistorical sense. And as such, it can reveal, or perhaps denaturalize, common assumptions about how archaeology was practiced, how their works related to those of their male counterparts, and also how their relatively subdued position facilitated experimental or unorthodox methodologies. But soon I realized that I am not equipped to speed things up; I lack the tools, knowledge, and "authority" to do it. I am a curator of contemporary art and my field of practice allows me to rummage in other disciplines, but rummaging is limited. So, my intention is not to account for every woman archaeologist who has not been properly recognized, but to think about why research carried out by women matters and speculate on how it allows us to think differently about the past.

As a political, theoretical support I lean on Donna Haraway's 1988 article "Situated Knowledges: The Science Question in Feminism and the Privilege of Partial Perspective." Haraway states that "feminists don't need a doctrine of objectivity that promises transcendence," that "we [feminists] don't want a theory of innocent powers to represent the world," and that "we also don't want to theorize the world."[3] She defends an embodied, situated science that renounces any universalizing objectivist ambition—in the Western, rational sense—and realizes that "objectivity turns out to be about particular and specific embodiment and definitely not about the false vision promising transcendence of all limits and responsibility. The moral is simple: only partial perspective promises objective vision."[4] This perspective, in my view, problematizes the notion of an univocal "human perspective"—the dominant category of humanity has already been codified by white men—that sees things that become visible as isolated objects, and questions fundamental divides such as that separating (allegedly rational) subjects from objects, and nature from culture.

In her 2011 exhibitions *Este desorden construido, autoriza geológicas sorpresas a la memoria más abandonada* and *Figures don't lie but liars can figure* Mariana Castillo Deball takes the myth of Narcissus and Echo to unfold a secondary narrative that for me resonates here. She states:

> *I thought of Narcissus as an exhibition space, and Echo as a cave. The practice of finding images in stains on the walls and rock formations is closer to the imaginative nature of Echo, who tries to repeat what Narcissus says, but her voice gets inevitably distorted, becoming something else all the time.*
>
> *On the opposite way, Narcissus is a repetition device, trying constantly to confirm his image, through his reflection on the water. The consequences of this gesture imply a complete denial of the outside world, in order to confirm the uniqueness of the self.*[5]

A similar analogy could be made, I think, between the Western, male-dominated scientific paradigm and what Haraway defines as a feminist science. It is not so much about men and women, but about ways of

3 Haraway, 579.

4 Haraway, 582–583.

5 Mariana Castillo Deball, interviewed by Tobias Ostrander in *Parergon* (Berlin: Hamburger Bahnhof—Museum für Gegenwart, 2014), 129.

approaching reality, and claiming authority over interpretations made of it. In the first, scientific knowledge confirms and asserts an image of the world in which a series of made-up separations—that function as a distorting filter through which one sees reality as if detached from one's body—have been naturalized. In the second, knowledge production is not separated from "nature"—or from one's body—but it is embedded in its web of relations. In Ovid's *Metamorphoses*, Narcissus, after falling in love with himself and realizing the image he loves is his own reflection, wishes vehemently that he could separate from his own body, while the nymph Echo, humiliated by Narcissus's rejection, blends herself with the trees and inhabits the caves, responding to the sounds that reach her. This wish to separate oneself from one's own body reproduces the aspiration of "leap[ing] out of the marked body and into a conquering gaze from nowhere."[6]

Two archaeologists, Margaret W. Conkey and Joan M. Gero, asserted that "feminists, among others, have argued that rationality, with its attendant notions of separability of subject and object, dispassionate objectivity, and neutral transcendence of personal states, is a mythical conflation that never obtains in actual scientific practice and, more significantly, itself represents a metapolitics of power relations."[7] By rejecting the normalization of human behavior as the behavior of men, they discuss the different implications of taking into account gender prespectives and feminist stanpoints in archaeology, showing how the male gaze and internalized patriarchal structures are embedded in the very foundations of archaeology and the need to decode and recode them.

I recently saw a film called "The Dig" (2021), based on a "real event." Months before the outbreak of World War II, a well-off English woman, Edith Pretty, hires excavator—not an archaeologist, and the film points at the socially constructed categories—Basil Brown, to unearth a series of mounds in her estate. She has an intuition about one of them that turns out to be correct: that one contains an important Anglo-Saxon burial. Soon, archaeologists from London arrive and displace the excavator with their entitlement and pedantic manners. The film, using very conventional cinematic and narrative resources—attempted romance, normalized gendered behavior, and predictable social breakthroughs—points at a series of divides: between men and women, between urban and rural, and between institutionally endorsed knowledge and self-taught trade, which is also a class divide. It is such narratives that both help and hamper my intention, because while the film straightforwardly illustrates certain tensions, it oversimplifies them. By relating intuition to the feminine, it elevates the value of the feminine, but it also confirms gender stereotypes; by exalting the value of women's work in the particular dig—that of Peggy Piggott—it makes them victims of an unchanged power structure.

And those power structures are built on the foundations of socially constructed, naturalized categories. For anthropologist Marisol de la Cadena, feminism decenters the inherently patriarchally centered logos[8]

6 Haraway, 581.

7 Margaret W. Conkey and Joan M. Gero, "Programme to Practice: Gender and Feminism in Archaeology," *Annual Review of Anthropology*, 26 (1997): 428. This ontology of separation creates categories that contaminate each other in reality. In archaeology this divide is particularly questionable, as human remains get objectified and fossils enter the realm of cultural objects.

8 Marisol de la Cadena, interviewed by Helene Risor and Joseph Feldman on the occasion of her keynote lecture at the Centro de Estudios Interculturales e

that I think is at the core of the issue of how scientific truth is constructed and legitimized. Conkey and Gero claim that feminist debates in archaeology engage in "the very nature of humankind: essentialism, inequality and power relationships, social categorization, political economy, rationality and ways of knowing, ideology, meaning and symbol making, materiality and agency."[9]

These debates are of course taken even further by Black and Indigenous archaeologists and anthropologists that seek to dismantle systematic bias and propose engaging research objectives linked to justice and historical reparation. For example, Maya-Kaqchikel anthropologist Aura Cumes recounts her disagreement with an archaeologist who translated a passage of the *Popol vuj* on the creation of the Ki'che' society equalling the term *winak* ("person") to man, applying a patriarchal, Western bias to a text that did not use a specific gender, and therefore assimilating it to its episteme.[10]

Looking at the history of women who practiced archaeology in Mexico—with their work considered peripheral to larger archaeological research enterprises—it is difficult not to be anachronistic, not to try to imprint an initial feminist standpoint onto their intentions. I have chosen to focus on the work of only four women whose work can help us reflect on how they partook in the construction of archaeological knowledge: two Mexican (Eulalia Guzmán Barrón and Beatriz Barba Ahuatzin), one British (Adela Breton), and one American (Merle Greene Robertson).[11]

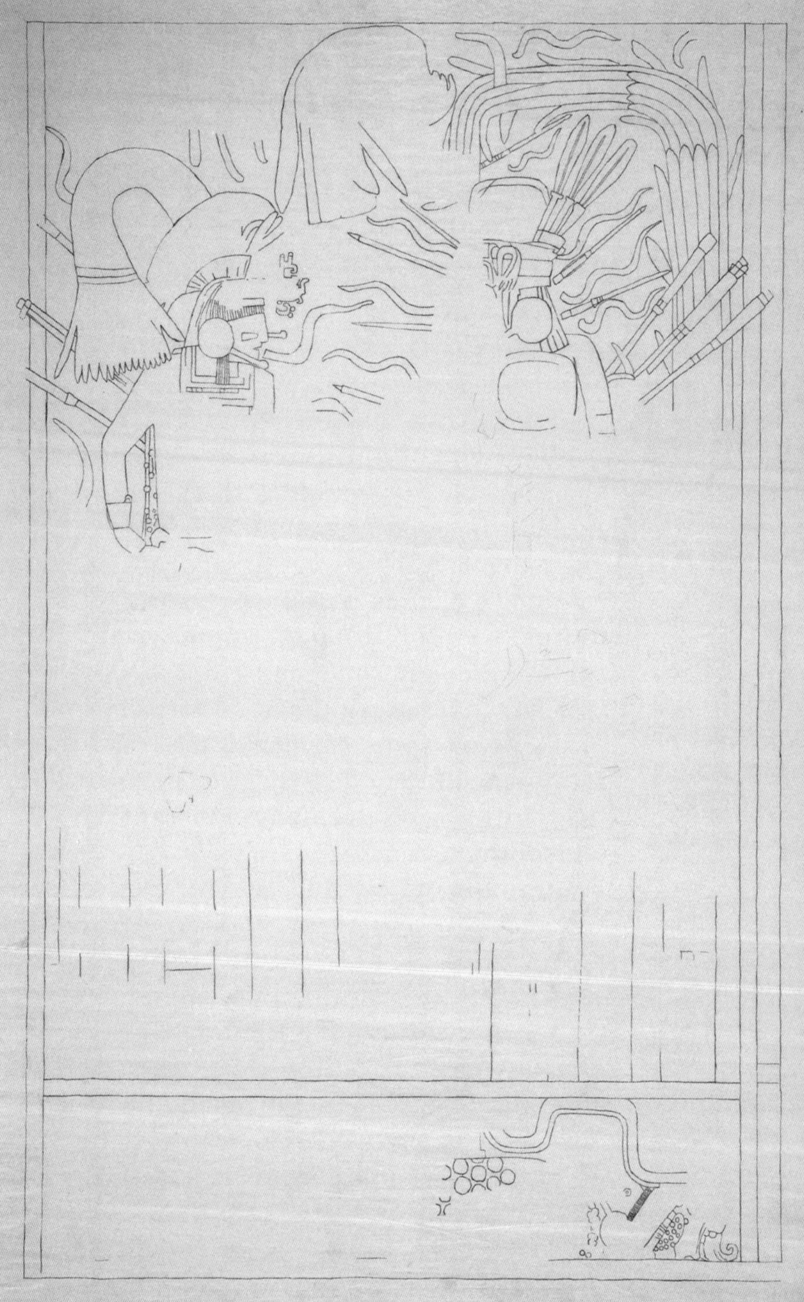

Indígenas, Chile, 2017: https://www.youtube.com/watch?v=ji4YdQORqOU&t=2s.

9 Conkey and Gero, 426.

10 Yásnaya Aguilar, "Entrevista con Aura Cumes: la dualidad complementaria y el *Popol vuj*. Patriarcado, capitalismo y despojo," *Revista de la Universidad de México* (April, 2021), https://www.revistadelauniversidad.mx/articles/8c6a441d-7b8a-4db5-a62f-98c71d32ae92/entrevista-con-aura-cumes-la-dualidad-complementaria-y-el-popol-vuj.

11 For a series of short biographies of women practicing archaeology in Mexico, see Paloma Estrada Muñoz, *Las mujeres en la arqueología mexicana (1876–2006) Logros, trabajos y aportes* (Editorial Académica Española, 2006).

2.
Adela Breton, (**1850–1923**), copy of a wall painting from East Wall, Upper Temple of the Jaguars, Chichen Itza, Mexico, red & black ink, Bristol Museum and Art Gallery, Bristol, UK

Adela Catherine Breton (**1849–1923**),[12] for instance, was an affluent British artist and archaeologist who travelled extensively during her lifetime and became involved in archaeology, attending several Congresses of Americanists. Her biography provides many opportunities to confirm her as an exception—an unmarried Victorian gentlewoman who ventured "alone" to many places around the world with a thirst for archaeological knowledge—and yet just as many opportunities to place her in a common narrative that needs to be carefully situated.

Breton travelled to Mexico several times between **1894** and **1908**, and her records of the murals in Teotihuacán, Acancéh, and Chichén Itzá have become very valuable testimonies of these paintings, whose uncoverings often brought about their deterioration or even destruction. She was encouraged by British archaeologist Alfred P. Maudslay to document the Upper Temple of the Jaguars in Chichén Itzá, which she did in her medium of choice, watercolor, "associated both with amateur lady painters and traveler artists who valued it for its portability."[13] Unlike previous, more general renditions of Chichén Itzá, and like Frederick Catherwood's, she "made full-size copies of the murals found at the Upper Temple [of the Jaguars] and wrote a paper about them . . . discussing the methods used in the original paintings and the identification of discrete styles which she argued may correspond to the hands of different artists."[14] Katherine Manthorne argues that, "unaware of what color choices signified to artists at Chichén Itzá, Breton instinctively realized that those choices were signifiers of meaning—both aesthetic and symbolic—and strived to reproduce them accurately."[15] Although the very idea of reproduction replicates scientific aspirations to truth-grabbing, I would like to apply a somewhat anachronistic notion to the fact that she sought to interpret color so vividly: I want to think that this approach amounts to showing a partial perspective, a care for detail and place that none of her contemporaries, including Mausdley, had shown. She was thorough and dedicated to her work and "dared" to review and rectify the findings of male counterparts such as those of Dr. Eduard Seler and Señor Antonio Peñafiel at another site, Xochicalco, about which she wrote a paper.

Although definitely renouncing the comfort of her life in Bath to travel through Mexico, where she slept in tents or inside the ruined temples, she enjoyed great privilege and the uncomfortable circumstances were a choice for her. An obituary of Adela Breton, written by E. N. Fallaize and published by the Royal Anthropological Institute of Great Britain and Ireland, reads: "In her early expeditions to the region [Mexico] she travelled on horseback over a country which more often than not was roadless, accompanied only by one Indian, who was devoted to her."[16] In one of her most commonly shown portraits in Mexico, Breton is sitting sidesaddle on a horse while a man standing next

12 For a detailed biography of Adela Breton, see Mary F. McVicker, *Adela Breton: A Victorian Artist Amid Mexico's Ruins* (Albuquerque: University of New Mexico Press, **2005**).

13 Catherine Manthorne, "Female Eyes On Latin America: Adela Breton (**1849–1923**). Yucatan Traveler & Recorder of the Mayan Ruins," *Colección Cisneros*, March **2021**, https://wayback.archive-it.org/4472/20220302062547/https://www.coleccioncisneros.org/editorial/featured/female-eyes-latin-america-adela-breton-1849-1923.

14 Manthorne.

15 Manthorne.

16 E. N. Fallaize, "Adela C. Breton," *Man*, **23** (Royal Anthropological Institute of Great Britain and Ireland, August **1923**), **126**.

to them is holding the reins. The "devoted Indian" was Pablo Solorio, Breton's guide in Mexico, whom she referred to as her "servant" and who travelled to Bath with her. According to Mary F. McVicker, "Pablo and Adela formed a close friendship. They were obviously compatible and liked and respected each other."[17] However, her privilege and affiliations stopped her from renouncing "to look upon the Mexican lands and peoples through an imperialist lens,"[18] which, in the end, was an imperialist, colonial one.

3.

Breton's thirteenth and last stay in Mexico was in 1908. The death of Pablo Solorio and the outbreak of the Mexican Revolution in 1910 would have probably stopped her from coming back. But that very same uprising made possible the emergence of women like Eulalia Guzmán Barrón (1890–1985), who is generally considered a foremother in the history of women archaeologists in Mexico. However, her biography is tarnished by murky circumstances that speak volumes about the power plays that have been enacted in the search for a Mexican identity. Guzmán was a schoolteacher and became an activist for the education and political rights of women, including suffrage, in the early twentieth century. She supported the Zapatistas during the Revolution and became interested in anthropology and archaeology; she assisted Alfonso Caso in the excavations in Monte Albán, Oaxaca, in 1932. Two years later, she was appointed Head of the Archaeology Department at the National Museum. The post-revolutionary years saw an emergence of a nationalist, essentialist Mexican State ideology seeking a unifying and unified Mexican identity; Eulalia Guzmán's work is very much inscribed in these efforts. She wrote her thesis on the "Essential characters of Ancient Mexican Art—Its Fundamental Meaning" following the idea of a Mexico whose integrity pre-dates colonization and is reconfirmed after the revolution. In 1949, two years after the discovery of the bones of Spanish conquistador Hernan Cortés, Eulalia Guzmán was commissioned to investigate the alleged existence of the burial of Cuauhtémoc in the small town of Ixcateopan, Guerrero. Guzmán and her team found archaeological evidence of the bones of Cuauhtémoc—according to some, she was under pressure from the government to do so—which served a nationalist surge that found in the image of Cuauhtémoc a revamped Aztec mirror in which to reflect the image of modern Mexico. Soon after her finding, a commission analyzing the bones established that they did not belong to Cuauhtémoc and that, furthermore, they actually belonged to at least four different individuals, including women and children.[19] The polemic surrounding the bones lasted several years and confronted different visions of Mexico, but in the end they were both profoundly patriarchal visions. Guzmán entrenched herself in the defense of the truthfulness of her discovery and was ridiculed by those who, claiming to be on the side of neutral scientific truth, accused her of tampering with it.

In 1955, writer Salvador Novo published a fictional dialogue between Guzmán and a young man she finds on her way to Ixcateopan. After a discussion between the two about the pertinence of her quest and the service it

17 McVicker, 46.

18 Manthorne.

19 For a detailed account of the incident, see Felícitas López Portillo T., "Hispanismo e indigenismo: la polémica de los (verdaderos) huesos de Cortés y Cuauhtémoc," *Revista de la Universidad de México* (December 1994), 22–29.

would do for the country, the young man asks her: "Aren't you afraid of finding him [Cuauhtémoc] anachronic, or so different from the image of him that has been forged that you would be forced to lie, just as you say have done the iconographists of his enemy Cortés?"[20] She insists nonetheless on the greatness of her mission and the success it will have:

> EULALIA: I'm sure. I will find them, even if I have to dig with my own nails. Even if they all deny it; even if they call me crazy and mock me.
>
> YOUNG MAN: Neither you, nor anyone. Because it would be like the certification of his painful death. It would be the same as likening him to Cortés, in a box, even an altar, no matter how splendid. And Cuauhtémoc has not died.
>
> EULALIA: How!
>
> YOUNG MAN: He will never die. The Spaniard didn't manage to kill him. Nor any foreigner. Cortés, Maximilian, Wilson . . . they all pass away, they die. Cuauhtémoc remains. He is exploited, robbed, whipped, cheated on, praised, humiliated, his treasures spoiled, he's forced to work his own lands. But he doesn't die. He is the land where you uselessly search for his remains, the air that caresses his black, straight hair, the water that pains his flowers, the dark flesh that knows to be quiet under the stars—and live on, deathless.
>
> EULALIA: What strange things you say! Who are you? What's your name?
>
> YOUNG MAN: You can call me, for instance—Cuauhtémoc.

Novo's drama shapes the idea that Cuauhtémoc is everywhere. He is the soul of the nation and doesn't need to be materialized in the recomposed body of a ruler. This was symptomatic of the post-revolutionary construction of an essentialized Mexican identity based on the supremacy of the Aztecs—a rhetoric that is enacted as well in the museological narrative of the Museum of Anthropology where all paths lead to the Mexica gallery.

4.

Women did not appear as specific subjects of history in Mexican archaeological research until later—and perhaps they have not appeared enough yet.[21] Mayanist archaeologists such as Tatiana Proskouriakoff (1909–1985) and Merle Greene Robertson (1913–2011) identified the fact that women were represented carrying bundles on several lintels at Yaxchilán, Chiapas, opening up a field of research. Like Breton, decades later, Merle Greene Robertson's work served to generate an archaeological record that has contributed to the understanding of Mayan history. She developed a "technique of recording monuments by means of rubbings, a method used by the ancient Chinese before newspapers were invented."[22] She

20 "¿No teme usted la decepción de hallarlo anacrónico, o tan diverso de la imagen que se ha forjado de él, que tenga que empezar a mentir, como dice usted que han mentido los iconógrafos de su enemigo Cortés?" Salvador Novo, "Eulalia lo encuentra," *Revista de la Universidad* (August 1955), 16. Author's translation.

21 Mexican magazine *Arqueología Mexicana* devoted one issue in 1998 to "Women in the Prehispanic World," but very few, if any, of the articles included take on a feminist stand. Only one of the authors is committed to gender archaeology that acknowledges women as subjects of history, but does not necessarily confront the androcentric bias of the field.

22 Merle Greene Robertson, *Never in Fear* (The Pre-Columbian Art Research Institute, 2006), 49.

arrived in Tikal as a tourist in **1961** while taking a break from her art studies in Guanajuato and became a lifelong Mayanist, recording more than one hundred sites in Guatemala and Mexico, working for American-funded research projects for four decades, until the **1990**s. She founded the Palenque Round Table (Mesa Redonda de Palenque), which would become one of the most important gatherings of American specialist knowledge in Mayan history.[23]

Also, like Breton, Greene arrived in male-dominated archaeology as an artist. Her rubbing technique created a very specific language that allowed her to build an impressive archive. After making watercolors and drawings, she came up with the idea of the rubbings. She fastened heavy rice paper to the stones and made it wet to then pound it into the stone. She used a silk-covered cotton ball (with sumi ink) or her thumbs (with oil paint) to rub the paper that would later be removed from the stone when completely dry. Greene developed a specific technique that responded to the materiality of the sites she studied, and invested herself in this colossal endeavor one stone at a time.

As an archaeologist, Greene did not seem to have been particularly interested in gender, but she did build a community that supported other women, like Linda Schele, in their professional development. She also nurtured a network of colleagues, both in the United States and in Mexico, with whom she grew professionally, and she was careful to acknowledge those who sustained her works locally. These practices of care, I am sure, greatly contributed to new ways of approaching the archaeological record, and also to the communities it belongs to.

In Chichén Itzá, Greene and her team "managed to do rubbings of the entire building [Lower Temple of the Jaguars], even the parts that Maudslay was not able to include." There they found "women warriors."[24] Greene's fleeting reference to the women warriors of Chichén Itzá makes me want to know more and to look for further information. She did not pay special attention to them, but her situated remark surely offers opportunities for musing. Although I did not find mentions of women warriors in Chichén Itzá—a Google search mainly yielded images of women standing next to pyramids—I did find articles about the political power Mayan elite women were able to hold both as rulers and warriors, mainly equalling it or comparing it to the power of men. But I crave evidence of other forms of power that perhaps remain invisible in the archaeological record and escape that "conquering gaze from nowhere" that Haraway talks about.

Jaguar Storage, **2014** and Tombstone with a jaguar bas-relief, **900–1200**, limestone, **108×92×32** cm, National Museum of Anthropology, Mexico City

5.

Beatriz Barba Ahuatzin (**1928–2021**) was the first woman to graduate as an archaeologist in Mexico, in **1955**, and led important campaigns for the labor rights of archaeologists who were underpaid. She initially trained as a schoolteacher and wrote a dissertation on the effects of inadequate furniture on the bodies of young children and their learning capabilities,[25] a topic that was considered irrelevant for many at the time but that showed her interest in societal issues and her commitment to the bettering of conditions of learning and research in the different fields she explored. She studied the high rate of female dropouts at the National School of

23 In **1995**, the National Institute of Anthropology and History took over the organization of the Mesa Redonda.

24 Robertson, **162**

25 The work was titled *Un problema escolar: el mobiliario* and was presented in **1953**.

Anthropology and History due to marriage at a time when women archaeologists' abilities were questioned on the basis of fitness. Barba founded the Mexican Association of Anthropologists and developed the project that would sustain the Heritage Law of **1972**. She was charged with the creation of the introductory gallery of the new Museo Nacional de Antropología between **1962** and **1964**, and then laid the foundations for the

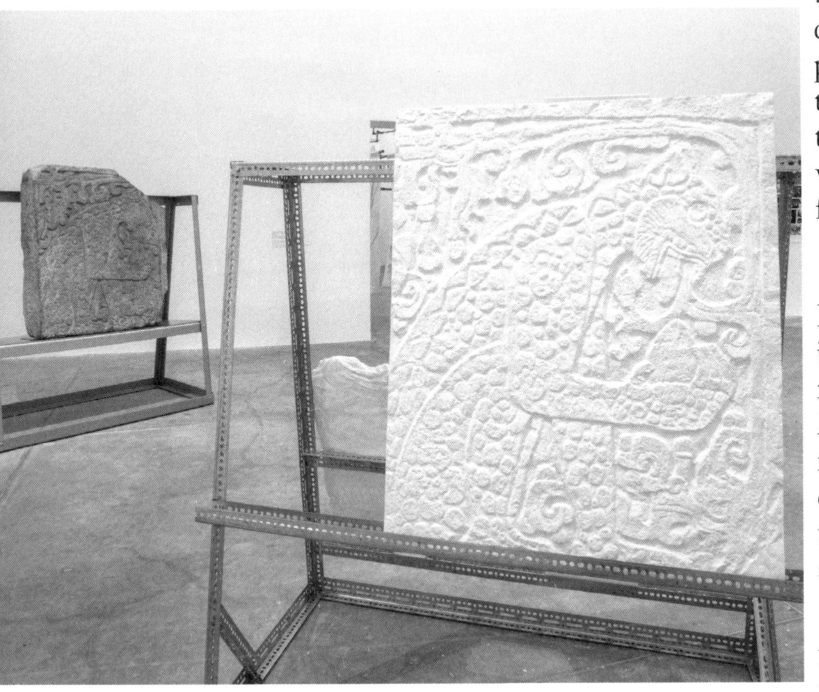

Museo Nacional de las Culturas.[26] As a teacher, archaeologist, ethnographer, museologist, and organizer, she was able to build a transversal approach to knowledge that seemed to connect her to the present in a very engaging way.

She wrote about the importance of the grandmother in the Ki'iche' society[27], stating the relevance of matrilineality in the Preclassic period and finding a way to grant power to women beyond the patriarchal understanding of political power. She recognized the importance of elder women—and the continuity of their role in the present—in bettering the relationship to the ancestors and accumulated knowledge. As an anthropologist, she also took interest in magic thought and practices but in pre-Cortesian times and contemporary in Mexico City, which had been so far considered a marginal field of study.

6.

I doubt that I have made a strong point, and in the process of writing this essay I have realized how far archaeology in and about Mexico is from assuming a radical transformation of the field in which women's lives can be accounted for without the androcentric bias that crushes their power and considers them naturally subdued.

In superficially mentioning the stories of Adela Breton, Merle Greene Robertson, and Beatriz Barba, I have not tried to show them as feminist foremothers, but rather to partially see their methodological approaches as "Echoist" practice. In the case of Eulalia Guzmán, I believe she got caught in the Narcissian temptation to create a distinct image of a fabricated reality called Mexico.

26 The INAH paid homage to Beatriz Barba in **1994**. On the occasion, her husband, the archaeologist Román Piña Chan, wrote a heartfelt biography of her. The memoirs of the event were published as *Homenaje a la doctora Beatriz Barba de Piña Chan* (Mexico: INAH, **1994**). On the occasion of her passing, her former student Víctor Joel Santos Ramírez wrote an obituary: "Beatriz Barba Ahuatzin (**1928–2021**), una maestra ejemplar In memoriam." https://1library.co/document/y4jevj9y-beatriz-barba-ahuatzin-maestra-ejemplar-in-memoriam.html

27 Beatriz Barba, "La importancia de la abuela en la sociedad Quiché, en un mito de transformación y en otro de eterno retorno," *Estudios del México Antiguo* (Mexico City: INAH, **1996**), **13–23**.

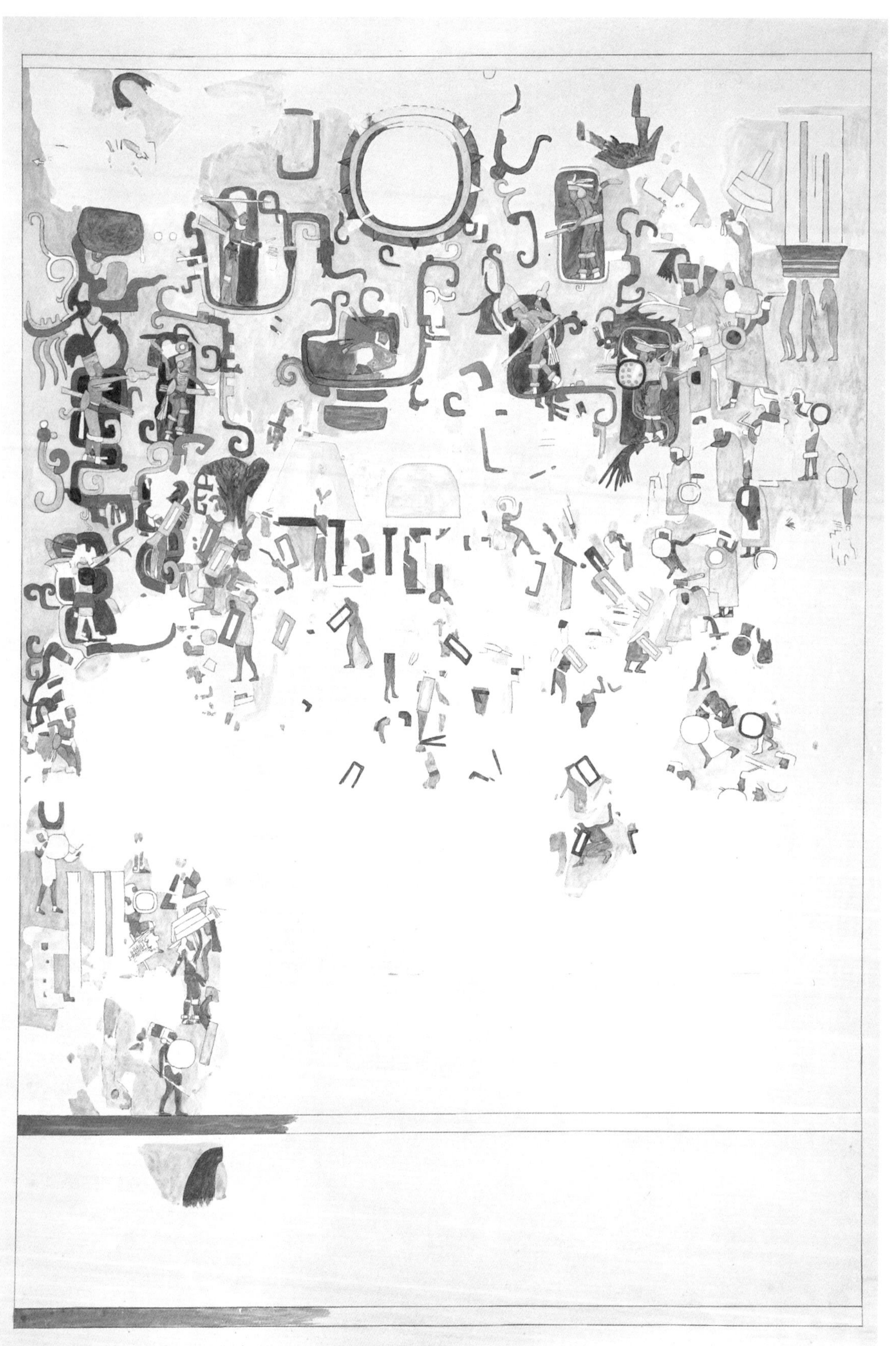

Adela Breton, (**1850–1923**), quarter-scale copy of a wall painting from the north wall, inner chamber, watercolor painting with red ink lines, Upper Temple of the Jaguars, Great Ball Court, Chichen Itza, Mexico

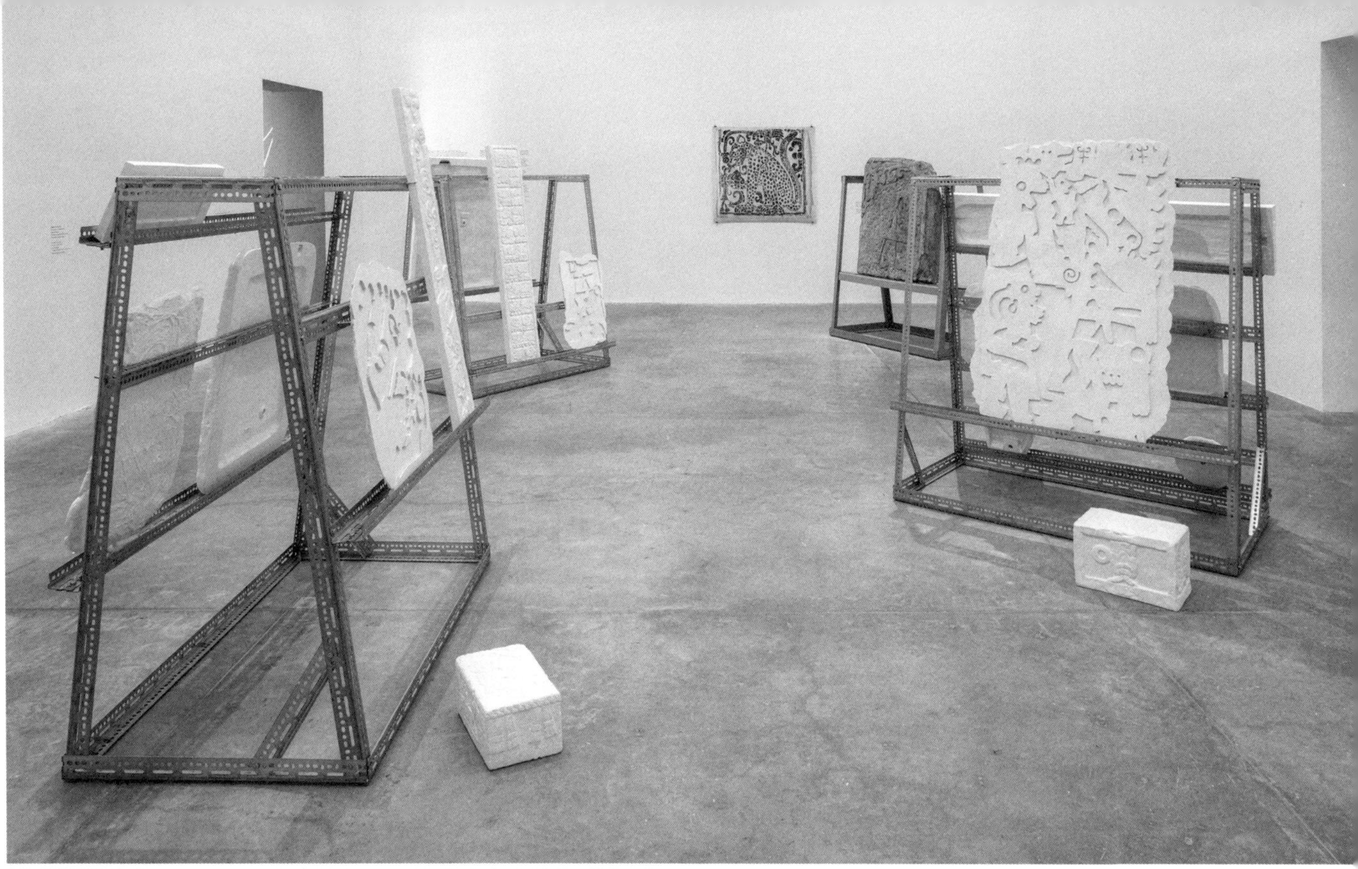

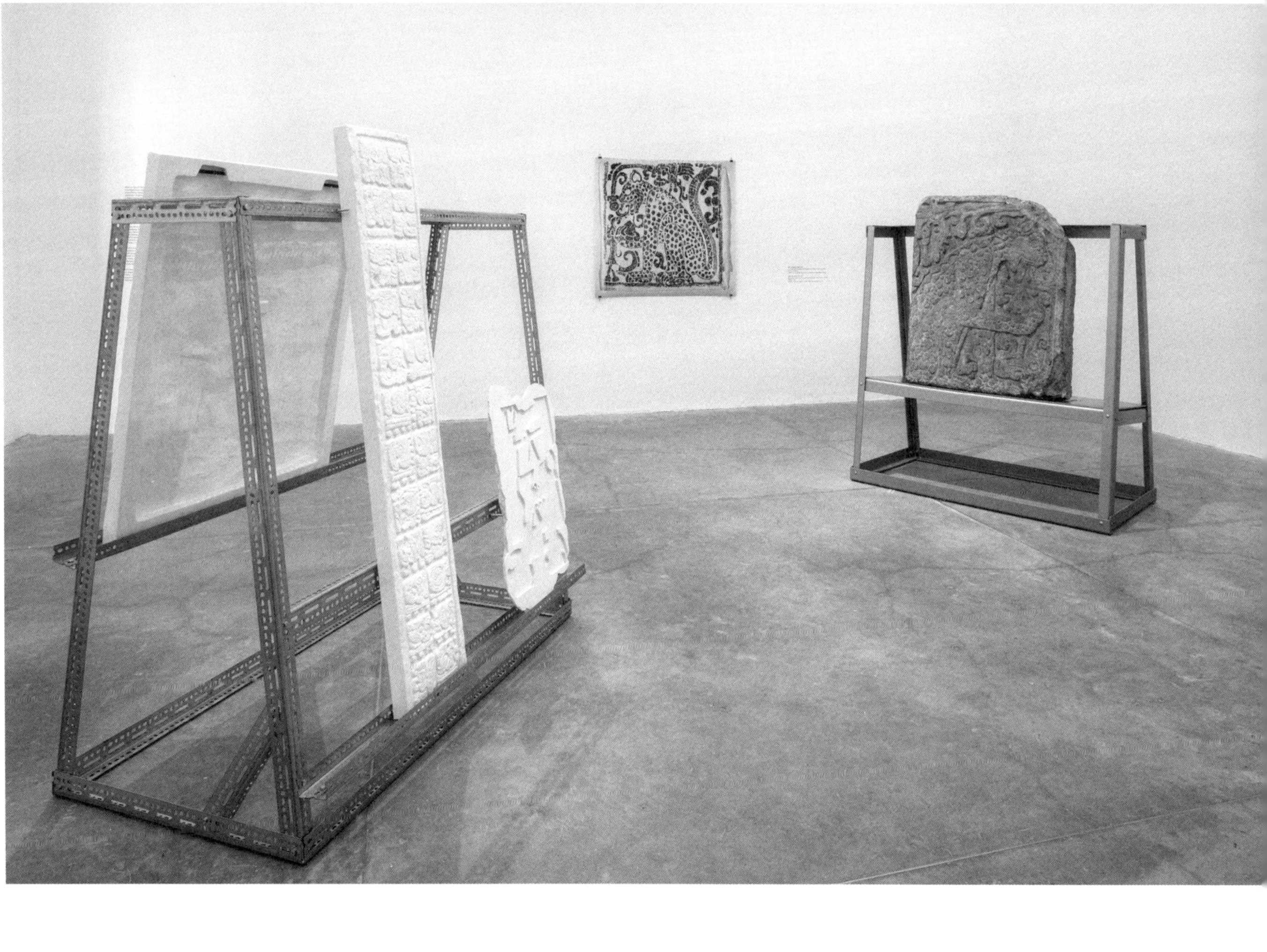

Installation views of the exhibition *Amarantus*, **2021**, MUAC, Mexico City

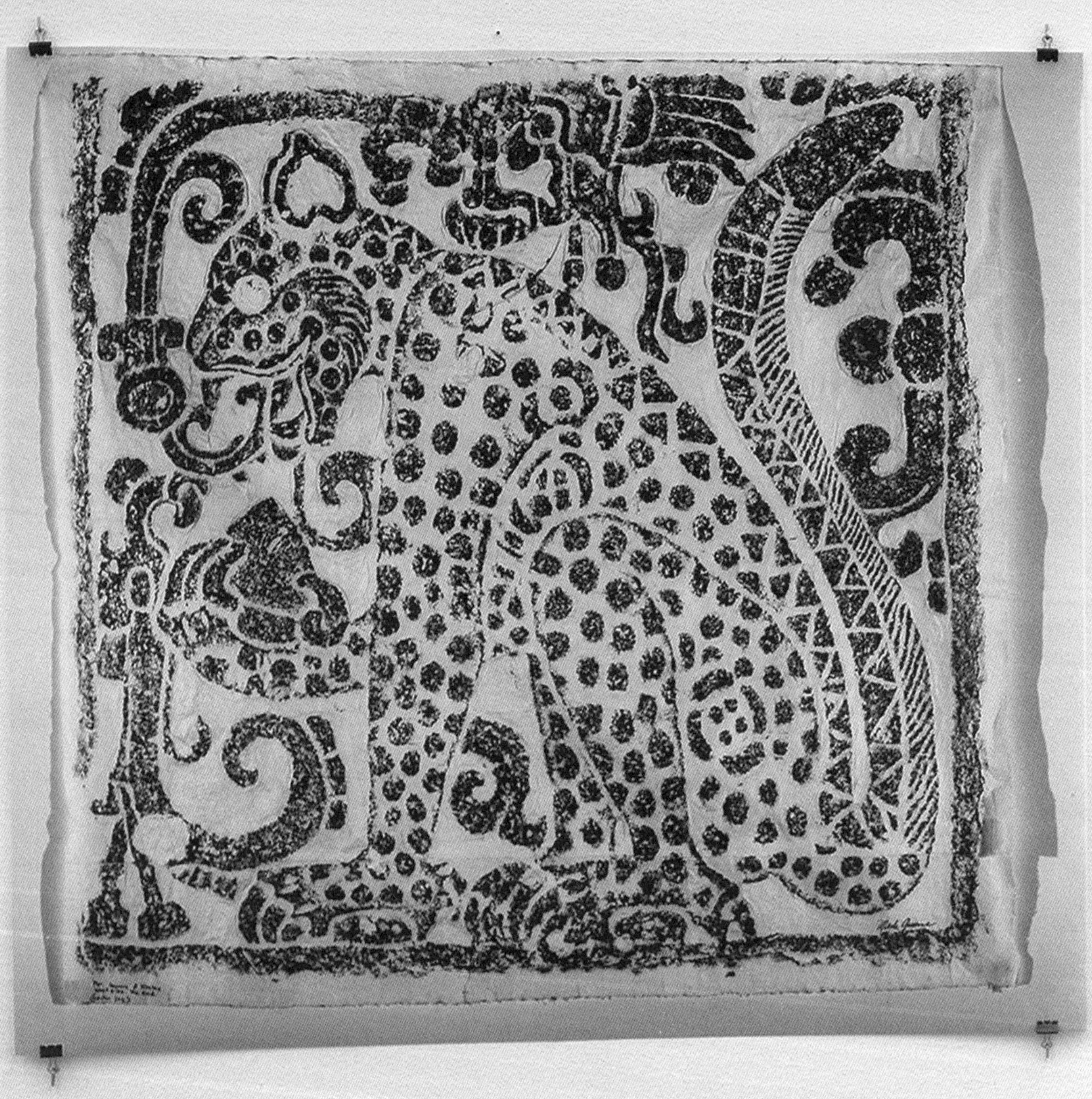

left: Reproduction of the rubbing from the Great Ballcourt at Chichen Itza, mediados del siglo, Merle Greene Robertson, The Latin American Library at Tulane University, Tulane

right: *Tombstone with a jaguar bas-relief* from the Gran Plaza, Chichén Itzá, **900–1200**, limestone, **108×92×32** cm, National Museum of Anthropology, Mexico City

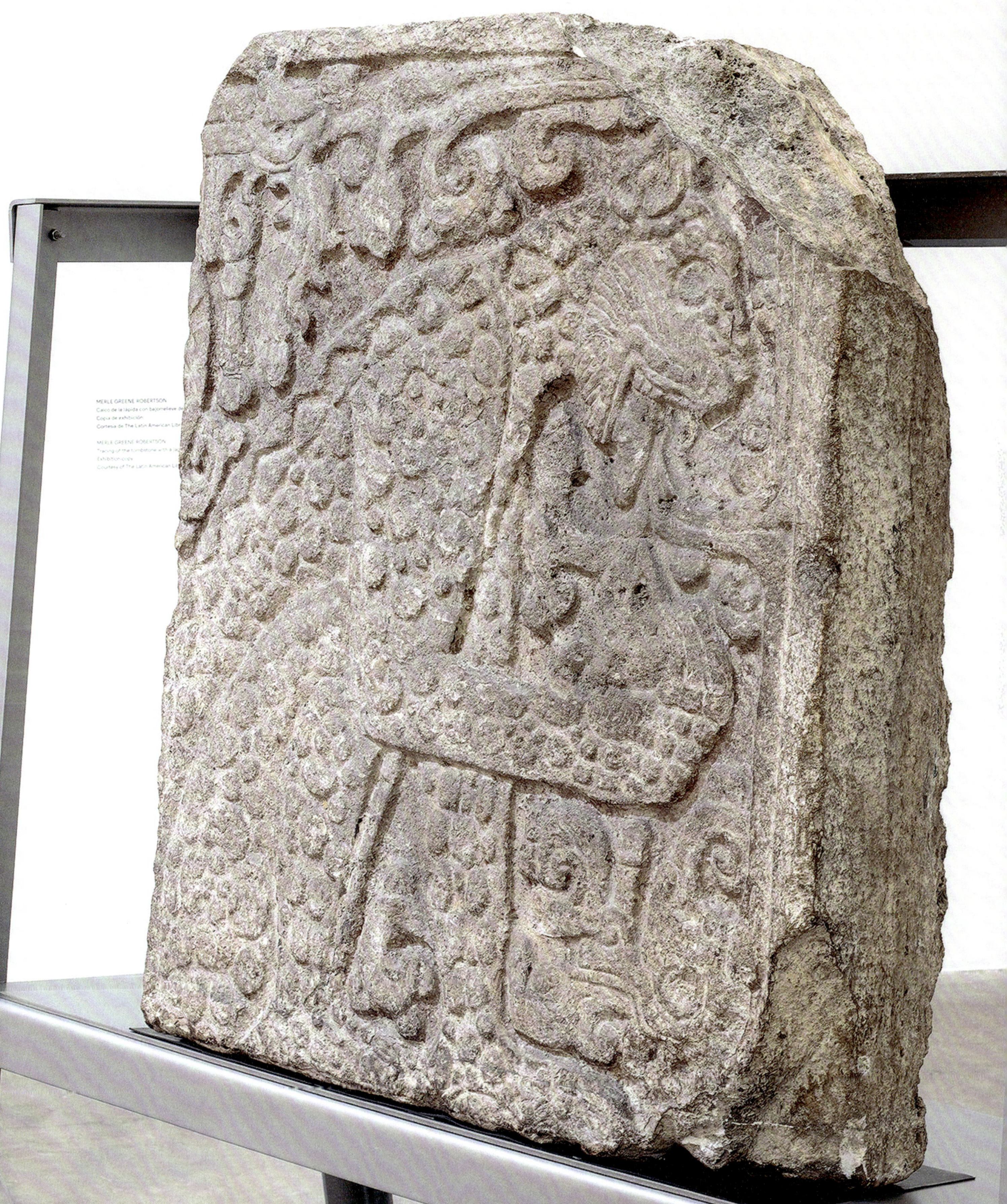
MERLE GREENE ROBERTSON
Calco de la lápida con bajorrelieve
Copia de exhibición
Cortesía de The Latin American
MERLE GREENE ROBERTSON
Tracing of the tombstone with a
Exhibition copy
Courtesy of The Latin American

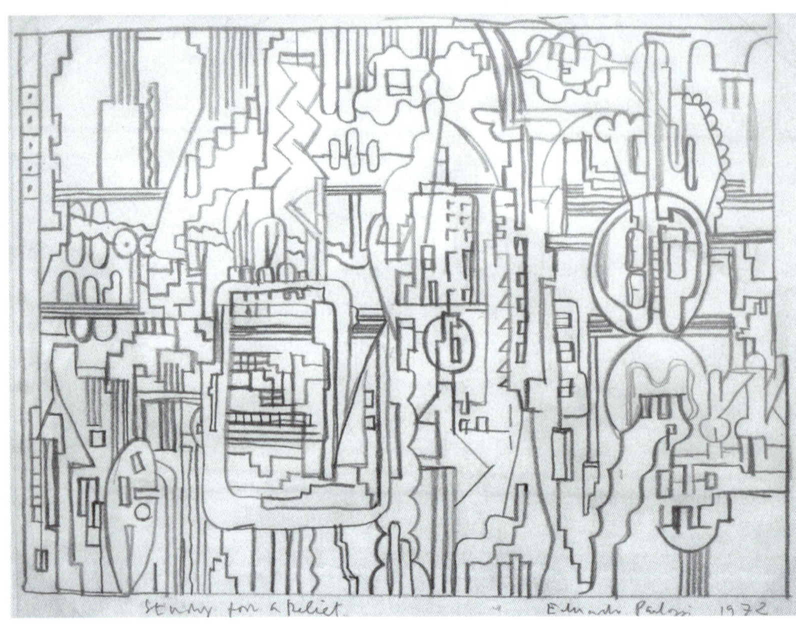

Eduardo Paolozzi, *Study for a relief*, **1972**, pencil on paper, **45×58×1.2** cm, Carrillo Gil Art Museum, Mexico City

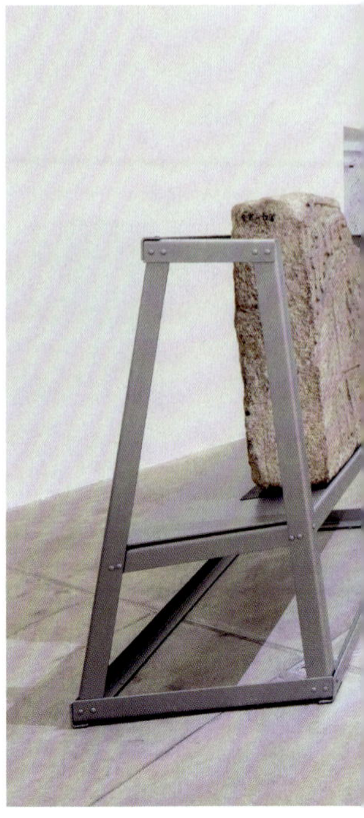

Hieroglyph Storage, **2014**, **150×150×80** cm, *Amarantus*, **2021**, MUAC, Mexico City

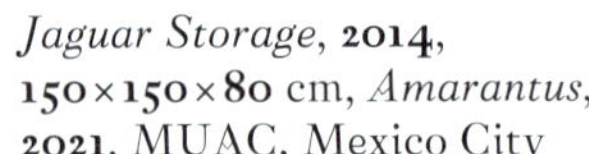

Jaguar Storage, **2014**, **150×150×80** cm, *Amarantus*, **2021**, MUAC, Mexico City

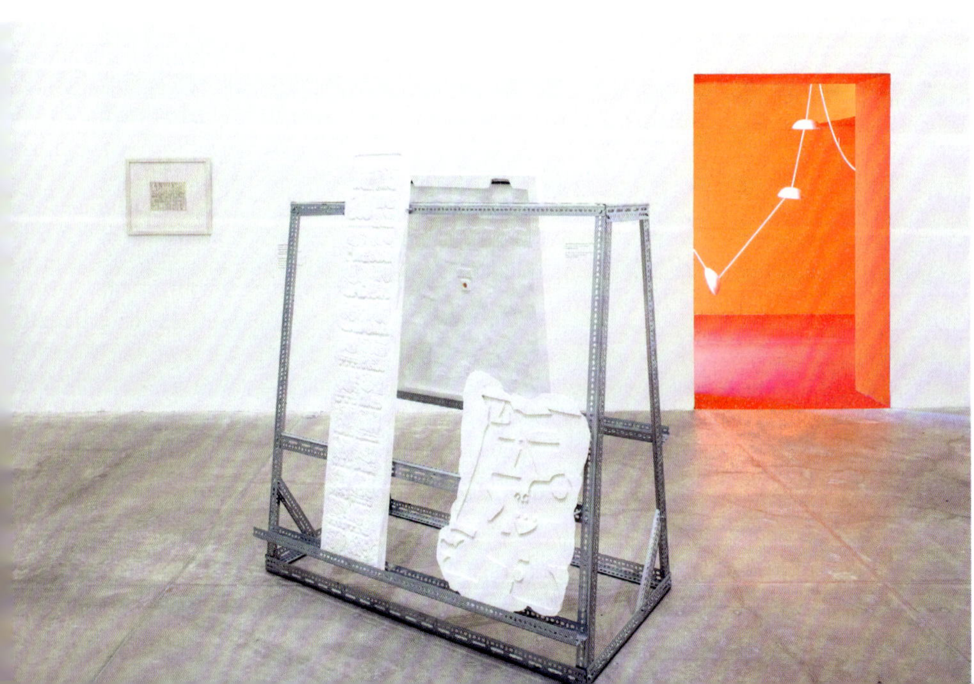

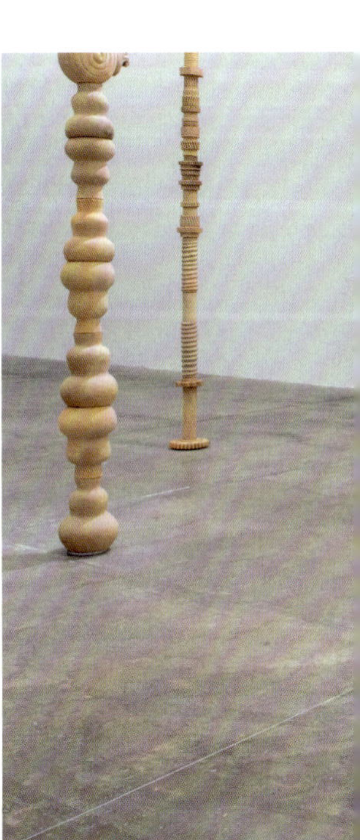

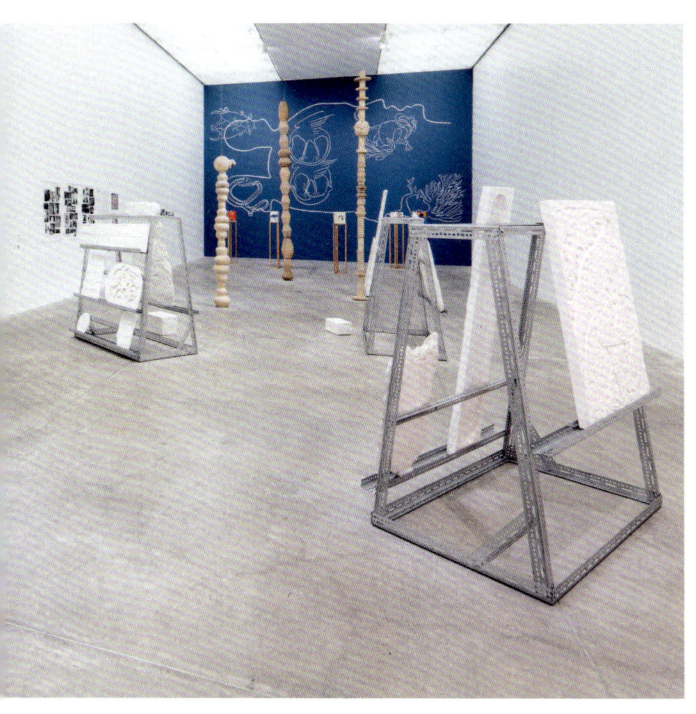

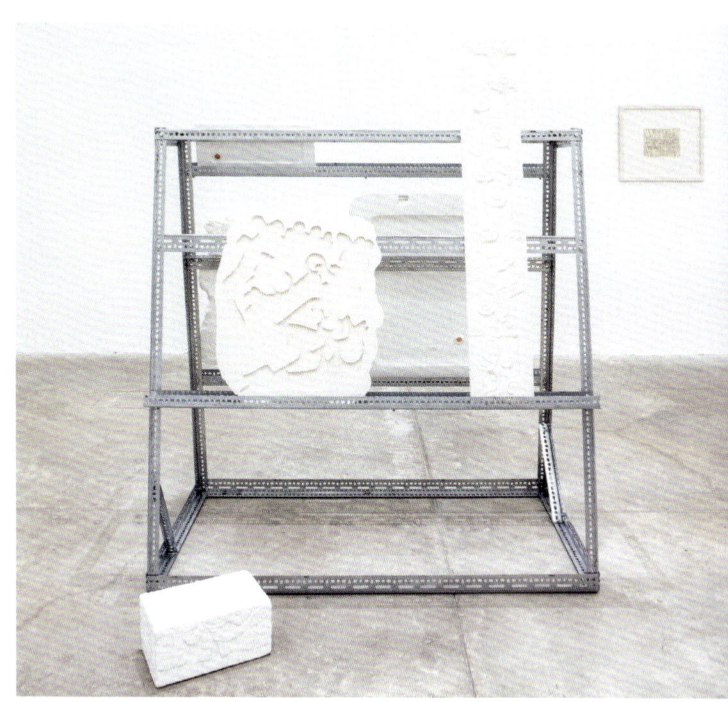

Papantla Storage, **2014**, **150×150×80** cm, *Amarantus*, **2021**, MUAC, Mexico City

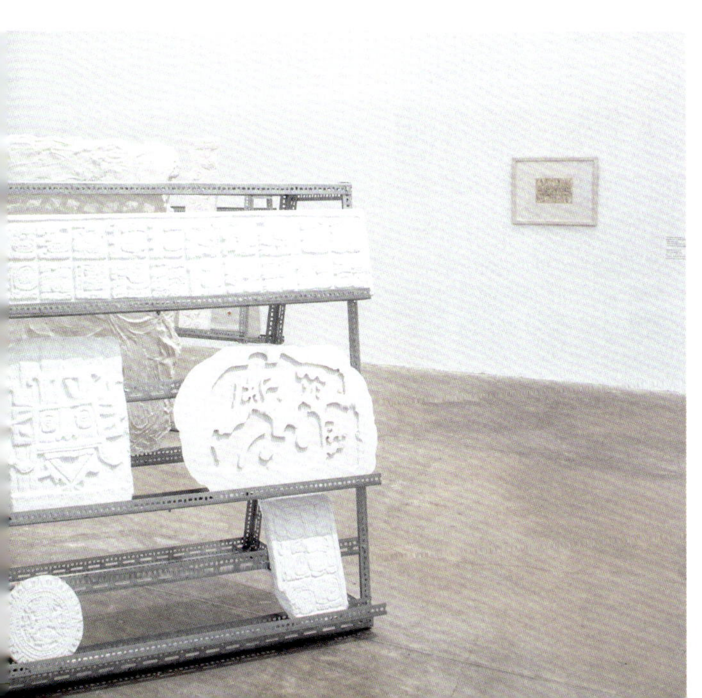

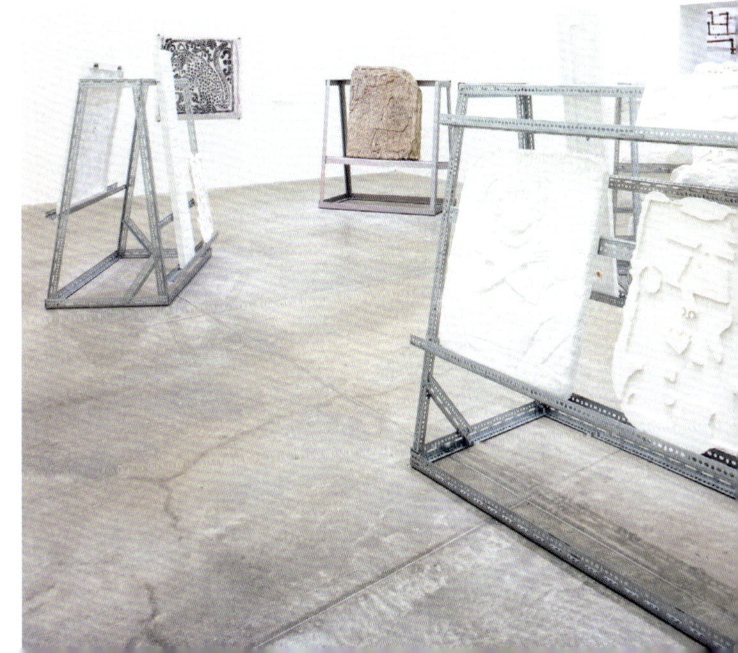

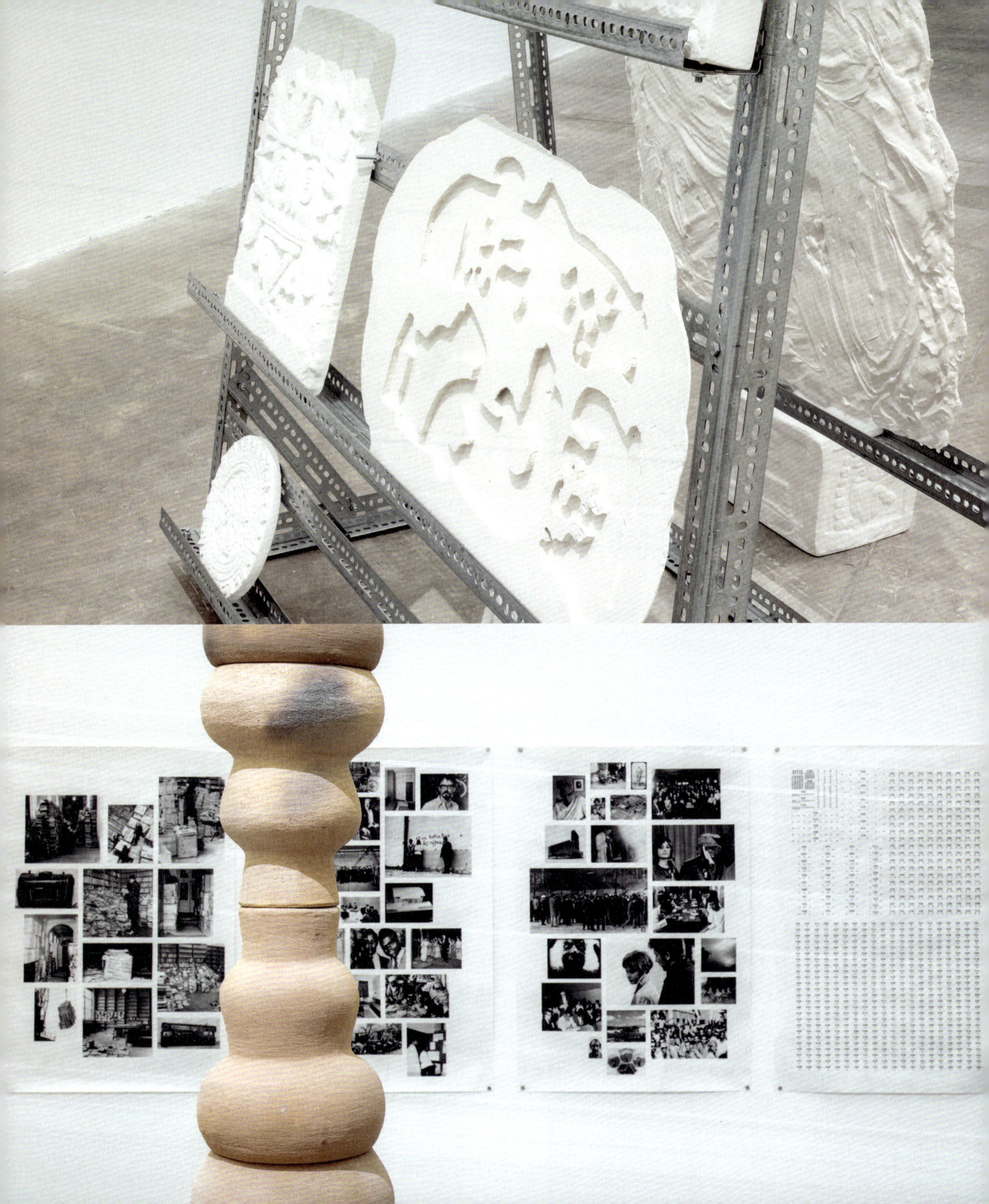

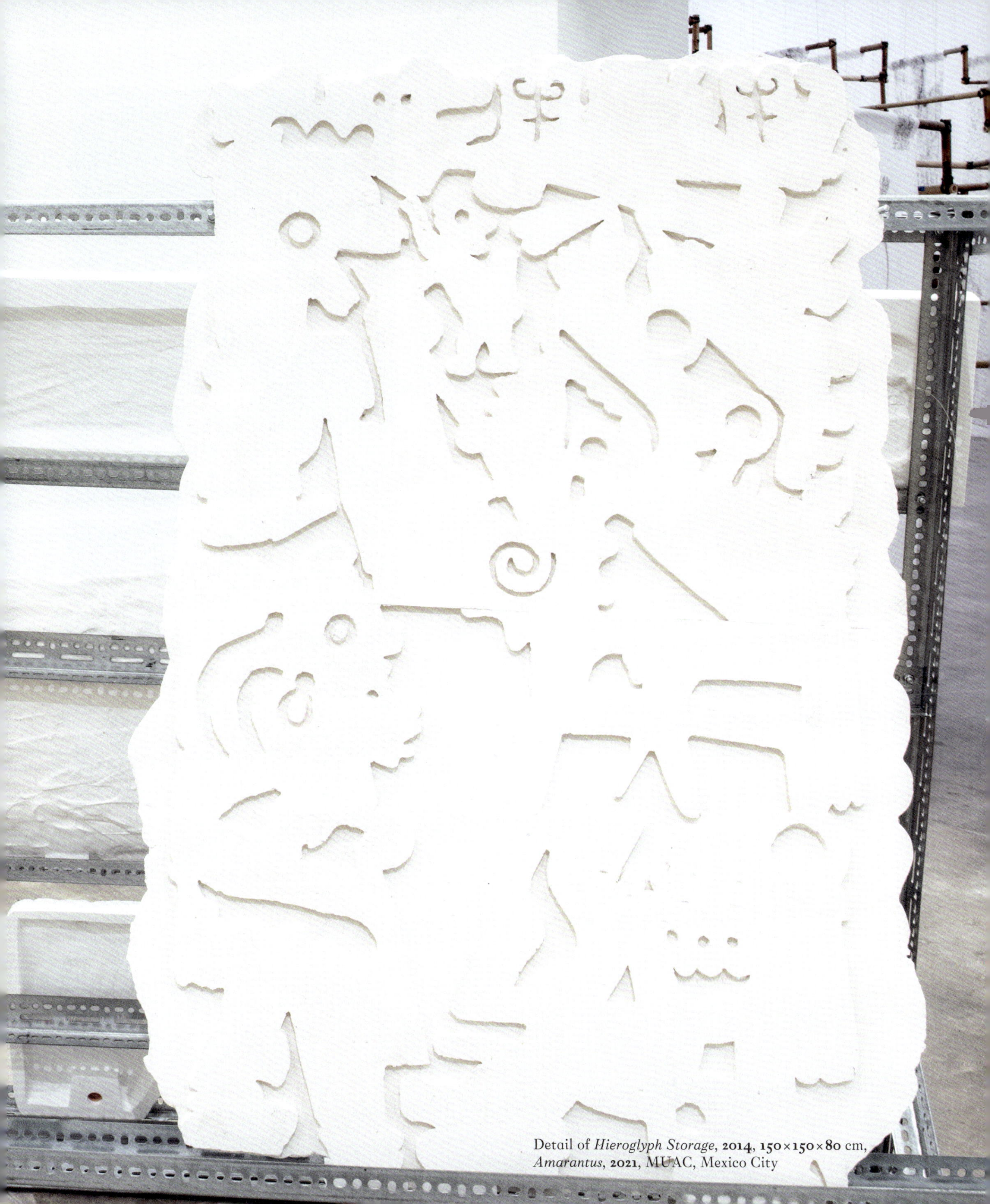

Detail of *Hieroglyph Storage*, 2014, 150 × 150 × 80 cm, *Amarantus*, 2021, MUAC, Mexico City

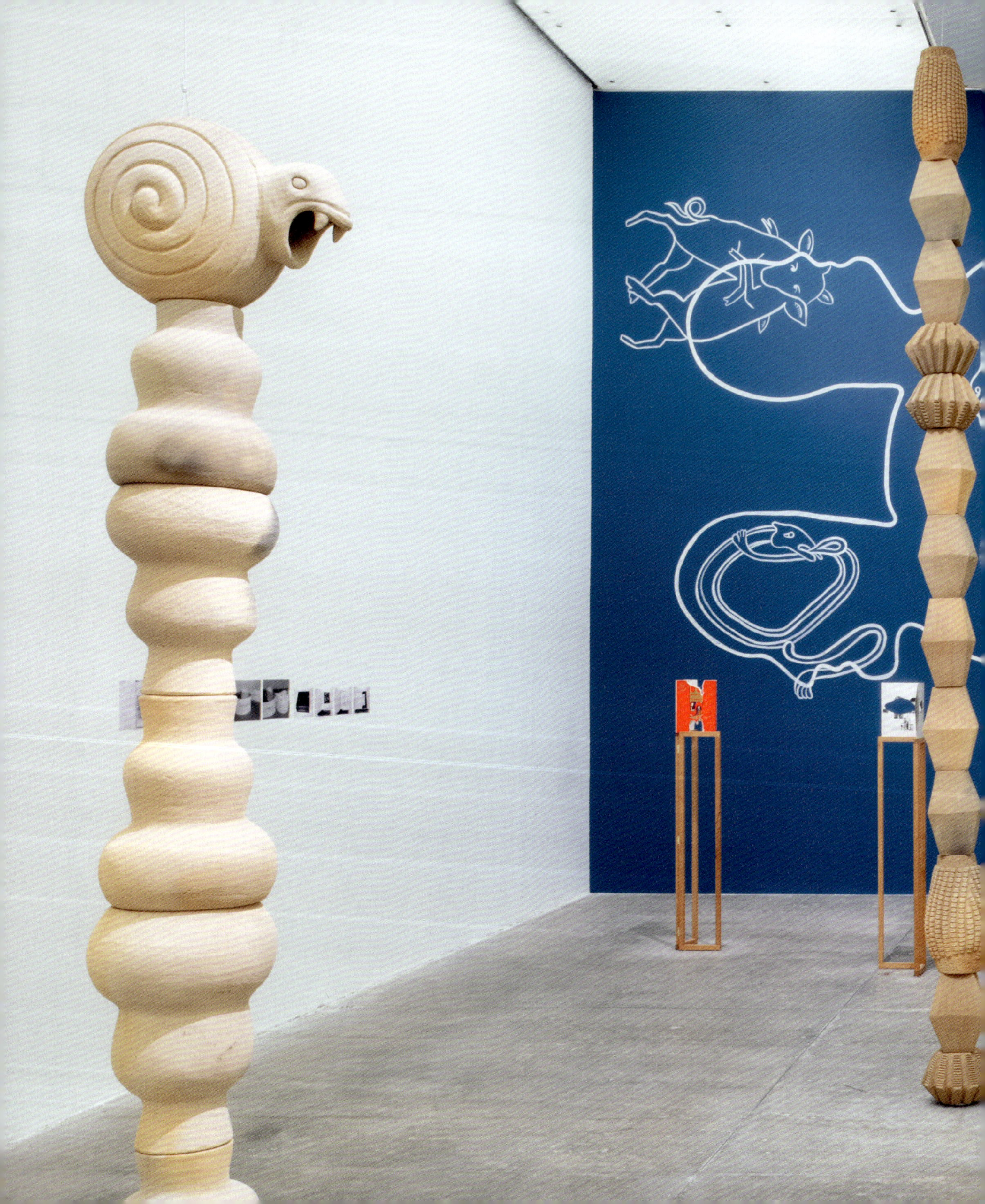

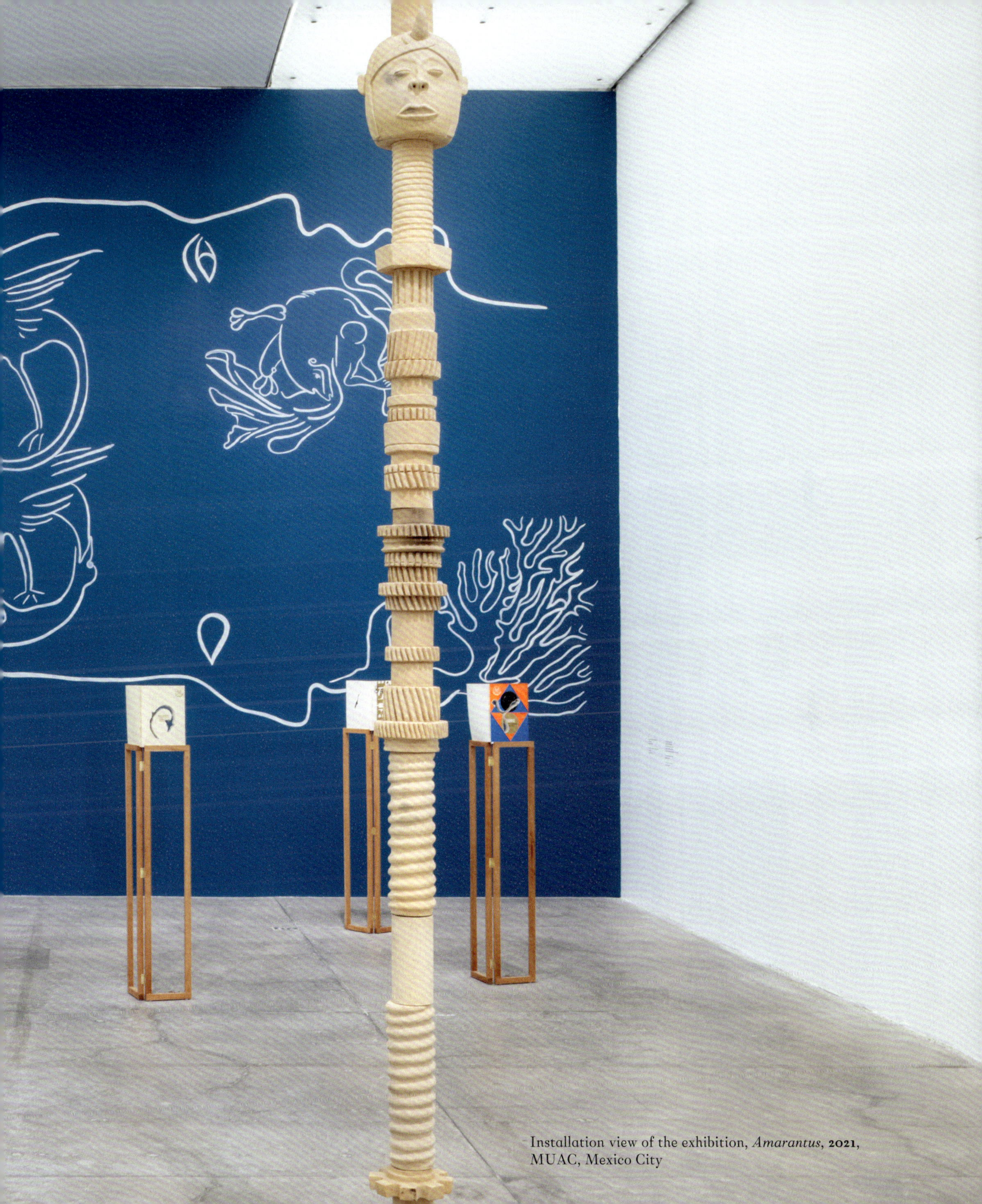

Installation view of the exhibition, *Amarantus*, **2021**, MUAC, Mexico City

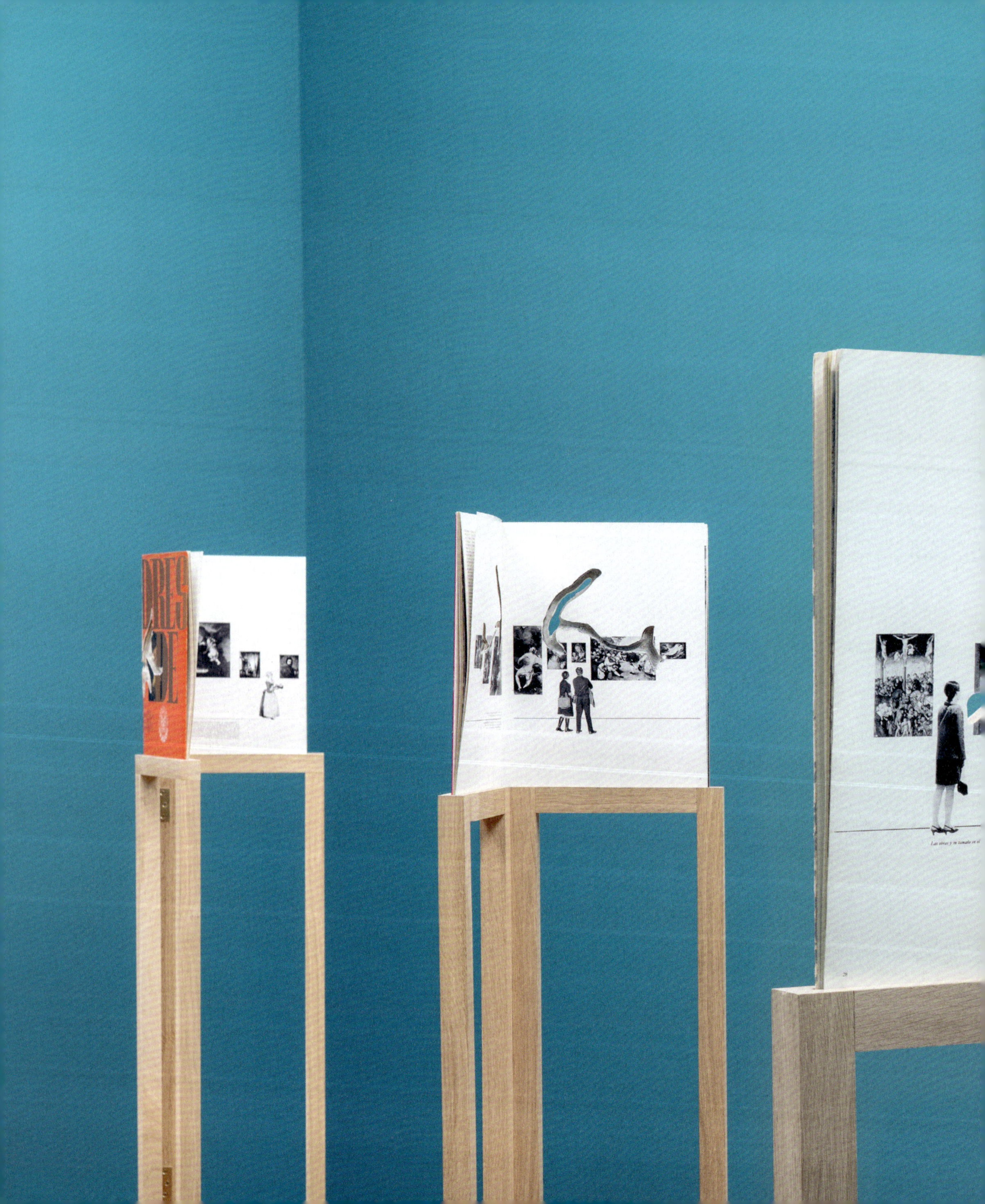

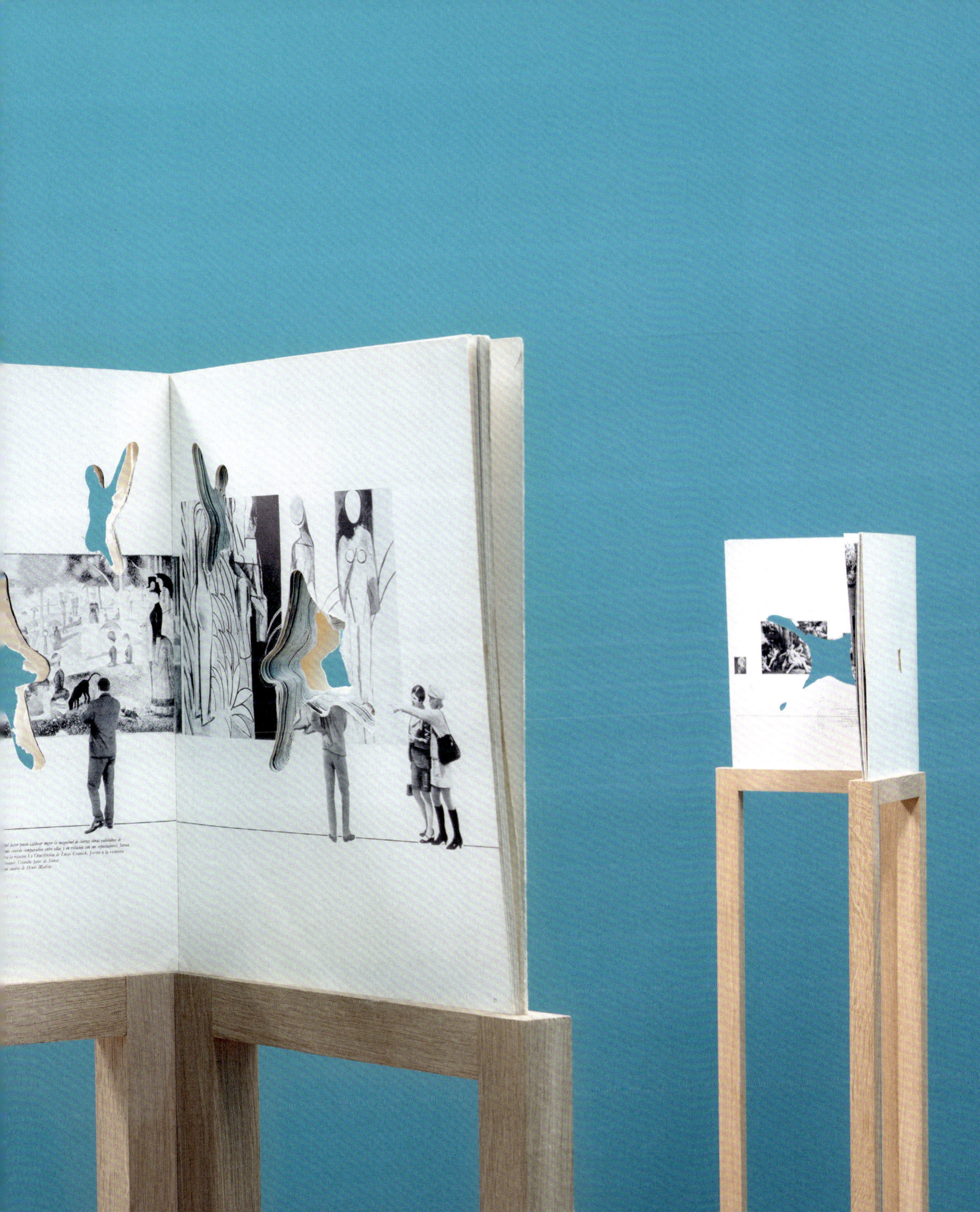

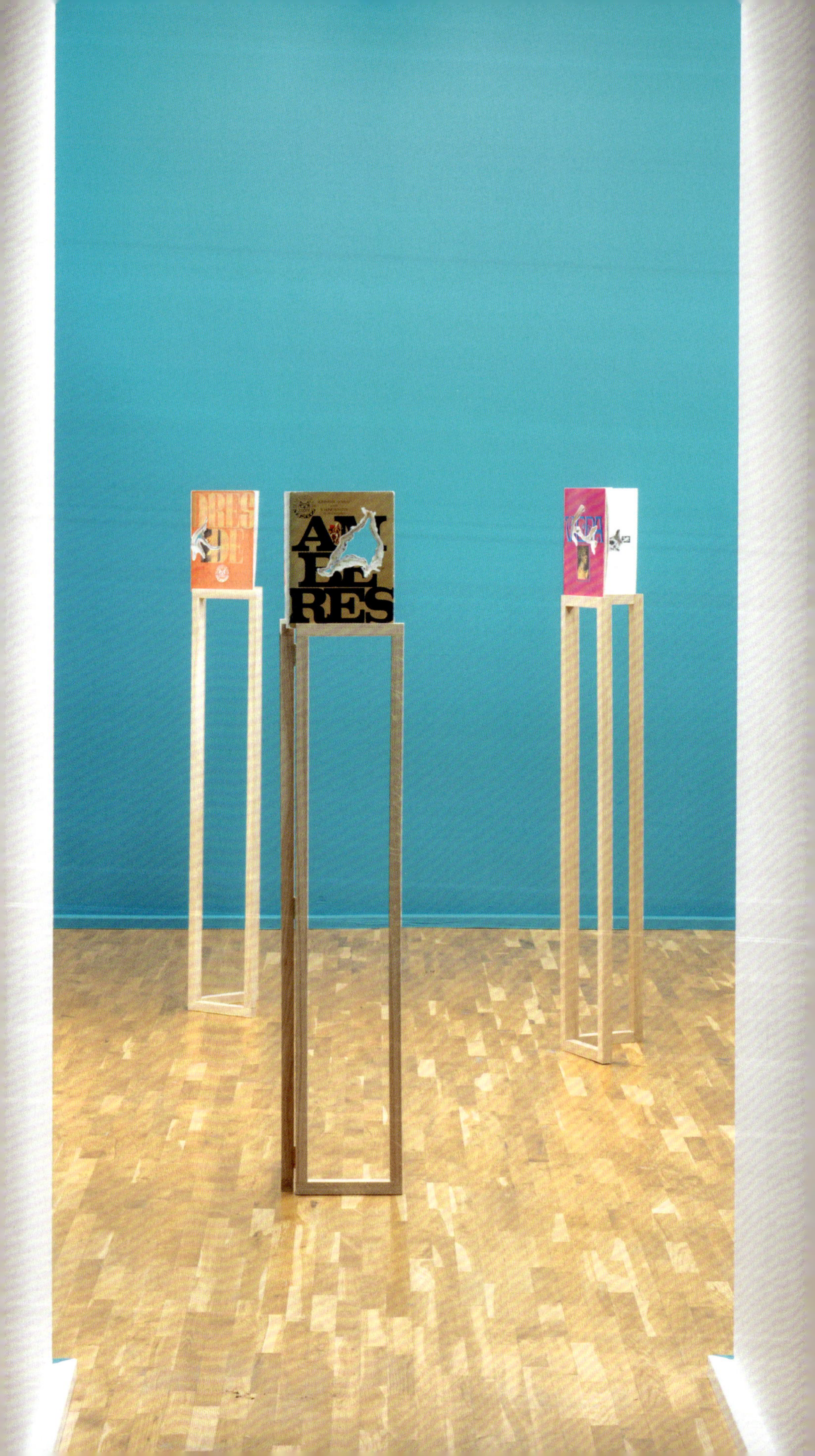

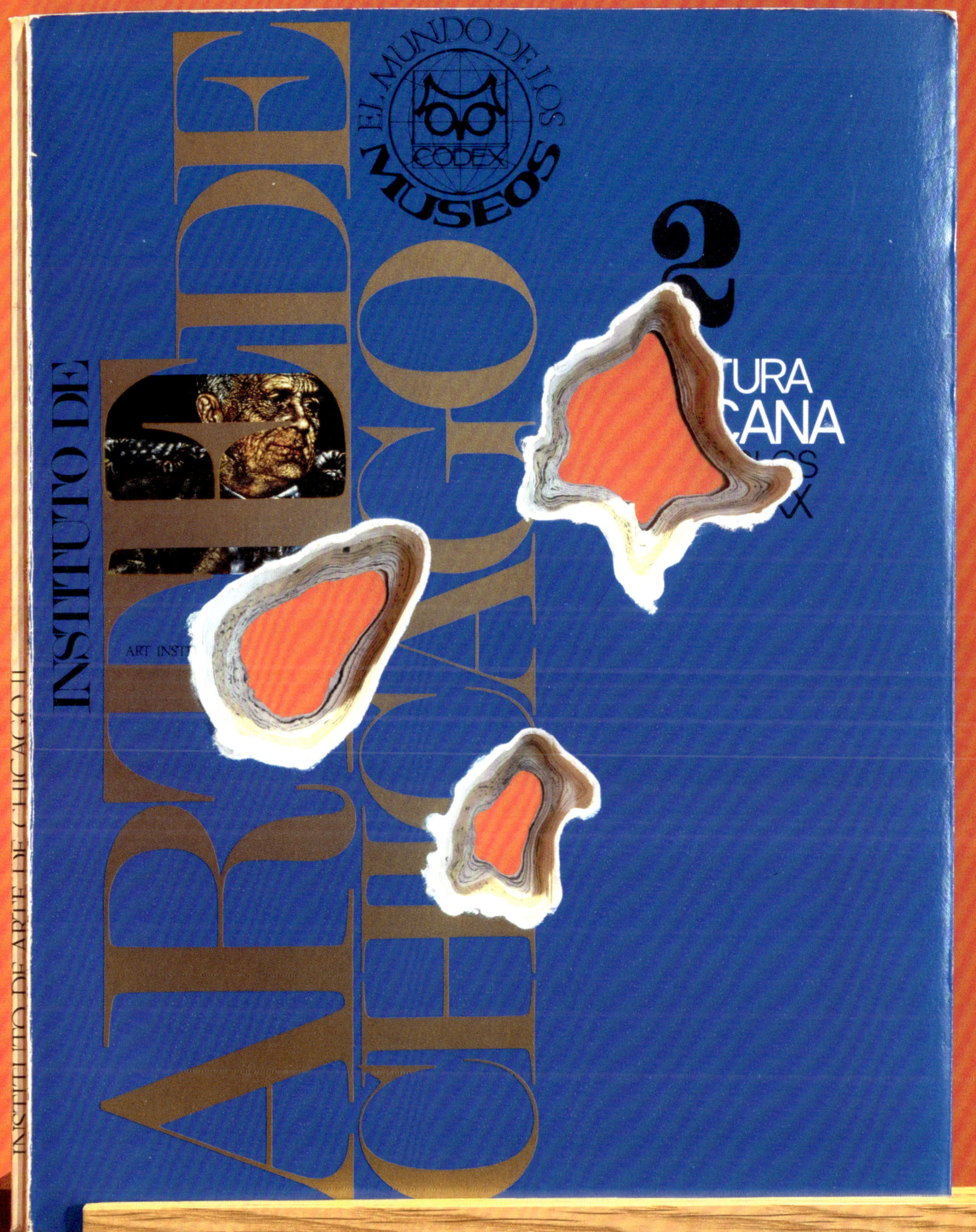

p. 40–42 *Do Ut Des*, 2009–2019, series of unique, drilled books from the collection *Great Museums of the World* on cedar bases, each 31×25×1 cm, *Amarantus*, 2021, MGKSiegen, Germany

p. 43 *Do ut des, Instituto de Arte de Chicago II*, 2019, *Point*, Kurimanzutto, New York

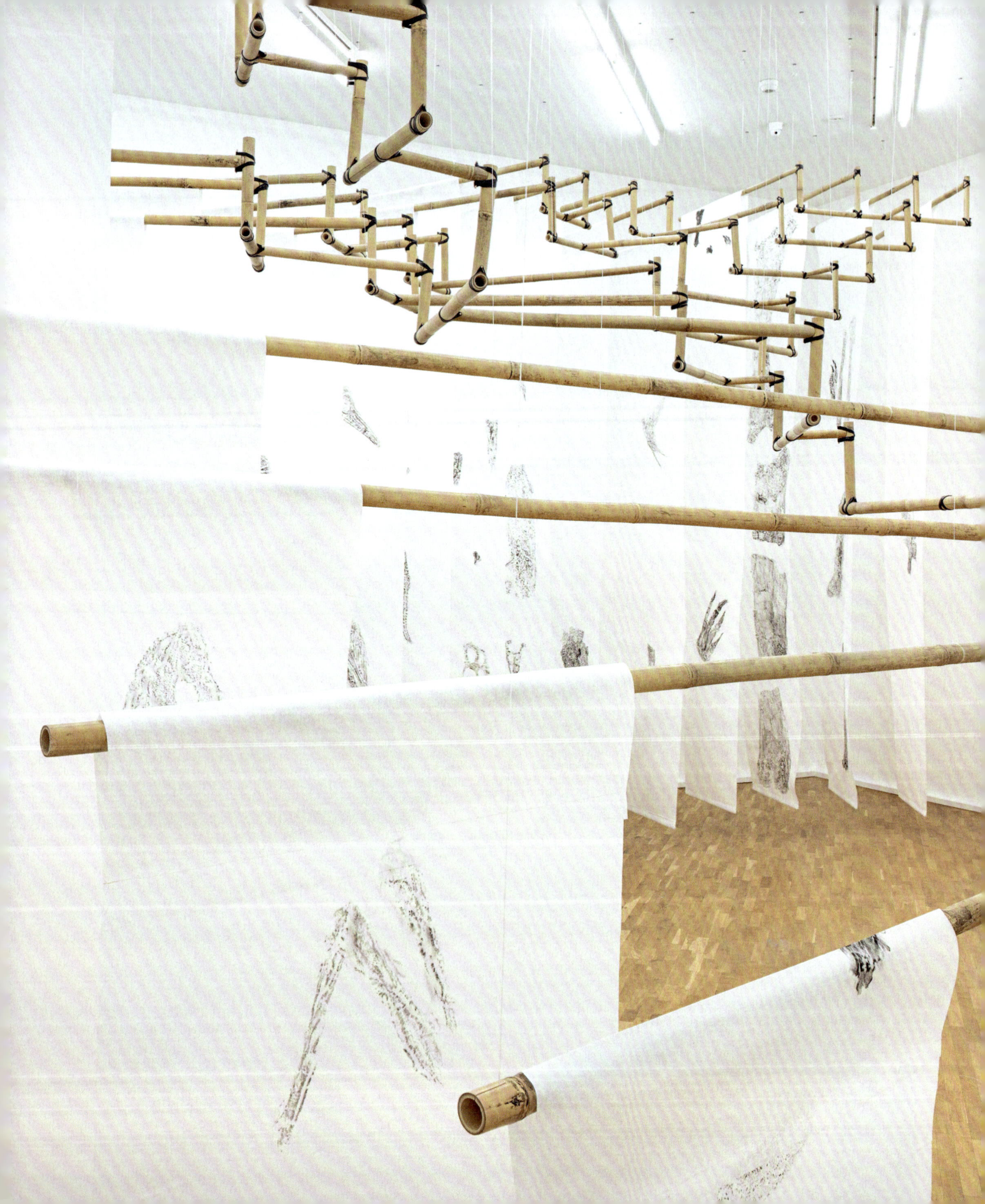

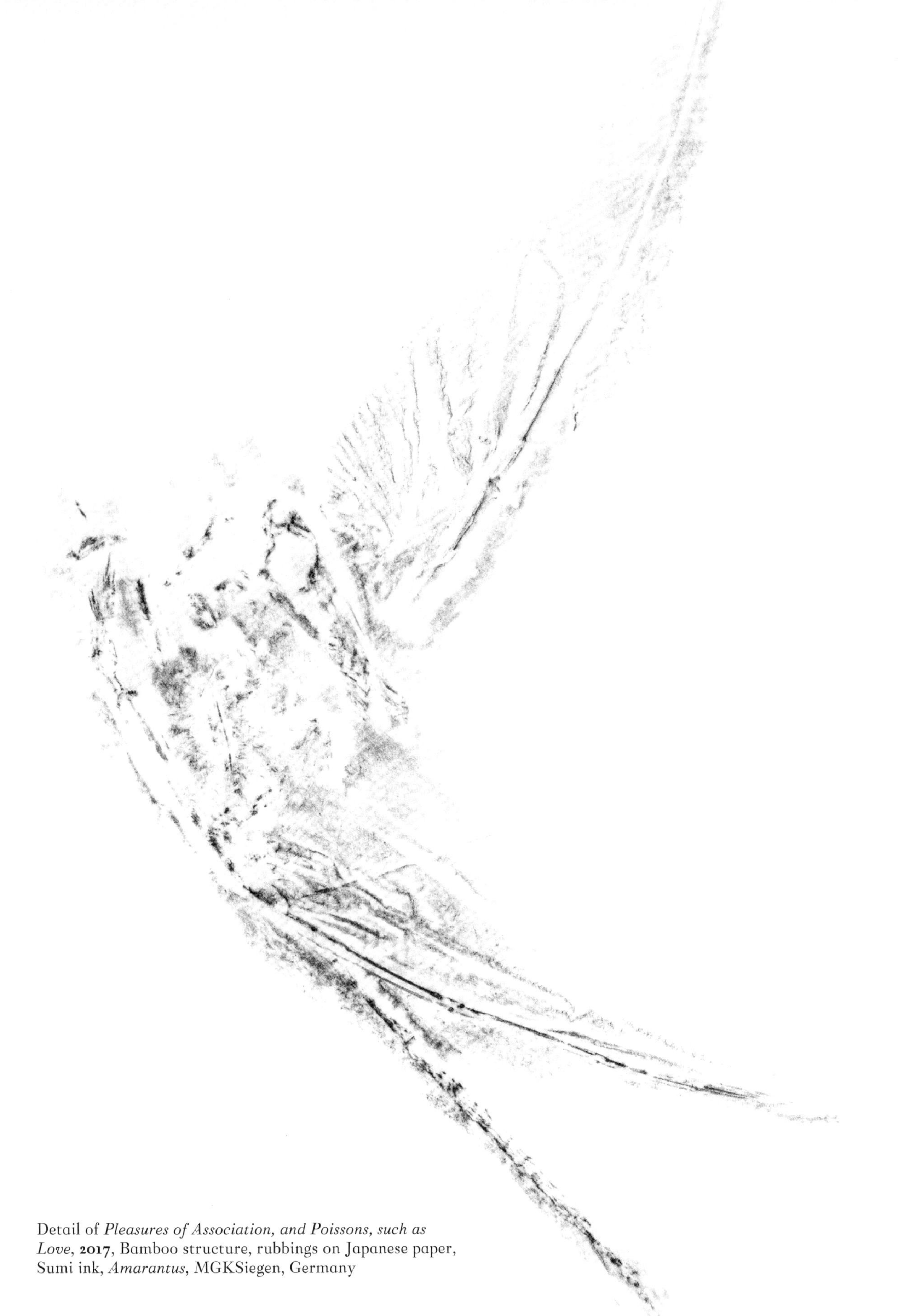

Detail of *Pleasures of Association, and Poissons, such as Love*, **2017**, Bamboo structure, rubbings on Japanese paper, Sumi ink, *Amarantus*, MGKSiegen, Germany

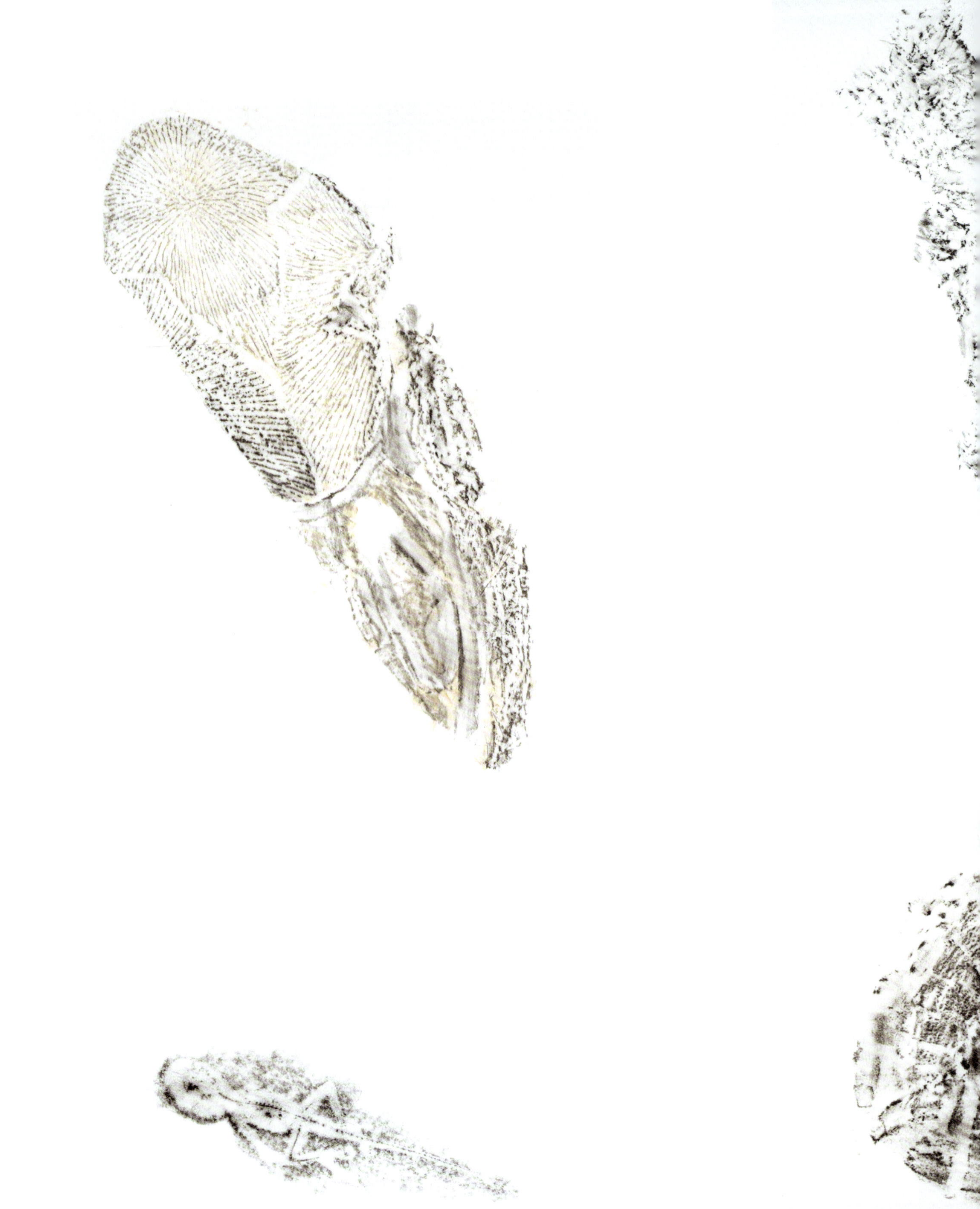

Details of *Pleasures of Association, and Poissons, such as Love*, **2017**, *Amarantus*, MGKSiegen, Germany, **2021**

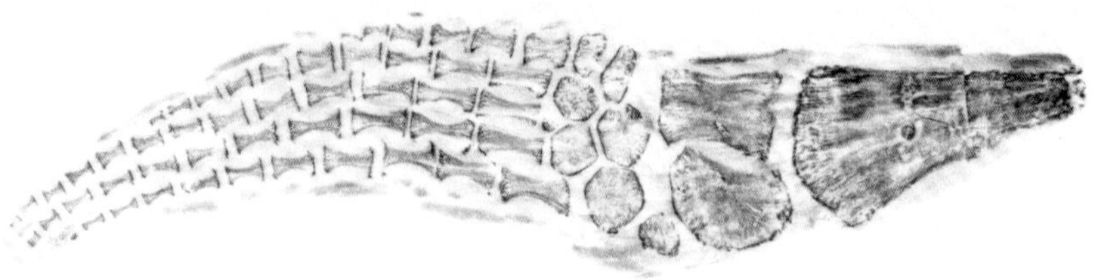

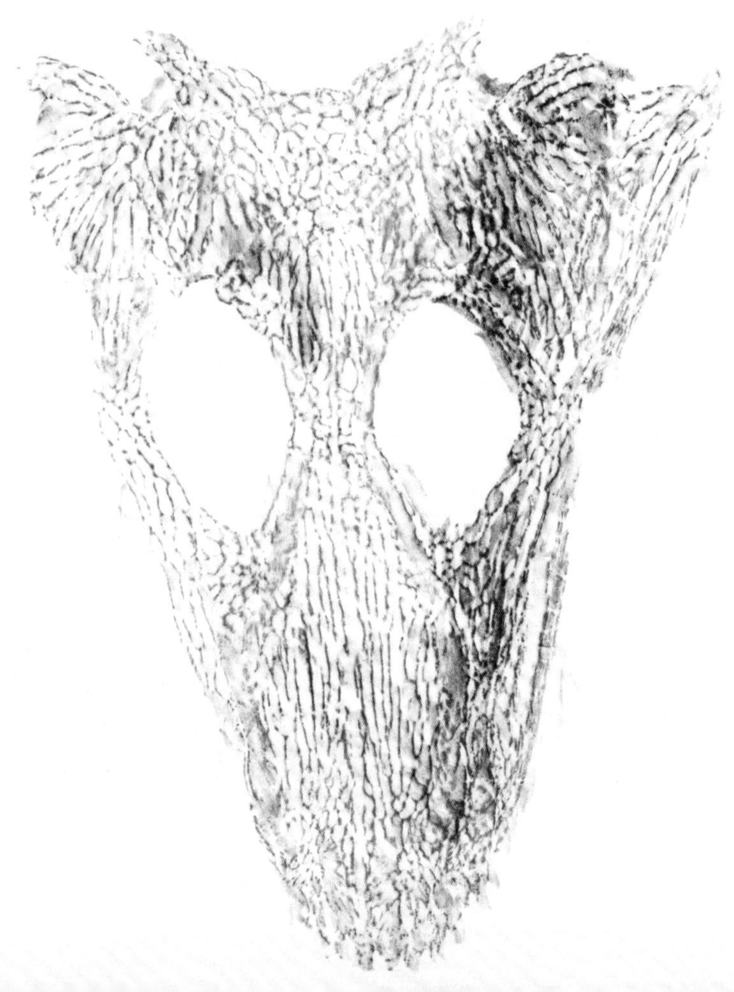

Details of *Pleasures of Association, and Poissons, such as Love*, **2017**, *Amarantus*, **2021**, MGKSiegen, Germany

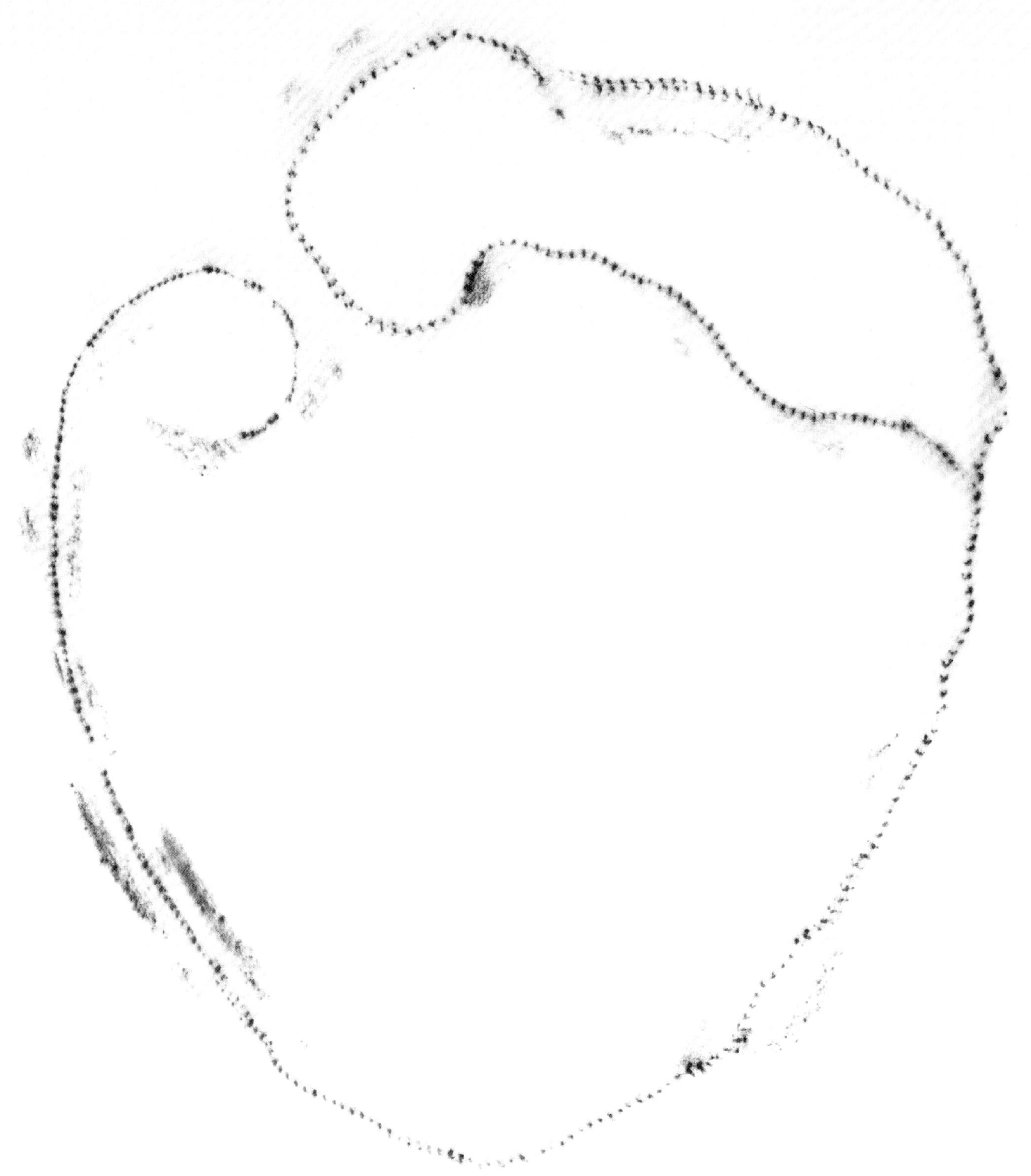

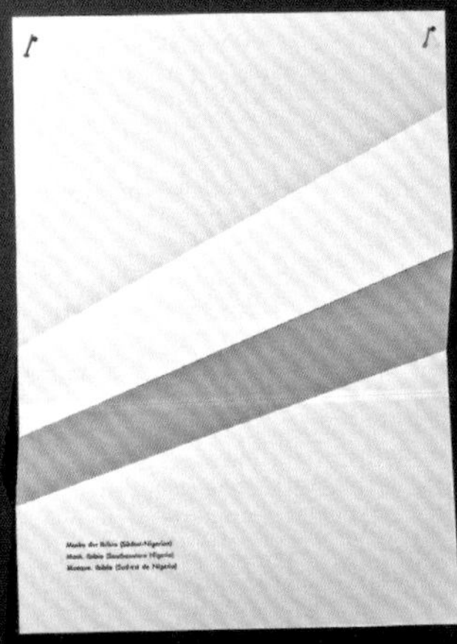

Falschgesichter, **2018**, series of **23** paper masks, folded glossy paper with printed text, *Amarantus*, **2021**, MGKSiegen, Germany

Maske der Ibibio (Südost-Nigerien)
Mask. Ibibio (Southeastern Nigeria)
Masque. Ibibio (Sud-est de Nigeria)

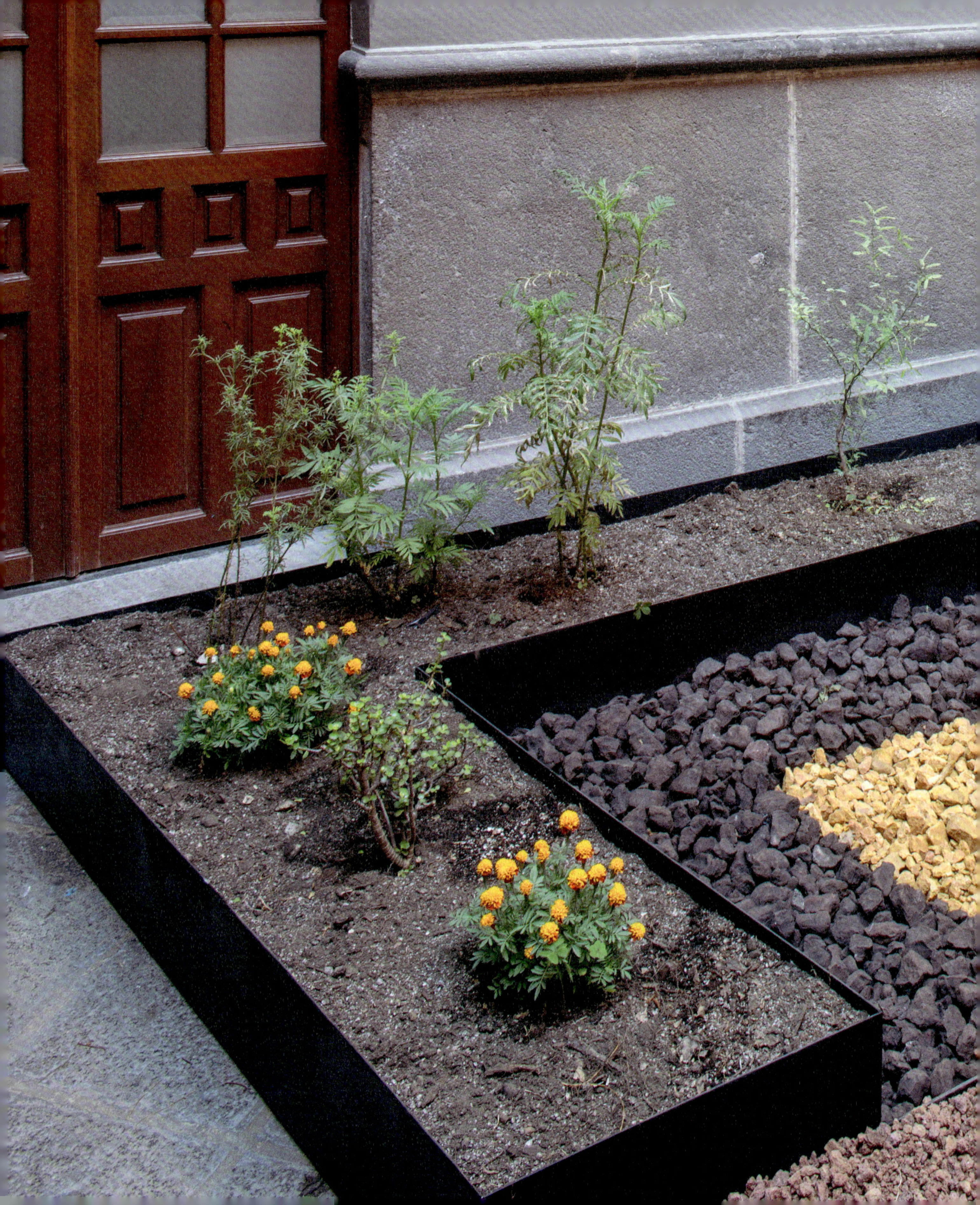

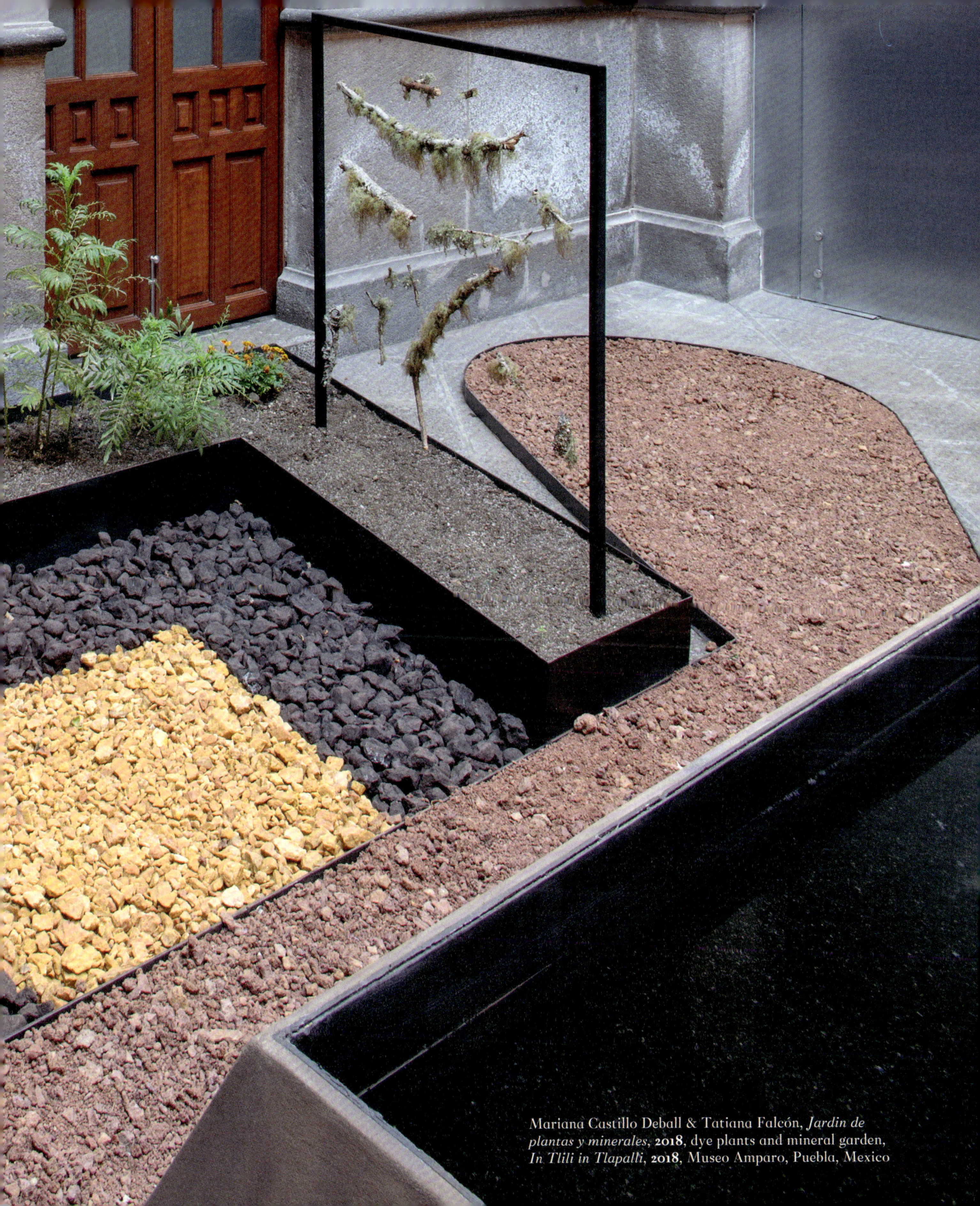

Mariana Castillo Deball & Tatiana Falcón, *Jardín de plantas y minerales*, **2018**, dye plants and mineral garden, *In Tlili in Tlapalli*, **2018**, Museo Amparo, Puebla, Mexico

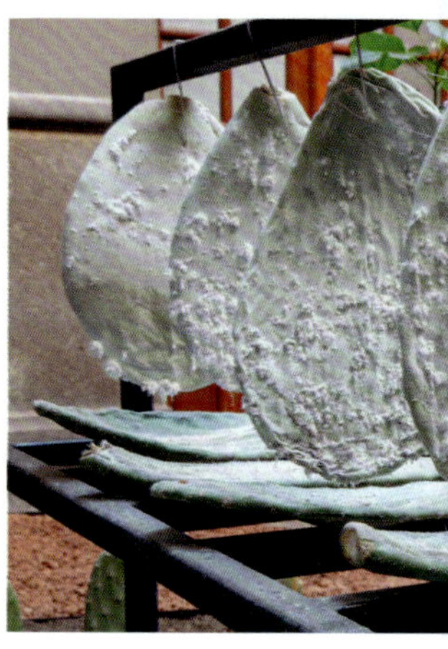

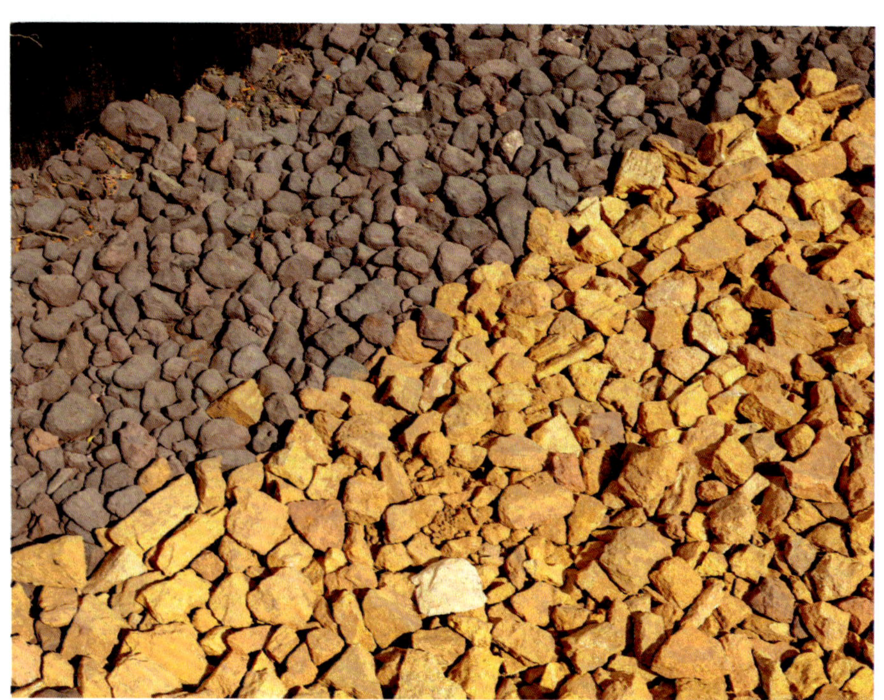

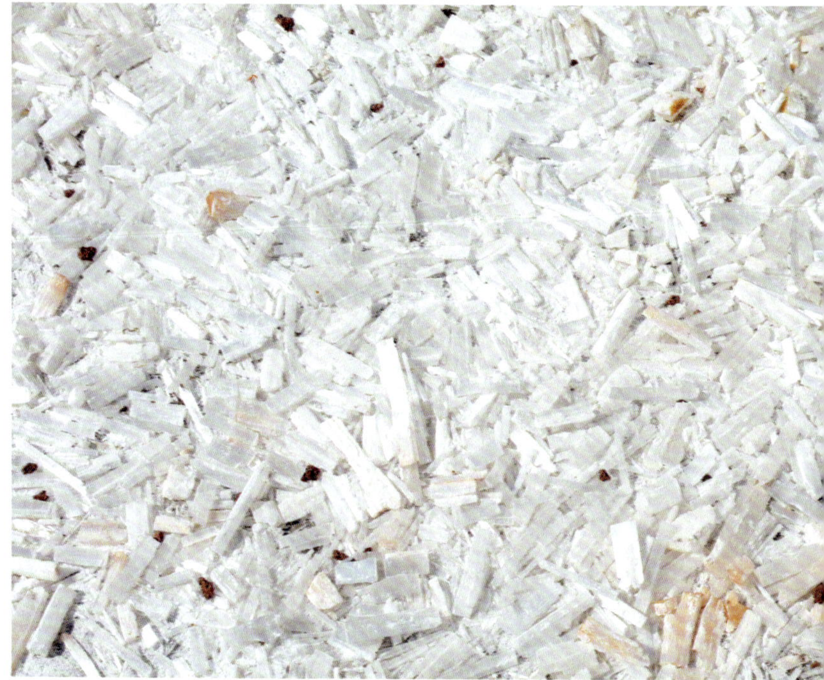

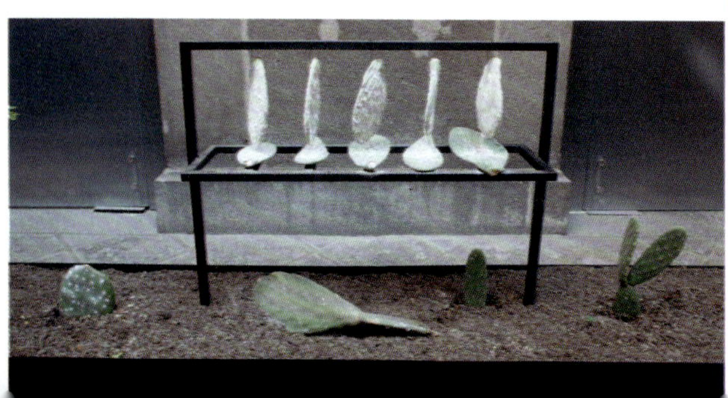

Mariana Castillo Deball & Tatiana Falcón, details of *Jardin de plantas y minerales*, **2018**, dye plants and mineral garden, *In Tlili in Tlapalli*, **2018**, Museo Amparo, Puebla, Mexico

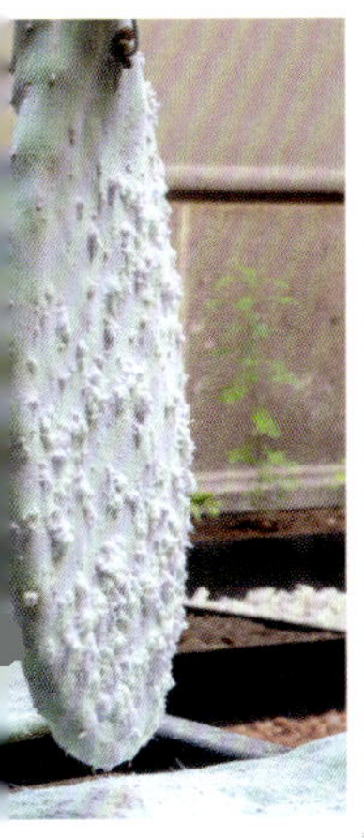
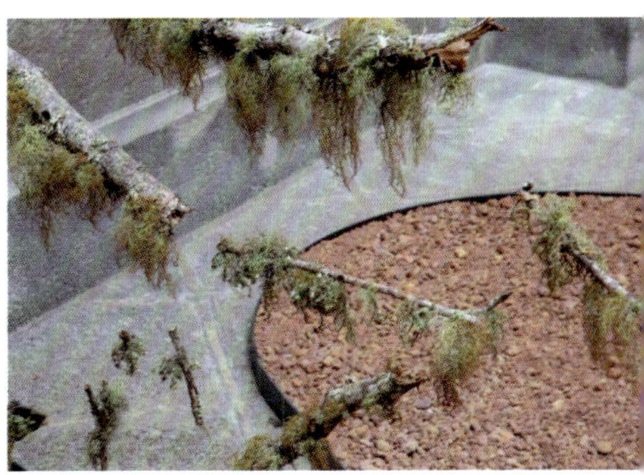
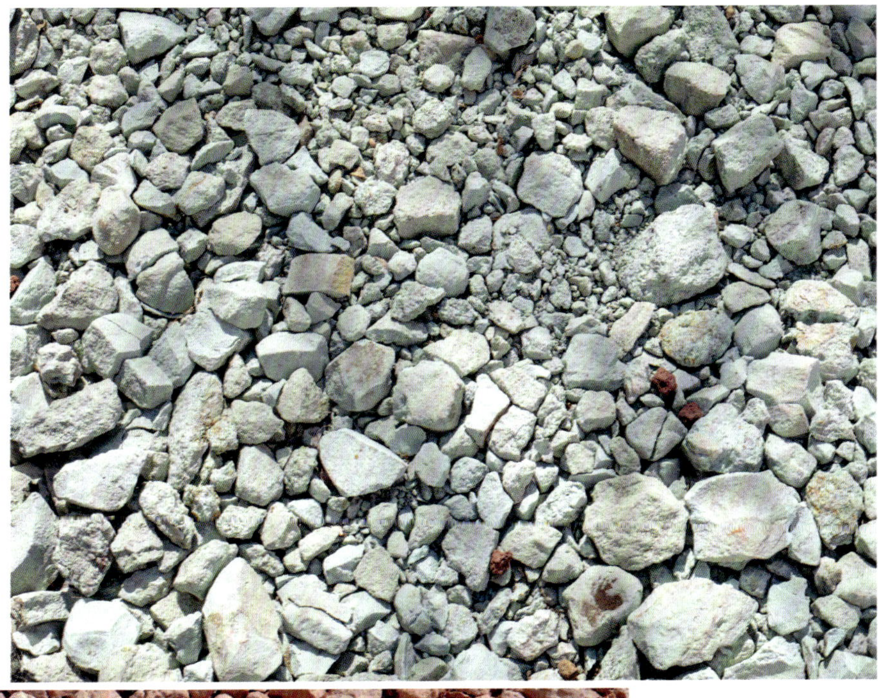
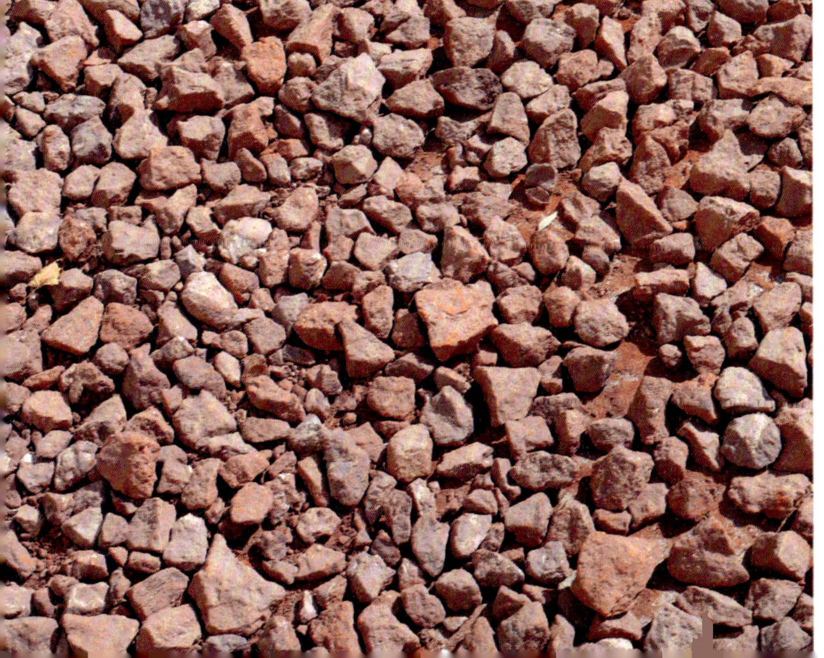
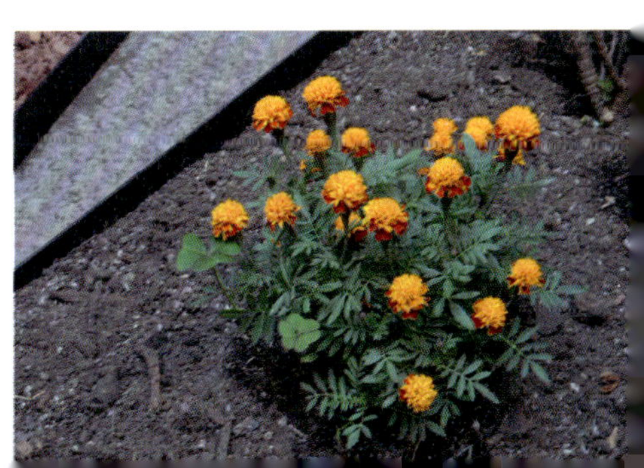

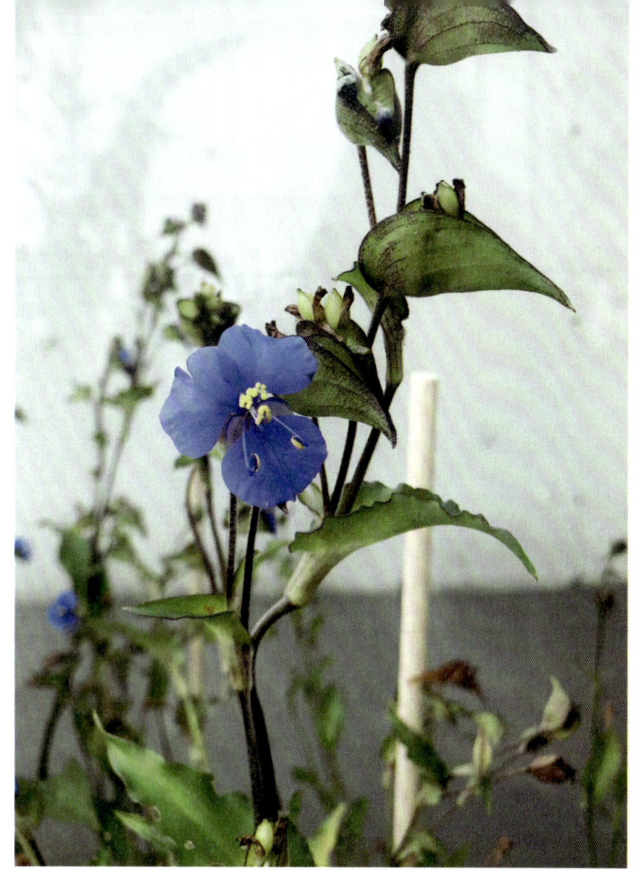
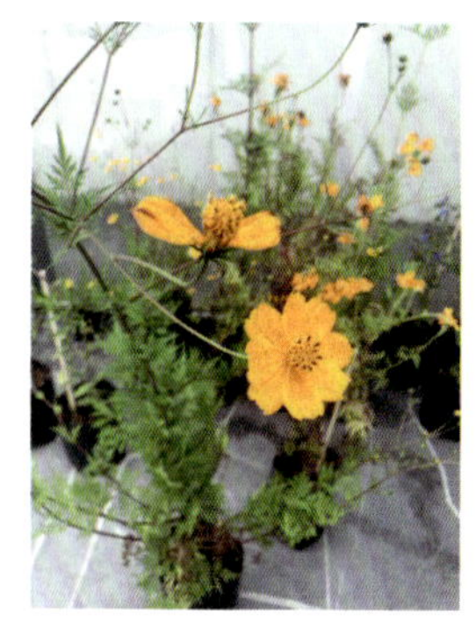
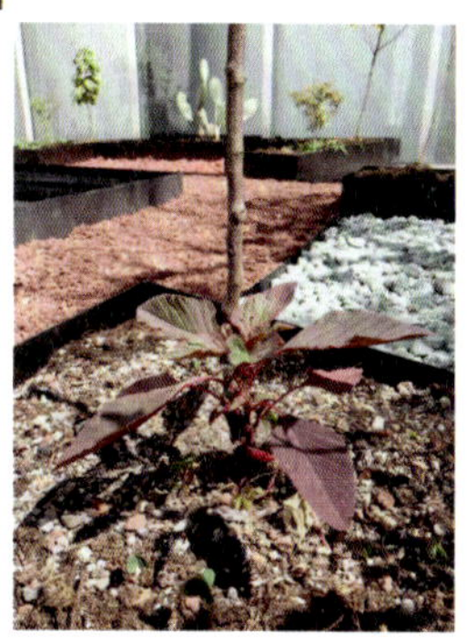
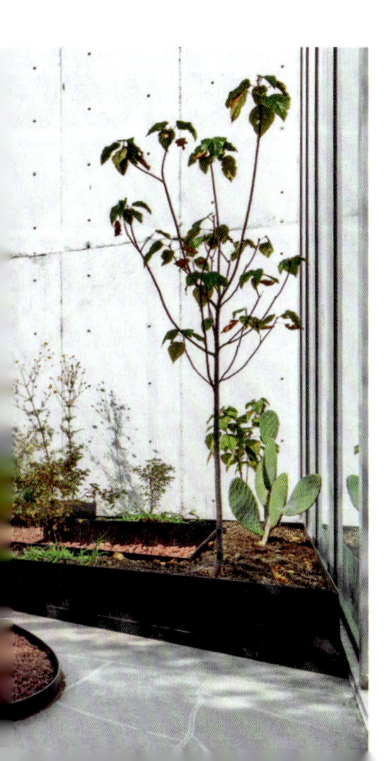
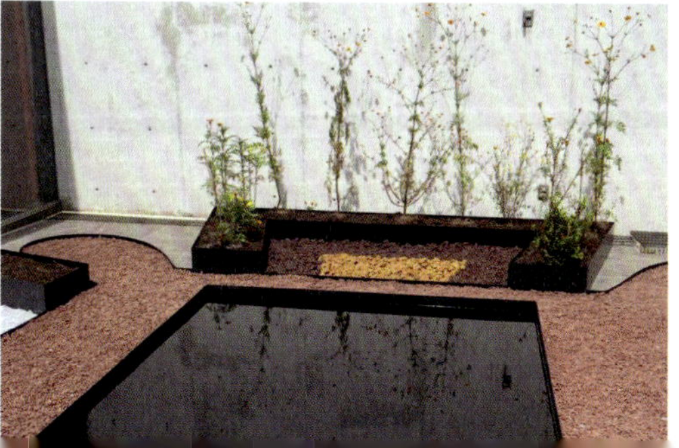

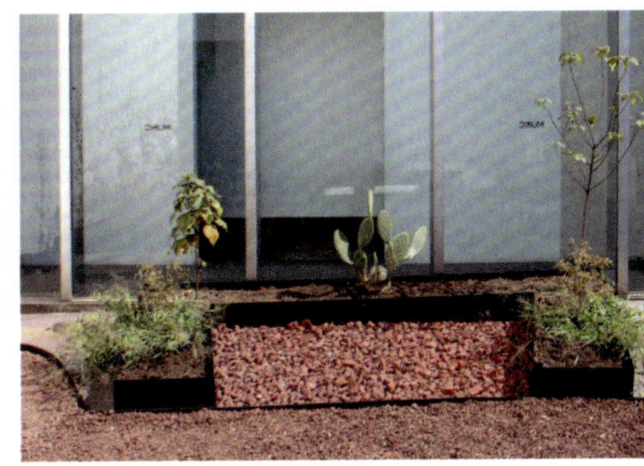

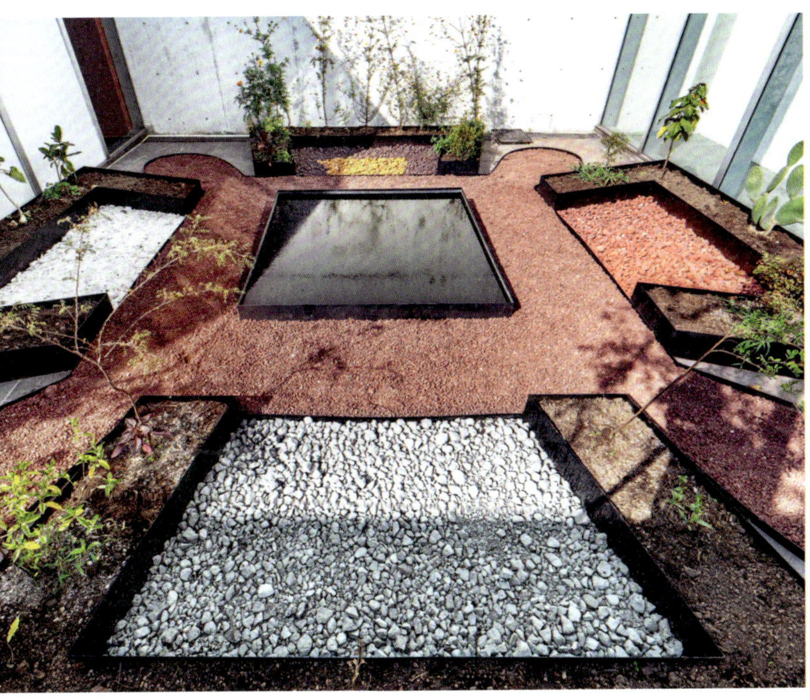

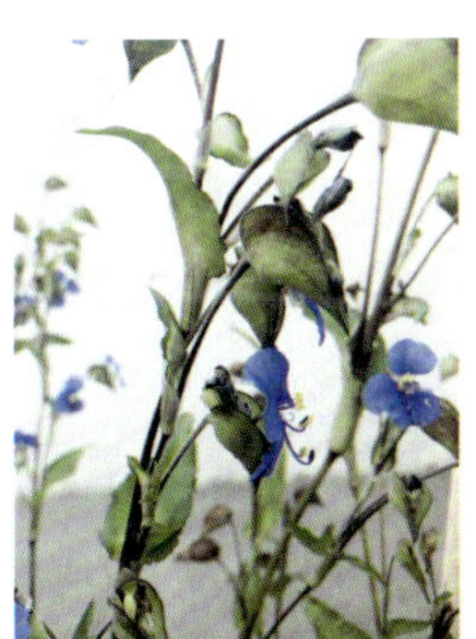

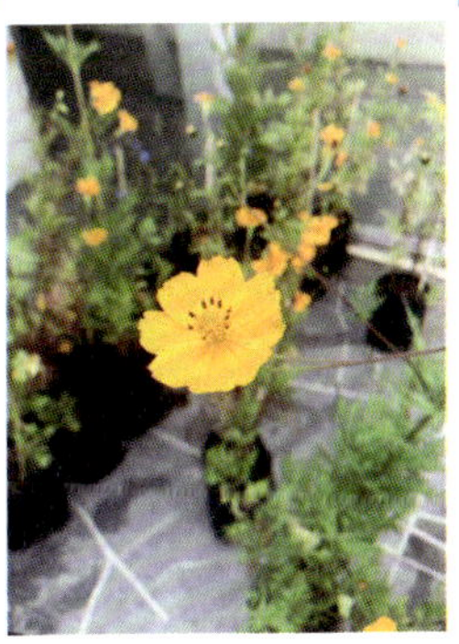

Mariana Castillo Deball & Tatiana Falcón, details of *Dye plants and minerals garden*, Amarantus, **2021**, MUAC Museo Universitario de Arte Contemporáneo, Mexico City, Mexico.

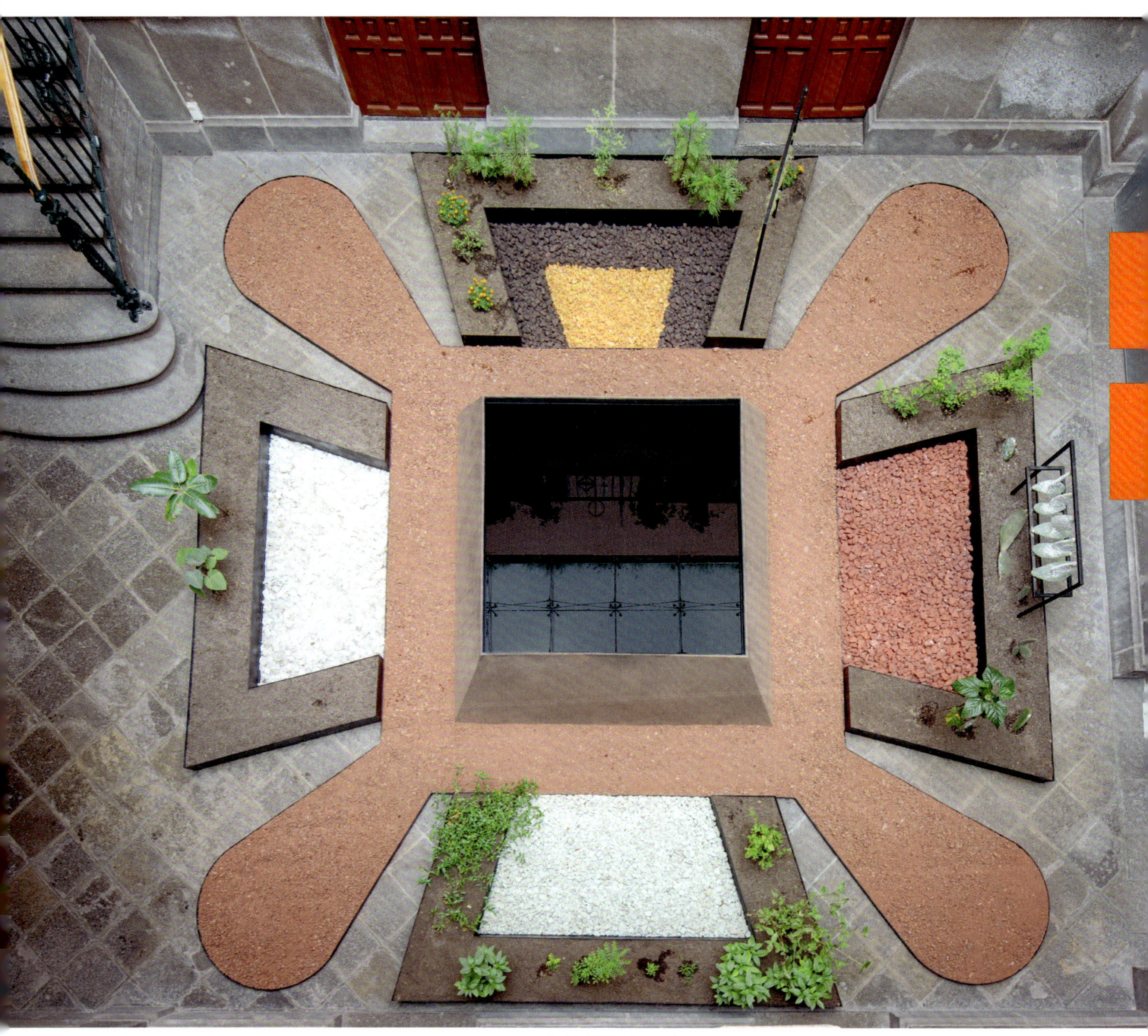

THE PAIN TER'S GAR DEN

TATIANA FALCÓN

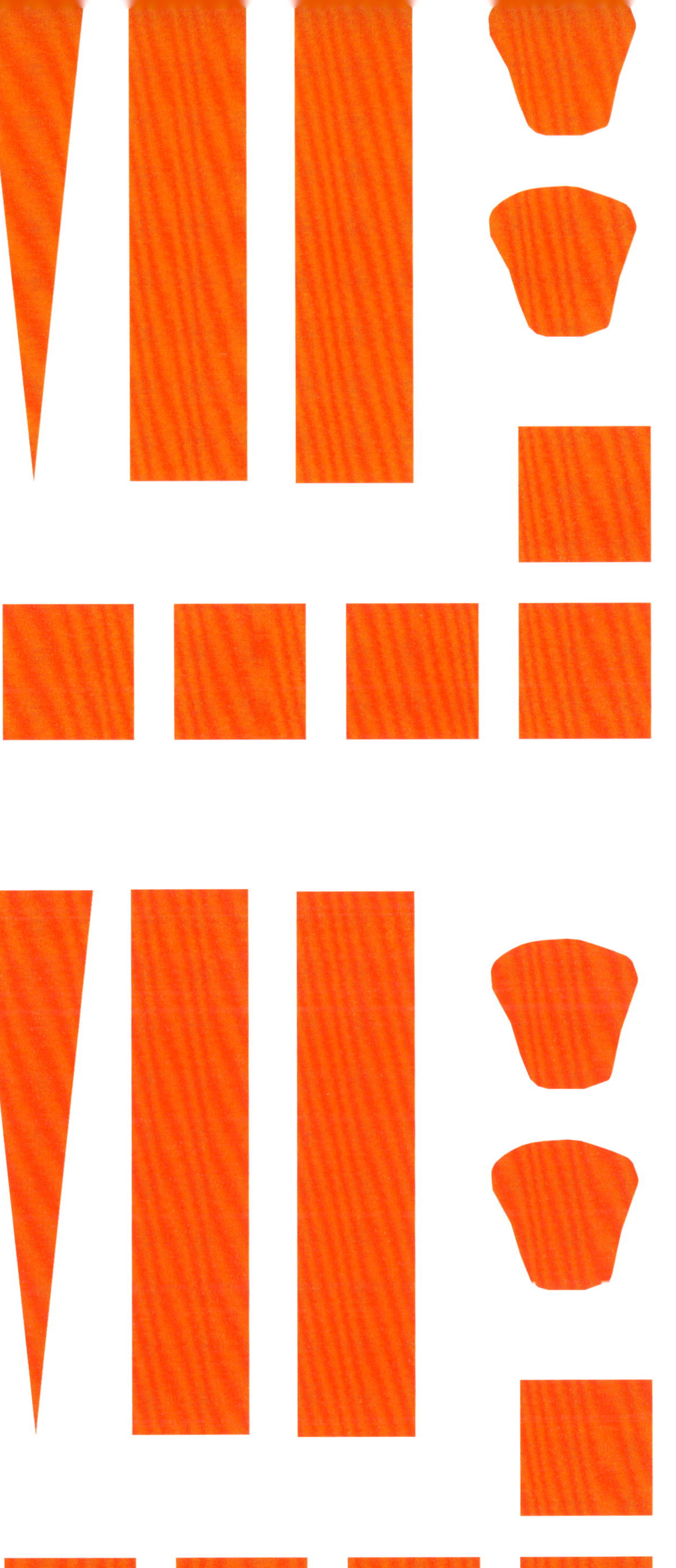

There is no historical record of a garden that has brought together all the dye-yielding plants like the one we made as part of the exhibition *In Tlilli in Tlapalli.*[1] *Imágenes de la nueva tierra: Identidad indígena después de la conquista*[2] (**1** September – **26** November **2018**, Museo Amparo, Puebla). We combined trees from different geographical areas, wild seasonal plants, bushes, insects, and lichens named in the *Florentine Codex*[3] as the sources of the most important colors used to make pigments—colored powders that yield paint when added to a binding agent—and dyes used by Nahua painters, dyers, and feather artists.

The spatial arrangement followed the *tonalpohualli*, the Nahua count of days, as recorded on the first sheet of the *Féjerváry-Mayer Codex*. According to this *tonalpohualli*, the course of time begins in the east, where the sun resides and which is a cardinal point associated with the color red. The raw materials documented in Chapter Eleven of Book **11** of the *Florentine Codex*, "On Colors, on All Kinds of Colors," and associated with

1 This text was originally published in Mariana Castillo Deball, *Amarantus* (Mexico: MUAC, **2021**), **182** – **203**. The editors mentioned refer to that edition.

2 *in tlilli* (black), *in tlapalli* (color): the black, the color.

3 The *Florentine Codex* is a bilingual work on two columns: the column in Spanish and the drawings are on the left side of the page, while the Nahuatl text is on the right. The quotes are from both the Spanish and Nahuatl texts. For ease of reading, both have been translated. Translations from Nahuatl are in italics. Citations from Spanish are taken directly from Sahagún, *Historia general de las cosas de Nueva España*, Book XI, fs. **216**r – **222**v, http://www.wdl.org/en/item/**10622**. A complete English translation of the Spanish text in the Codex has yet to be published. Translations from the World Digital Library are by the editors, whereas translations from the Nahuatl text are from Sahagún, *General History of the Things of New Spain*, **11** and **12**, trans. and ed. Arthur J. O. Anderson and Charles E. Dibble (Santa Fe: School of American Research, Santa Fe, **1961** – **1963**). Note that these volumes correspond to the Books X and XI of the *Florentine Codex*, respectively.

this quadrant are: cochineal (*Dactylopius coccus*), an insect of the *Dactylopiidae* family that is found on different kinds of nopales (prickly pear cactus, *Opuntia* spp.), whose females produce carminic acid from which the famous carmine red is obtained; young Mexican logwood trees (*Haematoxylon brasiletto*), endemic to the Isthmus of Tehuantepec region, whose wood—particularly the heartwood—is used in dye-making to obtain cherry tones; achiote bush (*Bixa orellana*), the seeds of which yield what Nahua colorists called "light red," and nowadays we would call orange. From the mineral kingdom we also included hematite (Fe_2O_3), which yields a blood-red pigment when pulverized.

According to the *tonalpohualli* in the *Féjérvary-Mayer Codex* (fig. 1), the next cardinal point in the count of days is north, which corresponds with the colors black and yellow. The main tree in this quadrant is mesquite (*Prosopis* spp.). These trees inhabit arid regions and are used to produce the color black, and their resin is used as a binding agent for painting. On the first sheet of the *Féjérvary-Mayer*, the mesquite represents one of the four cosmic trees that hold up the sky and serve as a bridge between the three levels of the world: heaven, earth, and the underworld. On either side of it are different plants from which yellows are extracted: three kinds of *cempaxóchiles* (Mexican Marigold, *Tagetes* spp.), the petals of which are used to produce different shades of warm yellow; and a plant called *zacapale* in Nahuatl (*Cuscuta* spp.), which looks like it is made of yellow yarn and grows like a vine. *Zacapale* has no leaves, which is why its name is derived from the word *zacate* (grass). In the past it was ground into a paste that was then molded into circular sheets for drying. Once processed, it was called *zacatlaxcalli* (*tlaxcalli* means tortilla), and this is how it was sold. Another source of yellow, with copperish tones, are lichens of the genus *Usnea*, whose

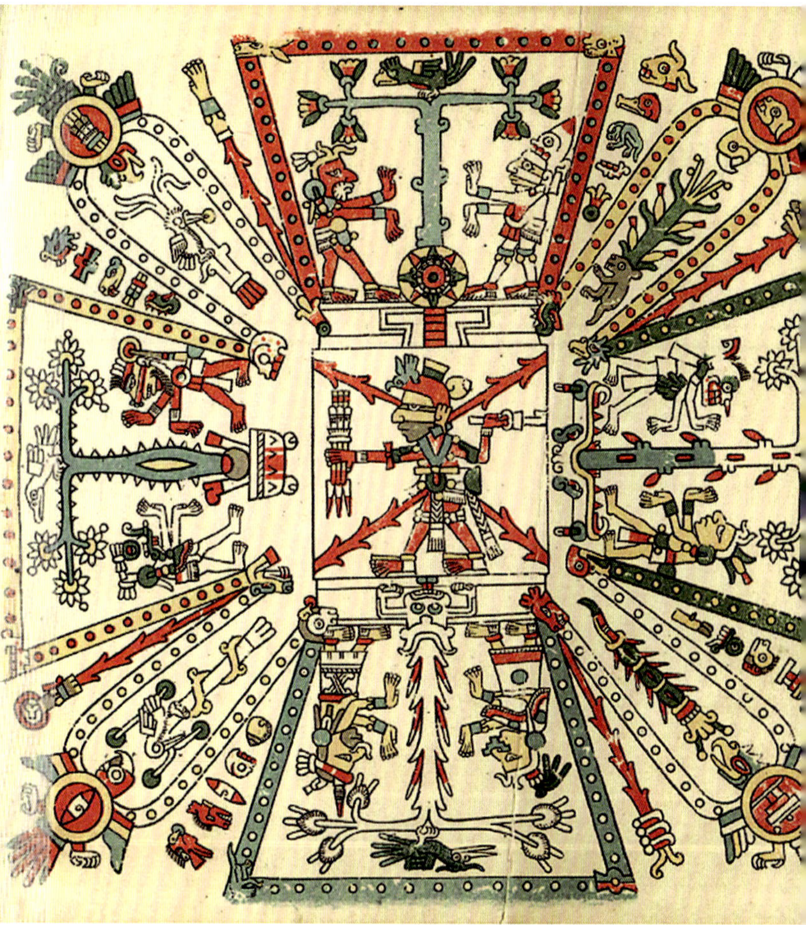

Fig 1. Once Known Creator, first plate of the Codex Fejérváry-Mayer. Reproduced with permission from the Instituto Nacional de Antropología e Historia, Mexico.

Nahuatl generic term is *quappachtli. Usnea* grows on both rocks and trees, but the word *quappachtli* refers specifically to species that grow on trees, and translates roughly as "tree fuzz." To finish up the space dedicated to the north, we included two iron oxide minerals, one black and one ochre, whose colors are the result of differences in their valences and in the quantities of molecular water they contain.

After north comes west, the place of the feminine and the color white. We represented this space with two different *amate* species, trees belonging to the Moraceae family from which paper was manufactured. In the pre-Hispanic era, *amate* paper and deerskin parchment were the two most common media used for making manuscripts. Often these media were covered with a thin layer of gesso (calcium sulfate, $CaSO_4$) or lime (calcium carbonate, $CaCO_3$); the latter was mainly used in the Maya region. In the chapter on color, Fray Bernardino de Sahagún's (1499–1590) informants mention that *chimaltizatl*, or translucent gesso, was the ideal material for preparing a leather or paper medium. In order to be used as a covering, it had to undergo a number of processes: calcination, pulverization, hydration, desiccation, and rehydration. The purity and luminosity of this mineral are reflected in the name with which it is now identified: selenite, or "moonstone."

The count of days ends in the south, and its color is blue-green. In this quadrant, we brought together three plants used to manufacture different shades of blue: *xiquilite* (*Indigofera suffruticosa*), from which indigo is extracted to produce Mayan blue; *matlalli* (*Commelina coelestis*), three-petaled flowers that only live for a day and whose juice is used to make the most precious blue; and Mexican honeysuckle, or *muitle* (*Justicia spicigera*), whose leaves were used to make greyish—and purplish—blue hues.

Contrary to what one might expect, there are no plant-based colorings to produce green hues. Chlorophyll decomposes quickly and is inadequate for both dyeing and painting, such that, in the past, green tones were made by combining blue and yellow. On the other hand, there are stones and soils that do present a greenish coloration. The use of azurite and malachite—basic copper carbonites—has been detected on mural paintings, but not on manuscripts. In the garden we opted for an iron mineral whose tonality is more reminiscent of the subtle green of jadeites.

Toward the end of Chapter 8 of the *Historia de los indios de la Nueva España*, Fray Toribio de Benavente, better known as Motolinía (c. 1482–1569), remarks: "The Indians make many colors from flowers, and when the painters wish to change from one color to another, they lick the brush clean, for the paints are made from the juice of flowers."[4]

This is certainly one of the most evocative images in Motolinía's writings, but it is falsehood, a way to call to mind an idyllic workshop scene. Motolinía took such a license in order to convey to his readers the existence of a different reality. Similarly, Amerigo Vespucci describes his fascination with the new reality in a letter addressed to Lorenzo di Pierfrancesco de' Medici, written in 1502:

> This land is very hospitable and full of countless big, green trees whose leaves never fall, and they all have a gentle, aromatic fragrance, and produce endless amounts of fruit, many of which are good-tasting and healthy for the body. The fields produce many herbs, flowers and roots, which are gentle and good, and for a time I marveled at the delicate fragrance of the herbs and flowers, and at the taste of these fruits and roots so much, that I thought myself to be near the Earthly Paradise: amidst all these things I would have believed that I was close to him . . .[5]

4 Fray Toribio de Benavente, "Motolinía," *Motolinía's History of the Indians of New Spain*, trans. and ed. Elizabeth Andros Foster (Berkeley: The Cortés Society, 1950), 19.

5 Amerigo Vespucci, *Cartas de viaje* (Barcelona: Alianza Editorial, 1986), 76–77. Translated by the editors (Mexico: MUAC, 2021).

But in spite of such surprises, from the beginning the Spaniards thought about practicality: seven days after having encountered the first island, still overwhelmed by the anguish of the crossing, Christopher Columbus was already thinking about the resources that could be extracted from these lands. At Cabo Hermoso he wrote:

> . . . and even as I saw this cape so green and so beautiful, like all the other lands of these islands, I scarcely know where to visit, I know not how to tire my eyes from seeing such beautiful vegetables and so different from ours, and I believe there are still many herbs and many trees of much value in Europe for the dyes they yield and medicines made from spices; but I do not know them, and this causes me great sorrow . . .[6]

It is not unusual that historians, soldiers, and monks would insistently refer to the wealth of natural resources. After gold and silver, spices and dyes were the raw materials that yielded the greatest economic dividends. In his *Historia de la conquista de México*, Francisco López de Gómara pointed out that "we should not forget the great quantity and variety of colors we have here that are sold, and the many others which are good and we lack, and they make from leaves, roses, flowers, fruits, roots, bark, stones, woods, and so many others that cannot be remembered."[7]

Twenty years later, Bernardino de Sahagún wrote about the commercial importance of cochineal: "This is the fine red (grana); this red is very well known in this land and beyond, and there is great trade of it as far as China and all the way to Turkey. Almost throughout the whole world it is esteemed and much valued."[8] But the American reality was also confrontational for them; the European paradigms on which knowledge was constructed had been turned upside down. This was a paradoxical reality in which, to foreign eyes, painters painted with the juice of flowers, and yet were ruled by pagan, sacrilegious, savage gods. Admiration and contempt, curiosity and terror, interest and disdain, came together in conflicts, disputes, and a sustained search for ways to make sense of this New World.

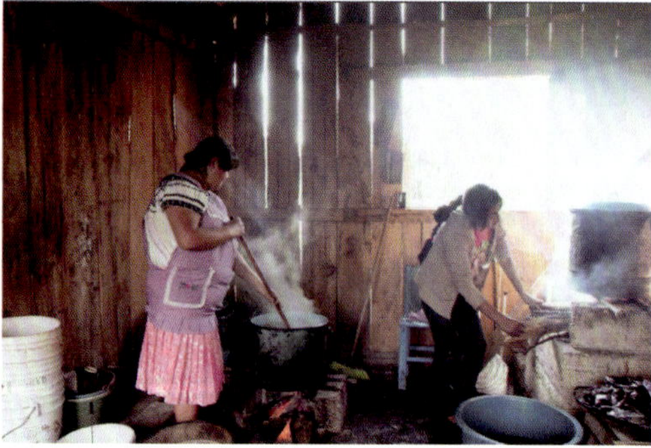

Fig 4. Manuela Lino's workshop, Hueyapan, Puebla, Mexico

Like any history of conquest, ours is full of abuses and contradictions. Today, it is still difficult not to feel a mix of admiration and offense. Because, despite the war, the interbreeding, and the epidemics that exterminated nearly eighty percent of the native population during the first forty years of contact, Mexico continues to be a multicultural, multilingual country that is also terribly divided and unequal. We are the outcome

6 *The Journal of Christopher Columbus (during His First Voyage, 1492–93)*, trans. and ed. Clements R. Markham (London: The Hakluyt Society, 1893), 52; translation by the author. Cf. Cristóbal Colón, "Viernes 19 de octubre," in *Relaciones y cartas de Cristóbal Colón* (Madrid: Biblioteca Nacional, 2006), 38, http://www.cervantesvirtual.com/nd/ark:/59851/bmcdj5b9.

7 Francisco López de Gómara, *La conquista de México* (Las Palmas de Gran Canaria: Red Ediciones, 2008), 164. Translated by the editors (Mexico: MUAC, 2021).

8 Bernardino de Sahagún, *General History of the Things of New Spain, Book XI: Earthly Things*, fs. 216v–217r, http://www.wdl.org/en/item/10622. Cf. note 13 below.

of complex, discordant, fragmented, and disrupted histories and realities. We are familiar with the images of the ancient gods, yet at the same time their forms continue to surprise us, and their underlying meanings remain a mystery. Maybe that explains why all that has survived of the indigenous past inspires similar curiosity to the one Motolinía, Sahagún, and Francisco Hernández (1514–1587) once felt, and now their texts guide us in attempting to grasp that which is inherently ours, yet altogether foreign to us.

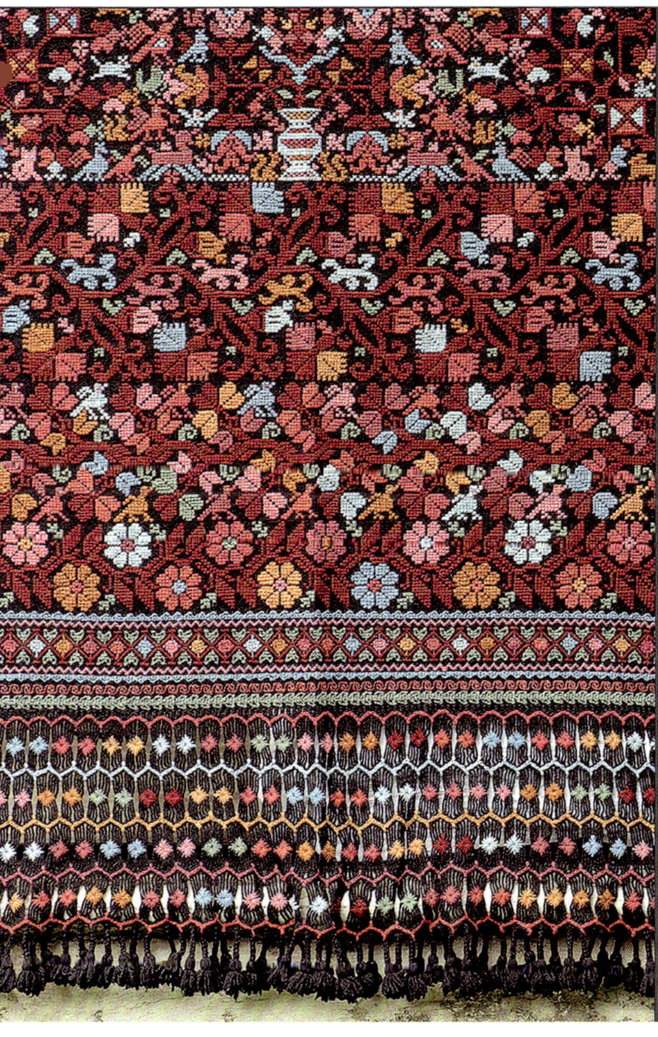

Fig 3. Manuela Lino's shawl

Although the indigenous ruling classes were able to negotiate and settle into the new order imposed by the conquerors, most of the population carried on with their lives as usual. They incorporated a new god and an ample calendar of saints' days to their pantheon, yet went on with their lives, shielded behind their languages, modes of organization, diets, attire, medicine, ways of doing things, and customs, and have endured in that way until now (fig. 2).

El jardín del pintor (*The Painter's Garden*) intended to be an homage to indigenous women and men who have studied and produced color. Dyers, painters, and alchemists who experimented and continue to experiment with different substances to find the ones that can be used to make pigments and dyes. It is also an homage to authors like Motolinía, Sahagún, and Hernández, who managed to transcend the barriers of their culture and immerse themselves in the New World, guided by their curiosity and their intelligence, and who sought ways to communicate with the people who lived here, leaving us invaluable texts documenting the history of Mexico. Finally, it is a tribute to the master colorists of the present day, especially to the memory of Manuela Cecilia Lino Bello (1943–2017).

When I met Manuela Lino in her home, I found her sitting on her living room armchair. She had a reserved appearance, a tiny and fragile complexion. I had not even yet sat down when she bent over to pick up two dark black plastic bags that she handed to me, saying, "You wanted to know about *tezuat*.[9] Open the bags and in one you will find the red, and in the other the green. We use the red to dye with cochineal . . ." And she continued speaking, barely giving me

9 The variant of Nahuatl spoken in Hueyapan omits the letter "l" at the end of nouns: *tezuatl*.

time to catch my breath, set up the tripod, and take out my camera to record her.

Her description of the leaves I had in my hands was so precise that it helped me to see details I would not have noticed otherwise: the difference in color between the stalk and the tips, the shininess and texture of the leaves, the differences between the upper and under sides, their symmetrical nervation . . . I looked at the leaves with amazement and then back at her, noting her white eyes that had gone blind fifteen years earlier, the movement of her small hands, and the way she touched her fingertips, as if recalling through touch the minute details of each plant.

Manuela spent her mornings going from her living room armchair to the kitchen and back again. From there, she instructed her assistant, Gloria, on what to buy for her meals, how to prepare the broth, or what material to have ready to deliver to the artisans who would be coming by later. She had the memory of an elephant: she knew where she had placed each object, to whom she had delivered what, how much money so-and-so owed her, who had samples of embroidered figures—her collection of prototypes was impressive.

In the afternoons she would go down to the dyeing workshop, which is now coordinated by her daughter, Cecilia, when she returns from her "official" job. There, Manuela kept track of everything that was prepared. With slight movements of her head, she turned her attention to different sounds and gave instructions to each of the artisans (fig. 3).

Hueyapan is located in the heart of the cloud forest of the Sierra Madre Oriental mountain range. It is a small town surrounded by pine and oak forests, and it is cold and rainy for most of the year. Manuela's workshop is a wood cabin with a gable roof, and the stoves are wood-burning. It is a dark space, because there are few windows, and because the soot from the wood has stained the walls and ceilings black. The atmosphere is dark and dense due to the woodsmoke and the vapor from the boiling pots; it is difficult to breathe. We talked about colors, exchanged recipes, and chatted about our families while the time-consuming process of dyeing was taking place.

When I reviewed the thousands of hours of recordings I made in the workshop, I was horrified to realize that there is nothing to be seen. So much smoke did not allow the camera to register the colors in the vats, even my own hoarse voice sounds unfamiliar, and I am taken aback at how often I blow my nose. Manuela is stolid in front of the camera; her movements and gestures are those of someone who has not seen herself or anyone else for years.

My encounter with Manuela is also important because of the correspondence between dying techniques in Hueyapan and the information compiled in the sixteenth-century documentary sources. Creating different shades of reds, cherries, pinks, and purples, made using cochineal (*Dactylopius coccus*), follows the same process that Sahagún and Hernández described half a millennium ago. It involves a plant called *tezuatl*, belonging to the family of Melastomataceae, whose chemical properties are still not entirely defined. Nevertheless, we know it is a plant that accumulates aluminum and contains a particular kind of tannin called ellagic acid. The combination of these two substances, with the carminic acid in the cochineal, produce cherry red and reddish hues, depending on the amount of cochineal used.

The recipe for fine reds recorded by Sahagún and Hernández is based on this same combination. In his *Historia natural de la Nueva España*, Hernández describes them as follows:

> Among the Mexicans there is a certain genus of prickly-pear cactus called *Nopalnocheztli*, for this reason, it is sown in places protected by nature against the depredations of cattle and beasts, little round worms, white on the outside and scarlet-colored within, which are sometimes born spontaneously and sometimes through human industry by applying eggs from the previous year to the new prickly-pear leaves. The Indians call them *nocheztli* while our countrymen call them *cochinilla* (cochineal), a name derived perhaps from *coccum* which is the species they belong to . . . The *nocheztli* can sometimes give a purple color, sometimes scarlet, depending on the preparation method. The outcome is thoroughly exquisite when it is ground with a decoction of the tree called *tezhoatl*, which we will discuss in due time, alum is added and the sediment is collected and then stored in the form of tablets . . .[10]

According to the sixteenth-century reports, the combination of *tezuatl*, cochineal, and alum was used to dye *tochomitl*—rabbit fur—and to make a pigment that, once dry, was compressed and kept in the form of tablets. In Hueyapan, today, wool is dyed; we do not know whether rabbit pelts and cotton were dyed there in ancient times, nor whether they used to make pigments. Regarding passing of knowledge from pre-Hispanic to contemporary Mexico, I can only offer coincidences or chain links to defend the hypothesis of a long tradition, interweaving data taken from diverse sources with the testimonies of the craftwork I have recorded (fig. 4).

The production of black cloaks using indigo is quite rare, from the point of view of technology. Hueyapan is one of the few villages in the world that has preserved this know-how. In this village, indigo is considered a special material, and to manipulate it dyers follow a series of prescriptions. Because of its properties, indigo blue (*Indigofera* spp.) is both a pigment and colorant at the same time. The colorant substance of indigo blue is called indigo and is insoluble in water, so it can be used as a pigment. The term "indigo" was used by the Romans to refer to the blue that was imported to Europe from India and the Near East. There are different vegetable species in nature that produce indigo; in Mexico, the most important one in terms of the quantity of colorant it contains is known as *jiquilite*, from the Nahuatl word *xiuquilitl* (*Indigofera suffruticosa*), but within Mexico's borders at least sixteen other endemic species have been identified.[11] Once extracted from the plant, the indigo is sold as a dry, hardened dark-blue substance with shades of violet. This characteristic allows the material to be transported to towns that are far from its place of origin.

Hueyapan does not have the right climatic conditions to produce indigo, so it is imported by way of specialized dyeing merchants. Manuela Lino explained that in the fifties, cochineal and indigo were purchased at the weekly market in Tlatlauquitepec, along with other ingredients, including alum,

10 Francisco Hernández, "Del nopalnocheztli o grana de Indias que nace en ciertas tunas," *Historia natural de la Nueva España*, I (México city: UNAM, 1959), 315–316. Translated by the editors (Mexico: MUAC, 2021).

11 Dominique Cardon, *Natural Dyes: Sources, Tradition, Technology and Science* (London: Archetype Publications, 2007), 354–357.

zacatlaxcalli, *tequesquite*, and ferrous sulfate.

Indigo is insoluble in water, so it cannot be used in dyeing without first undergoing a transformation. The chemical process is called reduction, and it implies removing the oxygen that occurs at its molecular level, which triggers a series of reactions that result in a soluble substance called indican. Indican is the precursor molecule of indigo, and it is found in this state in the plant before being extracted to produce indigo. It is a yellow-greenish substance that, when in solution with the thread or fabric being dyed, penetrates between the fibers and gets trapped there. Once the fibers are soaked in the indican solution, they are left to dry in the open air, so being in contact with oxygen transforms the molecules back into indigo. In a matter of minutes, the fabric turns green, then blue.

Blue dyeing requires at least five days of preparation. According to master dyers, women who work with indigo must be calm at heart and pure of body; otherwise, the transformation will not occur. Furthermore, those involved in the process must not be grieving the loss of a loved one, must not be menstruating or pregnant, and must abstain from sexual relations throughout the process; otherwise, the vat of dye will spoil.

In order to turn indigo into a soluble substance capable of dyeing, one must "stand the pot;" that is, bring together all the ingredients required to foster the transformation from indigo to indican, and maintain the pot at a constant temperature for three days to ensure that the reaction takes place. The reduction is achieved through a fermentation process. First, the indigo is left in water overnight to soften. The next day, the clumps are ground in a mortar with the help of water saturated with *tequesquite*. The alkalinity of the *tequesquite* helps to dissolve the indigo until it turns into a dense liquid without clumps. Then, into the dyeing pot go elderberry leaves (*Sambucus mexicana*, or *xomet* in Nahuatl) and yucca leaves (*ixot*), which aid the fermentation. The prescriptions also indicate adding one pine branch (*tatzcan*) that has been split into three parts, to avoid the evil eye, and one branch of *tepozán* (*Buddleia parviflora, tzayolitzcan*), to prevent it from being bewitched.

The leaves are layed creating crosses. On the first bed of herbs a "doll" is placed: a white cloth figurine that represents a human being with body, head, and limbs. The pot is blessed before adding some "seed": the liquid from previous dyeing processes that has been held back each time and mixed with the prior remnants. The old indigo is vital to set off the fermentation process of the new indigo, which will be added gradually from this point onwards.

Dyeing with indigo is perhaps one of the most admirable processes within the field. Old indigo gives life to the new indigo, and through a chemical metamorphosis transforms indigo into indican. The process is zealously watched over, as though protecting a gestation with magical spells. In Puebla's Sierra Norte, the Totonacs use paper figures as vehicles for prayers and as stand-ins for various domestic and natural deities. It is unclear whether the doll plays a similar role in Hueyapan. Having been unable to further investigate the role of the figure thus far, it seems to me that the process of dyeing with indigo presents strong parallels to the way the Nahuas of the Sierra Norte in Puebla conceive human gestation, as studied by Sybille de Pury-Toumi in the 1990s. This author explains, "the decomposition of matter has a reciprocal relationship with its re-composition, both for the plant and animal kingdoms, and thus for humans as well. Human pregnancy would correspond to this same representation: the development of the seed—the fetus—would entail the decomposition of the fruit—the mother's womb. As Nahuas conceive it, the process of fermentation is a process of decay or decomposition."[12] Pot/womb, fetus/doll, and the sprout that breathes life to the seed/fermented *añil.*

The production of black cloaks in the ancient past is recorded in the *Matrícula de Tributos* where the province of Tlatlauquitepec is depicted as tributing black cloaks—the center of the tributary province that included Hueyapan. Another interesting fact is that those blankets were for the *tlatoani* of Mexico-Tenochtitlan, as indicated by the sign on the drawing of the blankets.

In Book 8, Chapter 21 of the *Florentine Codex*, Sahagún reports that, during the celebration of the annual feast in honor of the god Xipe Totec, Moctezuma rewarded his best warriors with wide black cloaks, four to eight for each one.[13]

We know that the *amantecas*, traditional feather workers, would send their children to the Calmecac to learn their craft. Some young women and men were sacrificed during the feast that honored the goddesses Xiuhtlali and Xilo—associated with their craft—an offering that occurred during the ninth twenty-day-cycle, *Tlaxochimaco*, corresponding to the period between August 4 and 23 in our calendar. At this feast, women would dance together and make flower offerings. In Hueyapan, the craftswomen celebrate Santa Filomena on the August 12, with dances during which men and women adorned themselves with flower garlands and danced the *Xochipitzahuac*, or "Petite Flower."

The ancient *amantecas* would ask for theirs son to become *tlamacazqui* (priests), and in this way they could acquire "eyes and heart" (this would mean "full consciousness," according to López Austin) to fulfill their capacities as artisans. In the case of their daughters, they would ask for them to be adept at manual labor, and in particular that they became good dyers, of both feathers and *tochómitl*.[14]

The garden was, to some extent, a whim, a fancy. We brought together plants from different regions and climates that would have been unable to survive without the help of a good gardener tending to the needs of each one. We chose to make a garden because studies of many indigenous codices have shown that many of the pigments used to color them were of organic origin.[15] We wanted to use those same pigments on the walls of the museum in order to create a pictographic dialogue between the past and the present, and at the same time to show their particular luminous and chromatic qualities. In so doing, we also reinforced the temporal bridge that Castillo Deball had established by constructing and disassembling the image on the first page of the *Féjérvary-Mayer Codex* through the intervention of the patio area, in the case of the garden, and through the pieces *Perfecto luna* and *Materia de los días*, located on the floor and walls of the

12 Sybille de Pury-Toumi, *De palabras y maravillas: ensayo sobre la lengua y la cultura de los nahuas (Sierra norte de Puebla)* (Mexico City: Centro Francés de Estudios Mexicanos y Centroamericanos, 1997), 145.

13 Alfredo López Austin, *Educación mexica: Antología de documentos sahaguntinos* (Mexico City: UNAM, 1994), 115.

14 Austin, 125–27.

15 Cf. *Códice Cospi*, Miliani et al. (2012); *Códice Féjérvary-Mayer*, Domenici et al. (2014); *Códice Colombino*, Zetina et al. (2011a and 2014); Falcón (2014 and 2019); *Códice Madrid*, Buti et al. (2014); *Códice Zouche-Nuttall*, Higgitt (2013); *Códice Borbónico*, Pottier et al. (2019); *Códice De La Cruz-Badiano* (1552), Zetina et al., 2008, 2011b; *Códice Azoyu I*, Zetina et al. (2011); *Códice Florentino*, Baglioni et al. (2011a), Magaloni (2011); Giorgi et al. (2014).

mezzanine. The first page of the *Féjérvary-Mayer* is a *tonalpohualli*: it represents the creation of space and time. There, the ordering of the days of the sacred calendar converge, a center is defined, the cardinal points of inhabited space are arranged in order, and the pathways that join earth, heaven, and the underworld are forged. It is a ritual calendar with **260** days, formed by combining twenty named days (*veintenas*) and thirteen numbered days (*trecenas*).

Unlike the clay and stone sculptures or mural paintings, whose colors almost always came from mineral pigments, indigenous codices made before the Conquest and during the colonial era could indeed be painted using the juices of flowers because the flexible, mobile medium allowed them to be stored away from sunlight, the main enemy of colors of organic origin.

Thanks to other historical records and to the chemical analyses carried out on a good number of pre-Hispanic and colonial objects, we now know that pigments made from flowers, fruits, woods, barks, leaves, lichens, and insects were primarily used for painting on paper or leather: books of divination, genealogies, tribute accounts, annals, maps, and so on, which all had in common the characteristic of being easily transported and safeguarded.

What were those colors? What tonalities did they produce? How were the juices extracted from the flowers and turned into stable, indelible pigments? Fray Bernardino de Sahagún wrote an entire chapter on this topic, titled "On Colors, on All Kinds of Colors," in Book **11** of the *Florentine Codex*, the most complete version of the *Historia general de las cosas de la Nueva España* (**1577**). It is a compendium that names and describes various substances used in the art of painting. The sum of information disclosed in the Spanish and Nahuatl texts, as well as the drawings in the codex, allow the reconstruction of some processes involved in pigment-making.

Only two flowers are mentioned among the materials used as colorants: *matlalli* and *xochipalli*. The petals of the former were used for "fine blue . . . a very pleasing color to look at . . . [It is] *blue and a bit green. It gives a lot of color. It is firm, good, of beautiful appearance, fresh, fresh, very fresh.*"[16]

The second flower produced "fine yellow": "this color is brought from hot climates where it grows . . . *It is a dyeing medium, a pigment, for beautifying, for making things radiant, for giving luster.*"[17]

Fig 2. *Para qué me diste las manos llenas de color, todo lo que toque se llenará de sol*, **2018**, pigment on plaster, *In Tlili in Tlapalli*, **2018**, Museo Amparo, Puebla, Mexico

Although neither of these two examples explain the processes for making pigments, the text dedicated to the *xochipalli* provides other relevant data: the material is imported and it is both tint and pigment. That is, it was used for both dyeing and painting. It is relevant to clarify this because it refers to a specific category of knowledge that has to do with what we now call natural colorants: colored organic compounds, which are soluble, and produced by living organisms—plants, insects, lichens, animals, and fungi—that can be extracted and transferred to other surfaces through an aqueous medium and that, therefore, are used to dye other objects. In addition to defining a concrete group of compounds, the category makes it possible to classify them according to different criteria. In the case of natural dyeing, the colorants can be divided into three groups, depending on the methods: **1**) direct dyes, which are applied directly to the fibers without any kind of preparation; **2**) dyes with mordants, which require some metallic salt to create unifying bridges—

16 Sahagún, **1577**, Book III, **217**v.; Anderson and Dibble vol. **12**, Book XI, **1963**, p. **240**.

17 Sahagún, **1577**, Book XI, **217**r; Anderson and Dibble vol. **12**, Book XI, **1963**, p. **240**.

chemical bonds—between the dye and the fiber; and **3**) fermented dyes, which require a process of reduction by fermentation, in order to transform the coloring substance into a soluble precursor before dyeing. Colorants can also become pigments when extracted and precipitated on insoluble, inert substrates, like clay, alumina (aluminum hydrates), and plaster. Chemistry classifies them according to their molecular structures: the main chemical groups present in nature are quinines, indigoids, carotenoids, flavonoids, and tannins. The key point here is that these classification systems help us to organize, explain, and transform the world that surrounds us, and the logics behind them bring us closer to specific ways of thinking and producing knowledge. With one system we can follow the procedures and reconstruct the ways in which painters and dyers used their raw materials; with the other system, we can identify the origin of the substances used to color indigenous paintings.

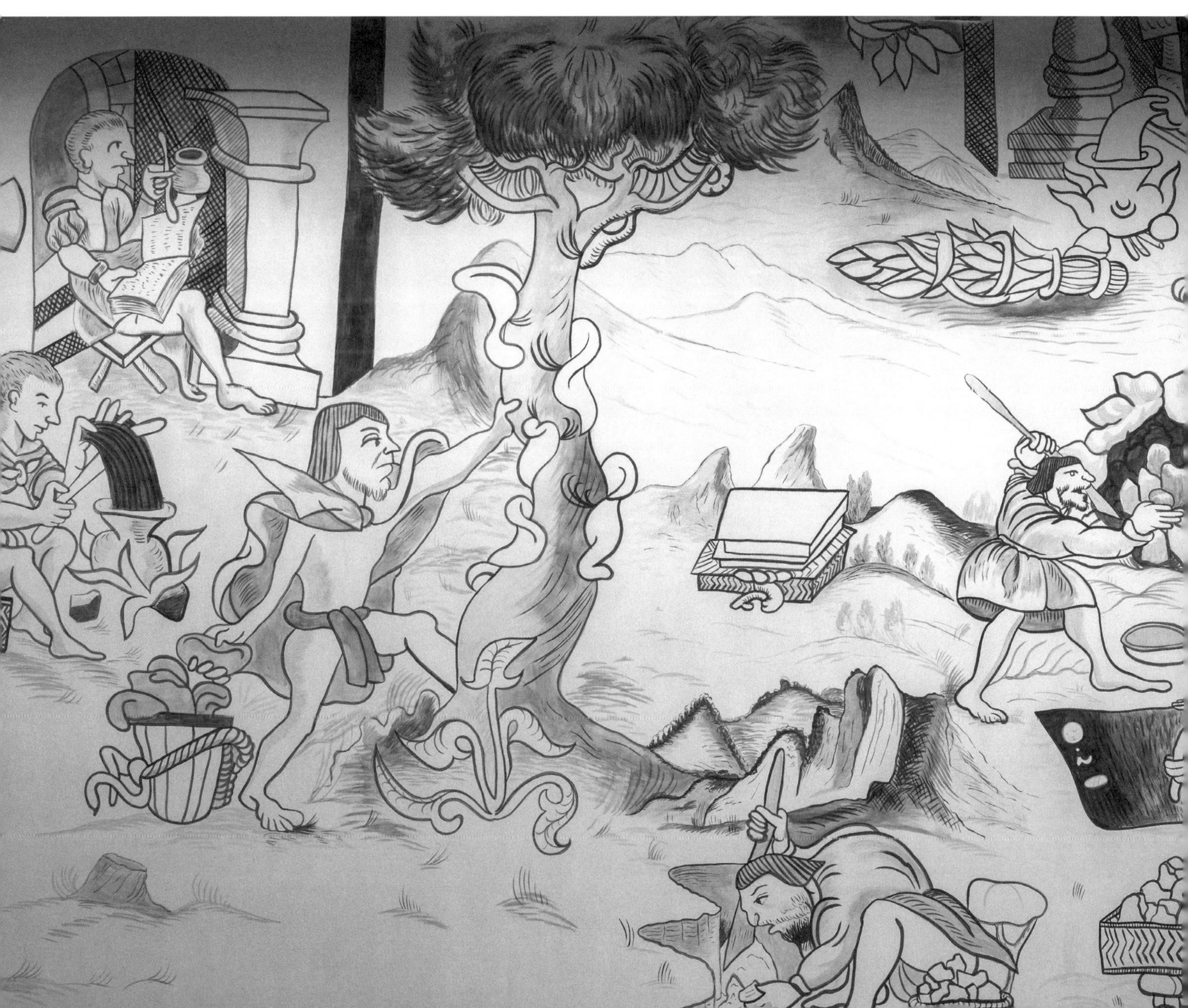

The first drawing associated with the *xochipalli* is a country scene in which a man cuts flowers that he puts into a basket. The bush he prunes is as tall as he is. In the second drawing, a painter-scribe, seated on the portico of a building with columns, holds a feather-pen to a blank piece of paper. Next to him there is a vessel and on top of it is a flower, similar to the flowers from the first drawing. Mountains are visible in the background. Both figures are wearing European clothing: a tailored, long-sleeved shirt with a round collar and a pleated short skirt. Their physiognomies and hair suggest that these are two different individuals. Is one the person in charge of preparing the pigments and the other the painter?

There are also two drawings associated with *matlalli*: in the first one the *matlalli* plant stands out, with its elongated leaves, intercalated curves and a flower with four rounded, symmetrical petals. The landscape in the background suggests that it grows in the wild. The fact that a plant is cultivated or grows wild determines the time it will take to germinate, grow, and be harvested. In a way, there is more control over cultivated plants, depending on the climatic conditions, the type of soil, and the rainfall in the region. Maize, for example, is cultivated

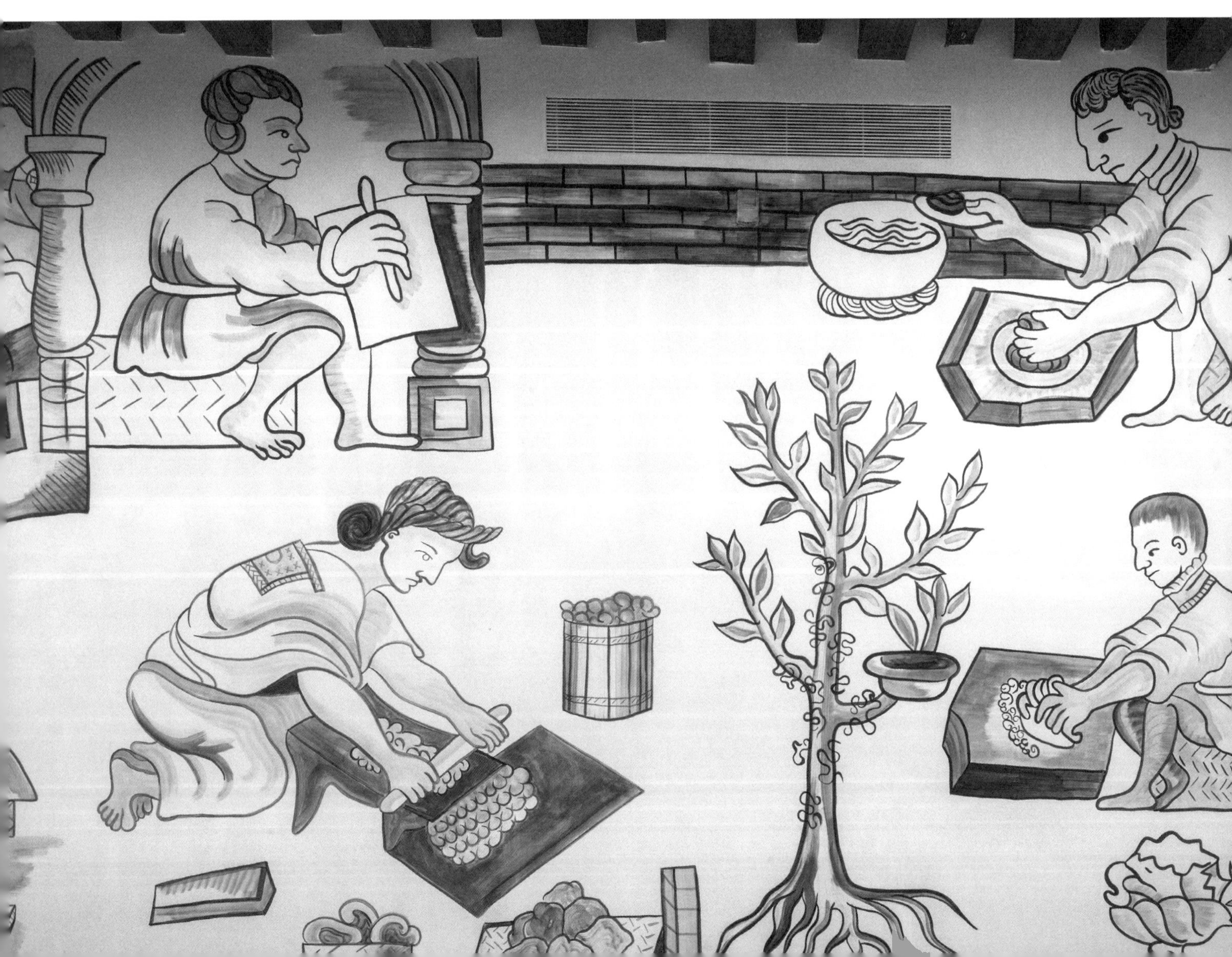

once or twice a year. In the case of wild plants, those who use them must know their growing cycles, even though these cannot be changed; they must be ready to collect the plant at precisely the right moment, depending on what part of the plant is needed (leaves, flowers, fruit, or seeds).

Francisco Hernández also recorded the use of these two flowers. As the head of Spain's first Royal Botanical Expedition (1570–1580), his job was to research useful plants in New Spain, so he recorded the colorant materials that were used by indigenous painters. Thanks to the letters he sent to King Philip II, we know that he collaborated with them and went through an apprenticeship period. The formal and taxonomic models of his collaborators had to be fitted to the needs and models of European record-keeping. In a letter dated November/December 1571, Hernández described the paints, writing: "More than 800 plants have been painted on paper, depicting their parts and in true to life proportions with more precision than before."[18] On March 31, 1573, he reported to his ruler that four volumes of paintings with the plants of New Spain had been completed, all of which had been painted on different occasions. He argued that the plants had to be studied in different seasons to understand their development and to ensure that they were the same plant and not a different one. He went further, writing that the plants were studied and painted at different times in order to add details like flowers, seeds, and fruits. In addition, he asks for the painters to be paid, as they helped regularly.[19] The collection of botanized plants and seeds from the first Royal Botanical Expedition is still kept at the Royal Botanical Garden in Madrid. Unfortunately, the paintings were dispersed by Philip II himself, who, as we know, used some of them to decorate the walls of the Escorial, which were then lost in the fire of 1671. Regarding the *matlalli* and *xochipalli*, the author provides the following information:

Para qué me diste las manos llenas de color, todo lo que toque se llenará de sol, 2018, pigment on plaster, pigment samples, *In Tlili in Tlapalli*, 2018, Museo Amparo, Puebla, Mexico

> [*Matlalli* is] a plant two cubits long, with fibrous roots, thin, cylindrical stalks, numerous delicate leaves, and flowers that resemble purple and blue violets. It is submerged in water for an hour and then squeezed, and that liquid is used to dye wool, they say, with sea-green or blue color. Some call this plant *matlaxochitl*.[20]
>
> *Xochipalli* is a plant six cubits tall, with long, thin roots, from which stalks the thickness of a finger grow, and on them sinuous, large leaves that somewhat resemble those of ragweed, and the flowers like those of *cempoalxochitl*, but small and colored yellow, with red. Only the flower is used, which is of a moderate heat (*calor*), agreeable in smell and taste, and fortifies the heart, combats illnesses of the womb, and cures ulcers, mainly on the mouth. It is used, above all, to dye wool and paint figures in a reddish yellow, for which it is cooked together with niter, and then the juice is squeezed out of it and strained, and thus serves painters and fullers as a colorant.

18 *The Mexican Treasury: The Writings of Dr. Francisco Hernández*, ed. Simon Varey, trans. Rafael Chabran, Cynthia L. Chamberlin, and Simon Varey, (Stanford: Stanford University Press, 2001), 48.

19 *The Mexican Treasury*, 52.

20 Francisco Hernández, Obras completas III, Historia natural de Nueva España, vol. II (Mexico: UNAM, 1959), Chapter XXI.

It grows in various hot places, and is a very common herb.[21]

We have, then, a flower that was used as a direct dye in the case of *matlalli*, and another that required a mordant to make its color fix, *xochipalli*. Hernández's text confronts us with another set of problems that are worth pointing out: the implicit ambiguity behind the names and adjectives that we use to designate a particular tone: "sea-green," "blue," or "reddish yellow" could refer to a vast range of chromatic possibilities. The botanical identification of plants to which he refers and the experimental reconstruction of procedures for making pigments and dyes are some of the most direct ways to understand what colors we are talking about.

Sahagún and Hernández mention other colorant materials of organic origin that do not come from flowers. The set of materials and manufacturing processes to which they refer is very similar. That is, the production of pigments was a specialized, well-defined, and noted practice. Sahagún associates the pigment vendor with those who traded with rabbit pelts (dyers) and with those who traded gourds—perhaps because these three specialists were located in a particular part of the market, as Hernán Cortés had described it in his second *Carta de Relación*. We know that the pigment vendors sold "dry colors and ground colors";[22] in other words, two kinds of pigments. On one hand were the organic ones, which are made from various organisms, both animal and vegetable. Given their nature, these needed to be extracted with water, and therefore required a drying process. On the other hand, mineral pigments needed to be submitted to different processes of grinding and pulverization—and sometimes purification and cleansing—turning stones into dust.

In Europe, "dry colors," or organic pigments, are called "lac pigments," because in oil painting they produce translucent strata and are used on the superficial layers of a painting as "color baths" that contribute to shading the colors of the underlying layers.[23] The translucent effect is due to the index of refraction of the lac pigments that is similar to linseed oil. Mineral pigments, on the other

21 Francisco Hernández, Obras completas III, Historia natural de Nueva España, vol. II (Mexico: UNAM, 1959), Chapter XX.

22 Sahagún (1577), Book X-21, 55r–55v, https://www.wdl.org/en/item/10621/view/1/113.

The Nahuatl version reads: "Twenty-first chapter, which telleth of those who sell colors, rabbit hair [material], and gourd bowls. The one who displays his merchandise with a large basket is the one who sells colors, various colors, dyes; a man who piles [small color baskets] on a large basket. He sells dried pigment, bars of cochineal pigment, cochineal mixed with gesso or flour, [pure] cochineal; light yellow, sky blue pigment; gesso, smoke-black, dark blue pigment; alum, *axin*, chicle, bitumen-mixed chicle, rust red; *tlilxochitl, mecaxochitl, uei nacaztli, teonacaztli*; opossum, opossum tail; small herbs, small roots; bitumen, resin, copal; *nacazcolotl, quimichpatli*; a blue coloring made from flowers; copper sulfate, iron pyrites."

"The seller of rabbit hair [material] is a dyer, a user of dyes, a dyer [of material] in many colors. [Sometimes] he uses faded colors, and dresses [the material] with ashes. He sells good rabbit-hair [material], well prepared, harmonious, not dulled with ashes. He sells them in red, yellow, sky blue, light green, dark blue, copper ochre, dark green, flower yellow, blue-green, [carmine], pink, brown. [With these] he dyes, he provides color." Bernardino de Sahagún Florentine Codex: General History of the Things of New Spain, eds., and translators Charles E. Dibble and Arthur J. O. Anderson (Santa Fe, New Mexico: School of American Research/University of Utah Press, (1961) 1974), vol. X, 77.

23 A lac pigment is made by precipitating (or adsorbing) a colorant to an insoluble and relatively stable substrate. In the traditional (read: European) definition, it is said that this substrate is of alumina hydrate, but in practice this is very restrictive.

The most common European recipes follow a logic that is the reverse of the American one: the extraction of colorant is carried out with the help of an alkali—lye from ashes, limewater, urine—followed by adding alum to precipitate a colorant to a substrate of hydrated amorphous alumina.

hand—with the exception of ultramarine and gray-green, whose indexes of refraction are very low—produce opaque layers, regardless of the binding agent with which the pigments are amalgamated. The process by which a color dye solidifies and creates a pigment involves the addition of metallic salts, which bind with the colorant molecules to form a chelate. These salts tend to be the same ones used by dyers to fix the colorants on fibers.

Color merchants traded in many materials. Table 1 shows the names of the materials and the colors present in the chapter to show the variety of products that could be acquired in the marketplace.

The list of materials compiled in Chapter 11 of Book XI of the *Florentine Codex* complements the information gathered in Chapter 21 of Book X. As I mentioned above, it lists different colorant materials that do not come from flowers. The organization of the chapter suggests an order based on two criteria. The Spanish-language text classifies the colors according to their quality: "The first paragraph deals with cochineal red [la grana], and other fine colors."[24] In this section one finds cochineal (*Dactylopius coccus*), *xochipalli* (*Cosmos sulphureus*), *matlalli* (*Commelina coelestis*), *zacatlaxcalli* (*Cuscuta tinctorum*), and *achiote* (*Bixe orellana*). The Nahuatl text adheres to a different criterion, centered on how the colors are prepared: "First paragraph, refers to how all the colors are made." As the Nahuatl subtitle indicates, the indigenous-language text includes more information related to the processes of manufacturing the pigments.

In the second paragraph, titled "On other tinting, not as fine as cochineal red; and on other non-fine colors" includes "not as fine" red from *palo de brazil* or *huitzquauitl* (*Haematoxylon brasiletto*); *nacazctolotl* (the seeds of the tree *Caesalpinia coriaria*), used to make ink for writing; *tezuatl* (*Miconia* spp.), a plant-based mordant used with cochineal to obtain the red tonalities of that dye; two blues, *tlaceuilli* and *xiuhquilitl* (extracted from *Indigofera sufrutticosa*) and a sky-blue pigment (*texotli*); a yellow-colored earth, *tecozauitl*; and smoke-black, *tlilli*, with a mineral mordant, *tlaliyac* or iron (II) sulfate. In spite of the fact that the combination of materials may seem somewhat arbitrary, in the second paragraph we encounter for the first time the explanations on the combinations of materials and processes, such that the Nahuatl title ("Second paragraph, which telleth of still other colors, so that it is seen how coloring is done") gives the first clues about the logic behind the explanation and presentation of the recipes.

Finally, the "Third paragraph: on certain materials for making colors," or "Third paragraph, on what colors are made with; on what improves them," includes the substances used as vehicles and support media for the pigments, as well as possible combinations for producing some secondary colors.[25]

With the painter's garden we refounded space and time, bringing about the writing of our own stories, germinating the seeds of the plants we were to sow. We constructed its center, burying the colonial source with a pyramidal platform, which is at the same time a smoky mirror. We aligned the lobes of the figure with the four cardinal directions and used the trapezium as parcels of land to sow the plants that produce the colors associated with each cardinal point.

24 Sahagún, *Códice Florentino*, XI, 216r., 218r., and 219v.

25 "Injc ume parrapho: oc centlamantli tlapalli itechpa tlatoa, iuh motta in quenin tlapalo. . . . Injc ei parrapho: itechpa tlatoa, injc mochiva qujqualtilia in tlapalli." Anderson and Dibble, vol. 12, Book XI (1963), 241, 243.

Table I: Names of colors and materials

Pigment	Nahuatl Name	Description
cochineal pigment	*tlaquaoac tlapalli*	In general, this term is associated with tablets of processed cochineal, although the term literally means "firm color," so, depending on the context, it can also refer to other materials.
cochineal mixed with gesso or flour	*tlapalnextli*	The Spanish version is associated with wild and modified cochineal; both possibilities yielded an ashen color, different from the chili red or blood red that was extracted from fine cochineal.
(pure) cochineal	*nocheztli*	This referes to fine cochineal, which comes from domesticated insects (*Dactylopius coccus*).
light yellow	*zacatlaxcalli*	This is also the name of a parasitic plant (*Cuscuta* spp.).
sky blue pigment	*texotli*	To this day, there is no consensus about the nature of this pigment. Some of us believe it is a mineral pigment (Hernández, Meabe, Falcón); others that it is a lac pigment (Dupey).
gesso	*tetizatl*	
smoke black	*tlilli*	
dark blue pigment	*tlaceuilli*	Associated with indigo blue (*Indigofera sufruticosa*).
alum	*tlalxocotl*	Disulfate of aluminum and potassium. It is used as a mordant.
axin	*axi*	Yellowish wax substance made by boiling worms (*Coccus axin*)
chicle gum	*tzictli*	
bitumen-mixed chicle gum	*tlaaxnelolli*	
rust red	*tlauitl*	
bitumen	*chapopotli*	
resin	*tecupalli*	
copal	*copalli*	

Pigment	Nahuatl Name	Description
	nacazcolotl	An ear-shaped fruit (*Caesalpinia coriaria*) that is used in dyeing because of its high tannin content.
a blue coloring made from flowers	*matlalin*	Name of the flower (*Commelina coelestis*) and a particular shade of blue. In Spanish, *azul fino*.
copper (or iron) sulfate	*tlaliiac*	Used in dyeing to make a colorant fix and change its shade. Some authors believe this is iron(II) sulfate.
red	*chichiltic*	Chili red.
yellow	*coztic*	
sky blue	*texotli*	
light green	*quiltic*	
dark blue	*mouitli*	This is also the name of a plant (*Justicia spicigera*) from which blue and purple shades are made. It is used as an adjective for indigo blue in the chapter on color, so it might refer to a shade of violet blue.
ochres and yellows	*quappachtli*	The Castilian version renders this as *color leonado*, "tawny colored." It is made from various lichens of the genus *Usnea*. The tonal variants can be classified using nomenclatures of hair color that run from chestnut to blond.
dark green	*iapalli*	
flower yellow	*suchipalli*	It is believed that it was extracted from the flowers of the *Cosmos sulphureus*, even though from Hernández's descriptions it could also refer to a kind of wild marigold (*Tagetes tenuifolia*). It yields orange tonalities.
blue-green	*quilpalli*	
carmine	*nochpalli*	
pink	*tlaztaleoalli*	
purple	*camiltic*	

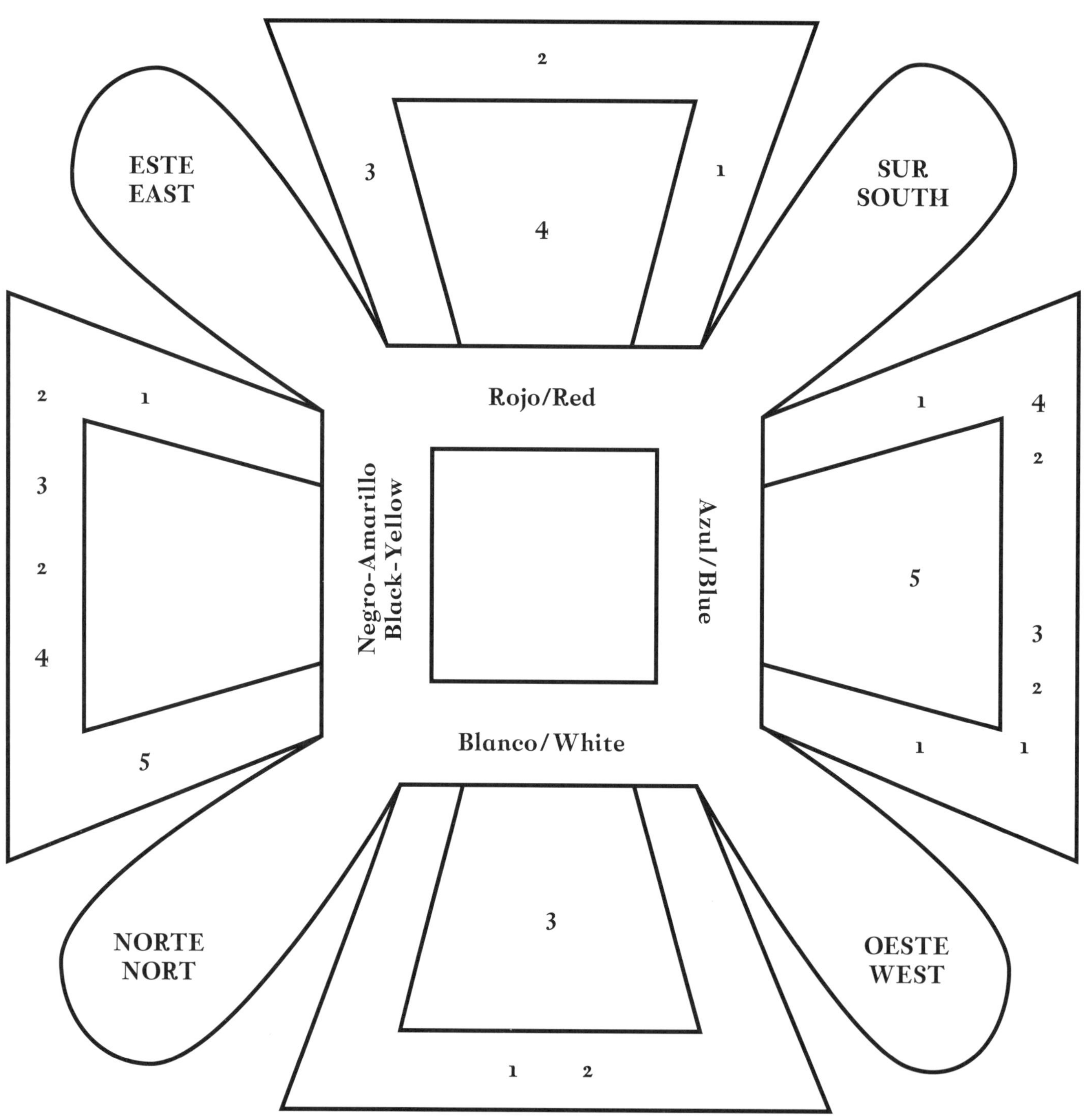
2
ESTE
EAST
3
1
SUR
SOUTH
4
2
1
Rojo/Red
1
4
2
3
Negro-Amarillo
Black-Yellow
Azul/Blue
2
5
3
4
2
Blanco/White
1
1
5
3
NORTE
NORT
OESTE
WEST
1
2

Jardín de plantas tintóreas y minerales
Plant and Mineral Garden

Blanco/White
1. Amate prieto/Brown amate
2. Amate amarillo/Yellow amate
3. Selenita/Selenite

Negro-Amarillo/Black-Yellow
1. Liquen/Usnea lichens
2. Cempoaxóchitl (Cempazuchil)/Mexican marigold
3. Mezquite/Mezquite
4. Xochipalli/Cosmos flowers
5. Zacatlaxcalli/Dodder
6. Óxido de hierro/Iron oxide

Rojo/Red
1. Achiote/Annatto
2. Grana cochinilla/Cochineal bug
3. Palo de Brasil/Haematoxylum brasiletto
4. Hematita/Hematite

Azul/Blue
1. Matlalli/Commelina coelestis
2. Muitle/Mexican honeysuckle
3. Añil/Anil
4. Yerba de pollo/Commelina
5. Celadonita/Celadonite

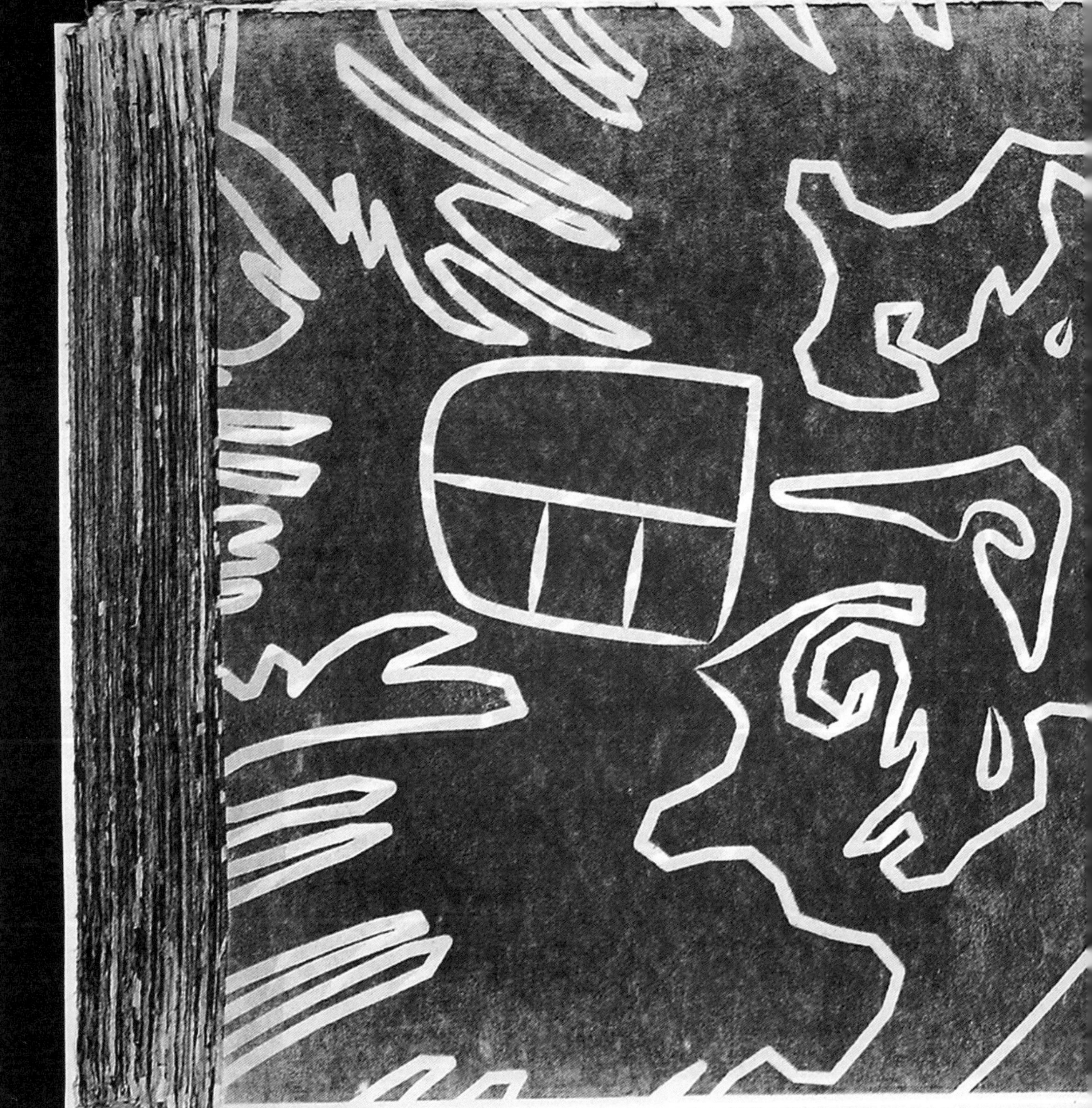

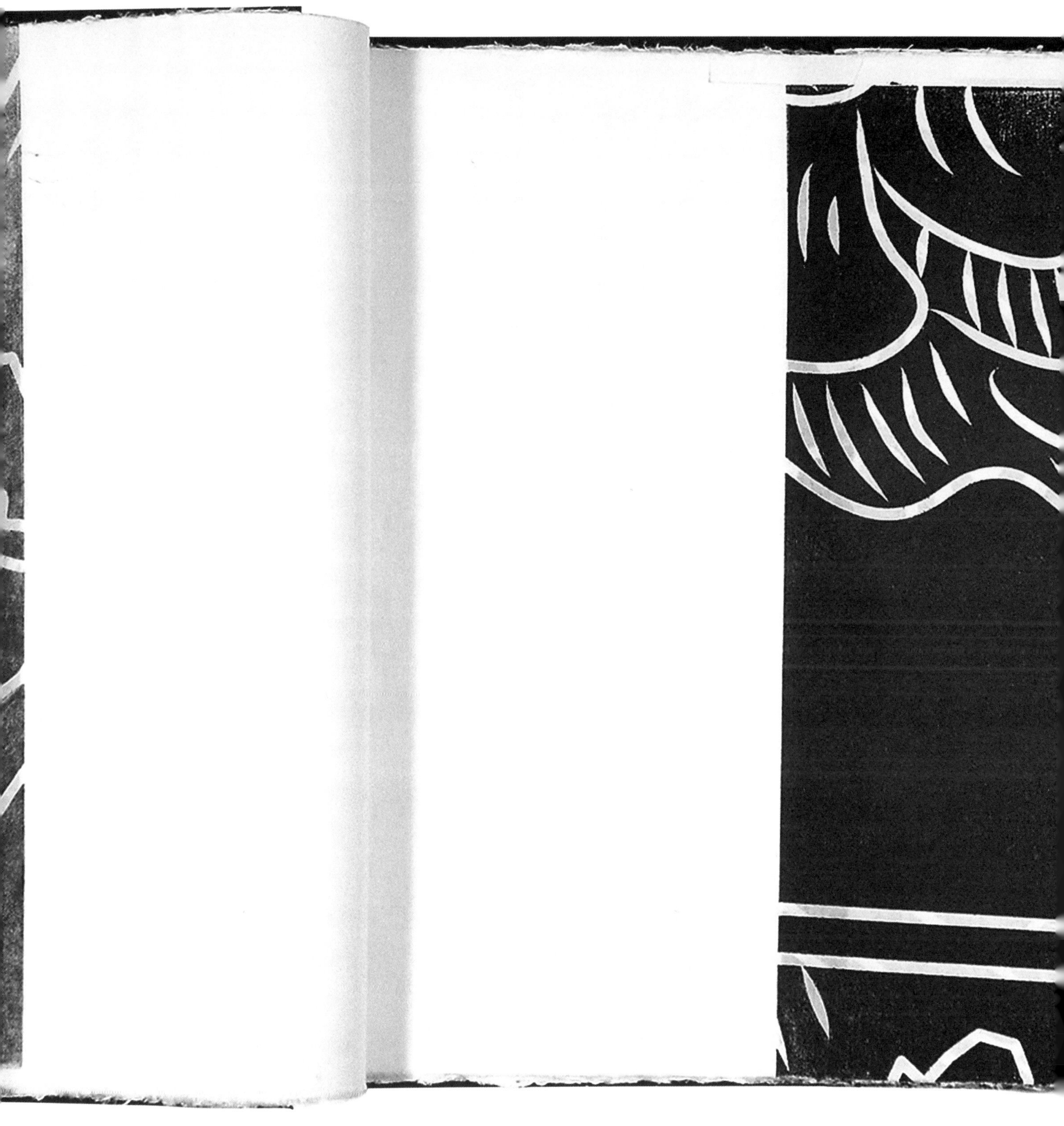

Atlas, Nuremberg Map of Tenochtitlan, **2013**, book-bound woodcut prints, Hosokawa paper **39**g, **450** paper sheets

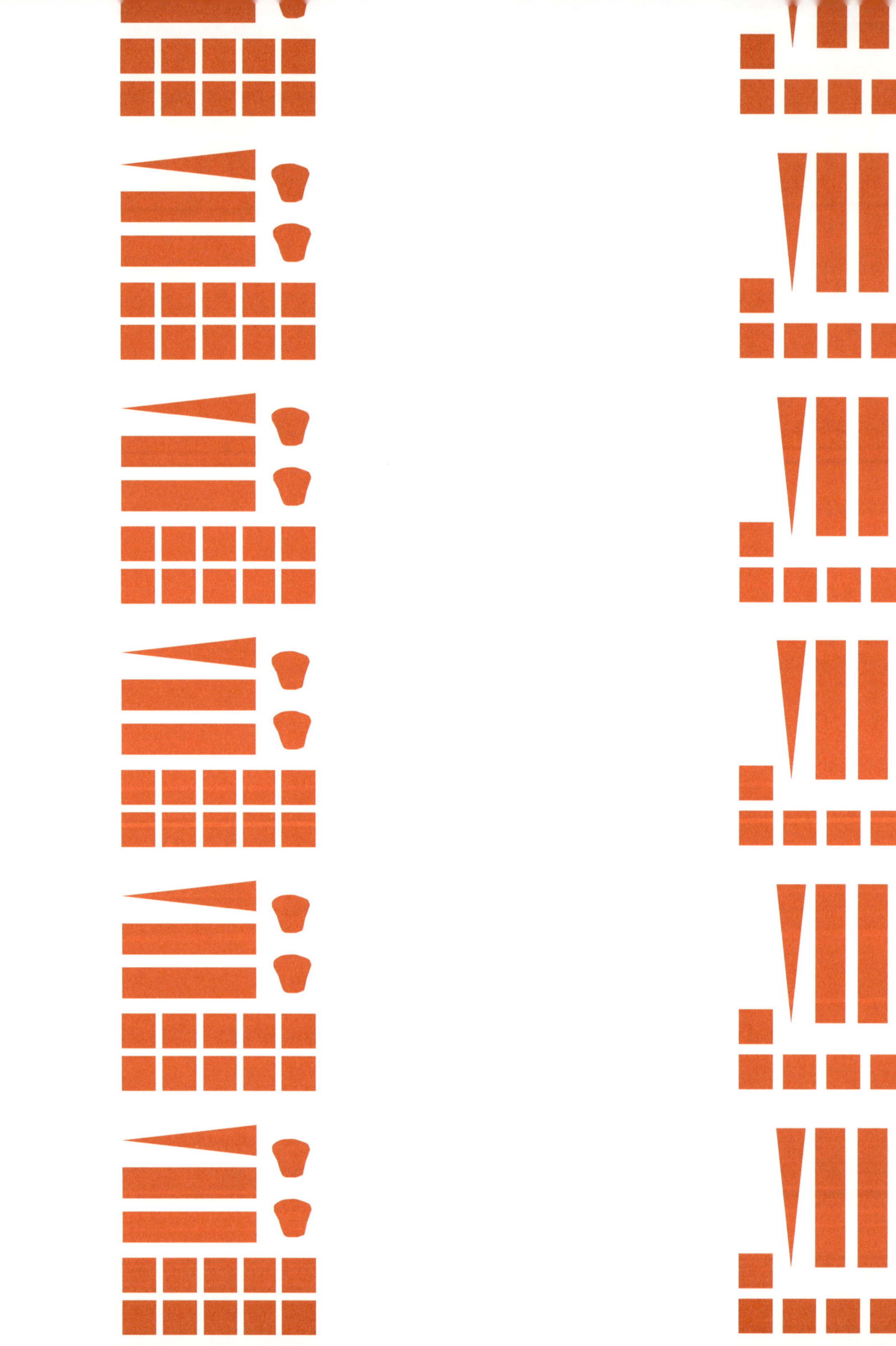

CARTOGRAPHIC PRESENCE IN THE WORK OF MARIANA CASTILLO DEBALL

BARBARA E. MUNDY

In her three pieces, *Nuremberg-Tenochtitlan*, *Teozacoalco*, and *Vista de Ojos*, Mariana Castillo Deball takes as her source material three important maps created in the wake of the Spanish Invasion of Mexico in the sixteenth century. All three maps were imbricated in the establishment of the Mexico as a colony of Spain; as I write this, Mexico is engaged in a painful commemoration of the 500th anniversary of the brutal conquest of the Mexica (also called the Aztecs) that brought an end to autonomous Indigenous rule. The Invasion and its aftermath led to the establishment of a present-day world order: a "First World" of European nations was created by the forcible extraction of the wealth and coercive control of the labor of the "Third World." In returning to these maps created in the wake of these world-altering events, maps designed to express European hegemony, Castillo Deball reworks them in unexpected ways. She blows up their scale to engrave them onto sheets of plywood, creating prints that are bound into books she calls "atlases"; she sets them on the floor to create an immersive viewing experience. All of these operations—engraving, printing, mapping—are a direct reflection of the ways that Europeans created the Americas as an object of knowledge, particularly Castillo Deball's homeland of Mexico, which was christened "New Spain" after the Invasion. Maps and printed atlases allowed the Americas to be made visible as a series of measured and (it seemed) scientifically derived lines on a sheet of paper, and allowed European readers and viewers visual mastery of the geographic expanse of the American continents, a "new world" in their eyes.

But rather than celebrating the progress of the science of cartography, or mourning the destruction of Indigenous autonomy, these works by Castillo Deball offer a mediation on the relation of knowledge about things and their representations. Through pointing to embodied experiences (of others, of ourselves), she also underscores the often unacknowledged role that embodied experience plays in knowledge production. By gesturing to Indigenous sources, she returns to the non-European roots of Mexico and knowledge about Mexico, and in her working practice, she alludes to the distinct history of print within modern Mexico.

MINING THE SOURCES

The sixteenth-century map that inspired the floor piece that is part of the installation *Nuremberg-Tenochtitlan* (**2013**) and later in *Amarantus* (**2021**) was printed in Nuremberg in **1524** (fig. **1**). It was a woodcut, a kind of relief print. Its unnamed creator traced an image onto a solid block of wood, and cut away the background, leaving the cartographic image raised up from the background block. After being inked and pressed against a damp sheet of paper in a press, the cartographic image was imprinted onto the sheet. Hundreds, if not thousands, of copies of the same image could have been made via this simple technology of relief printing.

The image printed in **1524** contained two maps. On the left was a schematic view of the Gulf Coast of Mexico, and on the right the map shows a bird's-eye-view of the Basin of Mexico. At the center is the great city of Tenochtitlan, the Mexica (Aztec) capital city. It is surrounded by a great lake, and smaller cities cluster around the lake's shores. This bird's-eye projection is not consistent, and features of Tenochtitlan are shown in elevation, including the great pyramidal temples that rose to over ninety feet high, in the center of the city. These two maps were meant to illustrate a letter that the conquistador Hernán Cortés wrote to his monarch, Charles V of Spain, describing his entry into, and the splendors of, the great Indigenous city, one of the largest cities in the world in the sixteenth century. But by the time the map was first printed in

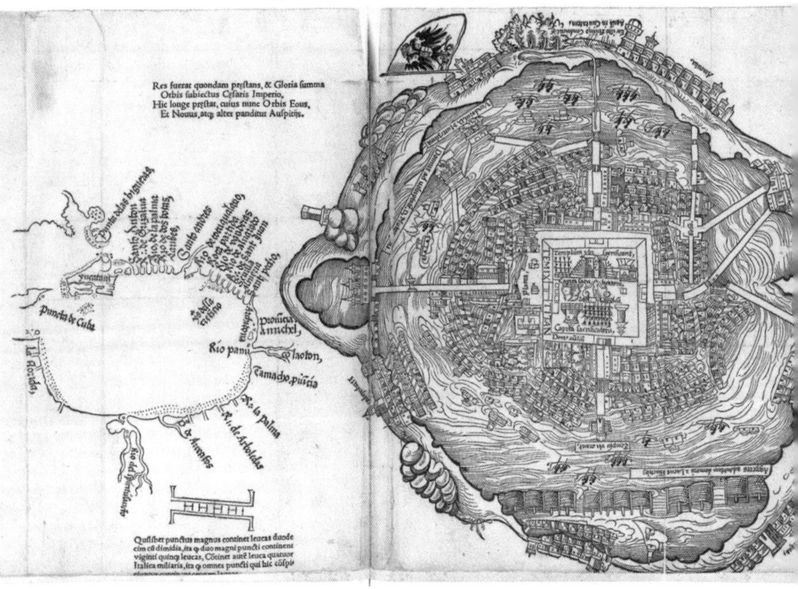

Fig. 1 *Map of Tenochtitlan*, **1524**, woodcut, printed in Nuremberg, Germany

Nuremberg in **1524**, the city had been captured by Cortés and his Indigenous allies. While mostly showing the city as it appeared before Cortés's arrival, the Nuremberg map also signals its conquest by including a battle standard, with the double-headed eagle of the Spanish Habsburg, at the top (fig. **2**). Tenochtitlan was renamed Mexico City by its new Spanish overlords, and it is the birthplace of Castillo Deball.

Another (less famous but equally important) map of Mexico City inspired *Vista de Ojos*, *(**2014**, fig. **3**). This map, called the Uppsala Map (earlier known as the Mapa de Santa Cruz) shows exactly the same area as the Nuremberg map—the Basin of Mexico with Mexico City at its center—but was created by a team of Indigenous painters, called *tlacuiloque* in Nahuatl, the Indigenous language of Central Mexico. These artists were heirs to a Mesoamerican painting tradition, as well as trained in new modes of representation coming from an exposure to

European artworks. Armed with first hand knowledge of the water systems of the Basin, the urban plan of the city, and the activities of the tens of thousands of inhabitants, the painters of this map combined a bird's-eye view, facade elevations, and narrative vignettes to offer a snapshot of life in the city in around 1540, a generation after the Spanish Invasion. The original map was painted on two large sheets of parchment and was presented to Charles V in the 1550s. Soon after, it slipped from public view for about two hundred years. Then, a visitor found it in the university collections of Uppsala, Sweden, where it is found today. Originally attributed to the Alonso de Santa Cruz, the Spanish cosmographer who made a copy of the map in 1550 and wrote his name on its surface, it was not until 1938 when it was recognized as being the creation of Indigenous artists. And it was not until 1974 that color lithographic plates of the map, prepared around 1900, were finally printed, thus making the map known and available to a larger public. The story of this map thus reveals how Indigenous knowledge, like that about the Basin of Mexico, was suppressed and overwritten in the historical record of the Spanish empire.

The map that inspired *Teozacoalco*, a work first shown at the New Museum in New York in 2019, comes not from Mexico City, but from the southern state of Oaxaca, where the Indigenous languages of Mixtec and Zapotec are still actively spoken in traditional communities (fig. 4). Around 1580, a printed questionnaire was sent out by the government of Philip II of Spain (the son of Charles V) to all overseas Spanish territories. The questionnaire was the Spain-based government's attempt to systematically collect information about its transatlantic possessions, mostly with an eye to their economic potential. One of its questions requested a map, the emergent instrument of imperial knowledge. One of the printed questionnaires reached the town of Teozacoalco, which today is home to some 1,225 people in the state of Oaxaca. In the sixteenth century, however, it was much more populous, and the capital of a small kingdom, whose indigenous rulers were Mixtec speakers. In Teozacoalco, the local painter, almost certainly a native speaker of the Mixtec language, pasted together twenty-three sheets of European paper to create a work the size of a large bedsheet, and on its surface inscribed a large circle. Within the circle, the painter rendered the roads, rivers, and ranges that pertained to the kingdom of Teozacoalco. Along the edges of the circle, the painter carefully set the pictographic toponyms (place-names) of the places that served as boundaries between Teozacoalco and neighboring kingdoms. In columns outside the map and within it, the historic rulers of Teozacoalco appear, the map offering a record of royal lineages stretching back to the tenth century. Although commissioned with the aim of serving Habsburg imperial ambitions, this map is like a Trojan horse, slipping evidence of an antecedent Indigenous Mixtec kingdom into the Spanish official archive.

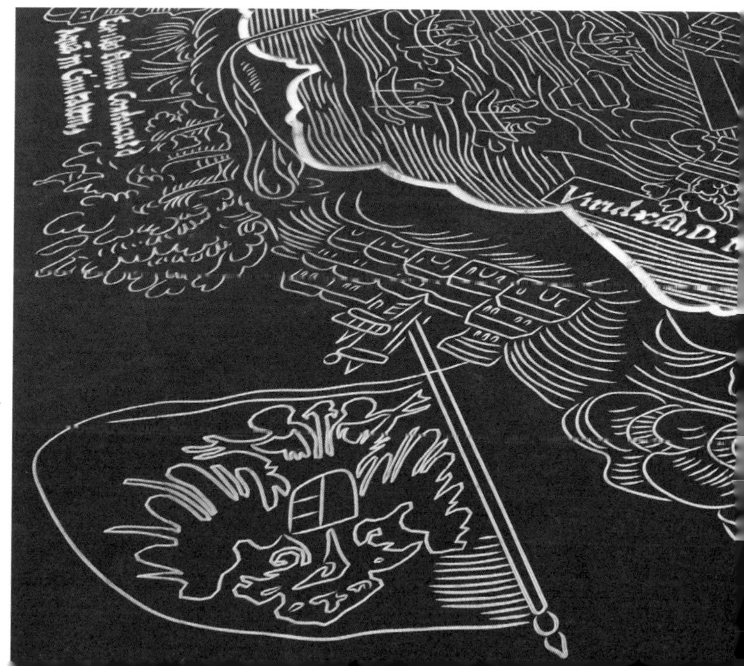

Fig. 2 Mariana Castillo Deball, detail of *Nuremberg Map of Tenochtitlan*, 2013, CNC engraved wooden floor

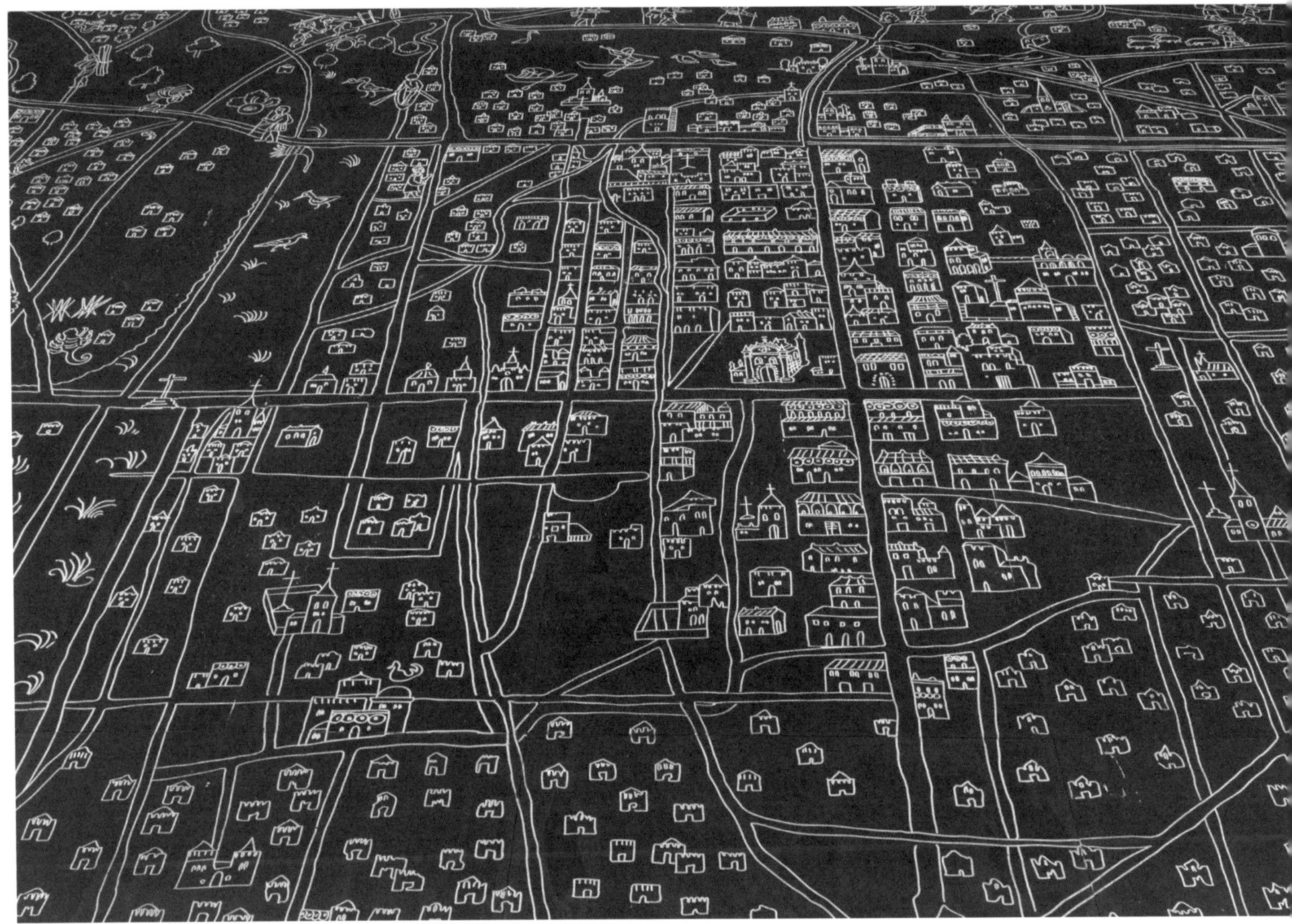

Fig. 3 Detail of *Vista de Ojos*, **2014**, CNC engraved wooden floor

THE PRINTED IMAGE AND THE CONSTRUCTION OF KNOWLEDGE

Castillo Deball's techniques in creating these floor pieces, which begin with an engraving process, are novel in their own right. And they also offer a point of reflection on the relationship between her artwork and the source material, particularly in the role of the printed image. For it was prints—cheaply produced in multiples—that allowed Europeans to first learn about Mexico during the globalization of the sixteenth century, and it was prints that determined how Europeans came to understand Mexico as an exotic, and at times, barbaric place.

Castillo Deball adapts the basic technique of making a woodblock print. After transferring a drawn image onto a wooden substrate, she cuts away the lines of the image. Modern tools distance her hand from the acts of drawing and of cutting. As she describes it:

> First I trace the image in the computer, converting it into a line drawing that can

be read as vector lines. This means that the image has no pixels, just pure line. Then I make a grid based on the [layout of the] exhibition space, decide the size of the wooden panels, and place this grid in the computer together with the line drawing. Afterwards the CNC [computer numerical control] machine engraves the lines into each wooden panel.

The process of cutting the image into the wooden panel is the reverse of a traditional woodblock, where the background is cut, leaving the raised lines of the image. The large wooden panels, with the lines cut out by the CNC router, are then inked, and pressed against large sheets of paper. This process creates prints that reproduce the source image, but transforms it from positive to negative.

Just like the sixteenth-century prints, Castillo Deball's pieces are workshop productions. Figure 5 captures the process of making the prints for *Nuremberg-Tenochtitlan*. The photograph was taken in **2013** inside the large Berlin studio Castillo Deball rented to create the work. In the center, Anna Szaflarski inks one of the large wooden panels, using a roller to apply the greasy ink in an even layer. In the upper left, Ayami Awazuhara gently picks up a sheet of dampened paper from a stack—one pair of clean hands and one pair of dirty hands being the rule of the print shop. She will bring it over to lay upon the inked plate, to create a monotype, later to be bound in an atlas. The drying sheets from earlier iterations of this same process are seen, hanging like clothes from a line, to the right of the photo. Once the impression has been taken, the dirty

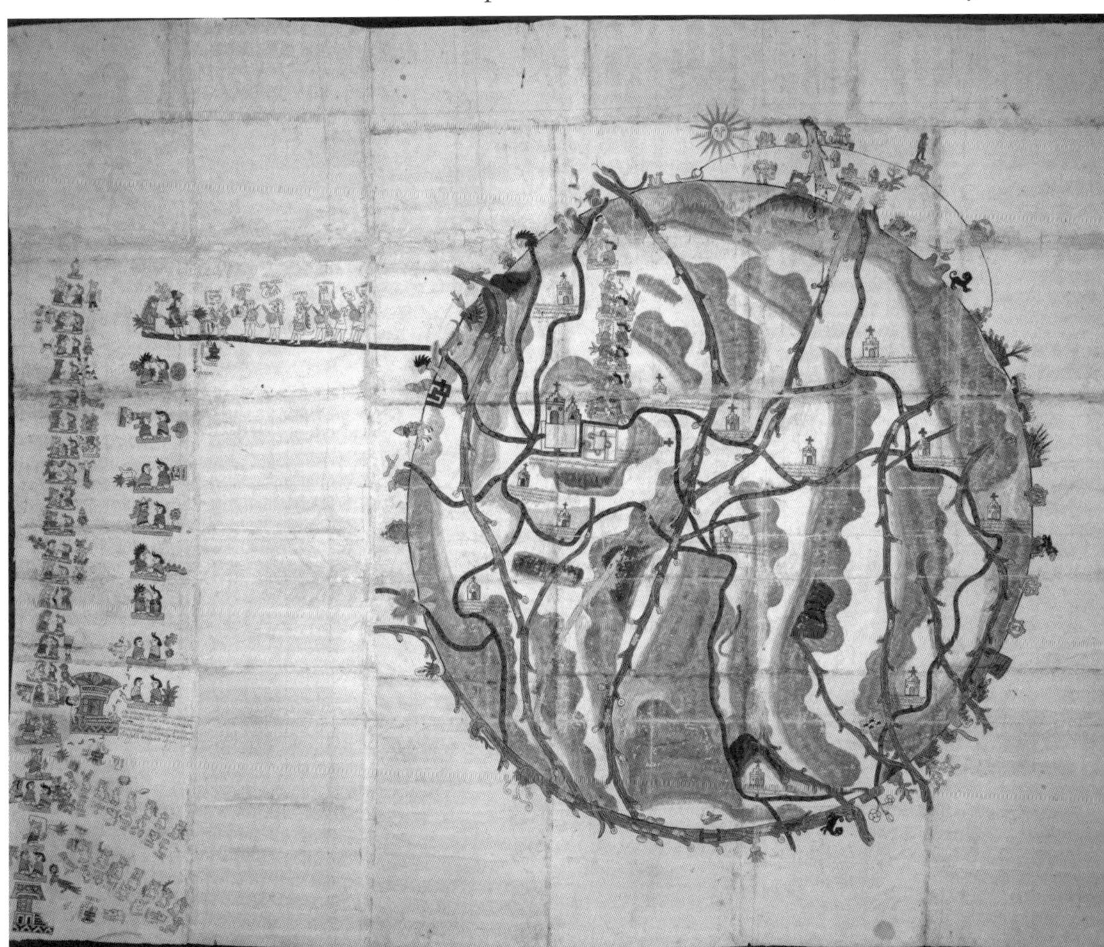

Fig. 4 *Map of Teozacoalco,* **1580**, European paper, **144×177** cm, San Pedro Teozacoalco, Oaxaca

hands in the team will move the plate against the wall, the residual ink creating a black surface.

A stack of drying plates can be seen behind Awazuhara. The plate casually leaning on top of the stack is a significant one, containing an enduring trope for how Europe viewed the American continent. It is a fragment of the center of the Nuremberg map, showing the great twin temples that once stood at the heart of Mexico City (fig. **6**). In the leaning plate, framed between the separators, is the depiction of a headless human figure, which was likely a rendering of an Aztec sacrificial victim. Within the context of Tenochtitlan, such human sacrifices replenished the living world with necessary energy for the survival of living beings. But when broadcast through Europe via the print in the early sixteenth century, the image of sacrifice provided the Spanish king and Catholic Church a needed rationale for the Conquest of Mexico. The knowledge provided by the map was inevitably bound up in ideology.

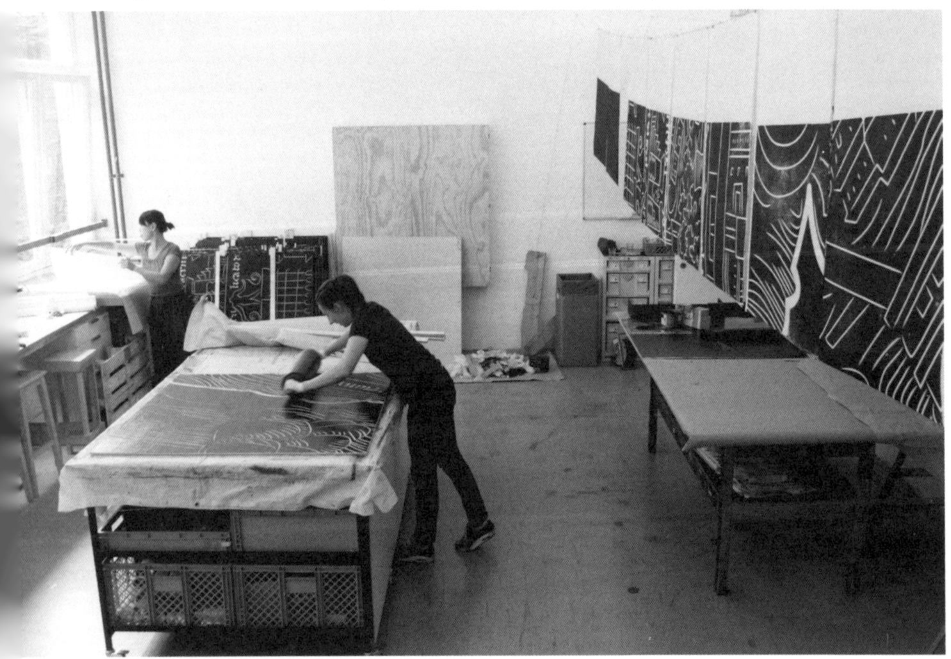

Fig. 5 Printing of *Atlas, Nuremberg Map of Tenochtitlan*

The prints that Castillo Deball drew from these plates were bound into a large book that she calls an "atlas," a word coined in the sixteenth century to describe a book of maps or charts, the kind of book that offered the viewer, in a single volume, access to knowledge of a huge territory. Like all of Castillo Deball's works, the atlas implicitly questions the relationship between the image (or diagram) and the reality it represents, as well as the way "scientific" knowledge is produced and disseminated. While the demand we make of most atlases is that their pages offer partial views of a recognizable geographic expanse—and, taken together, offer an image of the whole—(the "Americas" or the "World"), the pages of Castillo Deball's "atlas" frustrate our expectations. The scale is so immense that it is difficult to know what we are seeing, and the arbitrary cropping imposed by the dimensions of the plywood sheets makes it clear that the pages do little more than refer to the engraved plywood, rather than an expected referent of a geomass. The promise

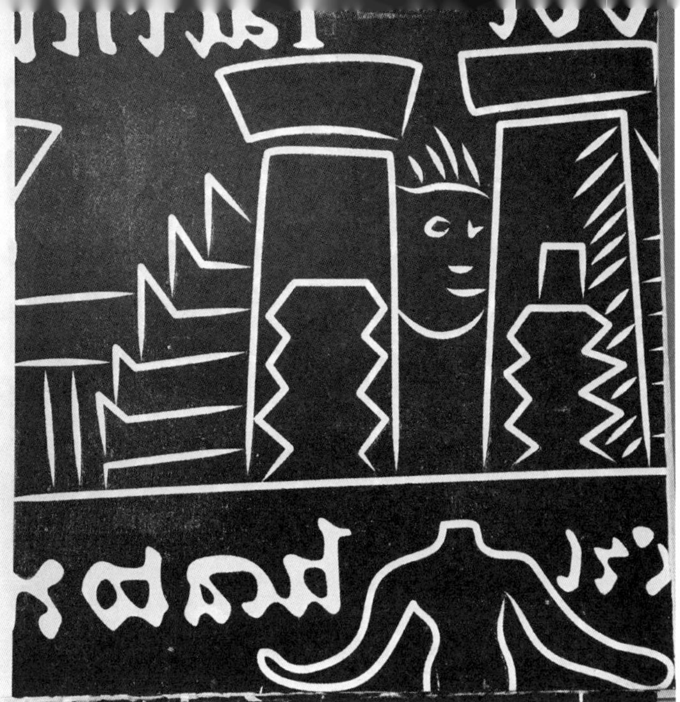

Fig. 6 *Atlas, Nuremberg Map of Tenochtitlan*, 2013, book bound wood cut prints, Hosokawa paper 39g, 450 paper sheets

of total knowledge that an atlas is meant to offer slips further and further away with each turn of its pages.

EMBODIMENT

While the historical records created at the time of Europe's violent conquest and subsequent colonization of Mexico thread through Castillo Deball's works, she also introduces a counter-narrative to conquest through the presence of the Indigenous body. The costumes included in *Amarantus* (2021) can be traced to *chinelo* dancing—a spectacle first performed in the colonial era, and continuing to the present day. Often staged during Carnival, a time of role reversals, Indigenous villagers would don masks and costumes and perform elaborate burlesques of their Spanish overlords. In 2013, Castillo Deball designed five *chinelo* costumes for a live dance performance at the Matadero in Madrid. When she was asked to present work in Berlin at the Hamburger Bahnhof, she had the idea of bringing the 1524 Nuremberg map into a relationship with the costumes. The Bahnhof lacked the resources to commission new work, or to restage the *chinelo* dance, but they did have funds for the existing display. Castillo Deball created the floor pieces, presenting it as part of the display, rather than new work. The floor piece, with the engraved map, stretched from wall to wall in the gallery, replacing a gallery's traditional concrete or wood-plank floor, and viewers to the exhibition were expected to walk over and within the enormous topographic space defined by the map (fig. 7). They were thus immersed in of one of the most broadly known European images of Indigenous Mexico: barbarous Mexico, sacrificial Mexico. But punctuating this space were the chinelo costumes, burlesque visions of Spaniards, the absurdly grimacing masks set at the top of scarecrow-like frames, empty costumes lacking their animating dancers. Their presence makes present another version of Conquest history, still performed today, an embodied and living tale, where strutting conquistadors from Spain are revealed to be masked impostors, the official history of Cortés's map gathering the dirt from the visitors' shoes.

Indigenous embodiment also figures in *Teozacoalco*. Again, the map source came from the sixteenth-century archive, but this indigenous map spent most of its life secreted in another archive. When the map was published for the first time in **1949** by the Mexican archeologist Alfonso Caso, he proved that the figures appearing on the map were historically documented people, establishing the depth of historical recordkeeping in Indigenous Mexico. In Castillo Deball's rendering, the elements of the map—roads, rivers, pictorial toponyms, rulers—have all

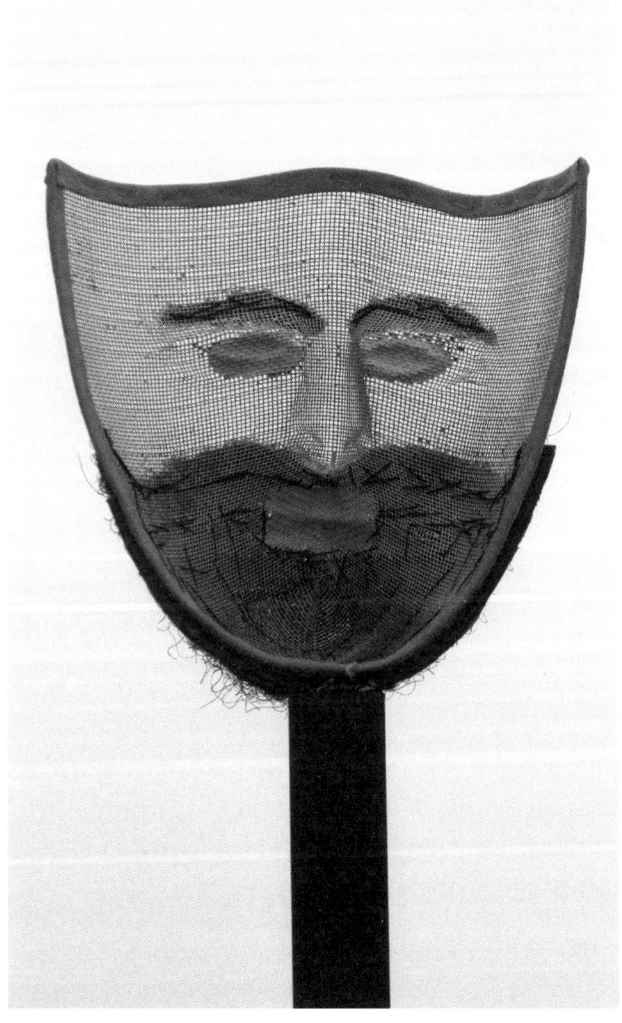

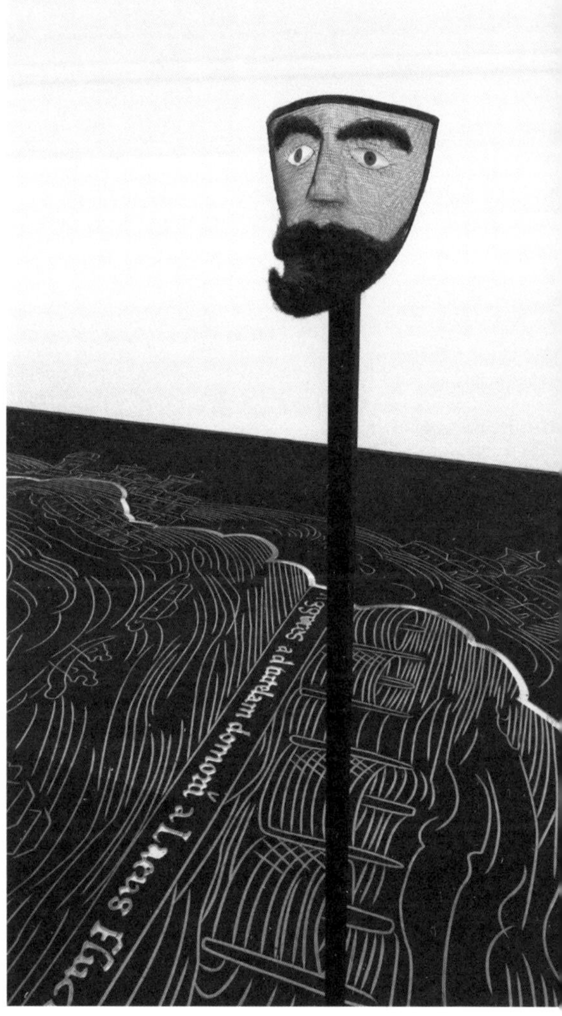

been inlaid into the plywood base, their colored forms on the original paper map translated into different colors of wood. Among the wooden inlay figures are the Mixtec kings and queens of Teozacoalco, including don Felipe de Santiago, a Mixtec noble who took a Spanish name when he was baptized, who was the seated ruler in **1580** when the map was made. The presence of his named figure was his way of staking his claim to the territory defined and made visible by the map. Castillo Deball's technique does much the same: the natural features of the landscape, the rivers and mountains seen in the map, are recast as wooden inlay, as are the human features, like the toponymic glyphs representing names in the Mixtec language, and the Teozacoalco rulers. All these figures, be they men or mountains, are embedded in the wooden substrate so as to be inseparable from it (fig. 8). Castillo Deball chose to use woods native to Mexico—ash, poplar, red cedar and American walnut—for these inlays, a choice that was partly economic (some local woods were cheaper). But it also points to the enduring presence of Indigenous peoples across the landscape of Mexico, and their embeddedness in the conception of Mexico as a nation.

INDIGENOUS PASTS, NATIONAL PASTS

The deep indigenous past of Mexico was the source for another one of Castillo Deball's pieces, where a vector image was engraved with a CNC router into large wooden panels that were then printed. The source for the piece *Tamoanchan* (first displayed at Pinksummer, Geneva in 2013) was not a map, but a pre-Hispanic fresco mural from the Mesoamerican city of Teotihuacan, made around the third century. Only fragments of the ancient mural survive, but after its recovery from the Tepantitlan complex in 1942, archeologists used these fragments to reconstruct (and to imagine) a whole. The full-bodied figures found in the painted reconstruction, carried out by Agustín Villagra in 1971, betray nothing of its originating fragments. That reconstruction is now a centerpiece of the display devoted to the art of Teotihuacan at the Museo Nacional de Antropología in Mexico City, inaugurated in 1964 to offer the deep Indigenous history that preceded (and prefigured) the modern nation. Castillo Deball's work, named *Tamoanchan* for a Mexica idea of paradise, used the Villagra reconstruction as the source of her engraved floor panels, which she had painted in black to make the image visible. After de-installation, the plywood panels served as the basis for printed images. But rather than printing the entire panel, Castillo Deball tried to capture the fragmentary nature of the mural itself by inking only the parts of the panel that corresponded to the original. Made only with pressure of the hand, these prints are a testimony to the fragmentary knowledge that lies beyond the seemingly robust images created of the Indigenous past for the service of the nation.

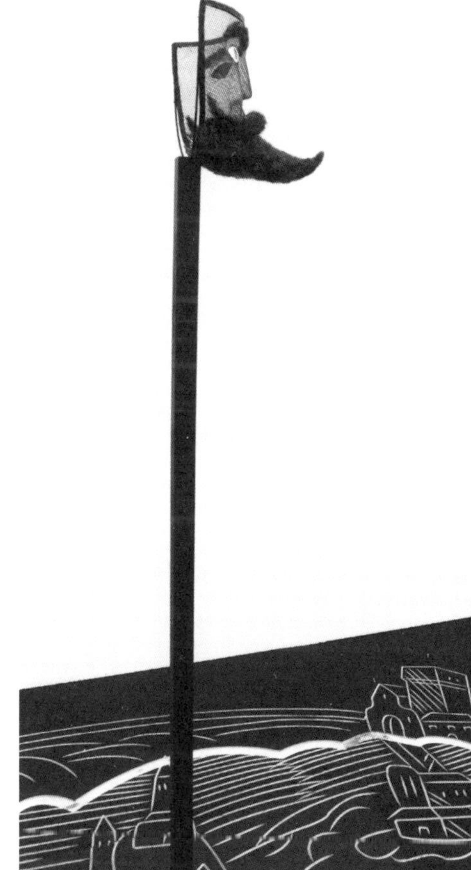

Fig. 7
Nuremberg Map of Tenochtitlan, 2013, CNC engraved wooden floor, costumes, embroideries, masks

THE COUNTER-HEGEMONY OF PRINT

Castillo Deball's attraction to the printed map of Nuremberg was its ubiquity. "I saw it everywhere," she says. And indeed, the print is to be found in many histories of Mexico, often to represent the former glory and complexity of the Mexica capital that stands as forerunner to the present glory of

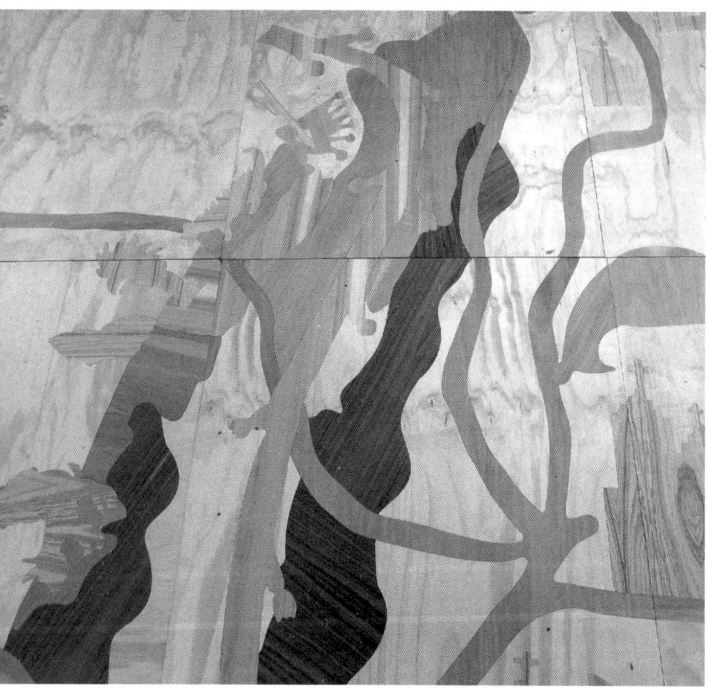

the Mexican nation. In the moment of its first creation, it meant something different. The presence of the Habsburg battle standard flying over the region signaled the capitulation of the Mexica to Spanish forces. Versions of it circulated for over three hundred years in European publications, and this circulation helped make the Nuremberg map represent a hegemonic view—an American continent under Europe's control.

But in the context of Mexico, Castillo Deball's use of the print means something quite different. Castillo Deball was trained in print techniques in art school, and her formation was marked by the unique twentieth-century history of print in Mexico City. Following the Mexican Revolution (**1910–1920**), a group of leftist artists (Leopoldo Méndez, Luis Arenal Bastar, and Pablo O'Higgins) founded a print workshop in **1937**. The founders' goal for the workshop, the *Taller de Gráfica Popular* (TGP), was to cheaply create didactic images for urban workers and rural campesinos, addressing real-world problems. Their output ranged from anti-fascist posters to scenes of peasant dislocation. Over time, the TGP attracted artists from across the Americas; the US-born Elizabeth Catlett joined the TGP in **1946** and worked with it for twenty years. It offered a model for radical printmakers throughout the Americas, no less for its socially engaged imagery than for its radically democratic and non-hierarchical modes of production. Today, fine-art print shops are still very much a part of the fabric of Mexico City's artistic world, and surfacing in Castillo Deball's works, created both in Germany and in Mexico City, are the legacies of both of these traditions.

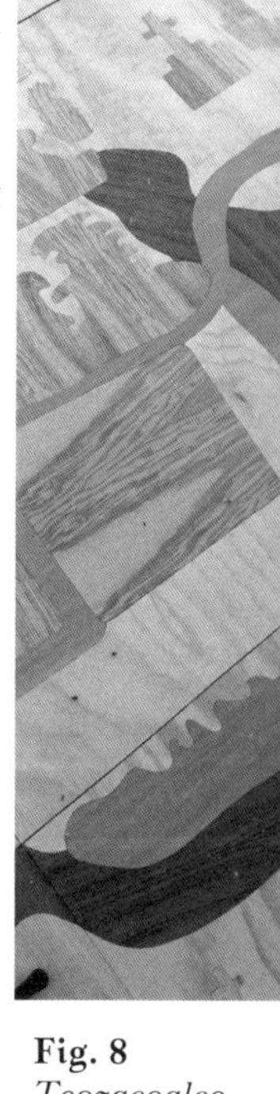

Fig. 8 *Teozacoalco Map*, **2018**, inlaid wood floor installation with pine plywood, ash, poplar, red cedar, and american walnut, *Finding Oneself Outside*, **2019**, New Museum, New York

MAP OF THE WORLD

In a short story by the Argentine writer Jorge Luis Borges, he offers an account of a map of exacting precision, so exact that it was a one-to-one scale, each inch of the map representing an inch of real space. The account is fictional, but Borges attributes it to a Spanish writer (Suárez Miranda) writing in **1658**, an era coinciding with the apex of Habsburg global power. It was also an era when European cosmographers and navigators were searching for more sophisticated means of measurement, like gauging longitude. These would, in turn, produce maps of greater accuracy, allowing them to know distant parts of the globe. Borges's story reveals that his perfect map, undergirded by "scientific" precision, is, in truth, a relic of imperial hubris. Rather than producing knowledge of the kingdom, its exactitude renders it useless. The map's fate? "In the western Deserts, tattered Fragments of the Map are still to be found, Sheltering an occasional Beast or beggar."

I could not help but think of Borges's story when I encountered Castillo Deball's work *Vista de Ojos* at the Los Angeles County Museum, where it was on display after being acquired by the museum in 2017. *Encountered* does little justice to the experience of her work, as the work is immense—each of the plywood plates measures almost four feet square, and 130 of them comprise the work. Set as the flooring, the work is meant to be walked upon, and the space of the map walked into. It is so large that the scenes underfoot envelop the gaze, and it is of a scale that gives the illusion of complete knowledge, like Borges's map. Indeed, the title of the work, *Vista de Ojos*, was the term used for the surveys carried out by Spanish government officials after the Invasion, often as part of expropriating Indigenous lands, and the viewer of Castillo Deball's work adopts the viewpoint of the colonial (and colonialist) surveyor, assuming a total knowledge about place that is part of the map's hegemonic promise.

But the circuits of this imperial, and imperialist, gaze are disrupted by the imagery set into the wood. It shows the Basin of Mexico, now occupied by the megalopolis of Mexico City, as it was in the sixteenth century, at the time of the Invasion. Underfoot, a bucolic landscape unfurls: Indigenous fishermen ply boats in the lake, and string up nets to capture fowl. The city, at the center, is comprised of well-ordered houses and streets, the same footprint that is found in Mexico City's historic center today. As someone who loves Mexico City and writes about its history in the era captured by the landscape in *Vista de Ojos*, but who does not live there, I found the work both engaging and unsettling. I was overwhelmed by feelings of deep familiarity and nostalgia, of knowing the place, as afforded by the map, as well as of deep alienation, as the past is a place to which one cannot return. Castillo Deball's work oscillates between the promise of images and the fragmentary knowledge that lies at their base; she presents European fantasies of global dominance and Indigenous critiques of those overweening presumptions; she brings together hegemonic and counter-hegemonic ways of knowing, without resolving the tensions between them. And she reminds us that one of the roles of art is to help us see more clearly the origins of the world we find ourselves in at present, and the nature of our relationship to it.

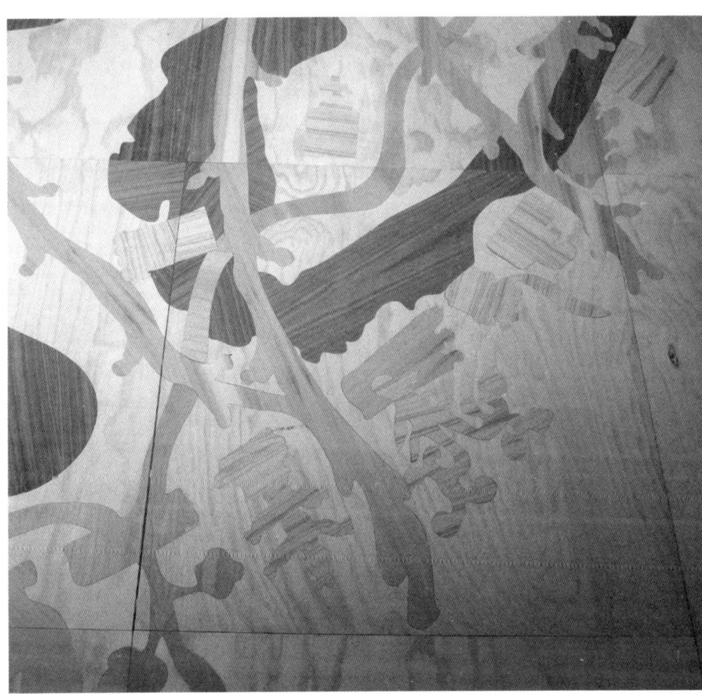

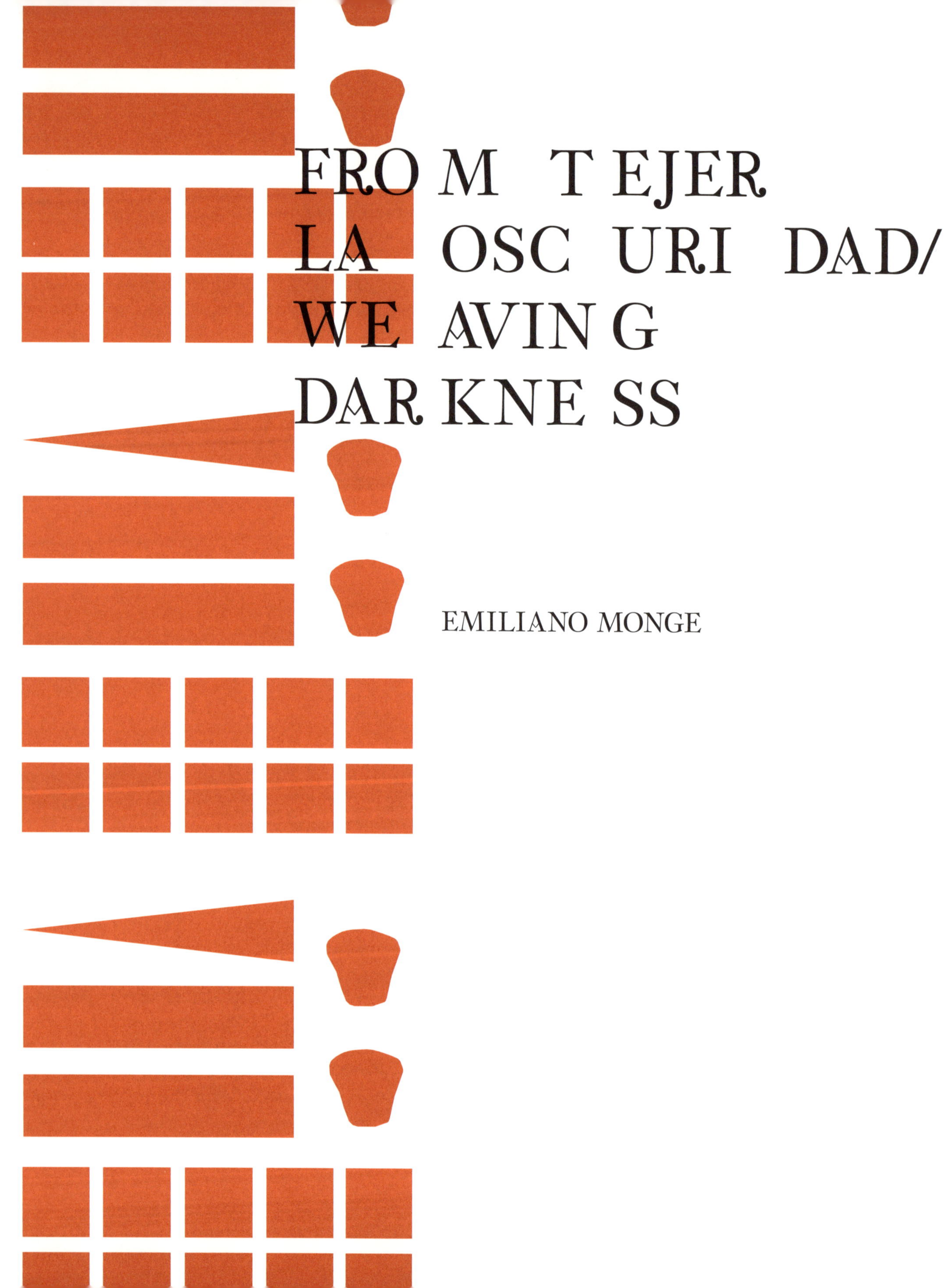

FRO M T EJER LA OSC URI DAD/ WE AVIN G DAR KNE SS

EMILIANO MONGE

To Make Us
(November **2031**)

I'm going to dive into our book! Counting my very first memory, I'll be one of us and I'll help to make us! Water. The first thing was water around my knees. Then the water at my waist, then at my neck, and finally the part where the ground was no longer there. The ever deeper zone and then the place just above the abyss, in the drowned throat of the earth. When I saw it, when I felt that empty space beneath me, I wanted to get out, to get back to shore as quickly as I could. But Mamá said no. She said: don't be afraid, Ana, you're not alone, I'm right here with you. Even so, I felt more and more afraid. What is it that scares you? The monster that lives down below, there in the depths. There's no monster there, she replied. Yes there is, he's yellow and brown, he has tentacles, arms, and spider feet, he has an iron mouth in the center of his body. And he has eyes on his lips. But no. That's in your head. You're imagining it. The monster is your thoughts. My thoughts? That's why you shouldn't use them. Because the monsters will come back anytime you think. Who would possibly say that to a young girl? I didn't want to think about anything, I wished to get to a state where my head would be forever blank. And I got there. One day, I stopped imagining, then I stopped thinking, then I stopped speaking, and finally I even stopped moving. So they brought me to this orphanage, where Mother and Laudo received me, and luckily, brought me to cabin sixteen. That's where Laya, Ligio, and Juana lured me out of myself, little by little, after sowing ideas and sparkles in my mind once again.

The Darkness
(February 2033)

We are the darkness. We were made on the eighth day. The day no one remembers. This was one of the two secrets Laya told me and asked me to write in this book, if we managed to escape, to get far away from the orphanage, to leave the besieged city behind. The other secret, in contrast, I cannot tell or write on these pages until we've crossed the mountains, found some coast and seen the sea. When we were leaving, just before we made sure that they weren't coming, that they'd give us a bit of time, Laya also asked me: remind the littlest girl of everything, help that girl give form to her memory. She is all of us.

Two
(18.686 / -98.181)

They advance forever seeking the night. Don't forget it, Ligio, the darkness is the only thing that is before but also after the light, Laudo told me when I surprised him hiding our book. I couldn't believe he had done it, that he'd have written despite our telling him not to. What are you doing, Laudo? I asked him in a low voice, but instead of answering me, he demanded: you should all go out there beyond where it emerges, to the place where the sun no longer appears. Then, after a couple of seconds, he added: I won't make it to the end of crossing this valley of statues with all of you. When silence surrounded us once again, Laudo hugged me, laughed without making a sound, and murmured: we call them statues because we don't know how else to name them, but they aren't made of metal or stone or wood. They aren't corpses either. Though at some point they were human, they aren't what we knew before as remains. They are a mix of both things, of effigy and plunder. When he finally let go of me, I noticed he had started crying and that his body was trembling. What's going on with you, Laudo, I asked him in a whisper, since I didn't want to wake the others nor alert those who'd begun to hunt us down again. They tried to flee, Ligio, to escape to the mountains or the caves, when the ocean of fire caught up to them, Laudo declared instead of answering me. After that, pointing toward the valley with his face, he stated: I'm going to get out of here, Ligio, my end has come and I shouldn't postpone it. Though I wanted to interrupt him, Laudo raised his voice, stepped back a couple of steps and said, turning around: you'll understand it when you read what I've written. Then, as I opened our book and looked for his words, I heard shouting in the distance and I cursed him for putting us in danger. Luckily, no sign of them appeared anywhere near us. And now I am here, writing what occurred yesterday though I shouldn't have been taking notes either. Laudo, however, sowed the seeds of his doubts in me. And now I don't know if Ayal is ready to be our memory, to be our book made flesh.

Five
(18.540 / -97.739)

Though Ayal will be our memory, before she can be it she'll have to know how. I told Ligio this last night, after we withdrew from the last city we pillaged. Those two are right, I told him later: we have to help her get ready. We have to teach her how to do it, I repeated, though I knew he was remembering my words. I had said them to him for the first time during Laudo and Bruna's funeral; we said good-bye to them as we are ordered to do in our most ancient books, the books we should not extract from our bundle: covered in ash we cried for them, holding one another we imitated the sound of their voices and *using one hundred and eighty medium-sized stones, round stones, white rock stones* we wrote on the ground "those who have gone will awaken again, when time joins together once again and the darkness will be restored, when before will be after the after will be now again." As I had not managed to convince him, I brought the issue up again a moment ago. When we are no longer, Ligio, when she is no longer either, only our book will remain and only it will be able to speak to those who are still walking. Perhaps Laya is wrong. And that's why we should also give it to Ayal. And that's why we should teach her how to use it, I pressed on, while we were looking for something that might be useful to us, among the suitcases we had found just a short while earlier. Obviously, I wanted to take advantage of the good mood that had suddenly possessed us all. And what was happening was that after so many years and so much suffering, you could glimpse, in the distance, the mountains we'd longed for forever. It was because of that, because all of us, including Ligio, felt that we should celebrate, though it also might have been that he saw the good sense in my words, that as he opened a suitcase out of which the calcified corpse of a small boy fell, he affirmed: You're right, Juana, Laudo,

Bruna and you are right. But it won't be me contradicting Laya's last words, he added, using his foot to turn over the corpse of the baby that had fallen to the floor. Then, leaning over to rip something from the corpse's neck, he concluded: you will be the one to give it to Ayal, and to explain to her how to use it. And before you do that, Juana, you should write it out in our book. That's why I've just noted all this down here.

Six
(18.311 / -97.203)

After a number of failed attempts, I, Ayal, who carries Laya our liberator in my name, tried again to do what Juana had asked of me. And though initially I thought I'd fail again, this time I was able to convince her. But it would be better for me to write things just as they were. After the last great fire, when the sky and the lightning changed color, I told Juana what Egidio had recounted to me. They became red and purple, sometimes we'd see them through some crack, I added, showing her that other fragment of memory, which Mila had shared with me. When we finally left the caves, though we didn't see the lightning anymore, the thunder was still audible, like applause inside our skulls, and I told her what Bruna had told me the same day she taught me to read the veins of the vascular system that crisscrosses the sky, as if wanting to prove to her, at the same time, that in my memory, in addition to carrying clearly the memories of the others, these were separate, that each one was its own independent story. Nonetheless, it was clear from Juana's face that I was not convincing her–she who would have been my mother if mothers still existed. That's why I recounted for her a memory that could leave no possible doubt, since she herself had shared it with me. A year after we would leave the caves, a fluorescent vapor emerged from the earth and covered the sky, like an incandescent sheet of cloth that blocked the darkness for months. It was the phase when increasingly more members left us. Though on her face, then, something changed, Juana told me: it seems good to me that you haven't forgotten those memories, but I don't know if your memory also preserves the pillars. The light has a beginning and an end; the darkness, in contrast, is always there, I told her then, in anger. Her god was an instant, while ours are before and they will also be after. Juana, however, did not want to agree. Though you remember and you preserve, you should write everything in this book because . . . because . . . who will speak to those who are left when your voice has gone dark? Resigned, I accepted what Juana wanted and I took this book, which, from that time forward, I have read many times. But it wasn't until today, nearly six months later, that I began to use it. To store here what I had been storing only in my head. And the thing is that also, today, something happened that made me finally understand the importance of not being, myself, the only one to carry our history. The importance of sharing it. There's no reason to continue fleeing, Egidio suddenly declared, as we fled from the last group of exterminators who would find any trace of us. Then, coming to a stop out of nowhere, and pointing way out in the distance, where those exterminators were barely a few luminous pinpricks, he added: they aren't even anything more than we are. And we aren't kids anymore, he concluded, handing someone else the baby he was carrying.

Twenty-three
(18.196 / -91.671)

Where is my voice? How would things have to be so as to continue storing our memory here?

This is what I was wondering for nine-and-a-half days, while we were crossing the final desert, this desert that wound up as a beach, the beach we were brought to by Biela, the woman who had seen the sea.

These questions, how ever, were not the right ones. Because the right question was this other one: or did it not have to be my voice? I discovered it almost without meaning to, I discovered it in an unexpected way. Contemplating the others while they were listening, just barely an instant ago, to what Biela was saying to us: those others, who have been there since some time ago, brought the wood.

And they, of whom I've already spoken to you, upon the sand, they began to give form to our boats, added Biela, before Sieno would pronounce the word for the bundle and before, also, Juana would have extirpated one more sentiment from our speech. Just then, I was saying, I realized. Just then I understood everything.

In addition to the written and spoken words, there are those that are taken as a given, I told myself while the others got to their feet and hurried: in no time the games would start again—taught to us by the sixth group that was slated to join with us: to place in combat two exterminators, with no weapons other than their hands and until only just one remained. In addition to the states that Lucho had shown me, there is this other state: the one that converts into a solid what another person might not be saying aloud.

How to use my voice? Where would I have to put it to extract from the others what has been secret, so that as well might be a shared memory, solid and fragile? These were the questions I had to ask myself and which, luckily when they came into my mind, arrived with their answers bound to them: our book will once again become everyone's. I will be, starting now, the person who forges us. I will be the one who Ligio, Juana, Bruna and Laudo, but also Madre and Laya, wanted me to be. The one who should give form to the words of the others. The voice without voice that will bestow weight on the voice of the community, I told myself then, caressing my womb and convincing myself that in this way I would know when the others would be ready to hear what I've shut up inside.

I will be, further, like the darkness, which can't be seen but makes us see the enveloping light, I said to myself later, noting that actually, rather, it was my womb that was caressing me. I will be like the silence, which cannot be heard but makes us hear the noises it contains I said to myself, too, and just then, feeling something in my womb that I hadn't felt before, I proclaimed: Lucho, he has to be the first one I place before us. Lucho shall reflect me and reflect us, like the voices of the gods reflect us in their books. And it will be Lucho, also, who converts me into that which I needed to be from the start: this book, I told myself in the end and at the same time I thought: I will also make sure that his voice and those of all of them, breathe like the first ones breathed, those who are in our most ancient books the voices from before the light.

Luckily, I had just finished finishing the final combat: there was just one single exterminator left standing when I ran to find Lucho. And, also luckily when I got to him, the dawn had assaulted the space:

Look, Ayal,

there on the horizon: finally
you can see them, finally
they are there, before
us: the sea and
its glimmers. Look at it everyone, let
your eyes get
used to their
wild reflections, and let also
all that silence enter
their ears:
there . . . there is where the new world begins.
That is our beginning and it is also our
end. This moment is the one that is
outside time.
Here what is lived and what is longed for collide, here they divide into
two and
our bewilderment is forever.
Look, look at the reflections! . . . Look how their
glimmers, all
of a sudden, fill
our enormous solitude
with the entire universe! And
look . . . also
look at your belly, Ayal,
you're finally
swelling!

Thirty-eight
30.324 / -20.469

Past: the instant
we entered the cave
revived in me that
other time they shut me up in a barrel. An instant
later, luckily
I realized: I understood that
there, inside that cave, I was not alone. That I would never again
feel alone. That,
finally, I was part
of another body, a body made of
many other bodies. And further, that here was proof: our
first darkness. Present: the final proof
has come: it will be even
more difficult than we had thought
to find the darkness
that awaits us. And the thing is that Lucho died this morning. But you
already
know this, Ayal,
because here among all of us
we know everything—this
news, in fact, precipitated the labor of your birth. Irineo, Ayosa, and
Bila took care of his body
on a blanket
they opened a channel in the body,
they emptied it, and before closing it up and cleaning it, they filled it
with his
most prized possessions: the pages
you ripped out of
this book, the snail stuck to a conch shell he found in the
first desiccated
valley we found, the
canine teeth of the wolf he never parted from, the map he drew
with Biela and the stone,
the tooth, the flute, the ring, the horseshoe
and the mouse skull he
inherited from Indrig: he, Lucho, was the only one who had been
permitted to board with
so many things. Then
they closed him up again, they

sewed him up with the thread he himself had spun, they slathered him
with whale fat and
they wrapped him with
the pelts, Ayal, he had chosen earlier. Future:
it will pass soon,
this pain, and they also will pass soon,
these contractions,
Ayal, he will be born healthy and you can petition before
the Council for them
to let you breastfeed him . . . no,
don’t say anything.
I promise you, Lila promises you
that you,
you’ll be allowed to do it: despite
the fact that you’ve kept
quiet, we know
that you’ll give birth to
the
darkness.

Thirty-nine
(33.016 / -16.338)

No, Ayal, it's not
like that.
The past, the present, and the
future are not
different things.
Nor are they
the only states of our
speech. Because
there is a fourth state. You say you don't
know what it is. But even so
you've been knotting it together on this journey. No, perhaps
those fires
were not our old
gods. Perhaps they were the new ones, signaling the way. Perhaps the
fourth state
might be our speech and might be
our destiny. Perhaps it might be
we ourselves. But that's fine. I won't speak to you of this any more, nor
will I
do what the others
have done. I,
Lara, will do only what I have
been doing here
with you, Ayal, while Lulo traps each word I say to you.
There you go, like that, shout as loudly as you can . . .
push as hard as you
must. No, Ayal,
it was not the earth we were seeking. You've done a fifth of úmeno
obstinated with
it, just two
eighths less than what you've done in your pushing.
But no . . . it wasn't the new
world either. It was just an atoll,
a tongue
of sand in the middle of the
ocean—. There you go . . . that's it, push harder, it's about
to come out. You pressed out the
water and I think I can finally catch
sight of . . . yes . . . it's his head! . . .

he's here! . . . Ayal!
You're about to . . . no . . . Ayal . . . Don't let yourself
give up now! Don't close
your eyes, Ayal! Don't stop
pushing either . . . don't
pass out!
Please! . . .
. . . you're about to
give birth . . . Ayal . . .
Ayal!

Forty
(31.978 / -13.086)

We've lost
hope, Ayal. I, Eneas, will
confess it to you
though I don't know if you can still
hear me. Whether it was
true or not that Lucho knew how to read the
the sky and the currents,
what is surely true is that there is no one
now who knows,
who dares even to say "I know how to do it."
And to make things worse,
it wasn't true that the darkness
lived in you, that
its seed inhabited you.
Your son was born dead and you have not regained consciousness, Ayal.
I'm talking to you without knowing
if there is something or someone in there who
might be listening.
And although I can try to write in this book, Ayal, neither I nor anyone
else,
among those who are still
left, among
those who are still going to the new world, none of us knows
how to use
this other system, these knots and these strands
that Evo taught you
to use.
Ayal, I don't
think we're going to get there,
I don't think
that darkness that was promised to us exists, and a
new world doesn't exist either. I think
the end
has come. And Ayal, I'm not the only one
who thinks in this way. The silence has eaten
our tongues, after it
turned you into
silence . . . What?
What did you say? Ayal? Are you
awake? Did you say
something?

Forty-one
(29.256 / -13.702)

Just barely
an instant ago, atop the covers,
the miracle we had been waiting for
occurred, the
one we'd
been longing for
all that time. Ayal,
the woman
who put me, Greta, in charge
of this book, the one who gave Eneas
the bundles that
had been Evo's,
opened her eyes for an instant and also opened her mouth, one second
before
she died there in her cabin.
She concentrated the entirety
of the force she still had left
to spit out, flapping, the word we'd been
begging for. The word
that would set the miracle in motion.
Suddenly, then, here up above,
our swaddled shape
started to shake, it scratched itself down one side and began
splintering apart, as if
it were
a clump of earth, no, the bark of an old tree or the cocoon
from a larva.
Finally, when it finished hatching, out of our shape
a bird emerged,
a black bird, nervous and alive. An ashen
crow which, as soon as
it took flight, caused Irineo to let out a shout:
toward
land! It's going to lead us
toward land!

Forty-two
(24.715 / -12.295)

We've been following
that bird
for days.
Perhaps because of that
we've finally stopped doubting
whether we will get
to the new world
or not. It flies, that crow, with more haste
than our boats
can manage.
But it never
gets so far away
that we can no longer see it,
that we can no longer continue
following in its
wake.

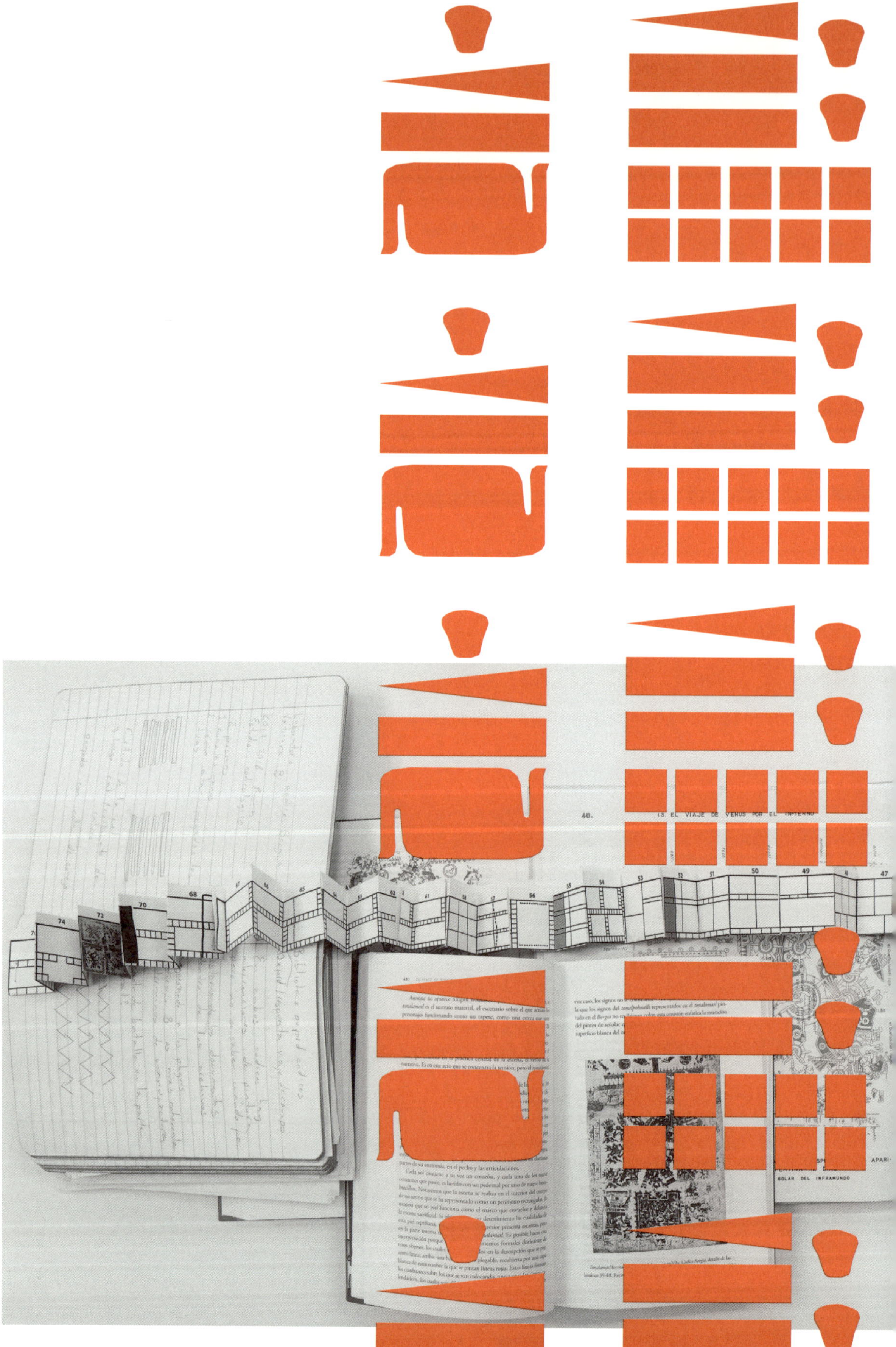

Photograph of artist's sketchbook, facsimile of *Codex Borgia*, and miniature codex made by Ana Díaz, **2021**

VÙ JÁ DE: BE YON D BO OKS

MARIANA CASTILLO DEBALL

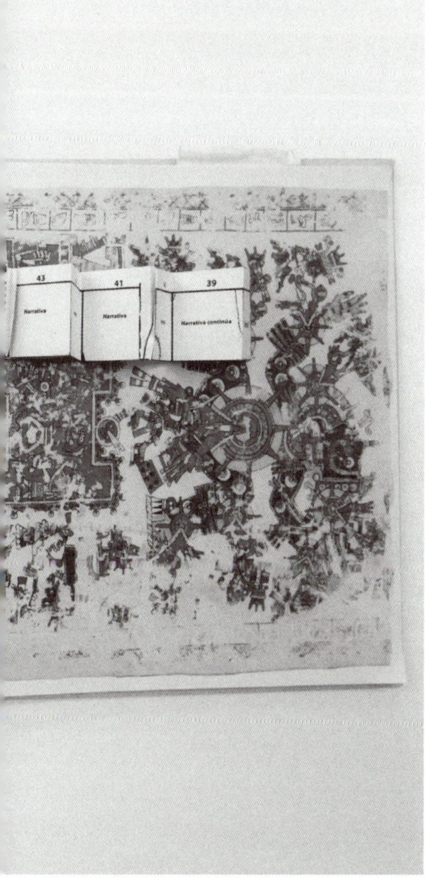

Dear Ana,[1]

I've stapled your miniature codex into the first pages of my *Ideal* red notebook. The last time we saw each other was at the Instituto de Investigaciones Históricas, when you invited me to participate in a workshop about the *Codex Borgia*.[2] You told us about your experience at the Vatican Library, where you studied how the different pieces of parchment that make up the object are bound together. There have been countless studies about the iconography, meaning, and history of this codex, but I don't think it had ever occurred to anyone to analyze how it was made.

You handed out scissors, paper, and glue, and we cut up and glued together the different parts to make miniature, photocopied versions of the *Codex Borgia*. Our replicas lacked the figures and drawings that characterize the codex; they were focused specifically on its material structure. Your interest in the making of the codex had to do with how it was used, how the different parts of the deerskin parchment were bound, whether

1 In memory of Ana Díaz Álvarez, renowned art historian who passed away in 2021 in Mexico City. Ana was an associate professor at the UNAM Instituto de Investigaciones Estéticas, where she taught courses in indigenous art history and Mesoamerican studies. She was the author of *El cuerpo del tiempo: Cosmología y tradiciones iconográficas del centro de México* and *El maíz se sienta para platicar: Códices y formas de conocimiento nahua, más allá del mundo de los libros*, and the editor of *Cielos e inframundos: Una revisión de las cosmologías mesoamericanas* (Mexico City: IIH-UNAM, 2016).

2 The *Codex Borgia* is one of the few codices that remain whose creation dates to pre-Columbian times. Though its origin is unknown, various researchers agree, because of its style, that it may be from Puebla, Tlaxcala, or the Mixtec region in Mexico. The *Codex Borgia* is an ancient *tonalamatl* (Nahuatl for "paper of days," or almanac) also known as *Codex Borgianus, Manuscrit de Veletri*, or *Codex Yohualli Ehecatl*. It may be consulted online at: http://www.famsi.org/spanish/research/loubat/Borgia/thumbs0.html.

there were traces of alterations or additions to the original object. You had observed that the format of the codex is quite large. Other codices are more portable, fitting in one's hands, and sometimes bearing traces of blood, which might mean that they were used during a ritual. I recall that you mentioned that, when you went to the Vatican Library, they only let you bring in a pencil and a small notebook to study the codex. The miniature version that we made with you was the result of the notes you took.

At the end of the session you and I decided to replicate the materiality of the codex, to work with a furrier to see how the parchment was prepared, folded, bound. We never did, though. I hope this imaginary conversation manages to communicate what I was never able to tell you.

As I was rereading your book *El maíz se sienta para platicar: códices y formas de conocimiento nahua, más allá del mundo de los libros*,[3] I found a couple traces of an earlier reading. The first is a bookmark. For the past several years, I've made a postcard to send out at the beginning of each new year. One side is printed with the numerals "**2018**" in a typography that I had designed based on the model of a mural of the plumed serpent; the back features a quote from *Coyote Anthropology* by Roy Wagner:

> COYOTE: Let me get this straight. A *déjà vu* is an uncanny experience, often associated with fatigue, of having had the same experience, or perception, that one is now having, at some time in the past. An experience that one could not otherwise recall without its possible recurrence in that way, as though the workings of memory and chance had somehow gotten confused with one another.
>
> ROY: An inability on the part of the past to predict the future, or at least its *own* futurity. So what, on that basis, is a *vùjá de*?
>
> COYOTE: Well, that would be the direct opposite: a *canny* experience, always identified with ebullience, on the part of that experience itself, that *it* had had *you* at some time before.
>
> ROY: Close, but no cigar. It would be an *in*direct opposite, with the roles of future and past, as well as those of perceiver and perceived, reversed.[4]

When I read *Coyote Anthropology* I was very intrigued. I understood very little and felt that translating it into Spanish would be the only way to apprehend the text. I contacted Roy Wagner in **2010** and proposed a collaboration involving his words and my drawings. We kept up a correspondence that lasted several years, which resulted in the publication of the book *Antropología del Coyote: Una conversación en palabras y dibujos*.[5] Translating is one of my favorite exercises. In the broadest sense of the word, my practice is to metamorphose substances into different media, for different publics.

Coyote Anthropology is a fable in which Roy Wagner and Coyote discuss the role of the anthropologist, the object of anthropological study, and transformations of reality. Relative to the bulk of anthropological

3 Ana Diaz Alvarez, *El maíz se sienta para platicar: Códices y formas de conocimiento nahua, más allá del mundo de los libros* (Mexico City: Bonillas Artigas Editores, **2016**).

4 Roy Wagner, *Coyote Anthropology* (Lincoln: University of Nebraska Press, **2010**), **24–25**.

5 Mariana Castillo Deball and Roy Wagner, *Antropología del Coyote: Una conversación en palabras y dibujos* (Mexico City: Surplus Ediciones), **37**.

writing, this book is exceptional, distancing itself from the academic language commonly used in the discipline. The book is also critical of the role of anthropologists in the communities they study because, far from being neutral observers, their presence alters the environments in which they work. *Coyote Anthropology* explores the complex dynamic of the anthropologist, who, by believing that he is doing fieldwork, and understanding otherness, ends up going through a process of personal transformation. Roy Wagner's notion of flexible time made me see that everything can be read upside down, and that time can be organized in different ways. Through his dialogues with Coyote, I realized that the body already knows our intentions before we put them in practice.

> COYOTE: And isn't what you are doing to me right now *anthropomorphizing* me, pretending that I am an anthropologist just like you? Heisenberg pointed out that we *interfere* with tiny particles in the very act of observing them, and so re-project our own intentions inadvertently upon the particle (or Coyote, as the case may be). But what he did not allow himself to concede was that the particle was doing the same thing back to him, for "it" had entered his own thought process as though it were part of his own neural net.
>
> ROY: Which, by that time, it *was*. Or, in other words, by virtue of the funda*mental* subject/object shift, *I got coyotes on the brain.*[6]

At around that time I started the project *Uncomfortable Objects*, conducting a series of experiments in which I blended the relationship between ground and figure, object and display mechanism. I worked primarily with scagliola and papier-mâché to make the pieces.

My *uncomfortable objects* function as fables that give voice to nonhumans: they imagine their voices, their consistency, and their temporality. Products of desire, research, or the imagination, they unhinge our conception of the world and force us to see from their perspective. What do nonhumans have to say about the world we have constructed around them? About our definitions, our manipulations, and our uses? What is left of objects after so much historical maneuvering, and what would their testimonies be if they could tell us their stories from their own perspectives? *Uncomfortable objects* can also be objects that have been destroyed, that do not allow themselves to be catalogued, or that have been held in the wrong category for centuries, Ana writes:

> The practices associated with the ancient codices have continued to operate for several centuries, but they have been modified and brought up to date for the context of each generation of users. We can therefore conclude that indigenous codices make up a *corpus* of dynamic, creative knowledge that integrates the use of different materials and objects, and affects various domains of life, objects that resemble books but fulfill other functions, in addition to recording written data that cannot be trusted to memory alone.[7]

One of the most persuasive arguments in *El maíz se sienta a platicar* is that the objects we call codices are not books, and that their function is much broader and more complex.

6 Deball and Wagner, 8.

7 Díaz, 15.

But what do you mean by that? When you describe objects that resemble books, but fulfill other functions, I ask myself whether books cannot be read in many different ways, or whether there are objects that start out as books only to become something else.

In the sixteenth century, Agostino Ramelli invented the first reading machine that attempted to facilitate the reading of multiple books at a time. In most cases, such facilitation attempts to reflect on the structure of the book, rather than attempting to replace it with a more effective mechanism. Many similar inventions were just sketches that were never built. The problem they pose is not technical; it is not a question of creating mechanisms in order to read "better," but rather of inventing other forms of reading and writing. Book machines are generally ephemeral contraptions, sketches, or simple implementations in the space of the book itself.

Raymond Roussel made a machine to read his novel, *Impressions of Africa*. The book itself is written using double entendres and little internal mechanisms that destabilize the tasks of author and reader. One of the methods that Roussel used in this work consists in turning the book's structure into an onion. Thus, in the middle of a description of the Egyptian desert, the narrative is suddenly interrupted to introduce a digression, a parenthetical other scene, which in turn is interrupted by another parenthesis, and so on. At a given moment, when the Canto is coming to an end, the parentheses return in the opposite direction and the onion closes. The points of entry and exit in the stories are different. One could probably journey through the onion in different ways, without repeating the same story at any point.

This image of an onion-book left me thinking about how to use the same mechanism in a collection of books, joined together such that one could peel each title off the onion as a reading mechanism. This image was the origin of *Never Odd or Even*. For the first stage of the project, I proposed an anthology of covers of nonexistent books in which I called upon authors from different disciplines to collaborate on a cover. *Volume I* (2005) includes twenty-four titles in a single publication, and volume II (2011) has thirty.

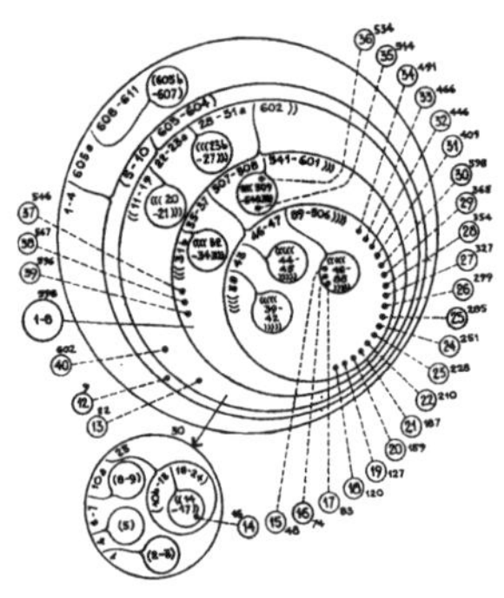

Schematic of the second chant of Raymond Roussel's *Impressions of Africa*, by Juan Esteban Fassio

> A literary journey through different themes, including: archaeology, gardening and contemporary ruins, magic, the history of technology, mysticism, tour guides, autobiography, archival techniques, monuments in motion, unpublished memoirs, tropical manifestations, intragenealogy, why the letter is all over the place, the taste of truth, the aroma of existence, conversations between a cardinal and a roadrunner, and many more![8]

At a second stage, during a series of events, I invited writers, artists, and academics to comment on one of the covers in the collection, such that the content of the titles would unfold. Each invitee was free to invent possible content based on the book cover of their choosing. The spirit of *Never Odd or*

8 Mariana Castillo Deball, *Never Odd or Even* (Berlin: BOM DIA BOA TARDE BOA NOITE, 2011).

Even involves creating fictions through collaboration. Each title functions as a catalyst and disseminator of new narratives; it is a metaphor for understanding how a gesture can expand, while symbolizing both dissolution and community. This project is an example of the different operations that I have developed in recent years to transform documents, histories, and biographies into spatial interventions and collaborative maneuvers.

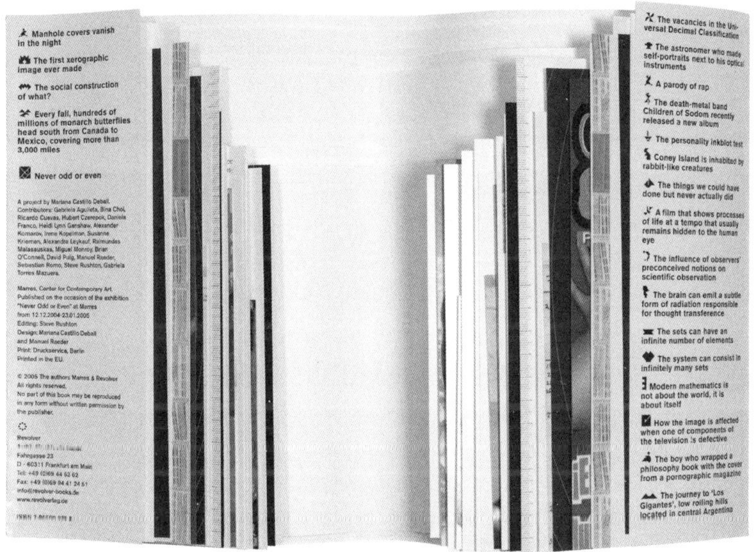

Never Odd or Even, Volume I, publication with contributions from several artists, 25 dust jackets, size various, max. 170×240 mm, (Berlin: Revolver, 2005)

The Wall and The Books, *Institute of Chance*, and *Interlude: The Reader's Traces* are three projects that also generate an expanded vision of the book and its reading. They draw on fragmented histories that could not remain bound in a single volume, so I decided to spill them out onto street corners, library corners, and archives so that they would, in a fragmentary way, occupy several spaces at once.

Ana, if we come back to your argument about destabilizing the identity of indigenous codices as books and define them as objects that resemble books but fulfill other functions, there is a crucial aspect that distinguishes them from the simple, playful exercise behind reading machines.

> There are two examples, one pre-Hispanic and the other colonial, of how the disappearance or destruction of indigenous books generated a classical rupture with ancient (lettered) knowledge, leaving a gap in history that could only be filled in by creating a new literary corpus: 1) the book burning undertaken by Tlacaélel in the era of Itzcóatl (the fifteenth century) with the aim of rewriting a new version of Mexica history; and 2) the burning of indigenous books undertaken by the ecclesiastic authorities in New Spain. Notable among these are the acto de fe in Maní, an event that is remembered for the destruction by Diego de Landa of hundreds of Maya codices, and the campaign by fray Juan de Zumárraga, the first bishop of Mexico, against idolatrous objects, including the *tonalamatl* and other memory-storing devices (so-called idols). These episodes continued throughout the entire colonial period.[9]

Despite the violence and scale of these actions, the destruction of these memory-storing devices did not succeed in putting an end to their histories. One could say that most of my projects take damaged, fragmented, or destroyed objects as their starting points. For each project I invent a personal equation, a key that invites a narrative to be generated out of absences.

These Ruins You See (2006–2008) is one example. In this project I researched the different elements that make up the *margins* or *context* of archaeology. The piece is divided into an empty museum space, an archive of

9 Díaz, 11.

documentary images, an audio guide, and a publication. The point of it all is not to exhibit and elucidate ancient Mesoamerican cultures or their ruins; on the contrary, it hinges on a meta-exhibition, an exhibition about the protocols and foundations of exhibition itself, or, more metaphorically, the negative space that surrounds objects on display.

> *These Ruins You See* meanders between politics, history, heritage, and identity, with the aim of finding the vestiges of archaeological practice in the present. Some of the most notable archaeological objects have led restless lives, moving between patios, warehouses, pedestals, display cases, museums, traveling exhibitions, and private collections. Archaeological representation is extended through copies, illustrations, textbooks, models, and souvenirs. Both the meaning and the authenticity of archaeological material are mixed up in this infinite chain of representations.[10]

This collection of empty display cases and narratives from different sources and temporalities reminds me of your empty *Codex Borgia*, in which there were just the marks where the deerskin parchment was cut and the sound of your voice narrating.

This project made me realize that I was not interested in objects, physical media, or histories, but rather in polyphony and the pastiche of everything, in the collective confluence of voices and vacuums, in absence as a catalyst of the imagination.

> The narrative of book burning functions as an originary myth that precisely exposes the moment and reasons that precipitated the end of an era, based on the extermination of its protagonists: the codices. The interesting thing about this myth is that it is not a narrative from the indigenous tradition, but rather the *horror vacui* resulting from the loss of books anchors its roots in European logocentrism.[11]
>
> In the Old World, books have not disappeared despite having also been the object of censorship and destruction throughout history. What makes the American case different? The answer does not seem to lie in the magnitude of the violence recorded in the different historical episodes, but rather in the nature of the knowledge at stake.[12]

Maybe these new codices are people, objects, and actions that manifest themselves every so often and then get dispersed.

Inside my copy of your book *El maíz se sienta para platicar*, I also found a photocopy of the first folio of the *Codex Fejérváry-Mayer*, representing one cycle in the count of the *tonalpohualli*, the Mesoamerican ritual calendar made up of twenty signs and thirteen numbers. Each day is a combination of a sign and a number that runs consecutively until 260 days have been reached. The image is a cosmogram presenting the earth made up of four cardinal regions and a center. Each color corresponds to a region of the cosmos and bears energies that move time and bring order to life on earth.

For the last several years I've been playing with this calendar to try to identify relationships between the measures of time and space. We could imagine that the duration of

10 Mariana Castillo Deball, *Estas ruinas que ves* (Berlin: Sternberg Press, 2008), 165.

11 Díaz, 16.

12 Díaz, 18.

a day is equivalent to the distance between someone's heart and fingertips. We could unfold this calendar and transform its original geometry.

I did my first experiment of unfolding the *tonalpohualli* in the exhibition *Them Inside the Skin* (2017), translating the first plate of the *Codex Fejérváry-Mayer* into twenty strips of metal, each perforated with thirteen circles to make up the 260 days. Each strip measures 270 cm, which amounts to two hearts, or *yolotl* in Nahuatl, one of the main Nahua measures used in construction. Each spatial coordinate corresponds to a color: east to red, north to yellow, west to green, and south to blue. The complete sculptural intervention amounts to a year occupying a space. The metal strips are connected with wooden joints and they go through the space sequentially, but they alter the space, as the calendar does through its correspondences between numbers and signs.

> The *tonalpohualli* system does not allow one to count the 365 days of the year, because its main function was to regulate, count, and order the emanations of the *tonalli* that circulate through the cosmos. That enabled each power or energy associated with a *tonalli* to imprint the day with a special quality: the day 7-reed, 9-movement. This calendar can thus be defined more as a qualitative temporal system than as a quantitative astronomical one.[13]

In 2018, Tatiana Falcón, Diana Magaloni, and I created the exhibition *In tlilli in tlapalli: Imágenes de la nueva tierra: Identidad indígena después de la conquista.*[14] Tatiana and I

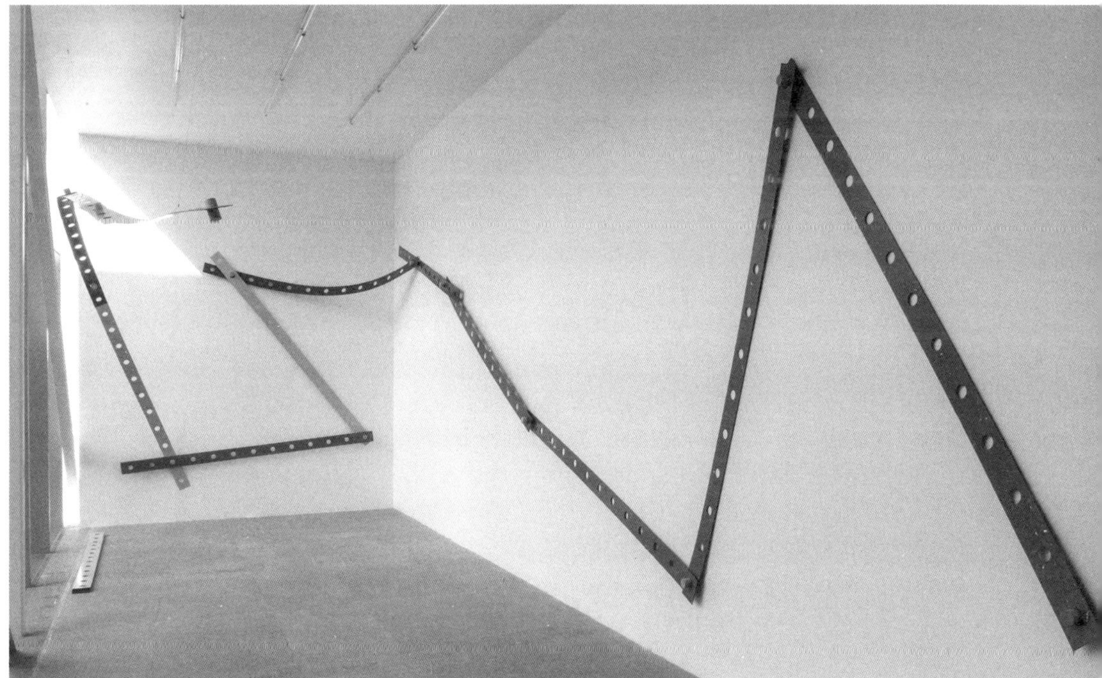

Tonalpohualli, Chicago, 2018, 20 perforated aluminium strips, wood joints, *Amarantus*, MUAC, Mexico City

the original composition of the calendar. The strips also feature a set of characters: deer, birds, and other figures I found at the flea market in Brussels and used to animate

13 Díaz, 30.

14 *In tlilli* (black), *in tlapalli* (color): the black, the color. It was on display from September 1 to November 26, 2018, at Museo Amparo in Puebla.

made a garden featuring plants and minerals used to make colors, based on the pigments that were used to paint the *Florentine Codex*. The architecture of the garden and the arrangement of the different plants were also based on the first plate of the *Codex Fejérváry-Mayer*. The present volume includes a text by Tatiana in which she describes the process of making pigments as well as how their usage continues. For the exhibition at the Museo Universitario Arte Contemporáneo (MUAC) we are remaking the garden. "There is no historical record of a garden that brought together all the dye-yielding plants like the one we made as part of that exhibition."[15] I feel that the garden has been the most radical transformation of a document that I have experienced, insofar as it became a space-time that grows and transforms.

While exploring the meanings and uses of plants for the garden, I came upon the title of this exhibition. In Greek, *amarantus* means "an imaginary flower that never dies." Amaranth is also one of the most important pseudo cereals consumed in Mexico, in addition to being an ingredient in different rituals. Amaranth seeds, or *huauhtli* in Nahuatl, were mixed with black agave syrup. After folding them together, an idol or *ixiptla* was made from the mixture. These edible figurative representations were embodiments of the sacred. Amaranth was prohibited by the Spaniards during the colonial era because of its connections to ritual.

Amarantus refers metaphorically to the objects I work with: objects that are damaged, absent, or outside their original context, but which nevertheless continue to live on through new uses and significations. Furthermore, edible amaranth figures speak to us of the *ixiptla* that gets incorporated into the body as nourishment.

One of the major pieces in the show, *Cocodrilo piel de los días*, starts off from a conversation that you and I had, in which you explained to me the meaning of plates thirty-nine and forty of the pre-Hispanic *tonalamatl* known as the *Codex Borgia*. Ana, I recall that you showed it to me on your screen, you explained that it was the skin of a

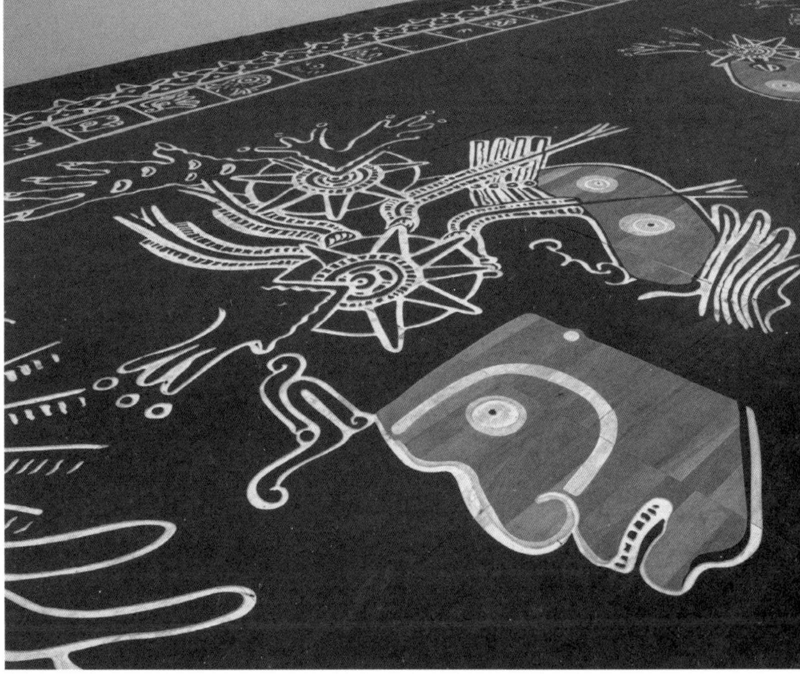

Crocodile Skin of the Days, **2021, 200** CNC routered wooden panels with veneer inlay, *Amarantus*, MUAC, Mexico City

reptile, and that the days were inscribed on its surface. It is a tapestry that contains time.

Perhaps you know this: in recent years I have made a series of engraved wooden floor tiles, which also serve as a printing matrix upon which the visitors to the exhibition can walk. Again, by changing the scale and materiality of the original documents, I generate a new experience or way of approaching the object. As a printing matrix it likewise becomes a device of graphic reproduction.

Generally, I have worked with maps and cartographic images. In this case I wanted to

15 Tatiana Falcón's text is included on p. 58 of this publication.

take up an image related to calendars and time that would gain a foothold in my obsession with generating chronotopes or spatiotemporal diagrams. Since you explained to me the meaning of the scene, I had already done several drawings and watercolors that were shown in *das Haut-Ich* in 2018. In your words:

> The scene represented on these two folios is very complex, so I will focus on two of the protagonists in this sequence. The image features an unfolded *tonalamatl*, whose function is not that of a book, but rather that of a skin that wraps around the scene of a sacrifice. In this case, the center of the composition is occupied by an anthropomorphic figure with black skin, whose body is distinguished by possessing nine suns, located on different parts of its anatomy, on its chest and joints.[16]

In order to transform the scene in the image that now makes up the floor, I focused on the two main elements: the reptile skin and the scene of the sacrifice. Generally, I compulsively draw the scene several times, in order to understand the image and make it my own, until I come to the feeling that it is alive.

Another reason why I chose this image is that the *tonalamatl* is drawn on the reptile skin.

> The image emphasizes that the *tonalamatl* is made of skin, not inert paper. This skin acquires a special quality, which implies the acquisition of a particular vitality that does not correspond to the skin of the living animal, nor to the dead skin that was flayed from the corpse. The *tonalamatl* transforms the skin into an artifact that belongs to another ontological dimension.[17]

Studying altered, destroyed documents that have been held in remote, inaccessible libraries and museums has meant working with printed copies, facsimiles, digital reproductions, and whatever is available. From the Western point of view, these copies are supplements of the original object, but they themselves have no value. I am convinced that each object, especially if it has undergone a trauma that is reflected in a group that protects it and keeps it in its memory and actions, is replicated in multiple formats, and all these representations are in a way part of the original, even if the latter no longer exists.

I was never able to make an argument for this idea on the basis of the Western epistemology of representation. Then I came across the Nahua concept of *ixiptla*, which encompasses all these different versions and regards them as part of the same tonal or expression of being. In my view, too, the ravages of colonization and looting have caused us to produce all these copies, as a means of holding and protecting, such that if one goes missing, we will still have multiple versions of it.

On the calendar, the deity Xipe Totec was often represented as a man who wore the flayed skin of another person on top of his own. The ceremony consisted in the sacrifice of the victim, and the transfiguration of the other person through the use of the skin of the sacrificed one. *Ixiptla* has been translated as "image," "delegate," "substitute," and "representative": it could be a statue, a vision, or the victim who becomes the god destined for sacrifice. The *ixiptlahuan* of the

16 Díaz, 41.

17 Díaz, 42.

same god could occur simultaneously, without the resemblances necessarily being identical.

Ixiptla derives from the Nahuatl particle *xip*: "skin," "covering," or "shell". It is the container, the recognizable presence, the actualization of a force imbued in an object: a being-there, removing the distinction between essence and matter, original and copy. A natural outer layer of tissue that covers the body of a person or an animal, skin can be separated from the body to make articles of clothing, vessels for holding liquids, or a surface on which to write. *Ixiptla* is the irresistible manifestation of a presence.

In 2014, I started the journal *Ixiptla* as a space of reflection in which anthropologists, archaeologists, artists, and writers collaborate in a discussion of models, copies, influence, and reproduction.

Maybe we are all *Mbo Xtá rídà* (skin people), as Hubert Matiúwàa suggests in his essay and poems, also published in this volume.[18] I learned about the work of Hubert Matiúwàa through Isadora Hastings, when I started working on the piece based on the *Codex Humboldt Fragment 1 / Codex Azoyú Verso 2*, a document that traces the tributes given by the kingdom of Tlachinollan, in the province of Tlapa, Guerrero, to the Mexica empire from 1486 to 1522. The codex ended up getting divided between Mexico and Germany: one part, the *Codex Humboldt Fragment 1*, was taken to Europe by Baron Alexander von Humboldt, who acquired it around 1803–1804 in Mexico City. Its counterpart, the *Codex Azoyú Reverso 2* was moved from the community of Azoyú in Guerrero to the library at the Museo Nacional de Antropología in Mexico City in 1940. Drawing on this codex, I made a ceramic mural for one of the galleries dedicated to Mesoamerican art at the Humboldt Forum in Berlin, which will house ethnographic collections and opened its doors in 2021.

In 2017, I contacted the collective Cooperación Comunitaria to help me adapt the piece in the context of the mountains of Guerrero, since that association had begun to work in the area, rebuilding adobe houses damaged by Hurricanes Ingrid and Manuel in 2013. In that region adobe is used as a building material, and Cooperación Comunitaria was interested in covering the buildings with raw earth tiles. After almost a year of tests they found the right mix, and now the outside walls of the buildings are covered in raw earth tiles, decorated with the design of reliefs taken from the codex.

I want to come back to your text, Ana, and to your argument about how the codices have become other things, other actions, and how it is that they operate in their specific context.

> By this logic, the *tonalamatl* was an instrument that, together with other (ritual) objects, shaped a history that encompasses the social networks that were generated, are generated, and will remain anchored in the landscape; a history of people who move around, and of emanations that flow over a tangible, recognizable space; a landscape that ties families, lineages, saints, ancestors, meteorological phenomena, and calendrical dates (spatio-temporal referents) in a complex knot that only locals can recognize and articulate without relying on books. Thus, the specialists who know the keys to time continue being responsible for carrying out the right ceremonies for interacting with local forces, in order

18 A selection of Hubert Matiúwàa's poems are included on p. 177 of this publication.

> to initiate negotiations before making an offering of food and pleasurable sensations, through colorful, perfumed objects perfectly arranged on the altar. These are the people who know the names of all the lords by heart, as well as the correct way to invoke them.[19]

I want to repeat your phrase "a history that encompasses the social networks that were generated, are generated, and will remain anchored in the landscape," since it seems to me that the concept of landscape solves the puzzle. That is where contemporary codices, as free expressions of a specific object or physical substrate, are expressed, precisely and ephemerally. Maybe they function like this by nature, or to protect themselves against possible destruction or disappearance. If there's only one object storing a given memory, its disappearance has terrible consequences. But if the object is distributed across various *ixiptlahuan* through forms, colors, people, histories, then it is more difficult to eradicate it in a single stroke.

In his book *La expresión americana*, José Lezama Lima talks about becoming-landscape as a particular characteristic of the Americas.

> Only what is difficult is stimulating; only the resistance that challenges us is capable of confronting, arousing, maintaining our power of knowledge, but really: what counts as difficult? Only that which is submerged in the maternal waters of darkness? An original without a cause, antithesis, or logos? It is form-in-becoming in which a landscape goes toward a meaning, an interpretation, or a simple hermeneutic, leading towards its reconstruction, which is definitely what marks its efficacy or disuse, its ordinancing force or its muted echo, which is its historical vision.[20]

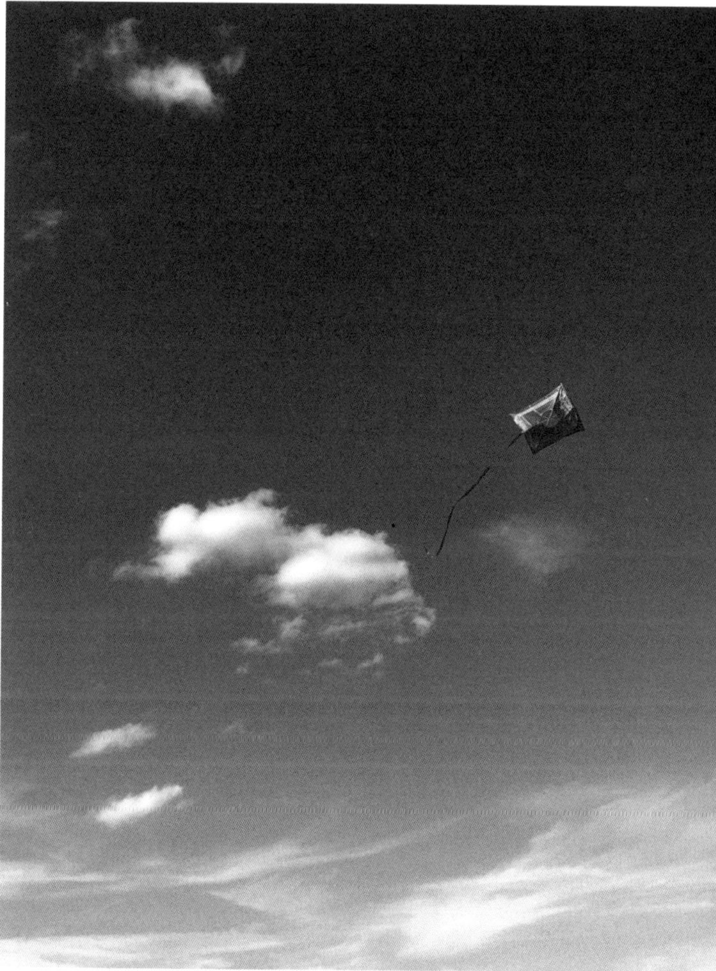

Papalote cocodrilo piel de los días (Crocodile Skin of the Days Kite), 2021, performative action in Tempelhofer Feld, *Behind the Screen*, Klosterfelde Edition, Berlin

A couple months ago, before traveling to Mexico to prepare this exhibition, I made a blue kite based on a Korean design that has an orifice at its center. I gather that these kites are flown in funeral ceremonies and that the spirit can escape through this perforation.

19 Díaz, 82.

20 José Lezama Lima, *La expresión americana* (Madrid: Alianza, 1969), 9.

Papalote cocodrilo piel de los días is an homage to your memory, Ana. You were a brilliant specialist in indigenous thought and art in central Mexico, who illuminated my path to start reading and understanding *tonalpohualli*. One of your favorite plates was the 39–40 of the *Codex Borgia*, which features a crocodile or a reptile whose skin features the symbols of the days of the *tonalpohualli* ritual calendar.

The kites flew in a collective action on July 30, 2021, generating new landscapes every time their circular windows allowed the wind to pass through them. Thus we bid you farewell on that day, and so I bid farewell to you for now. I hope that the pages of this book speak for everything we did not get a chance to say to each other.

Lovingly,

Mariana

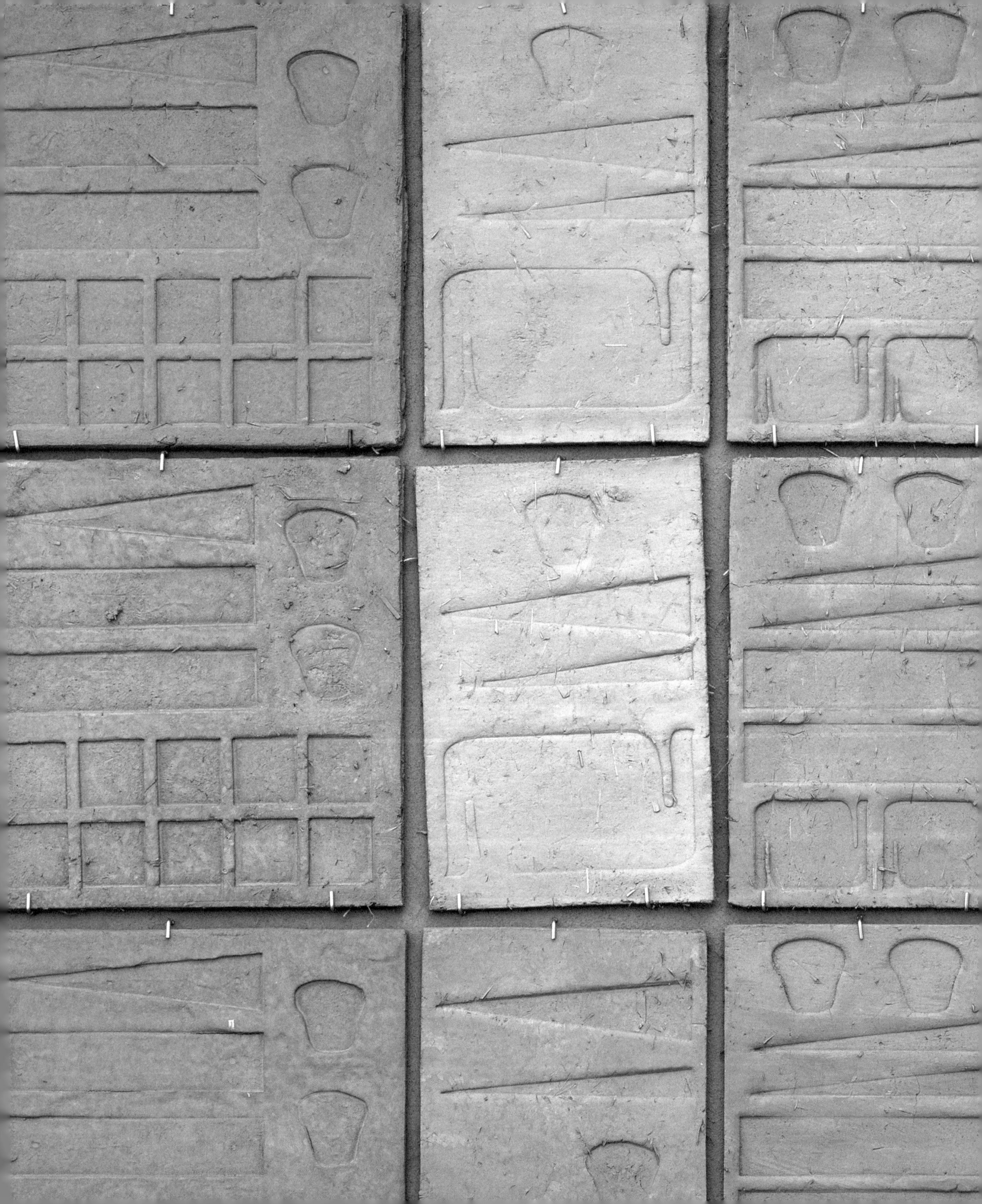

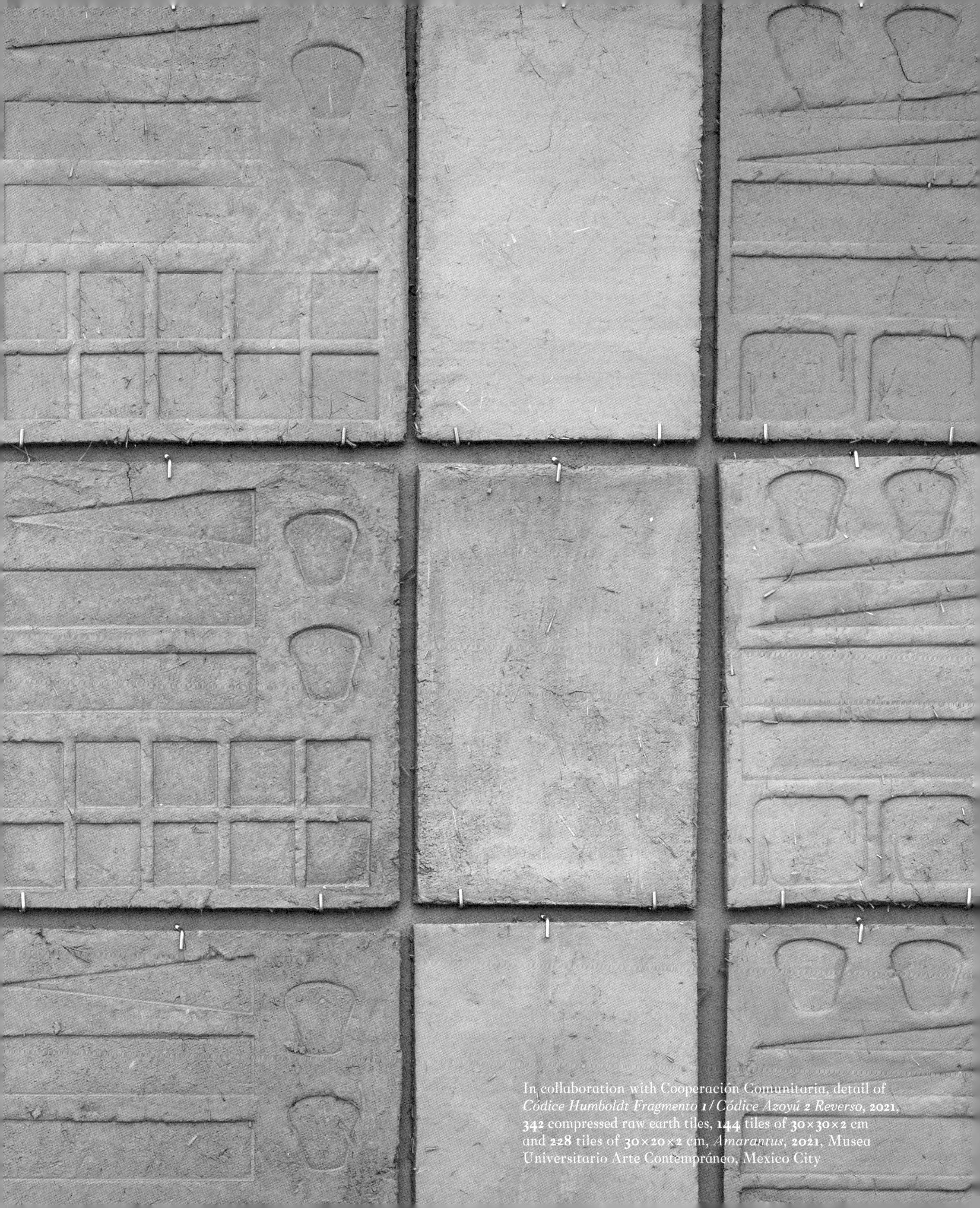

In collaboration with Cooperación Comunitaria, detail of *Códice Humboldt Fragmento 1 / Códice Azoyú 2 Reverso*, 2021, 342 compressed raw earth tiles, 144 tiles of 30 × 30 × 2 cm and 228 tiles of 30 × 20 × 2 cm, *Amarantus*, 2021, Musea Universitario Arte Contempráneo, Mexico City

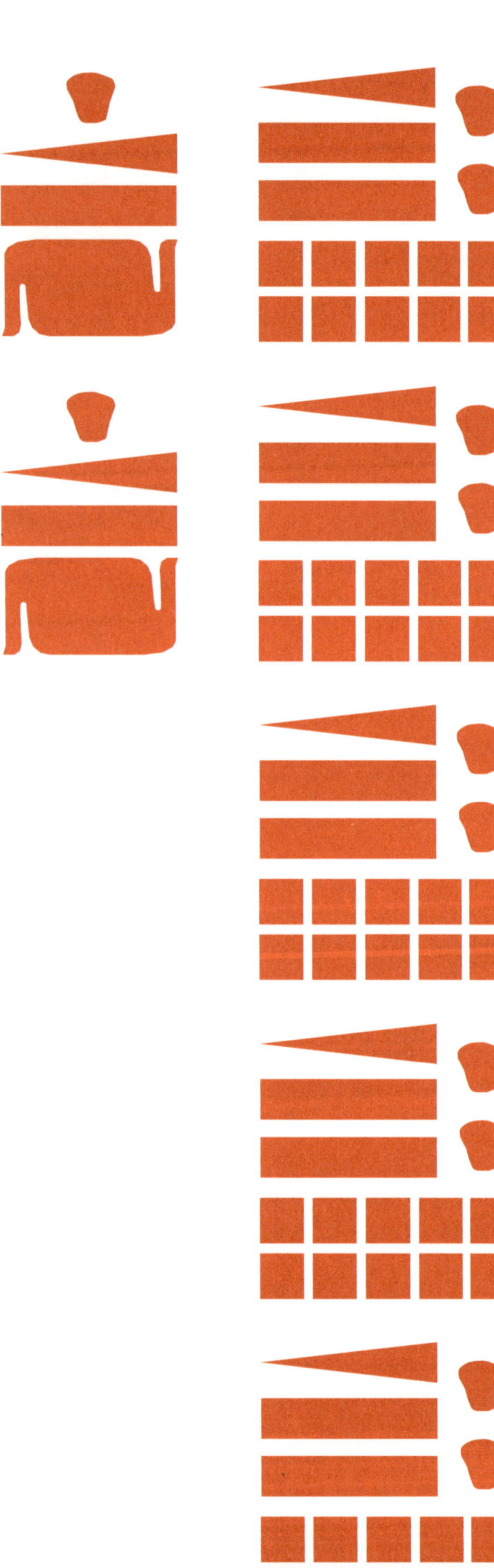
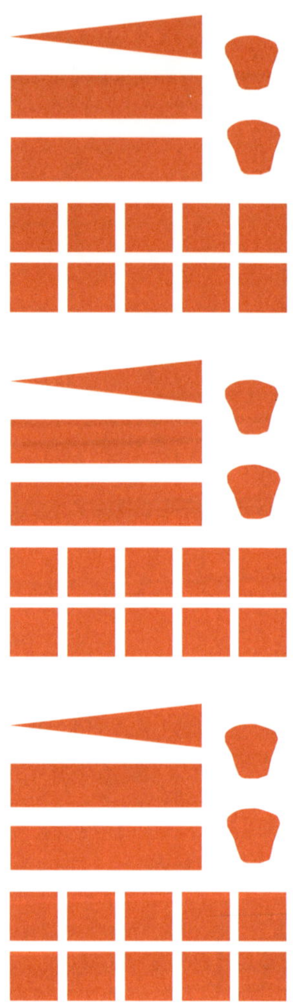

THE DOUBLE LIFE OF THE AZOYÚ CODEX

MARIANA CASTILLO DEBALL
ISADORA HASTINGS

Some documents have incredible stories: after being fragmented and divided up into different hands, they have crossed oceans and vast distances. Such is the case of the Códice Humboldt Fragmento **1** */ Códice Azoyú Reverso* **2**, *a document that traces the tributes given by the kingdom of Tlachinollan, in the province of Tlapa, Guerrero, to the Mexica Empire, from* **1486–1522**. *The codex ended up split between Mexico and Germany: one part, the Códice Humboldt Fragmento* **1**, *was taken to Europe by Baron Alexander von Humboldt, who acquired it in Mexico City around* **1803–1804**. *The other part, its homologue, the Códice Azoyú Reverso* **2**, *was brought from the community of Azoyú in Guerrero to the library of the Museo Nacional de Antropología (MNA) in Mexico City in* **1940**. *I used this codex to make a ceramic mural for one of the galleries dedicated to Mesoamerica, at the Humboldt Forum, a museum in Berlin housing ethnographic collections, scheduled to open its doors in* **2021**.

In **2017**, *I contacted Cooperación Comunitaria to adapt that piece in the context of the Montaña de Guerrero, since the association had been working in the area, rebuilding adobe houses that had been damaged by Hurricanes Ingrid and Manuel in* **2013**. *Adobe is the usual building material in that part of Guerrero, and Cooperación Comunitaria thought it would be interesting to cover the buildings with tiles made from raw earth. After almost a year of trials and errors, we hit the right mixture: the outside walls of the buildings now feature tiles made of raw earth, ornamented with reliefs based on the codex. The following is a conversation I had with Isadora Hastings, coordinator of Cooperación Comunitaria, about this process and the work that is now a part of the community.*

Mariana Castillo Deball

ISADORA HASTINGS (IH): Cooperación Comunitaria is a nonprofit organization that works in the Montaña de Guerrero as well as in three other states in Mexico: Oaxaca, Chiapas, and Hidalgo. Ten years ago, we started working in rural housing, revisiting traditional building systems and local materials. In addition to the building itself, we sought to recover production processes, analyzing the territory and the natural resources, and attending to sociocultural aspects, in order to improve the quality of life in the communities and reduce their vulnerability. This work involves an exchange of knowledge: on one side, the community's experience and all the knowledge it has generated over many years, and on the other, the technical knowledge that Cooperación Comunitaria can contribute, by reinforcing the houses and analyzing the territory, so that the communities can return to being self-sufficient and self-managed.

The specific project in Guerrero, on which we collaborated with Mariana, started in 2013 after Hurricanes Ingrid and Manuel, which destroyed a lot of the housing in an area where homes are still made with adobe. The Montaña de Guerrero, on the eastern side of the state, is the most seismically active part of the country, and winds there can reach up to 120 kilometers per hour. Three different indigenous groups settled there: the Nahua, the Ñuu Savi and the Mé'phàà. We have worked directly with the latter to rebuild their houses. We quickly perceived that in that area there was a high risk of landslides, so we did an analysis to find out whether it was necessary to relocate the houses, while recognizing that the causes of these disasters are deforestation, the use of agrochemicals that erode the soil, and the supplanting of forest-based economic activities by agricultural ones. This is why we acted holistically in the communities, working for two years before starting to rebuild the houses. Once the rebuilding was complete, we started to replicate this model in other communities. For the past three years our work has focused on building community centers and collective-use centers using reinforced adobe. To do so we have worked with the engineer Gerson Huerta, analyzing traditional building systems and reinforcing them so that they can withstand earthquakes and strong winds. The idea is to pass all this new technical knowledge on to the communities, so that they will then be able to apply that knowledge throughout the region.

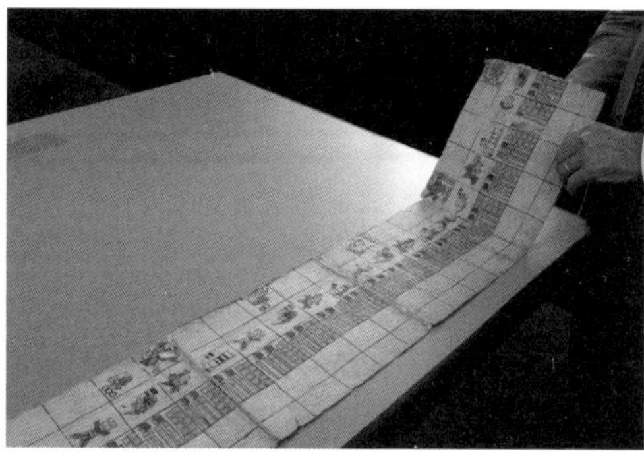

Codex Humboldt Fragment 1
Staatsbibliothek zu Berlin

For the last two years, we have worked with a group of teachers at indigenous preschools where the Mé'phàà language is spoken. They did not have a workplace because they are not administered by the Secretaría de Educación Pública (SEP), so they asked us to build them two community centers. It was a collaborative project during which they also learned how to reinforce adobe buildings. Another project of ours took place at the Universidad Intercultural del Estado de Guerrero (UIEG). In that case, students from eighteen different municipalities helped to build an environmentally friendly hall where they would be able to take classes. They learned new building techniques as well as safer reinforcement systems, a knowledge that they can now take back to their communities. These buildings—the environmentally friendly hall and two of the Mé'phàà preschool buildings—are where Mariana made the pieces that she is now going to talk about.

MARIANA CASTILLO DEBALL (MCD): *The Códice Humboldt Fragmento 1 / Códice Azoyú Reverso 2* was likely split up in one of two agrarian disputes that took place in the mayoralty of Tlapa during the early eighteenth century. At the time, a lot of the territories changed hands, and several documents were confiscated. *The Códice Humboldt Fragmento 1* was taken to Europe by the baron Alexander von Humboldt, after he acquired it from Antonio de León y Gama in the early nineteenth century. The rest of the document was dispersed until 1940, when it was acquired by Yrineo Germán, a descendent of Tlapa's ancient rulers. That piece of the document eventually caught the attention of Alfonso Ortega, a researcher at the MNA, who offered to trade the documents for a string of public projects and material goods. On the basis of these verbal agreements, he obtained the codices, which he brought to the library at the Museum.

The codex is a record of tribute payments made by the kingdom of Tlachinollan to the Mexica. Almost all the payments were made in gold—an abundant material in the region, even today—as well as in textiles. An envoy from the Mexica kingdom would come to collect the tribute every four months. The document includes records of what was paid along with calendrical information about feast days and special events.

Using this document, I made a ceramic mural for one of the Mesoamerican galleries at Berlin's Humboldt Forum, a new museum that will house the ethnographic collections. When I transformed this document to adapt it for this piece, I used as a reference the tributary registry, following the sequence of the entire document, including the sections that are now lost. The document is read from bottom to top, and right to left.

The parts of the document that are still lost—or perhaps safeguarded by the communities—appear as blank tiles. There are many

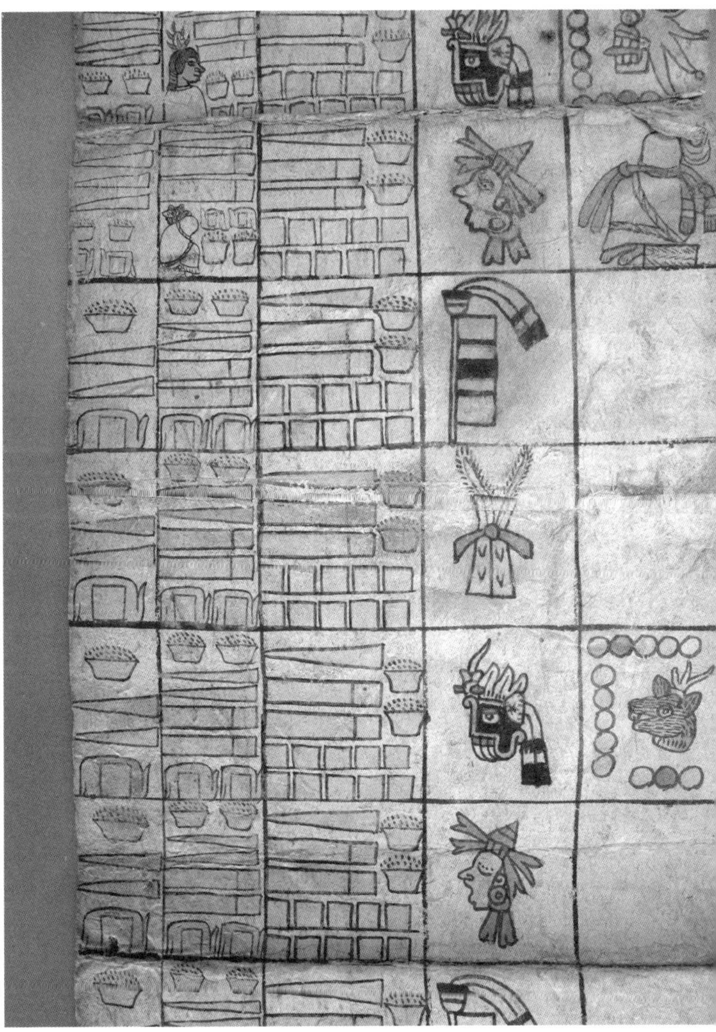

Codex Humboldt Fragment 1
Staatsbibliothek zu Berlin

communities that save such documents to use as titles for their land, or to keep them from ending up in big museums or libraries, because that would make them unavailable to the communities. By the end of the document, it appears that the Mexica were demanding so much tribute that the glyphs no longer fit within the grid because the quantities of gold and textiles were immense. The document ends in the first years of the

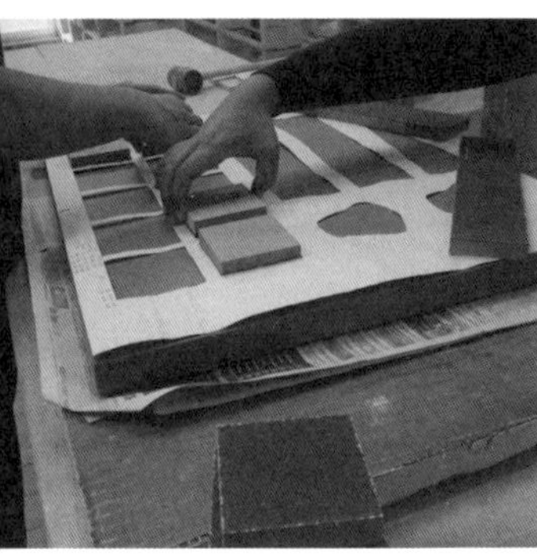

Spanish conquest, when the Mexica empire was defeated: simply, no one came to collect the tribute, so the document came to an end.

The piece at the Humboldt Forum is a ceramic mural measuring eight-by-ten meters and comprising 312 plaques corresponding to the grid of tributes. To translate

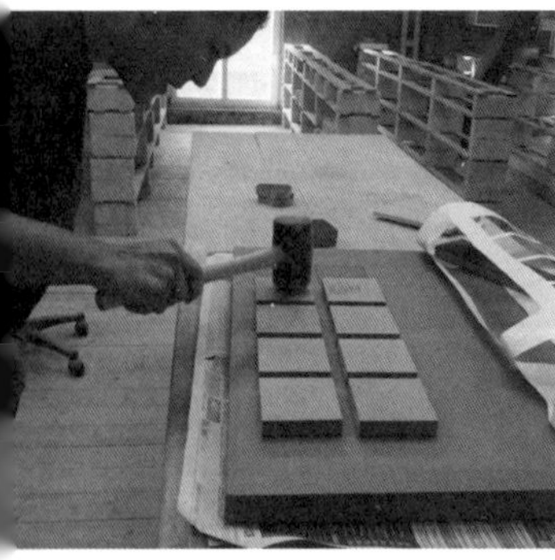

the glyphs corresponding to the gold and textile tributes, drawn on *Amate* paper on the original document, I developed a series of stamps in the shape of each glyph. These stamps have a textured surface that leaves a mark when pressed against a ceramic tile. The tiles were then stamped with these shapes, keeping the sequence of glyphs on the codex. The Berlin piece was reproduced in Golem, a ceramics workshop in Brandenburg that specializes in tiles, decorations, and reconstructions of historical monuments. It struck me that it would be interesting to do this project in Mexico because all of these documents are kept in libraries, museums, and universities, and indigenous communities have very little access to them.

One thing that particularly interested me is that the document is called *Códice Azoyú*. Azoyú is a region in southern Guerrero, in Tierra Caliente. The place where the document ended up has nothing to do with where it came from, namely Tlapa, a region in the northern part of the state. That observation gave rise to the idea of doing the piece in Tlapa, the document's original territory, together with Cooperación Comunitaria. One major difference from the Berlin piece is that we wanted to change the manufacture technique because in Guerrero, Cooperación Comunitaria has worked with reinforced adobe, so the idea was to use raw rather than baked earth to make this piece. That was a rather complicated process, since finding the right recipe was a whole challenge itself. We had to make sure that there weren't too many ingredients, that it wasn't too heavy, that it could then be attached to the walls without falling down, and that the reliefs made by the stamps would be visible, because the impression is very subtle, and the light has to be hitting the wall just right in order to really see the piece.

Process pictures in the ceramic workshop GOLEM, Berlin, Germany

It was very interesting to talk with the community and to show them the origin of the piece. I pursued this initiative independently of the museum in Berlin, although they supported its completion. I felt it was important to create a counterweight to the Berlin piece, made in a European museum with colonial collections, and what better way to do so as an artist than by going back to the indigenous communities and establishing a more relevant connection.

IH: The piece was done in three buildings: the environmental hall at the UIEG, the Community Center in La Ciénaga, and the Community Center in Ojo de Agua. These were overseen by the architect Jesús Álvarez, who has generated a lot of knowledge about the local materials in the area. We have been working hard to recover the technique of building with adobe because it is inexpensive, provides good insulation, and has a small ecological footprint.

Earth mural samples by Cooperación Comunitaria for *Codex Humboldt Fragment 1 / Codex Azoyú Reverse 2*, **2020**, in Ojo de Agua, Malinaltepec, Guerrero

From the outset, when Cooperación Comunitaria started working on the raw earthen tiles, we collaborated with the architect Luis Fernando Guerrero Baca of the Universidad Autónoma Metropolitana (UAM) Xochimilco, and the Instituto Nacional de Antropología e Historia (INAH). Luis is also a restorer, and he has a deep knowledge of building with earth. He's helped us develop a variety of building techniques. At first Mariana also developed these individual stamps for the tiles, but we quickly saw that it was complicated because each tile features a combination of stamps. Architects Jesús Álvarez and Cecilia Maldonado found a solution: making plaques with the stamps made it a lot easier. The plaques have the same depths in the material and were no longer uneven, because if you pressed it too hard, the tiles would break, as they are very thin. It was a very delicate work, and required a lot of labor and technique.

Although we were planning to install the tiles using a plaster of soil—which did work—Jesús wondered what we were going to do about the earthquakes. He and the engineer Gerson Huerta then came up with a more mechanical system of putting the tiles on the wall and preventing them from falling in the event of an earthquake, using nails of a particular size, hammered in a certain way, with a wire mesh inside the tile. Also, one of the main community promoters working in the Montaña de Guerrero, Grabiel Cantú, proposed that the women should make the tiles and be involved in this process, because the material was a lot like tortilla dough, and on that count they're the experts. All the material for making the tiles was brought to Grabiel's community, Obispo, which was the first one to be rebuilt after the earthquake.

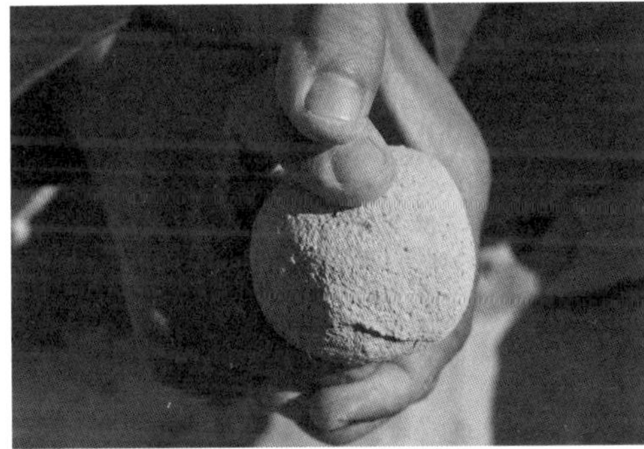

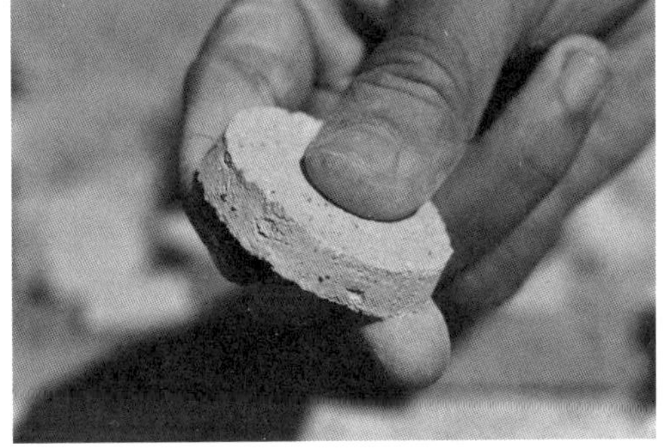

It's been very interesting for us at Cooperación Comunitara to work with you, Mariana, because it's the first time we've brought a work of art to the community. We are very

interested to know what it was like for you, since the process of manufacture is perhaps, in many cases, no longer something done directly by the artist, but there is nevertheless a very careful oversight of the production process behind it. For us it was very significant that the women made the project their own when they made the tiles, and that they made certain decisions about the production process. But for you, what was it like to be delegating the process from a distance?

MCD: I was always interested in this project being a collaboration: to propose the basic elements of the project and to introduce the community to the codex's history. In terms of construction and materials, I didn't have any experience working with adobe or raw earth. It was also essential that the architects, the community, and the women make the project their own, and come up with their own solutions, because it wasn't something that I commanded them to do, but rather something we were doing together. In that sense, that moment of letting go and giving them agency in the project really made it a collaboration rather than just a commission. I think that was crucial, and it meant that people worked on it in a different way, because they knew that ultimately it was their project too.

IH: In that sense, I think that the objective was achieved, because the work they did—the community, the architects, and Grabiel—was very detailed. On top of that, it involved learning something new, because it's not something they had done before. It's interesting to me that a lot of people have stopped to look at the piece and asked how it was made: there's an interest there and they like how it looks in terms of its construction. Another thing that's interesting to us is the way in which the different publics, in Germany and Mexico, are going to relate to these two murals: on one hand, it's going to be in a museum, where it's a work of art, and on the other, here in the mountains, the public will be the people in the communities themselves. The only thing left to do now is to put up a sign explaining its meaning, because it's part of their local history. It's interesting that they're getting acquainted with it in the context of what's happening today with the mining industry, and with everything that's going on in the area, but also as a piece of art that's becoming part of the architecture, part of the history of the place.

MCD: In fact, it was also special that, the last time I spoke to Cecilia, she told me that one day they were in the car and it just so happened that they were going to drive past Azoyú, because you're doing another project there. She said to Jesús, "Let's go to Azoyú to see if there's anything about the codex there." They ended up finding a cultural center where the codex is painted on all the walls, and there's a facsimile of it there, too. I think it was special that the Cooperación Comunitaria team got so involved in this research. Now they know more about it than I do!

Making the piece at the Humboldt Forum in Berlin and making it with you in the Montaña de Guerrero: there couldn't be two more different contexts. In the case of the museum in Berlin, it was a commission by the government for a collection of objects that have been acquired around the world. As I said before, there has to be a lot of mediation between the objects and the public. Obviously, it's a place where a lot of research is done, and it's about offering an explanation to the public about where those objects come from and why they're there, but it still ends up being alienating. If you go to a museum where there are eight hundred thousand objects from all around the world, you don't feel like you're in a specific place; you feel like you're somewhere that accumulates a lot of places from the rest of the world. By contrast, the Montaña de Guerrero is a much more specific context: it's about a community, a document. And that piece, which only concerns them, is much clearer and more transparent in that sense. That's why, for me as an artist, it was always very important to do that dual gesture. I do a lot of work with these indigenous documents, but in recent years I've been trying to generate that mediation and to return to where the object came from and ask, "Who's here?" and "Whose business is this?" Sometimes we think that museums only have dead objects that no longer matter to anyone, but that's not true. There are people, for example, in Malinaltepec, for whom this document is important, and together with them we could make a mural in these centers, develop a new technique and make history our own. And in that case, it belongs to everyone and no one. Everyone has the capacity and agency to rewrite their history. For me that was very exciting and moving.

IH: It's also meaningful for the communities to know that there's this document that's been split in two, between Berlin and Mexico City, and that it came from the Montaña de Guerrero. For them it's very important, especially in times like these, to know the history of tributes that, in a lot of ways, they're still paying to this day—now with their territory and their natural resources. We're very grateful to you for the initiative and for the way you made the piece, the fact that you allowed it to be produced there and to take on a life of its own with the communities.

MCD: On top of that, maybe there are people who still have parts of the document because, as I said, there's a third part that's still missing.

QUESTION FROM THE PUBLIC (P): How can we learn to build like you? How can we learn from you to listen to these communities and build based on what makes sense to them?

IH: We believe that people learn best through practice. To build with earth you have to touch it, understand its different types, plastic qualities, and textures. You learn it over time. We also have a series of building manuals for different techniques: adobe, wattle and daub, walls with rod structures filled with earth, etc.

P: What strategies could be taken in order to prevent History Museums—who keep these codices—from limiting the access to the communities where these documents came from?

MCD: Museums have a lot of strategies for making these documents accessible. For example, there are very extensive digitalization projects that make documents available online. Sometimes they make facsimiles. I've never seen the original codex; I've only ever seen copies, facsimiles, digital images. I do think efforts have been made, but the problem isn't digitalization, it's mediation: how to do it so that a specific community knows that the document is accessible online and that it exists, because if they don't even know it exists, they don't know how to look for it.

IH: It's also important to mention that in the Montaña de Guerrero there still aren't any telephones; there are barely any cell phones and the signal you get there is very weak. So, there's no access to the Internet. The way they get information and learn things there is very different from the way that happens in a city.

P: Could you say more about the experience of connecting and building relationships with the people in the communities where you work?

IH: There are two kinds of projects. One involves showing up to rebuild after a disaster, and the other is working with groups that have already coalesced around some production process. In our case, normally they reach out to us because they want us to help them build a space where they'll be able to carry out training workshops and develop their products. These are groups that we've accompanied for many years. It's very enriching because we learn a lot from them, from these living cultures, and we can also contribute some of the technical knowledge that we have. It takes time to build long-lasting relationships and for them to contribute to seeing what we might propose in order to improve their processes, whether in terms of construction or production. It's a very delicate issue, but when we're in a region we start getting to know more communities, more people, and the fact that we've worked in the same area for many years has allowed us to delve deeper into the territory and the knowledge of natural resources as well as into their culture.

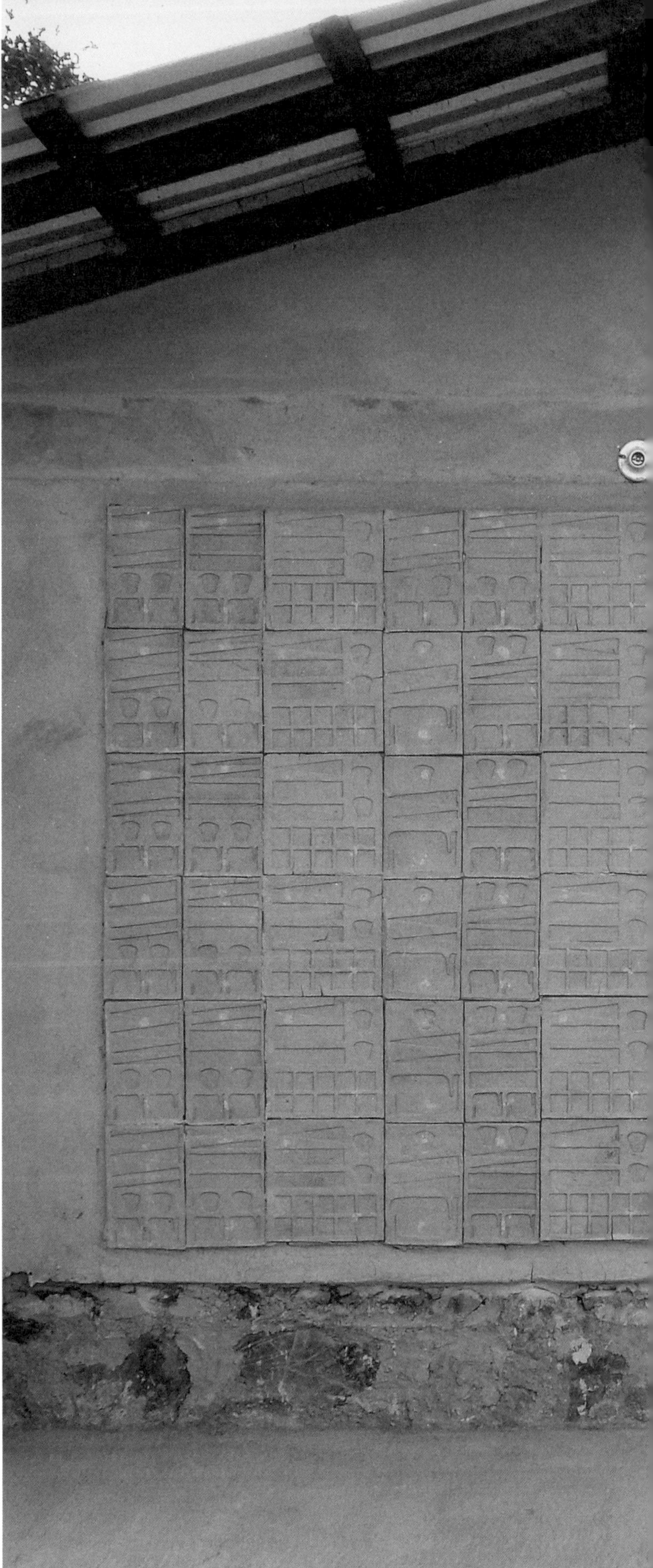

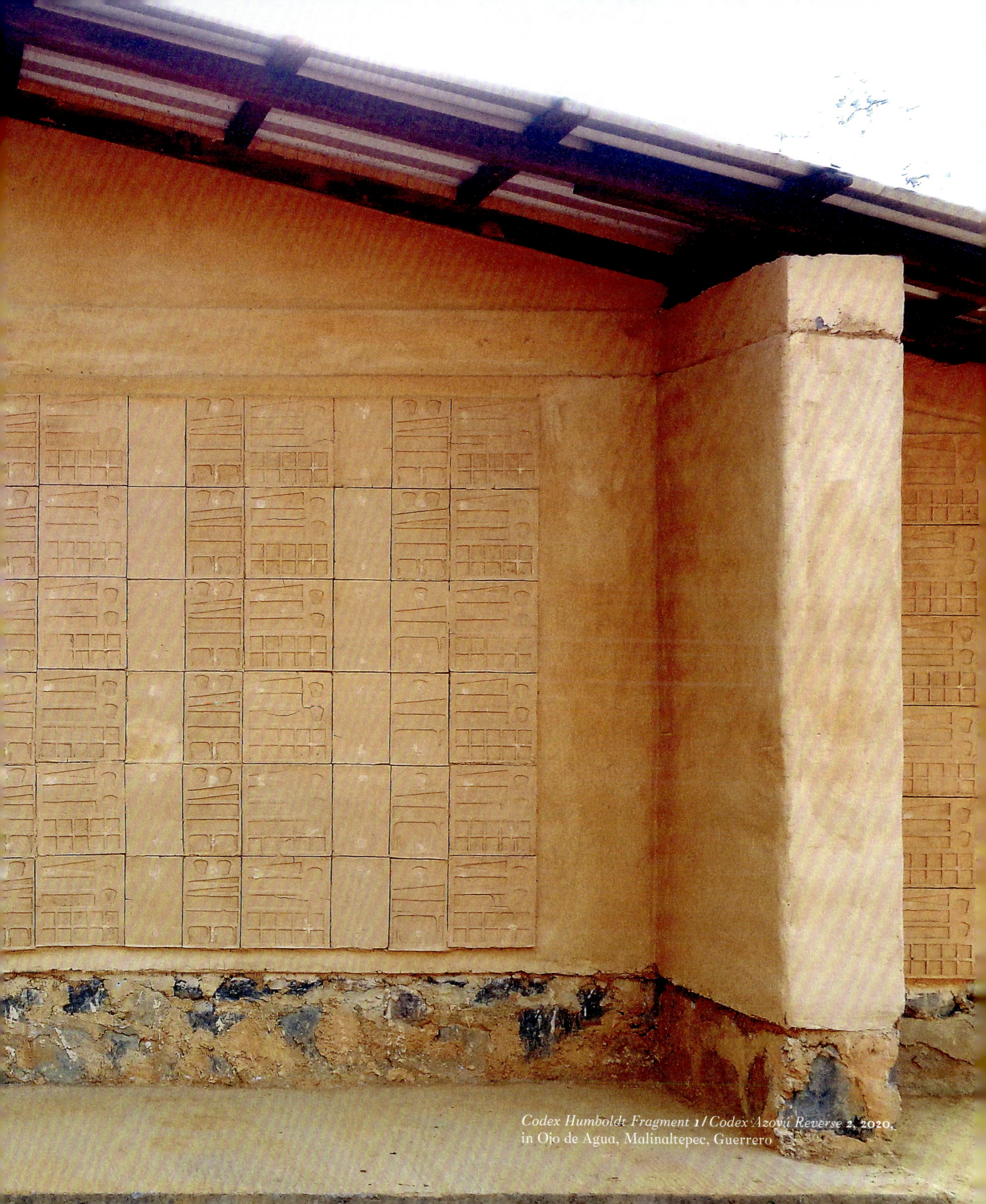

Codex Humboldt Fragment 1 / Codex Azoyú Reverse 2, 2020,
in Ojo de Agua, Malinaltepec, Guerrero

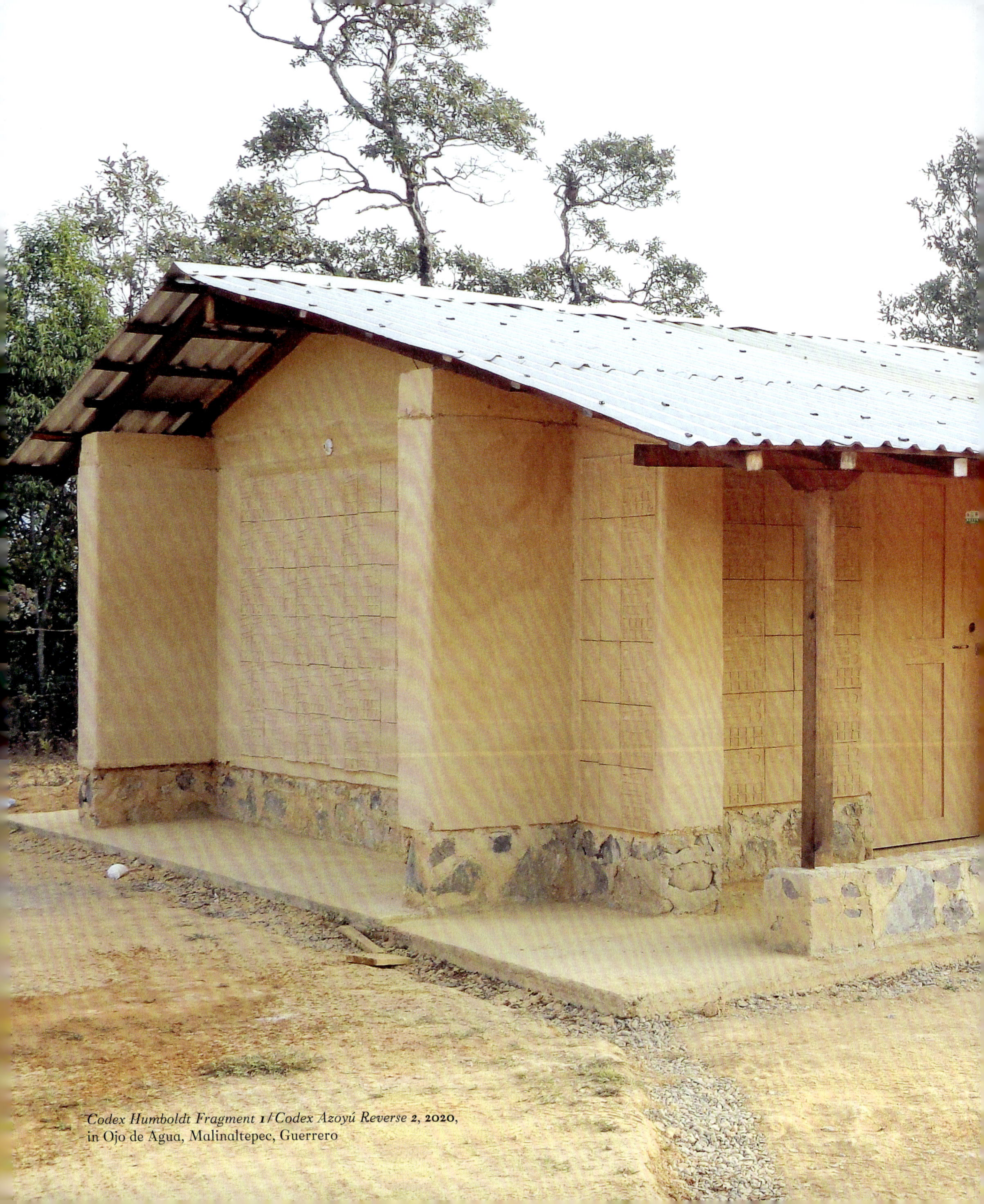

Codex Humboldt Fragment 1 / Codex Azoyú Reverse 2, 2020,
in Ojo de Agua, Malinaltepec, Guerrero

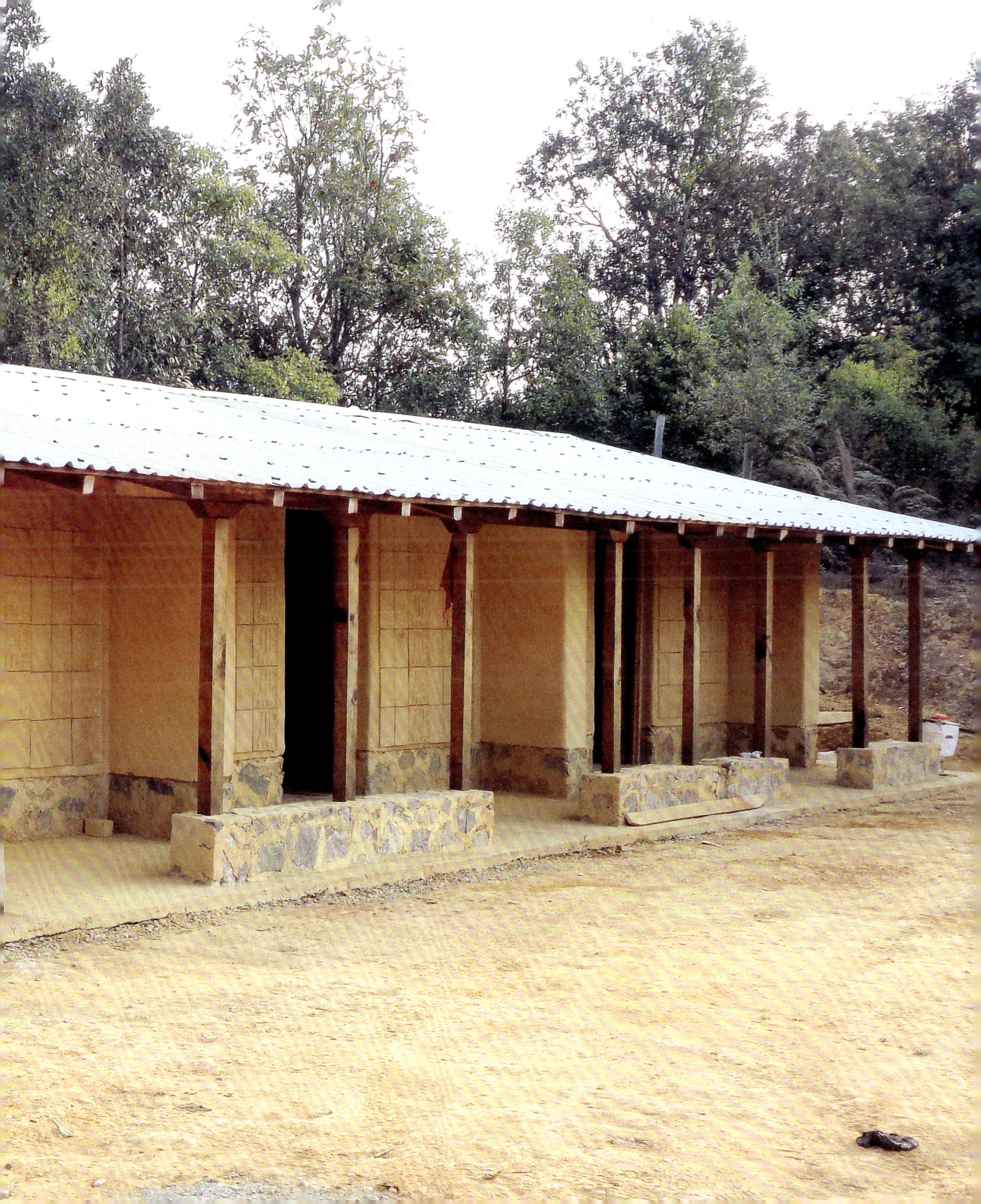

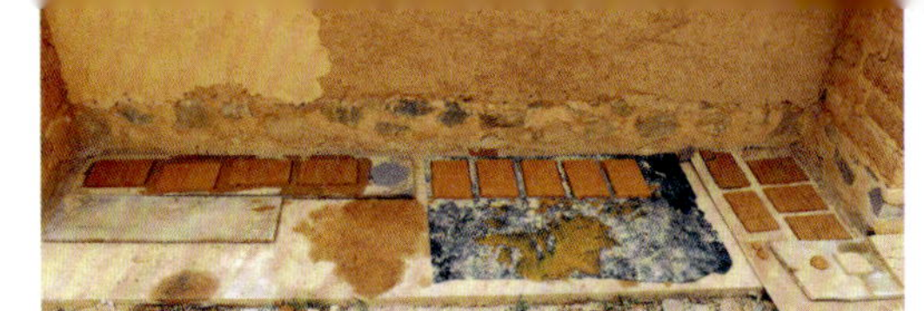

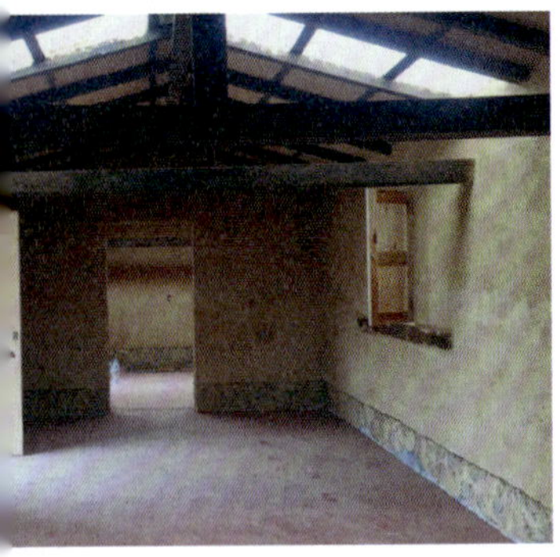

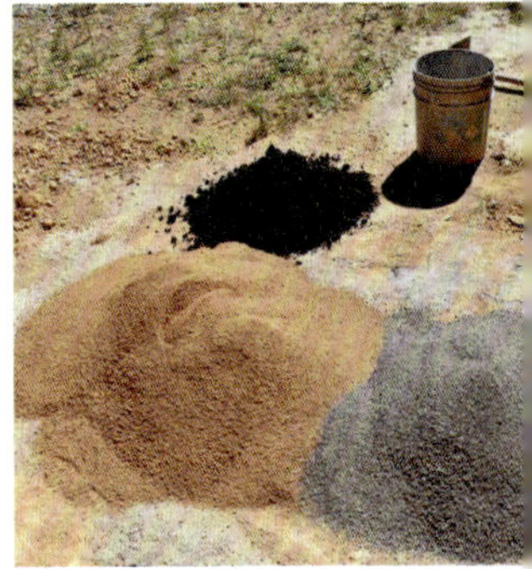

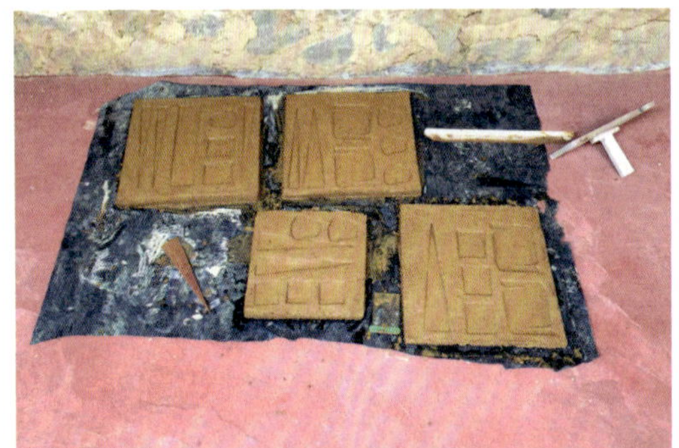

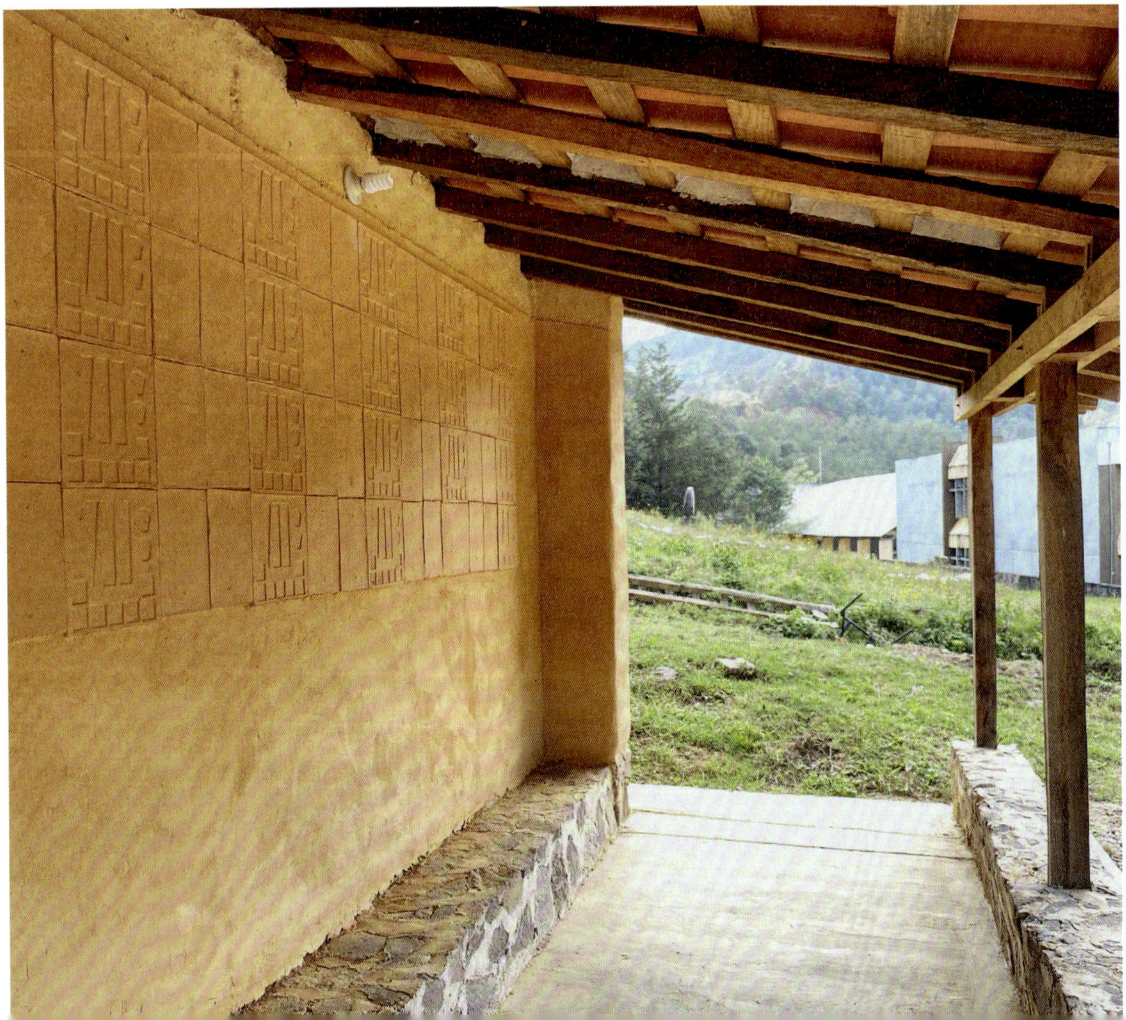

Details of *Codex Humboldt Fragment 1 / Codex Azoyú Reverse 2*, 2020, in Ojo de Agua, Malinaltepec, Guerrero

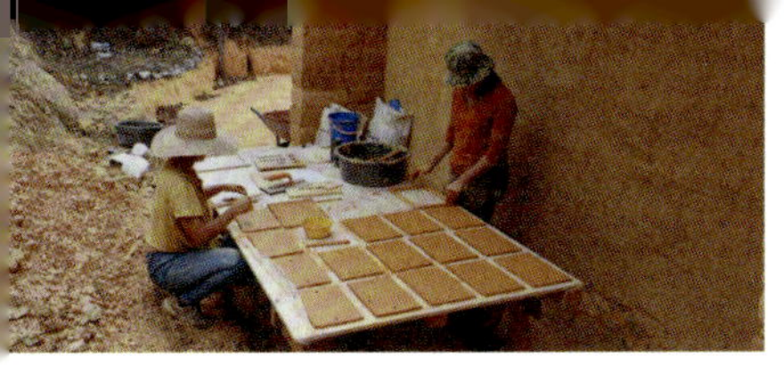

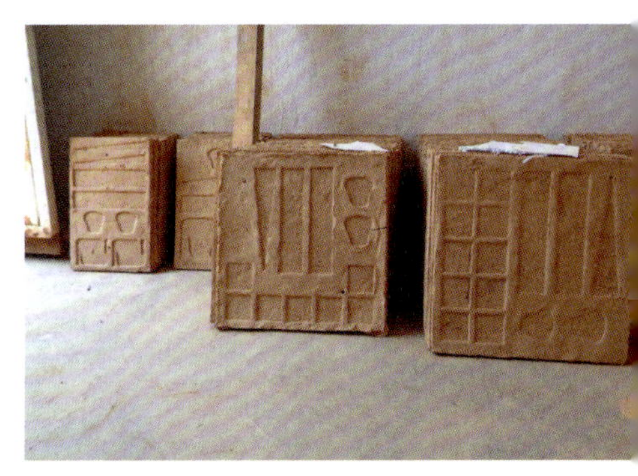

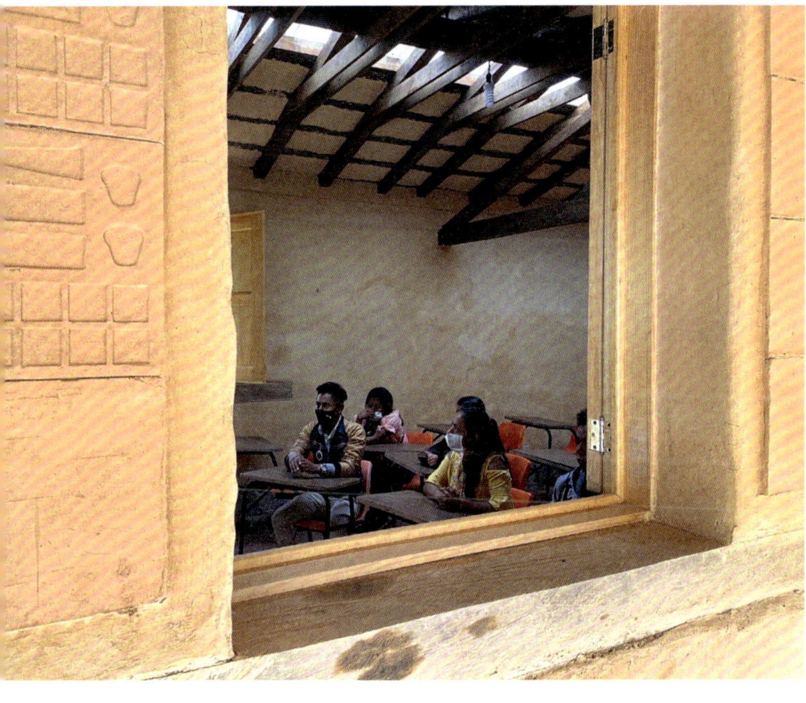

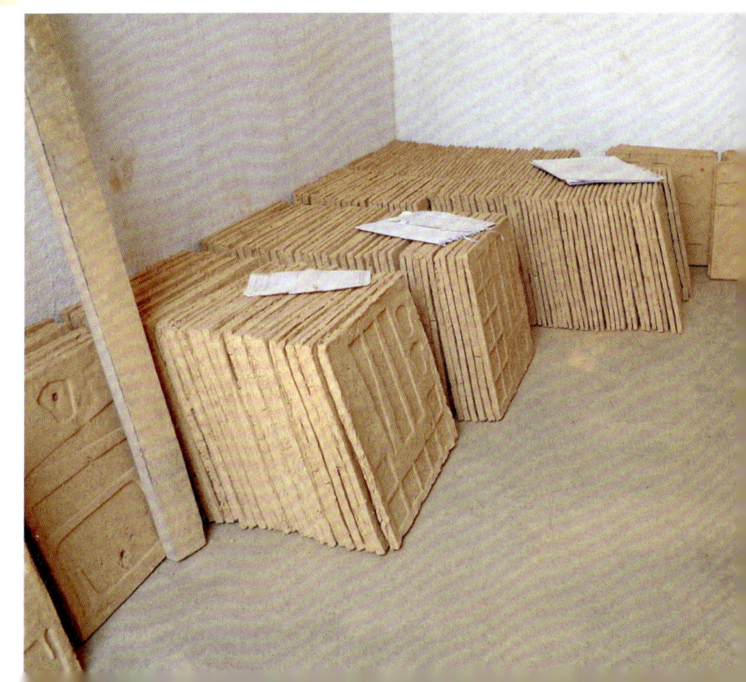

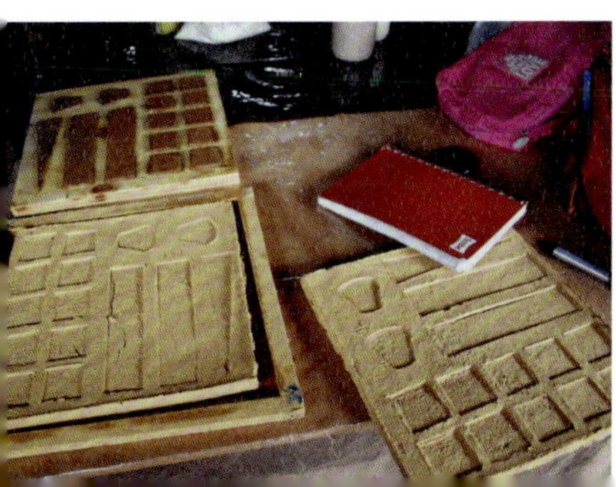

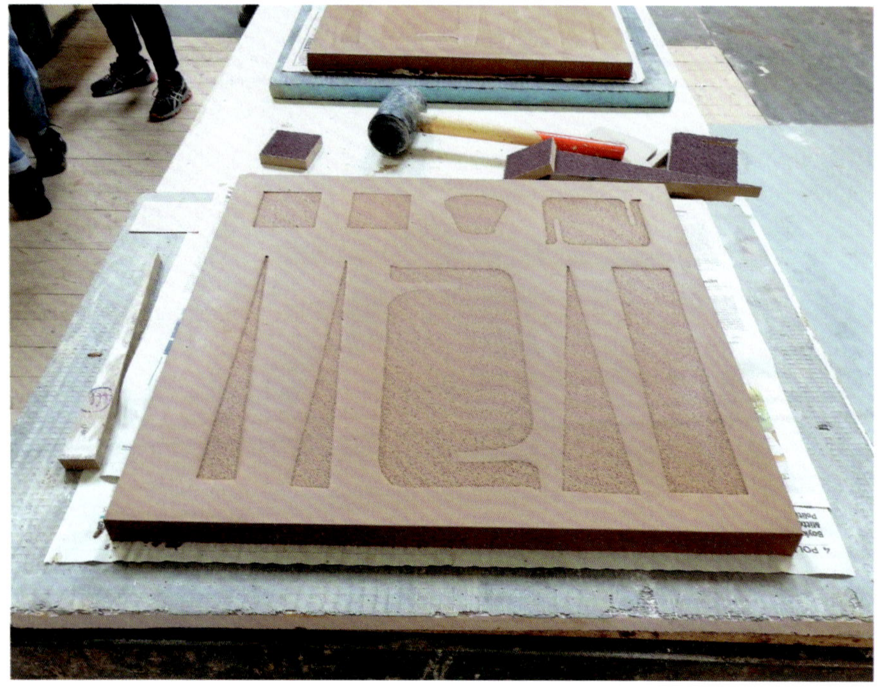

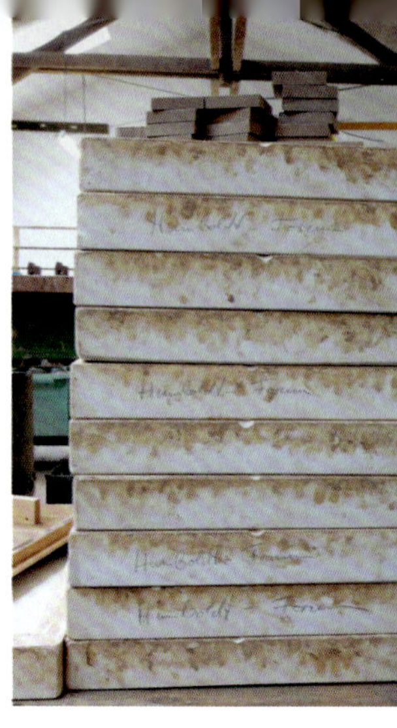

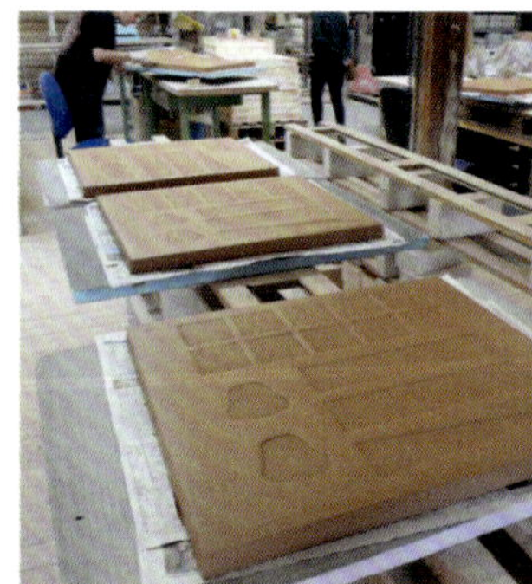

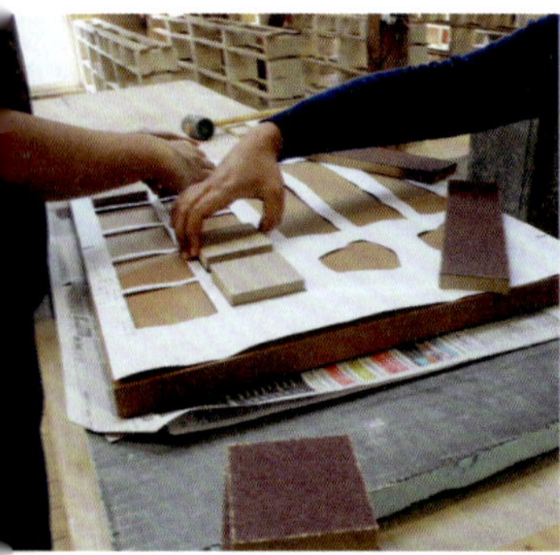

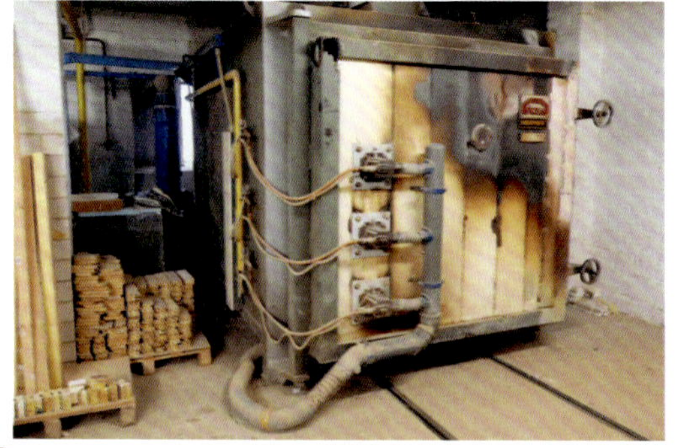

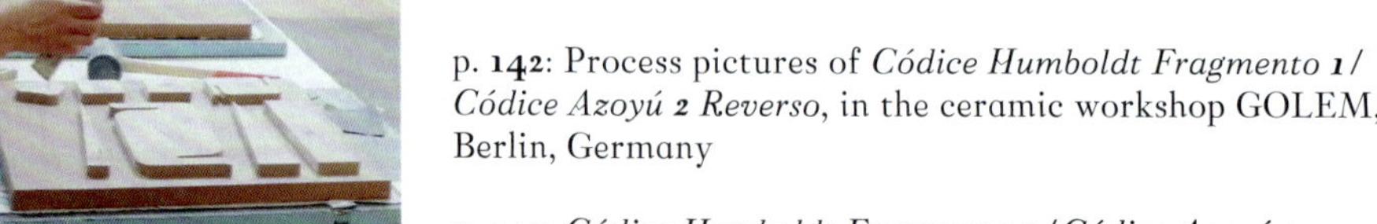

p. **142**: Process pictures of *Códice Humboldt Fragmento 1* / *Códice Azoyú 2 Reverso*, in the ceramic workshop GOLEM, Berlin, Germany

p. **143**: *Códice Humboldt Fragmento 1* / *Códice Azoyú 2 Reverso*, **2020**, Humboldt Forum, Berlin

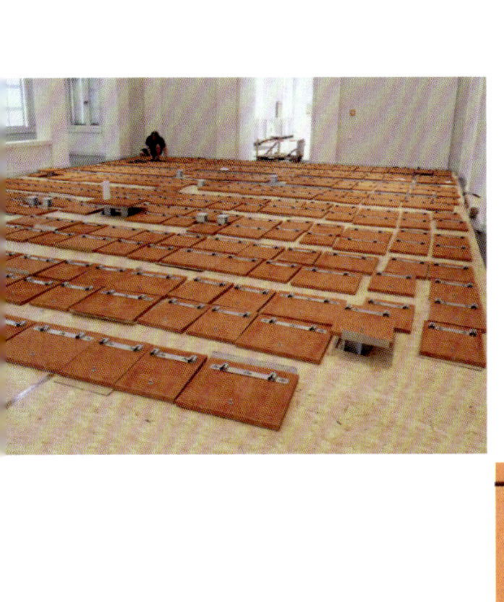
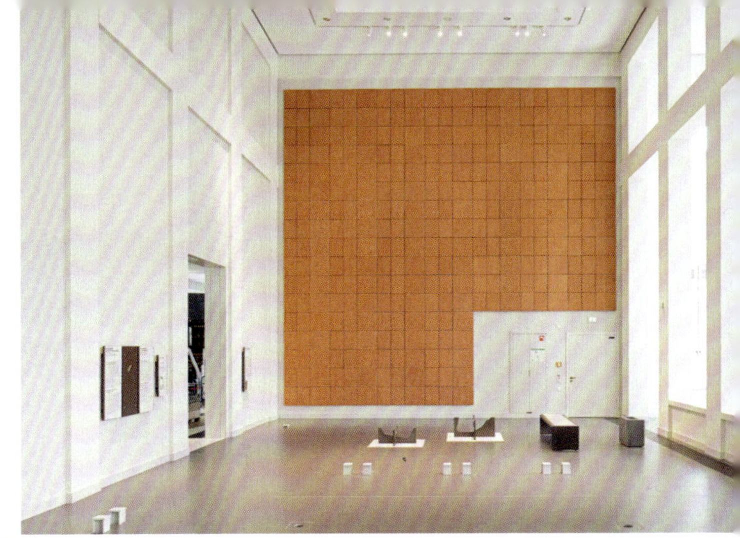
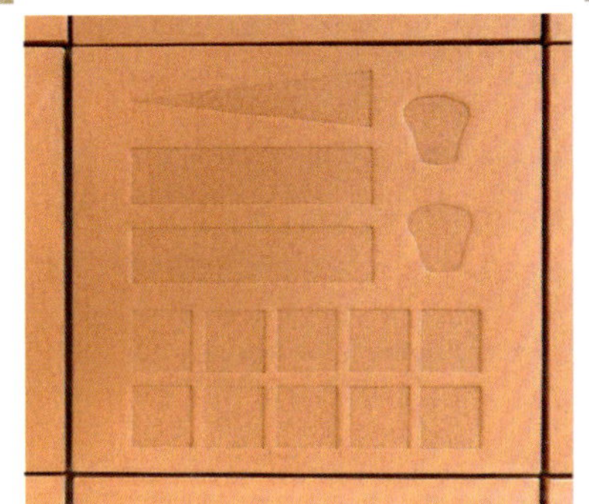
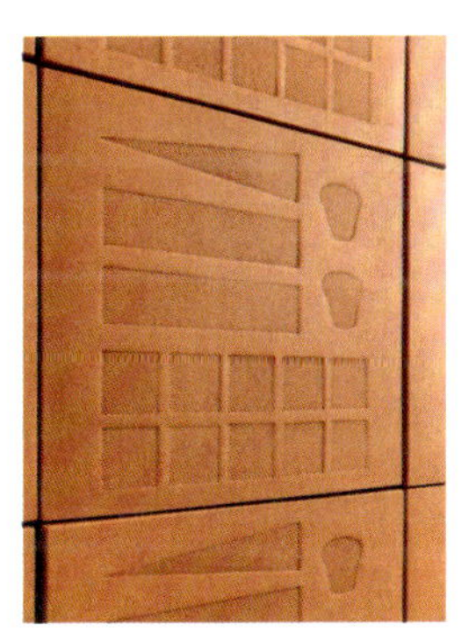
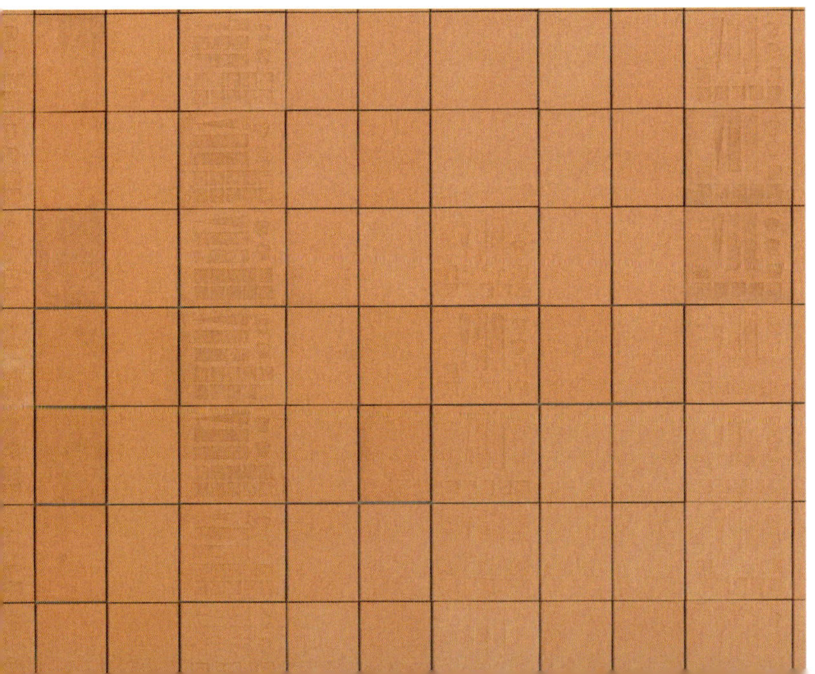
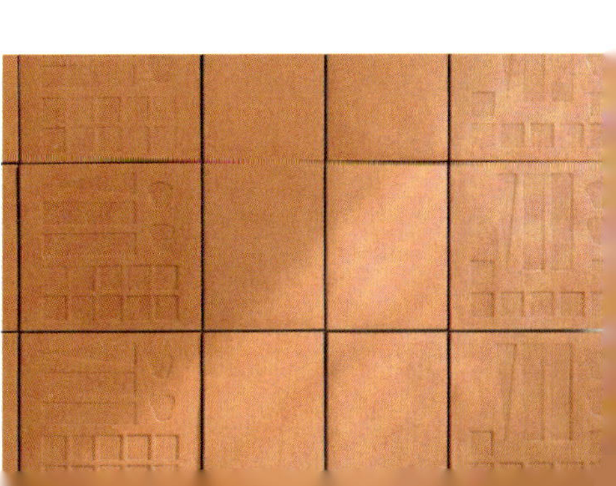

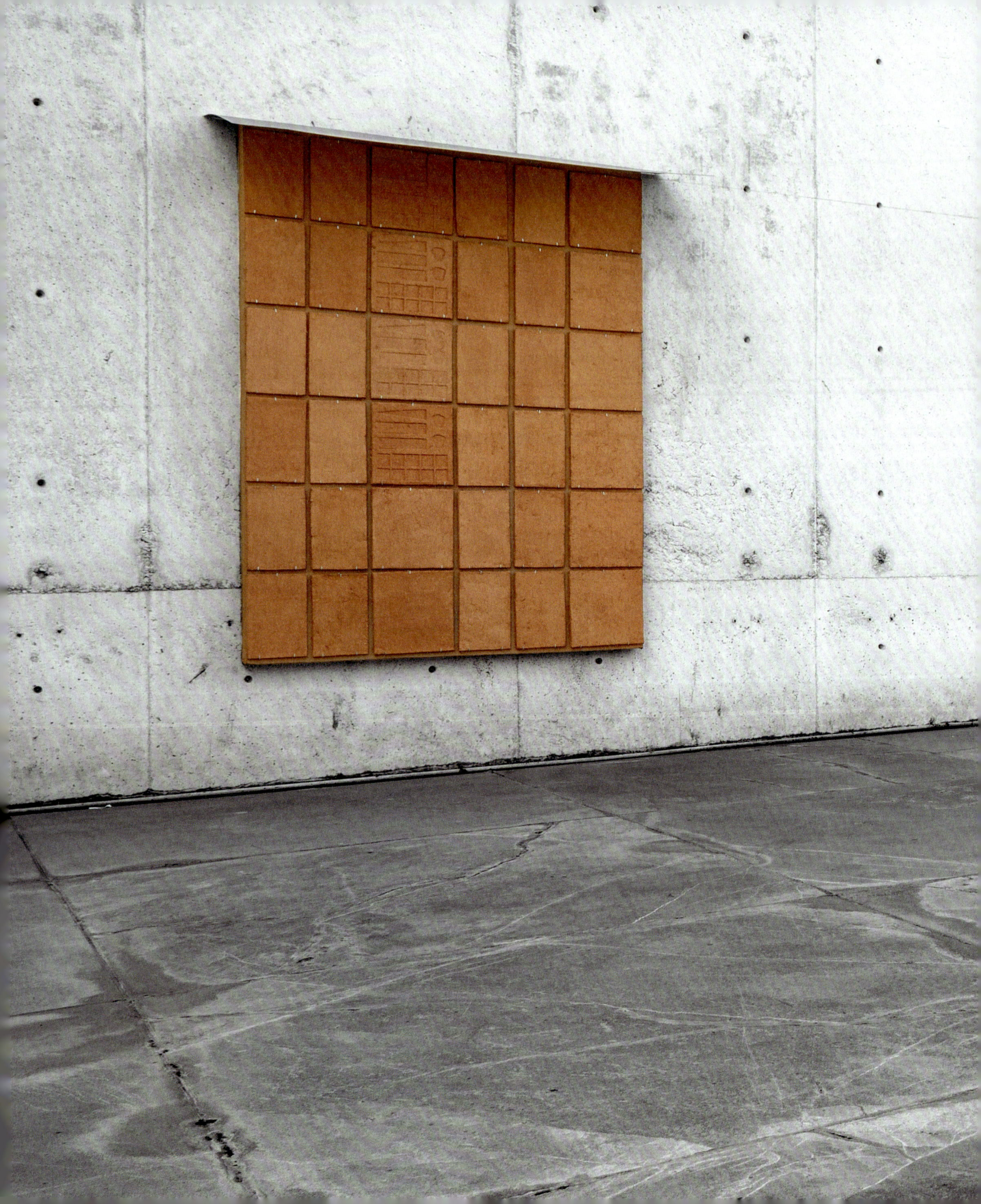

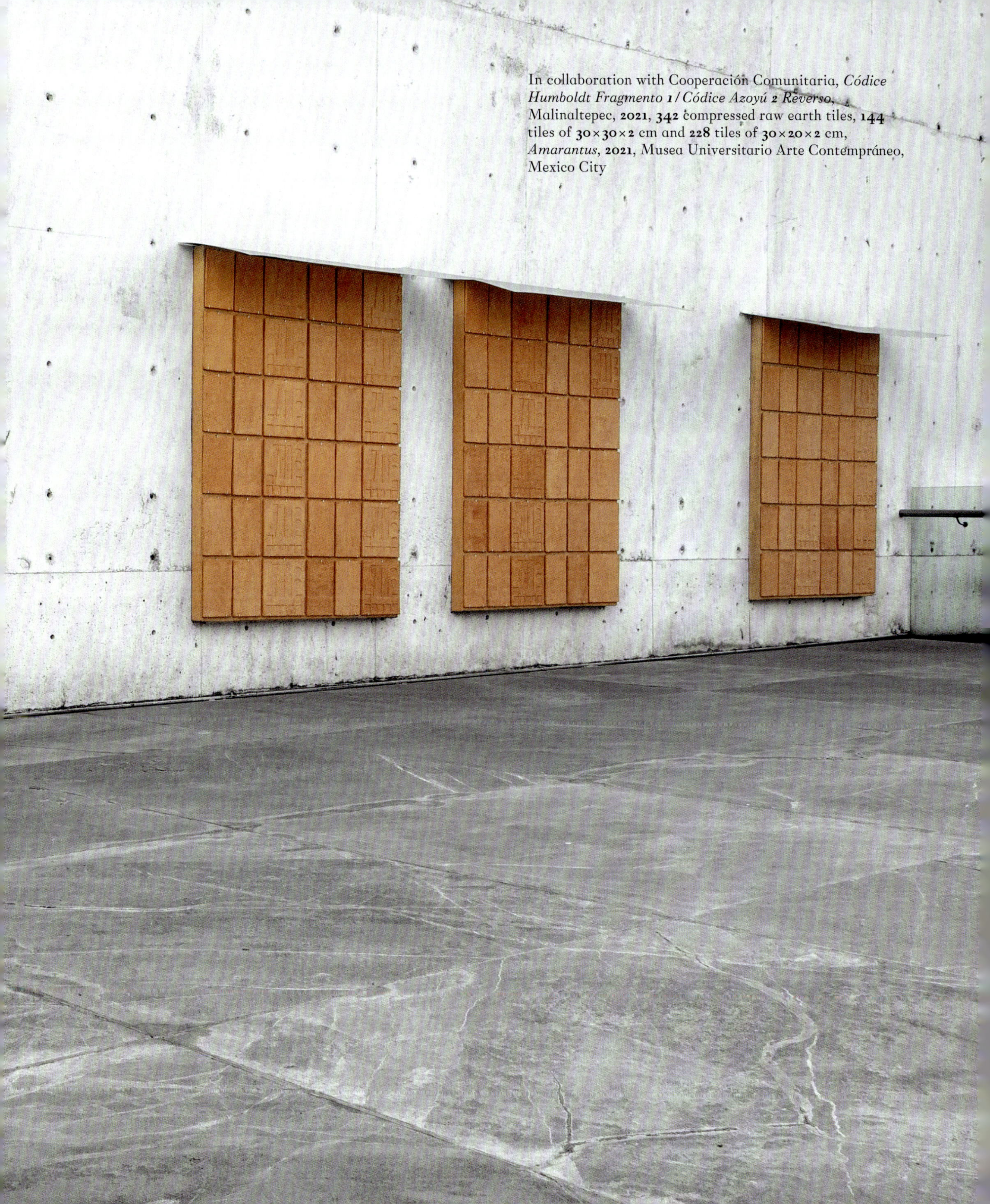

In collaboration with Cooperación Comunitaria, *Códice Humboldt Fragmento 1 / Códice Azoyú 2 Reverso*, Malinaltepec, 2021, 342 compressed raw earth tiles, 144 tiles of 30×30×2 cm and 228 tiles of 30×20×2 cm, *Amarantus*, 2021, Musea Universitario Arte Contempráneo, Mexico City

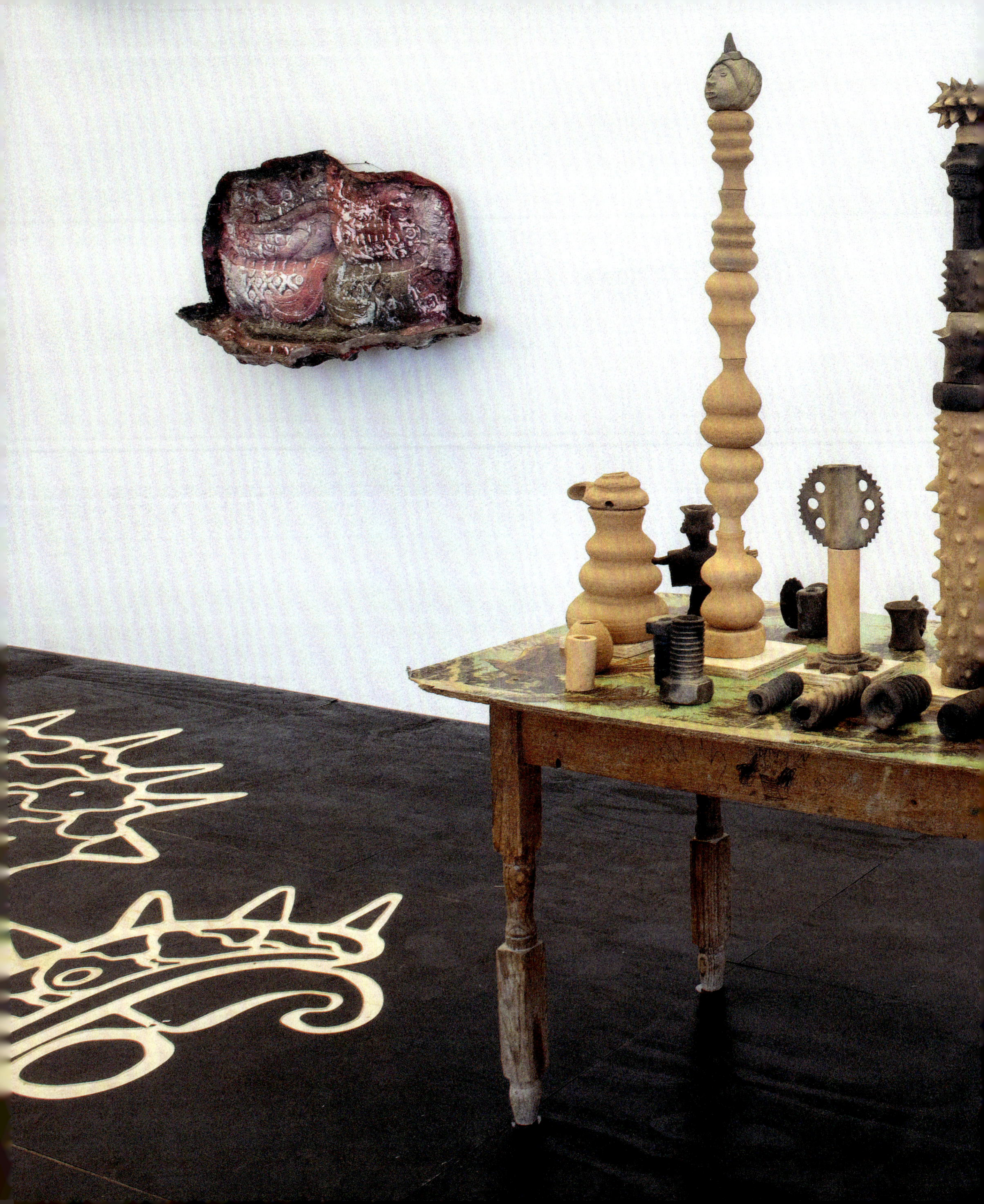

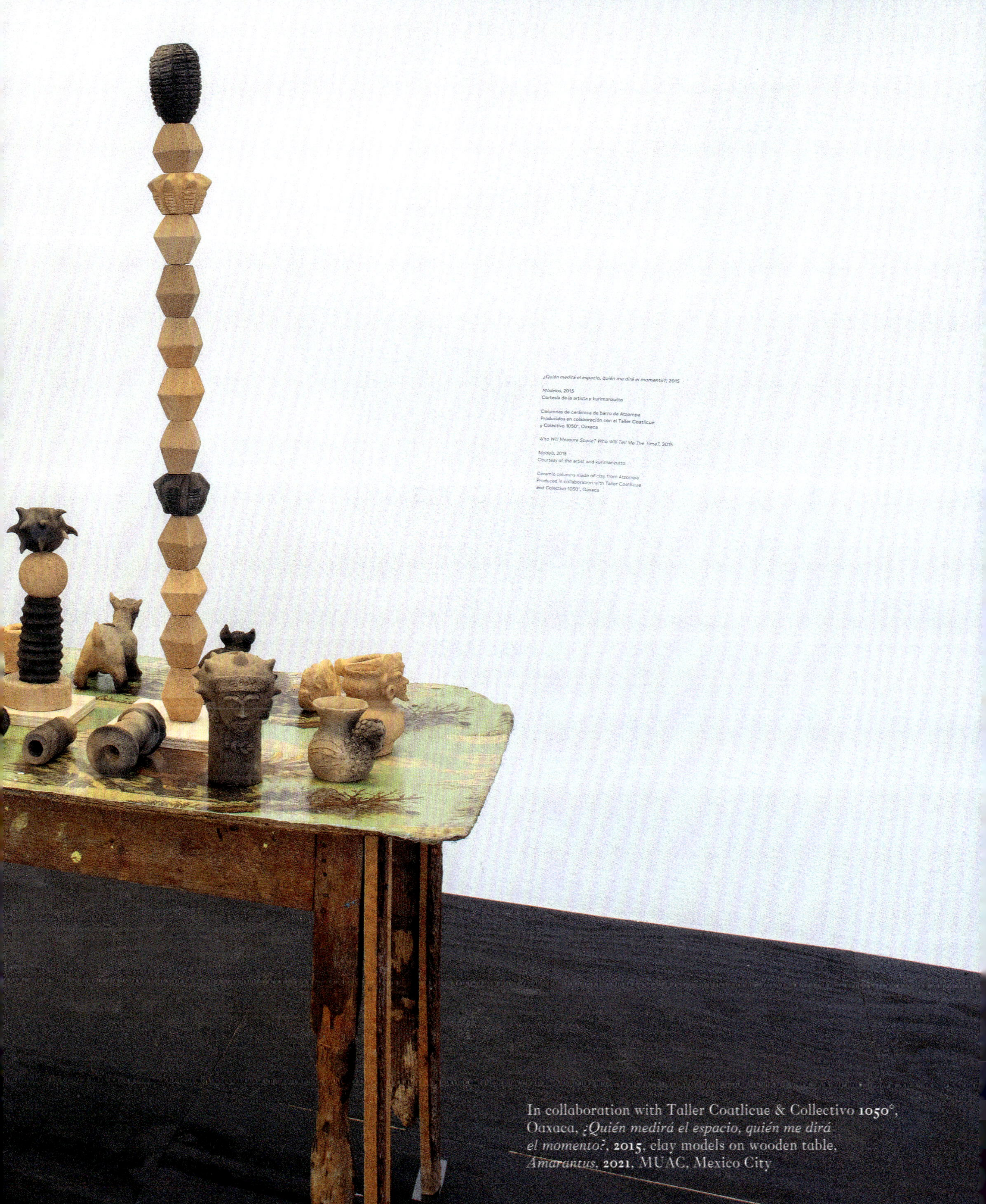

In collaboration with Taller Coatlicue & Collectivo 1050°, Oaxaca, *¿Quién medirá el espacio, quién me dirá el momento?*, 2015, clay models on wooden table, *Amarantus*, 2021, MUAC, Mexico City

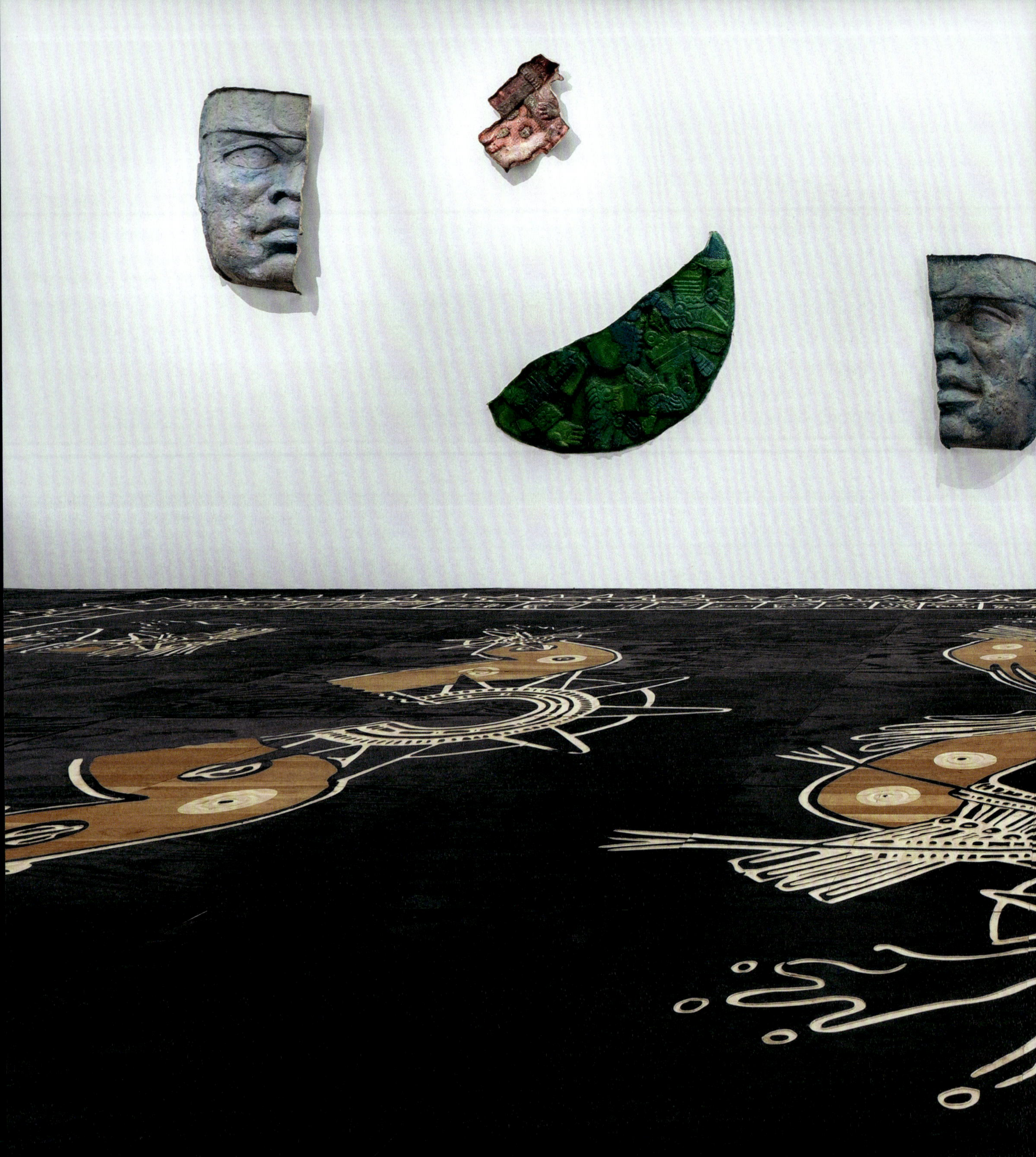

Installation views of the exhibition *Amarantus*, 2021,
MUAC, Mexico City

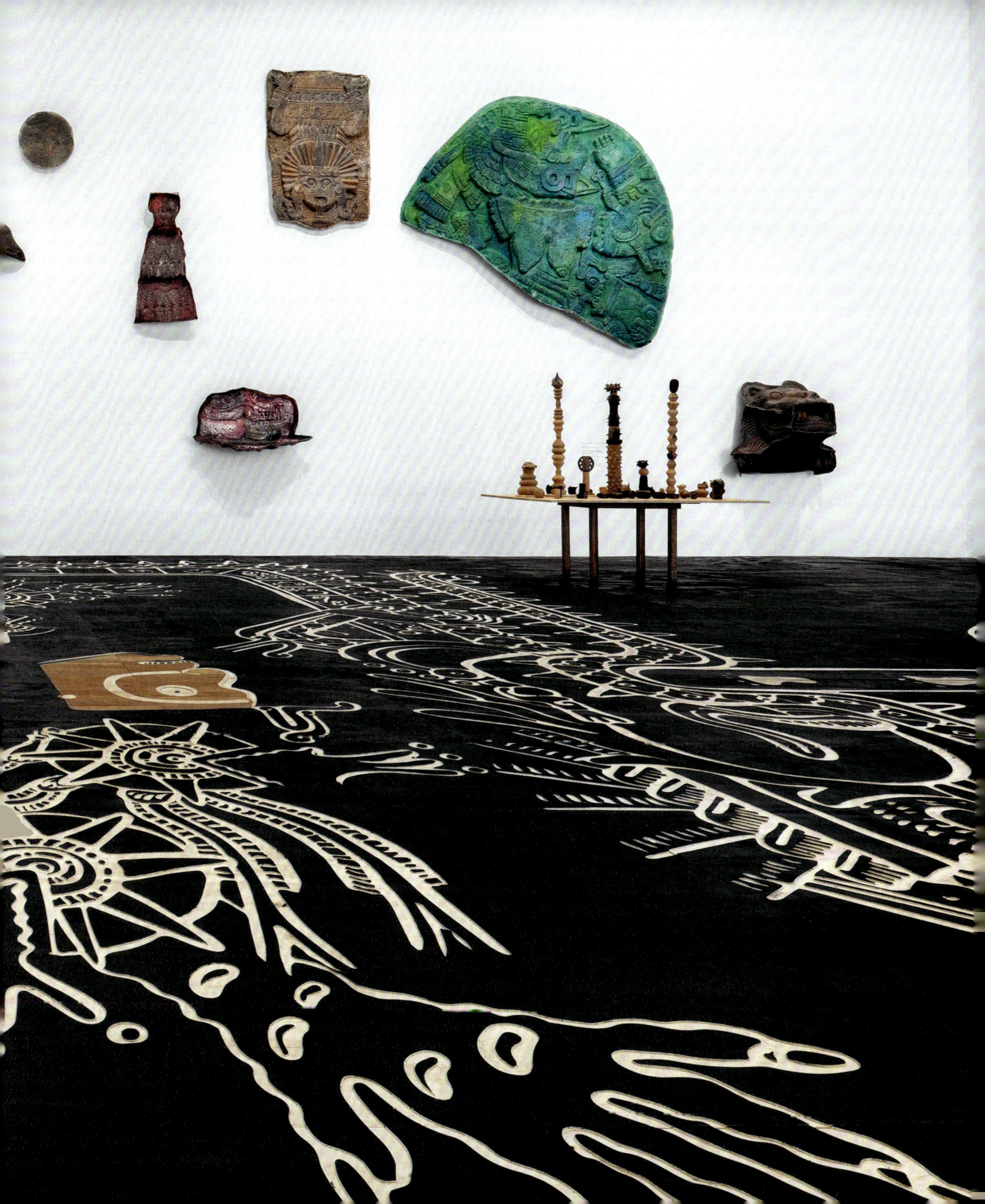

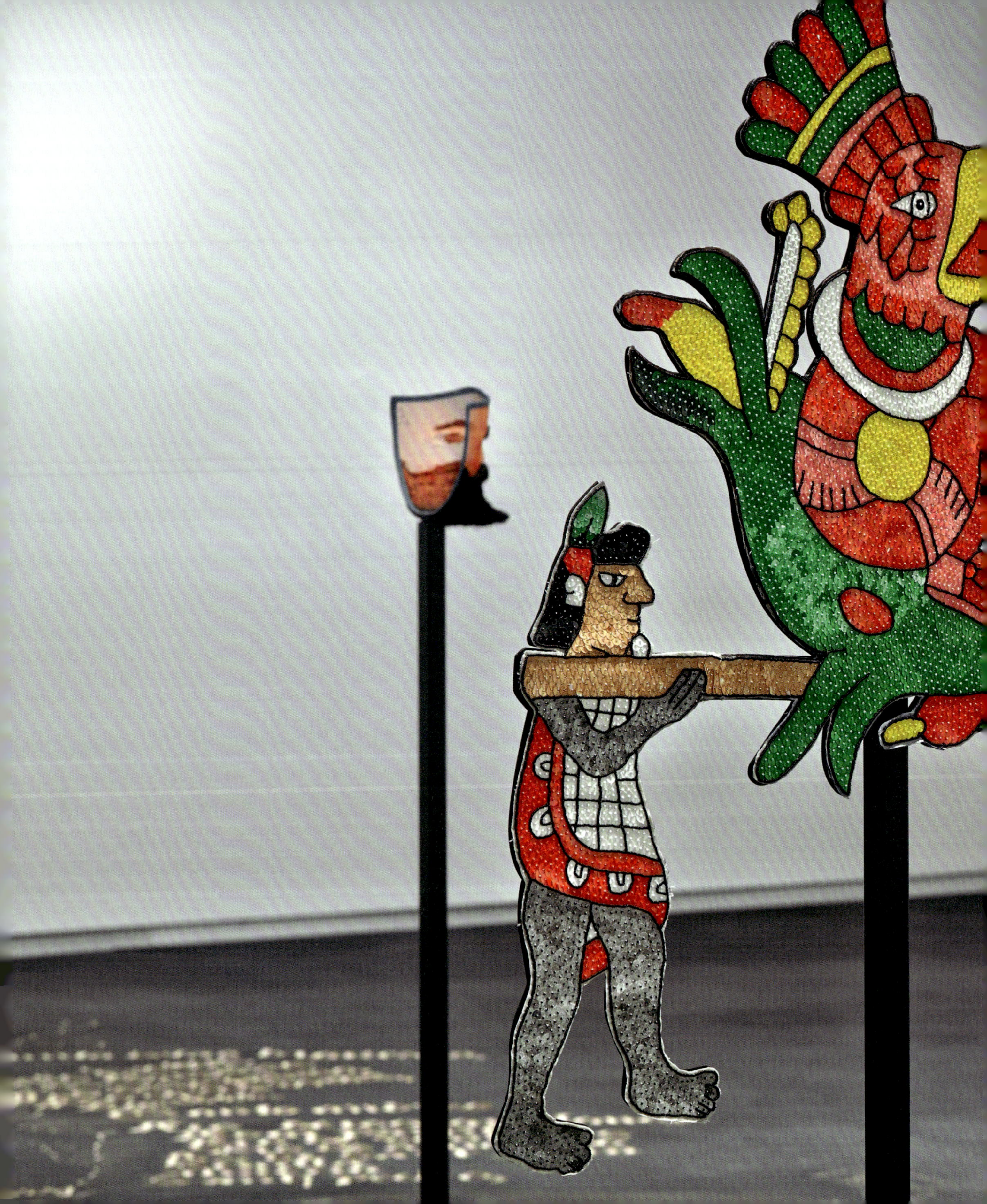

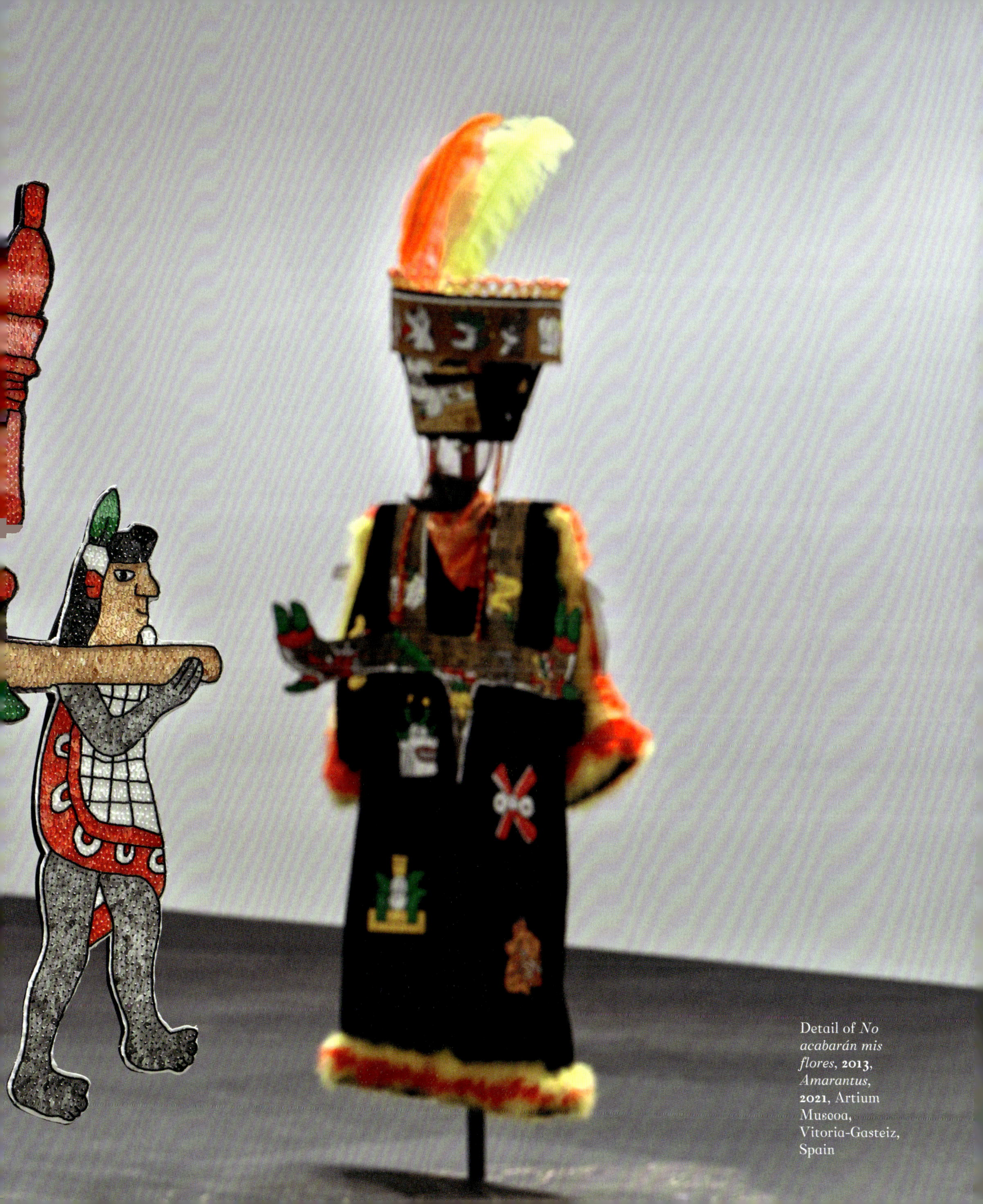

Detail of *No acabarán mis flores*, **2013**, *Amarantus*, **2021**, Artium Museoa, Vitoria-Gasteiz, Spain

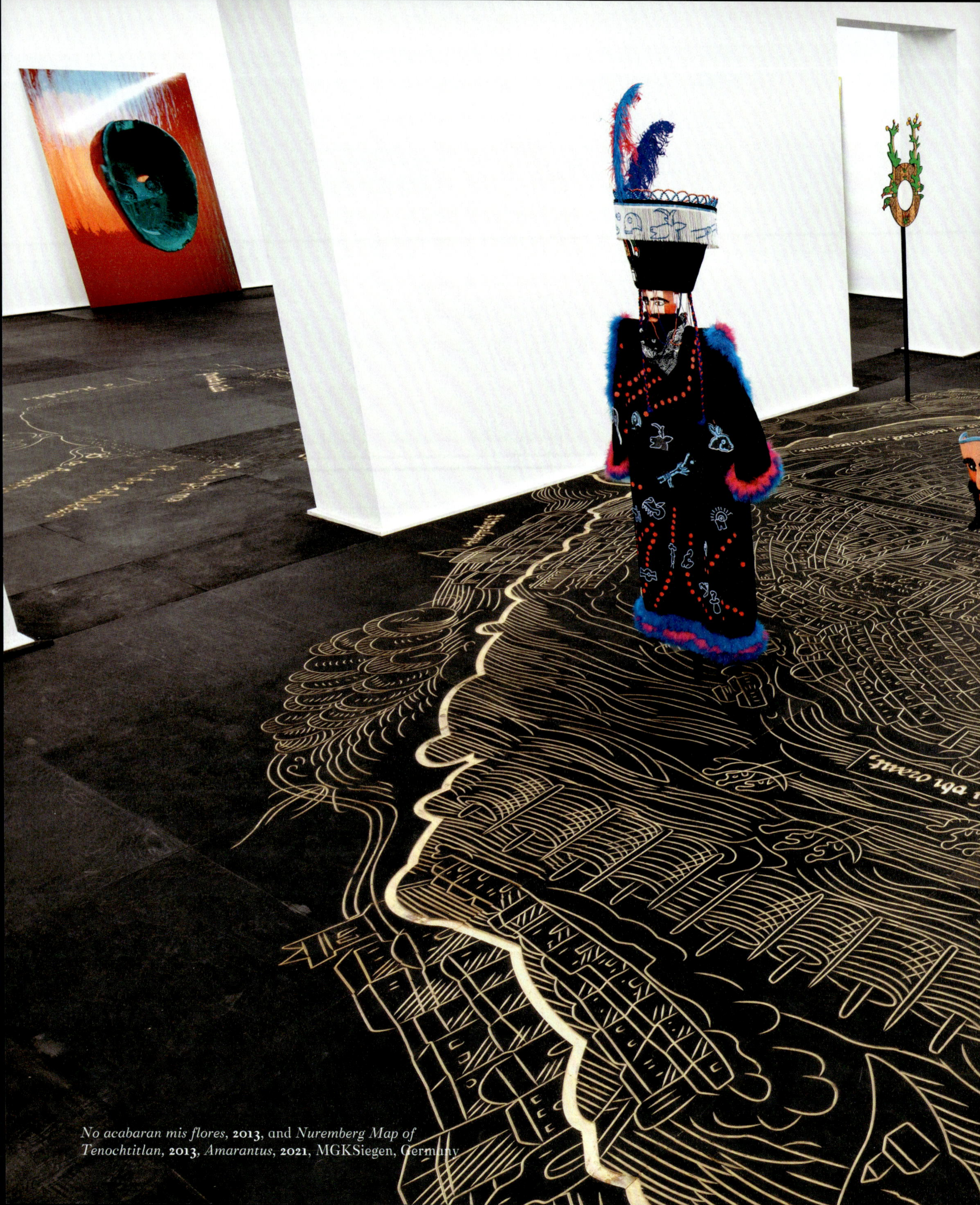

No acabaran mis flores, **2013**, and *Nuremberg Map of Tenochtitlan*, **2013**, *Amarantus*, **2021**, MGKSiegen, Germany

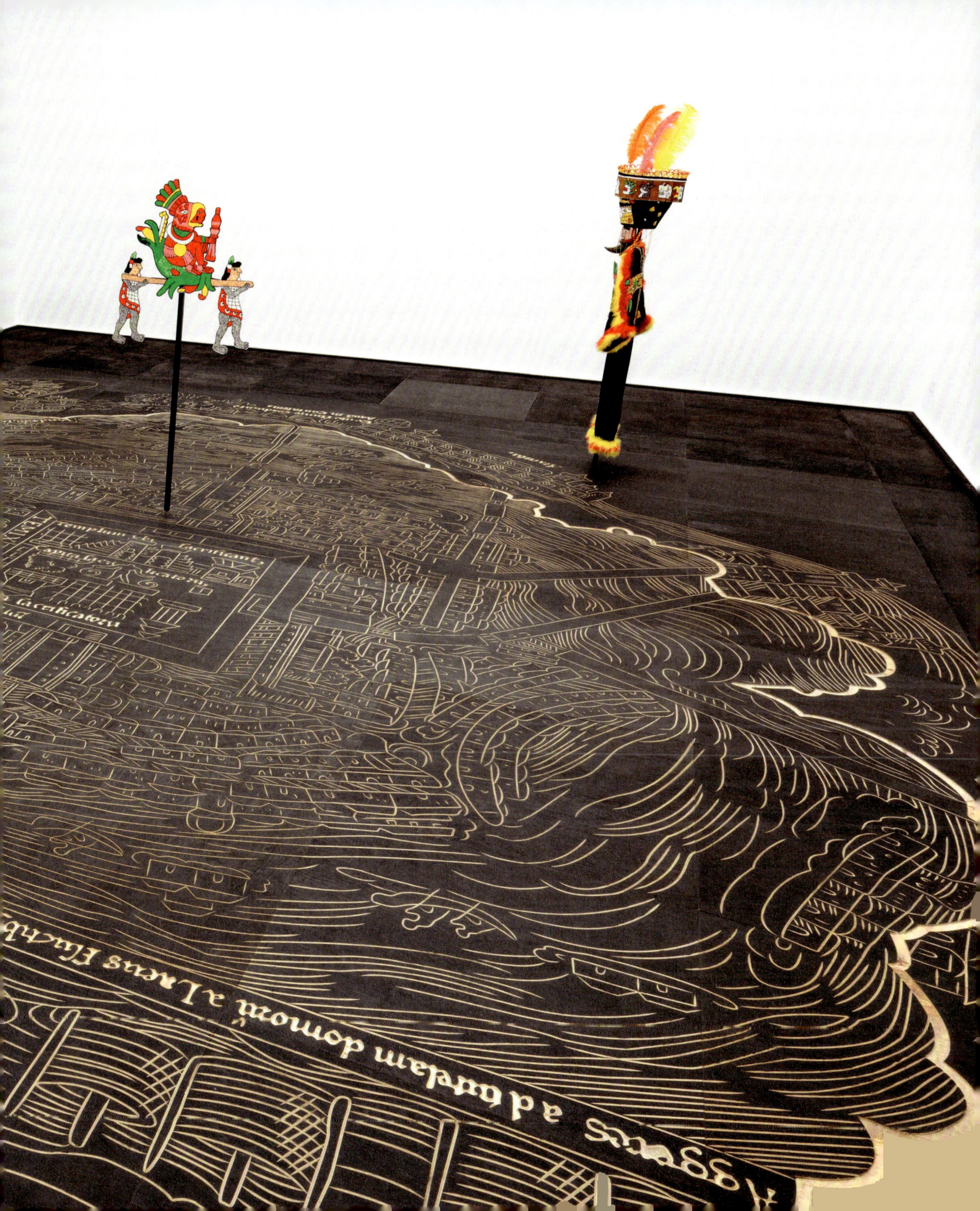

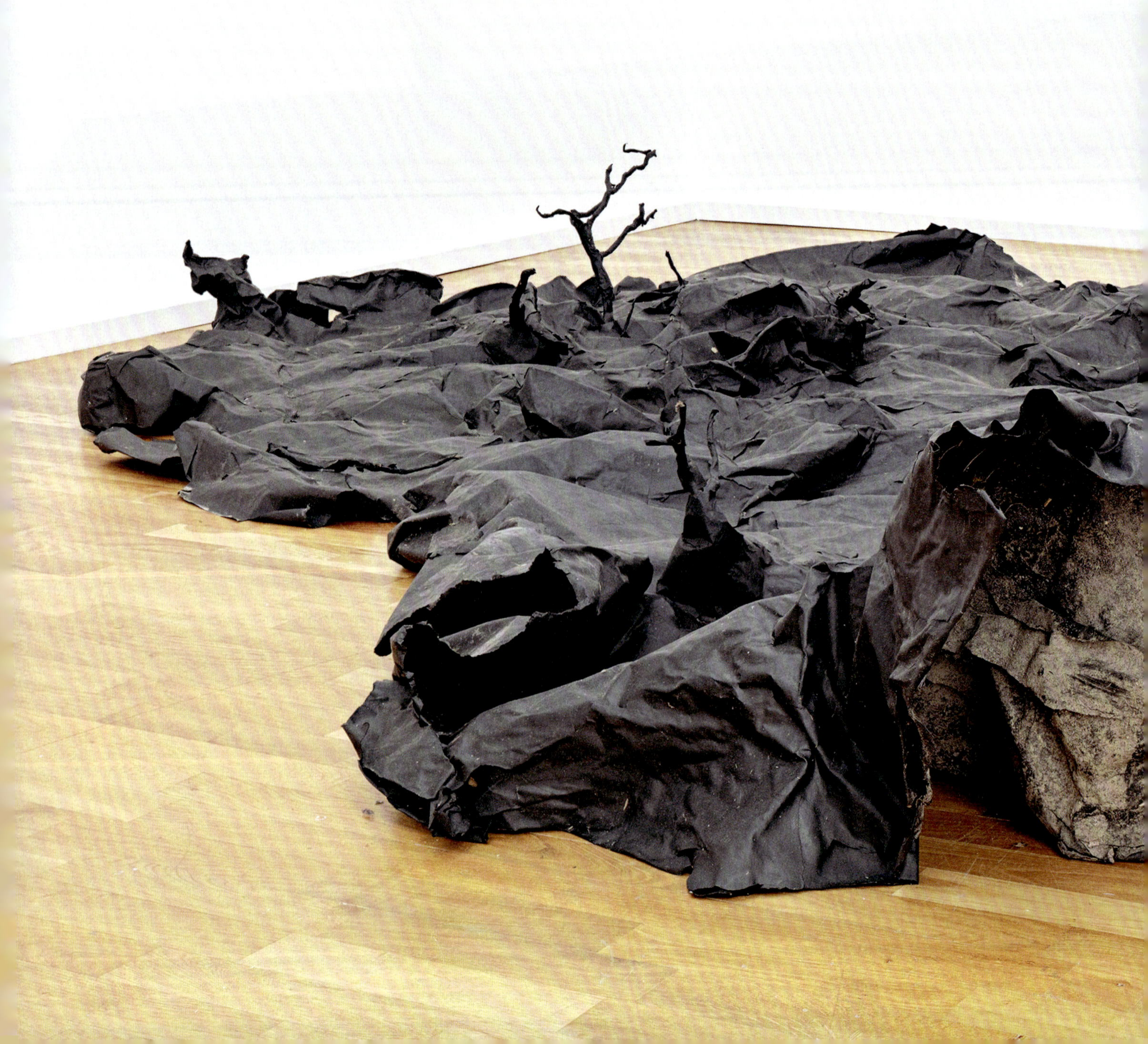

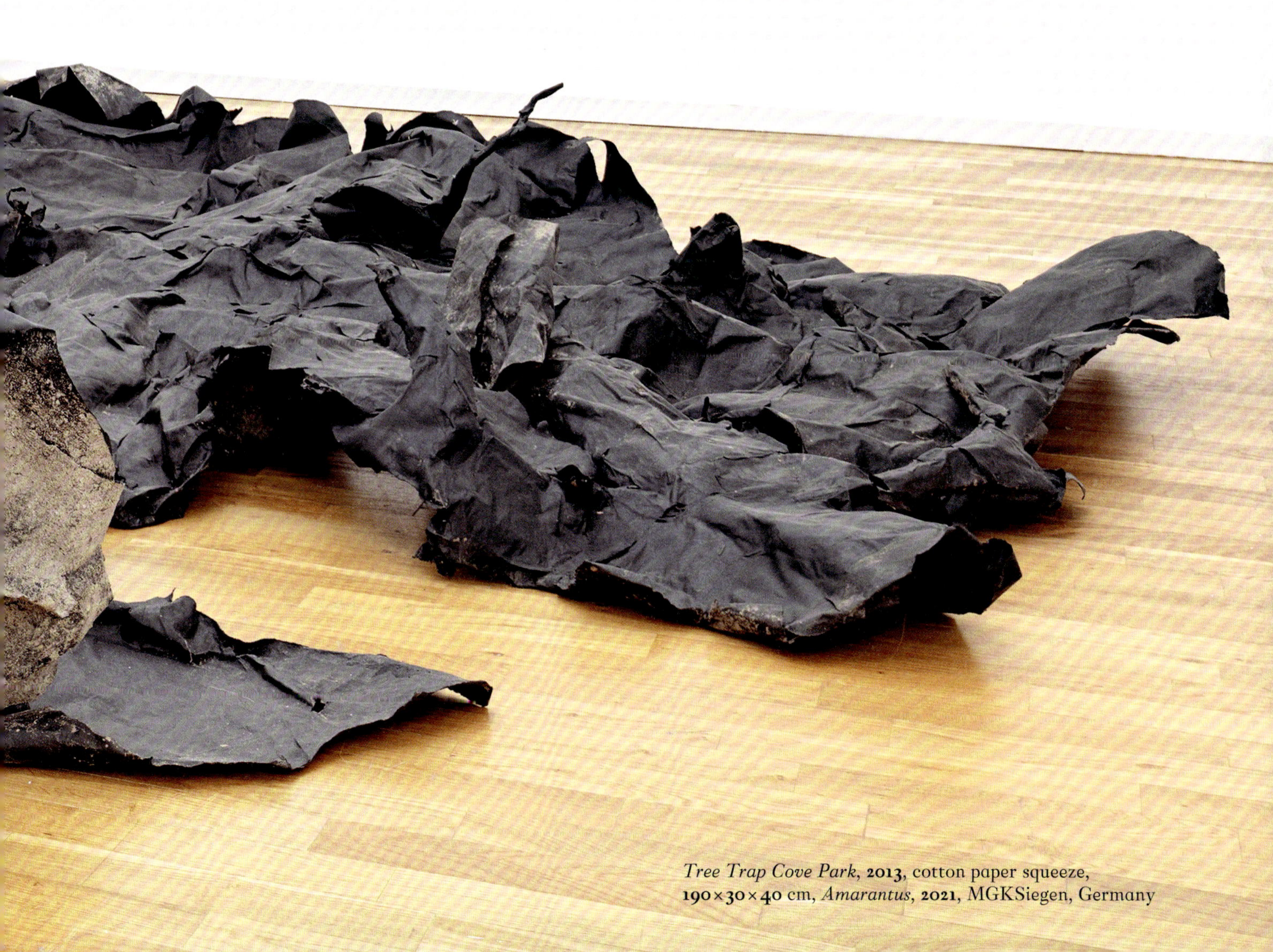

Tree Trap Cove Park, 2013, cotton paper squeeze, 190×30×40 cm, *Amarantus*, 2021, MGKSiegen, Germany

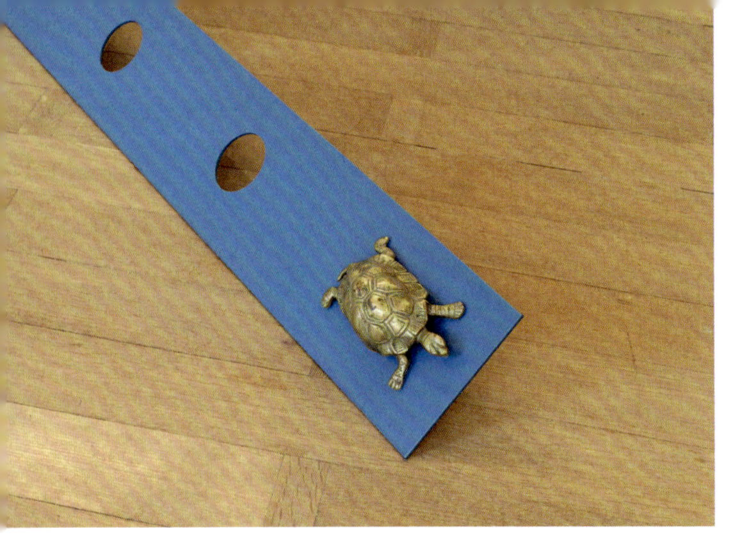

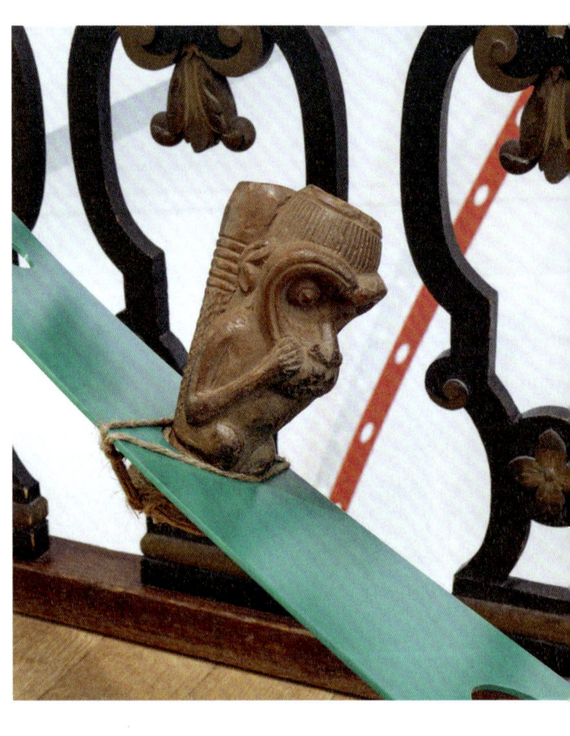

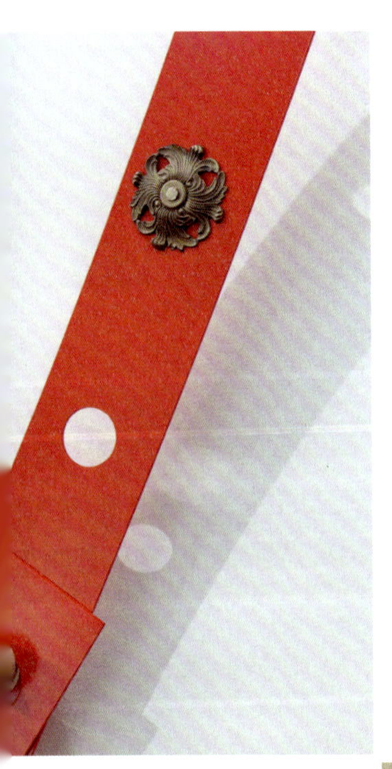

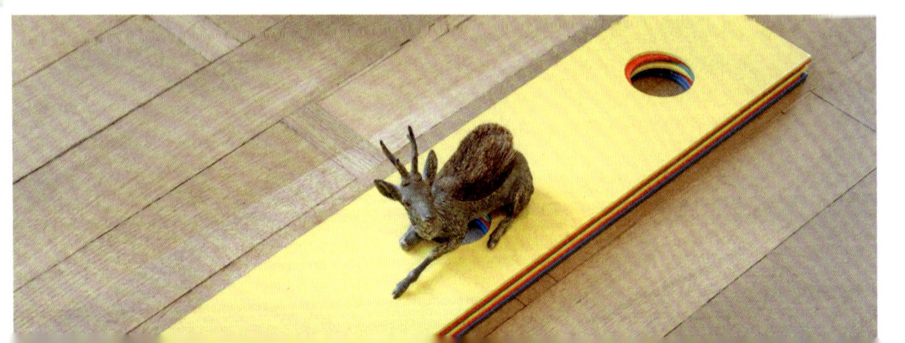

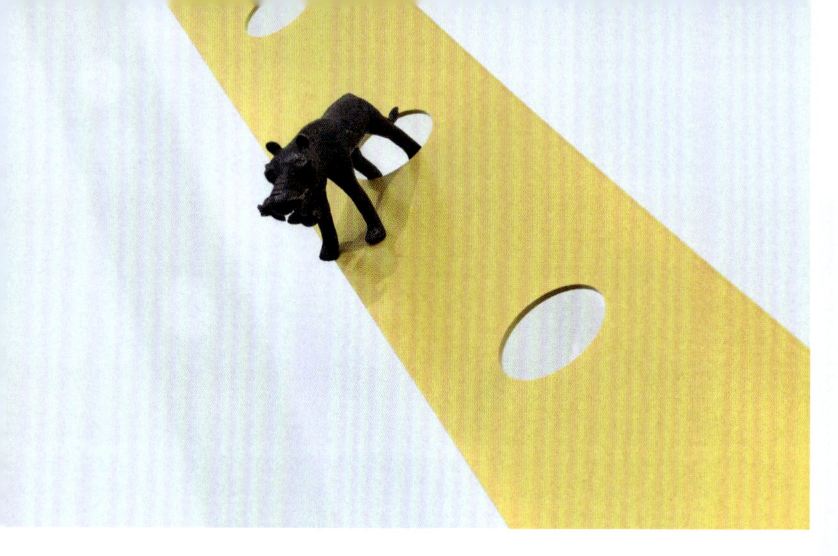

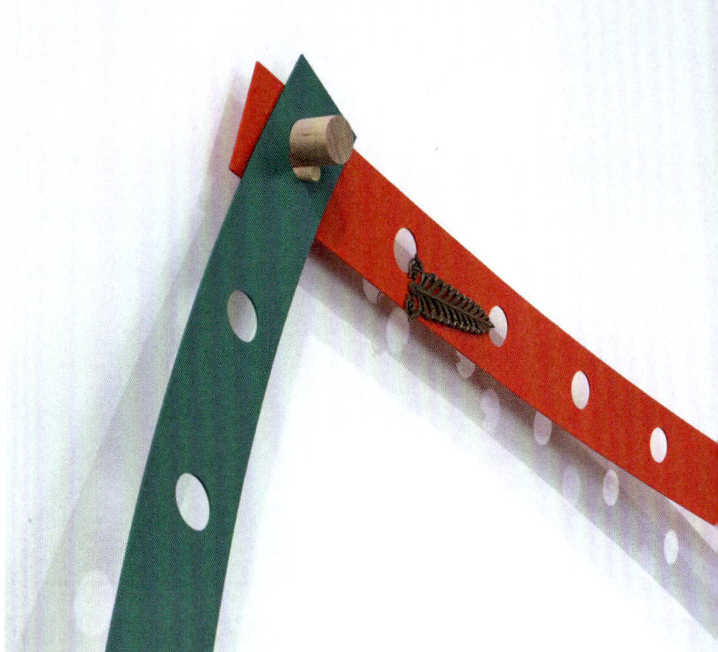

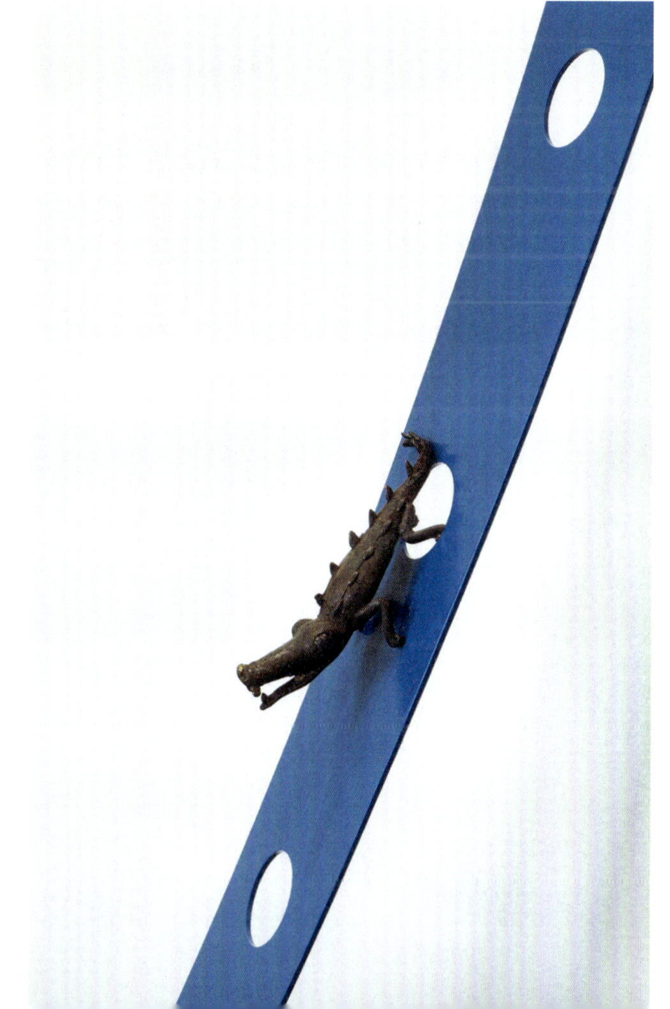

Tonalpohualli, **2017**, **20** perforated aluminium strips and wood joints with wood and bronze figures, **0.3 × 12 × 270** cm, *Them inside the skin*, **2017**, Mendes Wood DM, Brussels

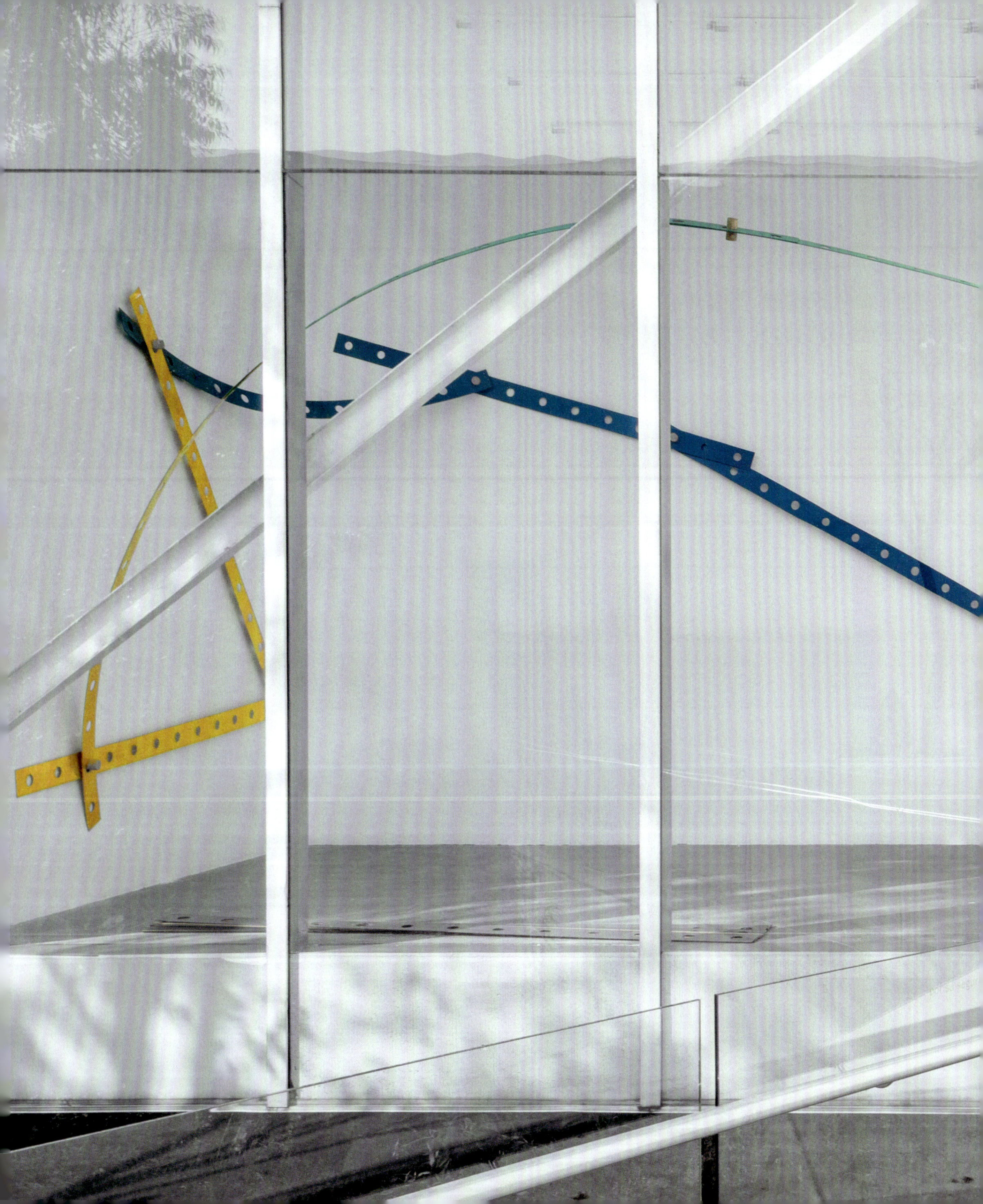

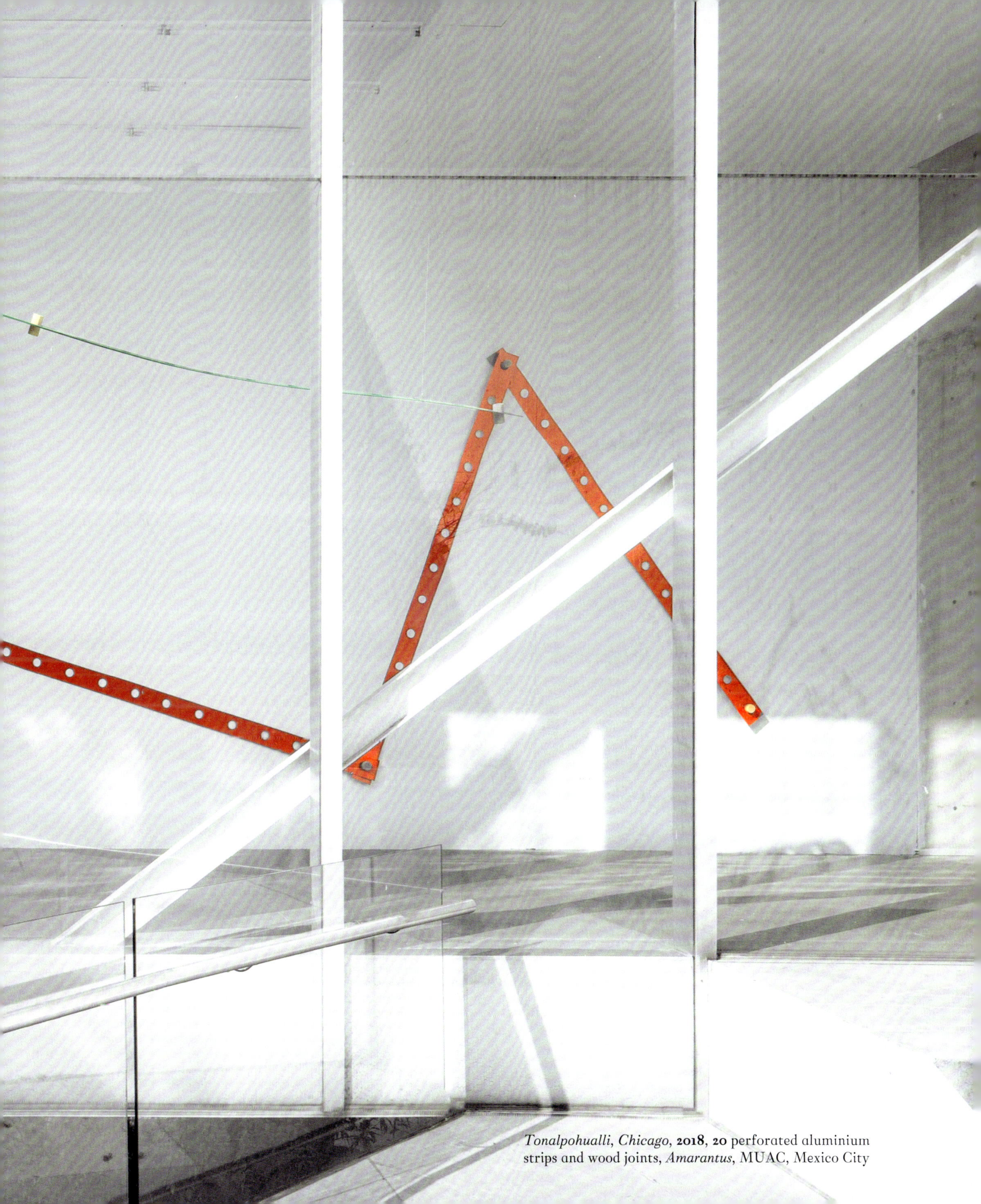

Tonalpohualli, Chicago, **2018**, **20** perforated aluminium strips and wood joints, *Amarantus*, MUAC, Mexico City

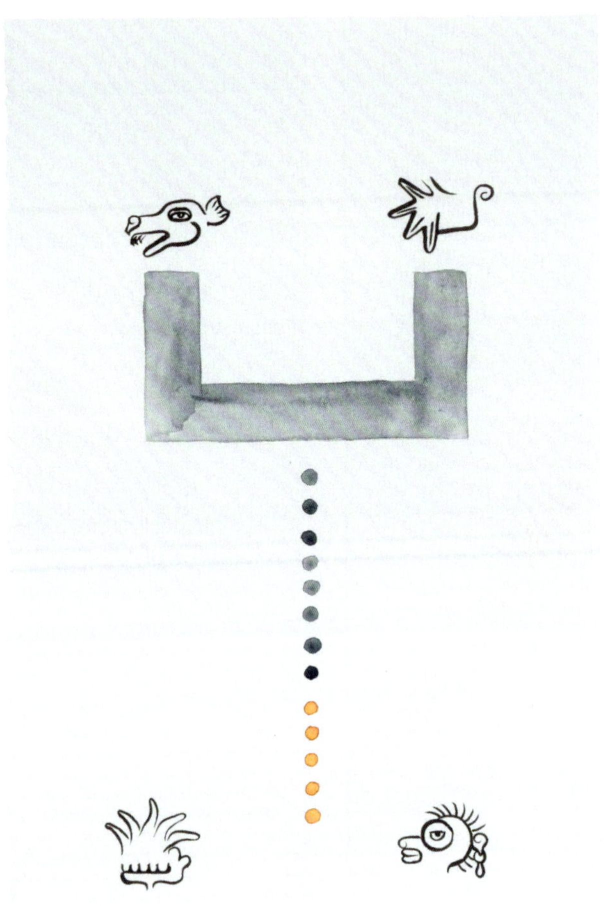

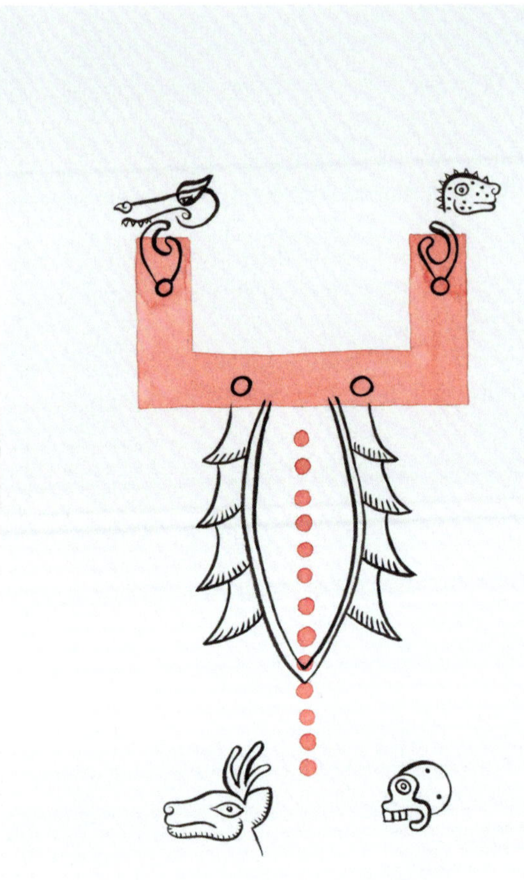

Scorpion Time and *Scorpion Time II,* **2018**, watercolor and ink on paper, **35** × **22** cm

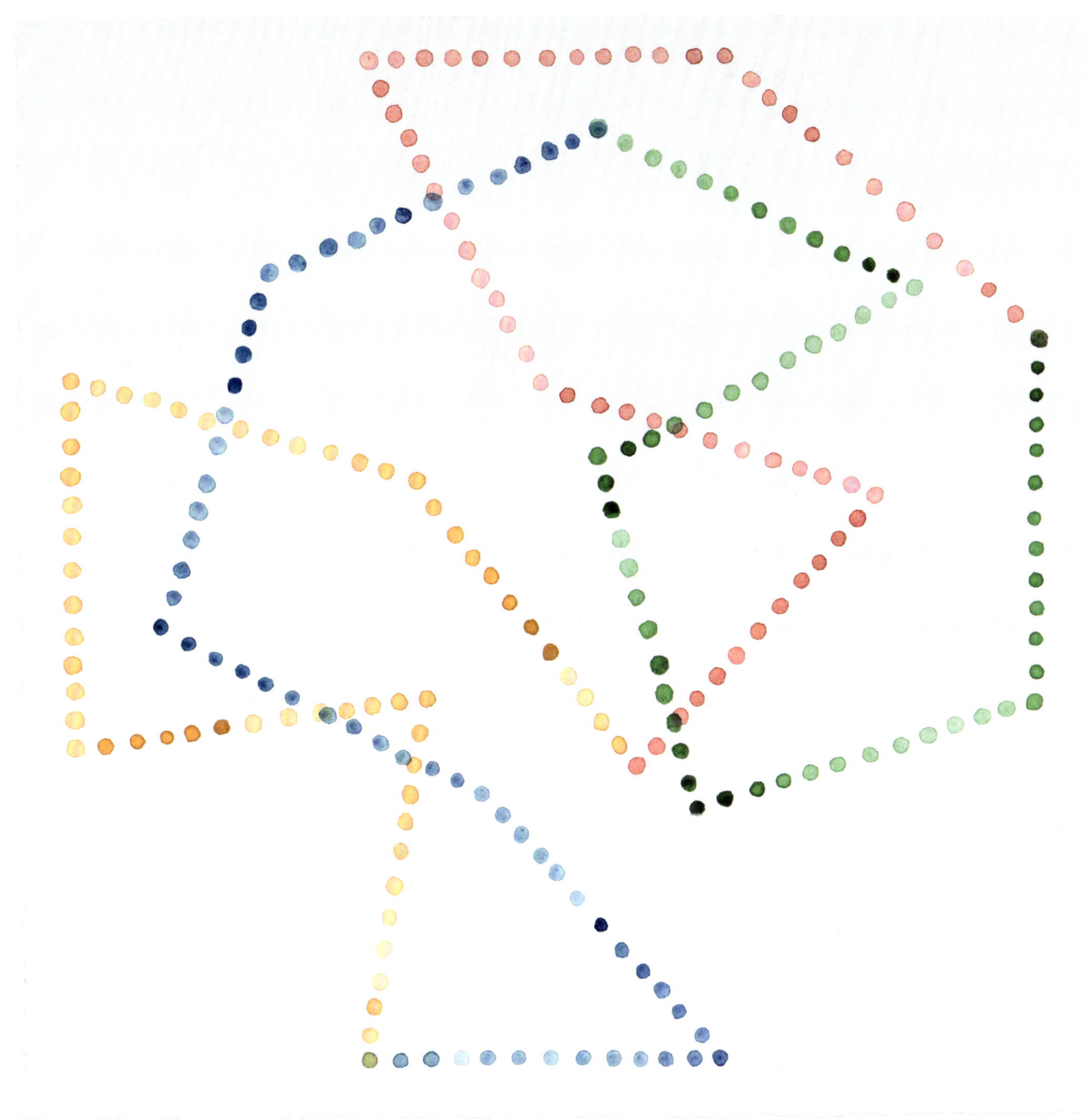

Tonalamatl V, **2018**, watercolor on paper, 35 × 35 cm

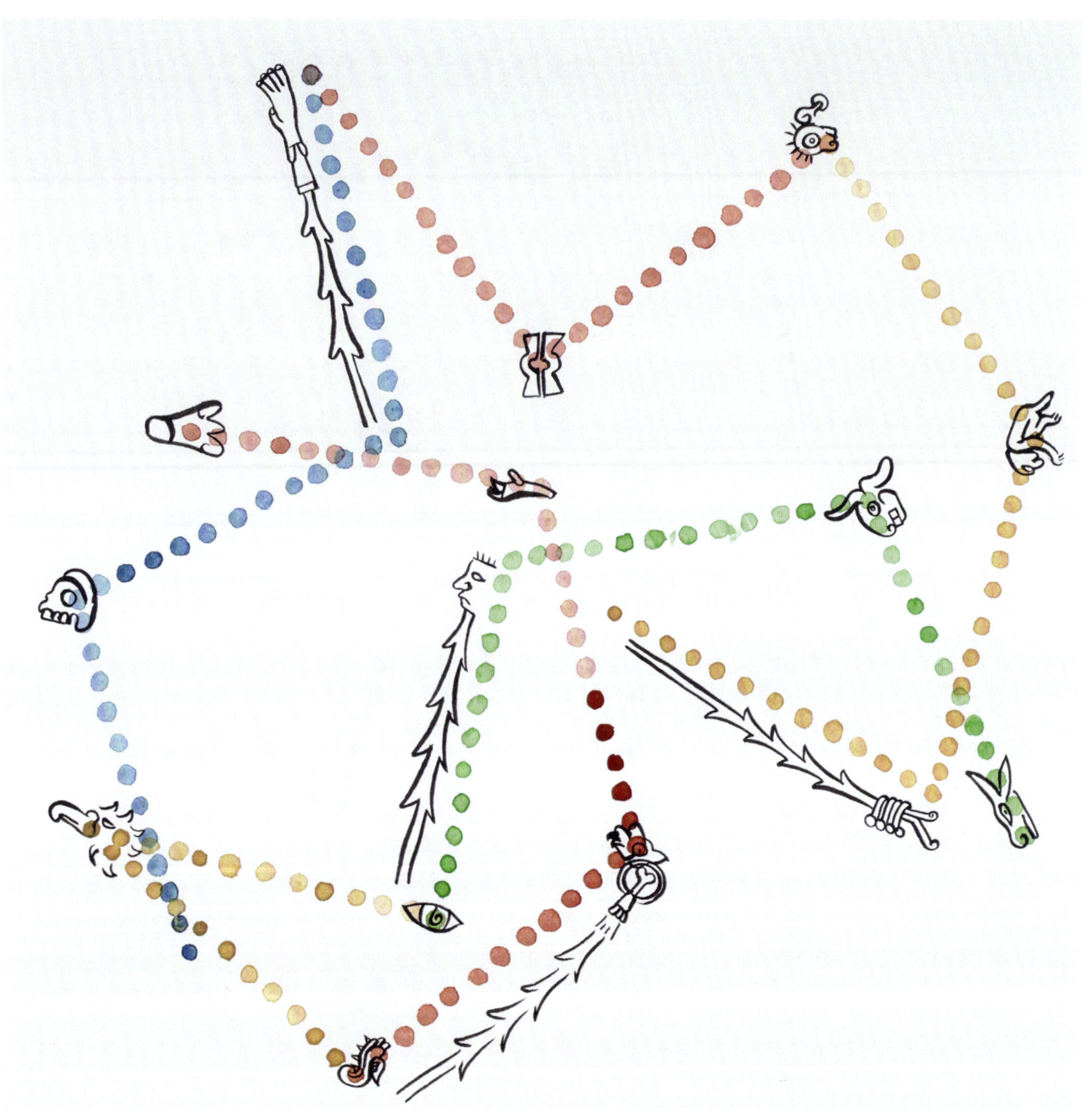

Tonalamatl II, **2018**, watercolor and ink on paper, **35 × 35** cm

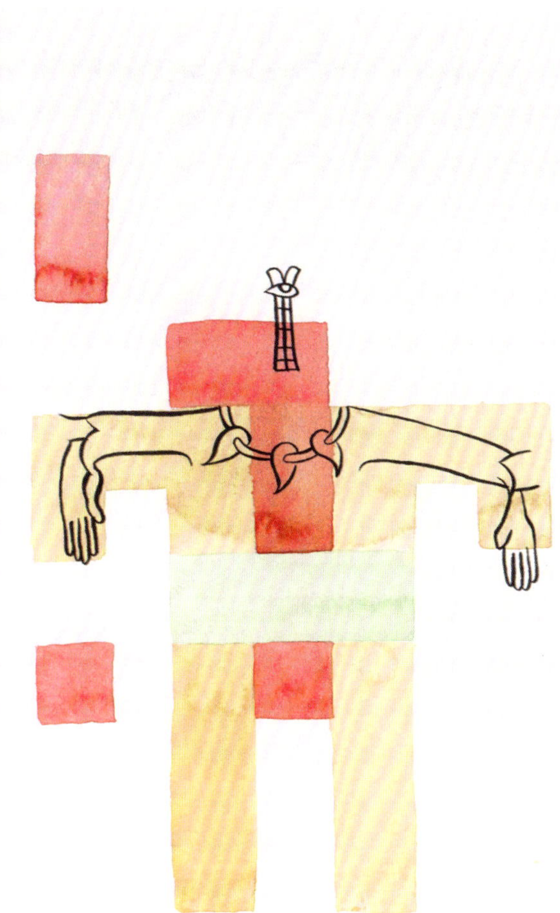

What's the matter with you, **2017**, watercolor and ink on paper, **35 × 22** cm

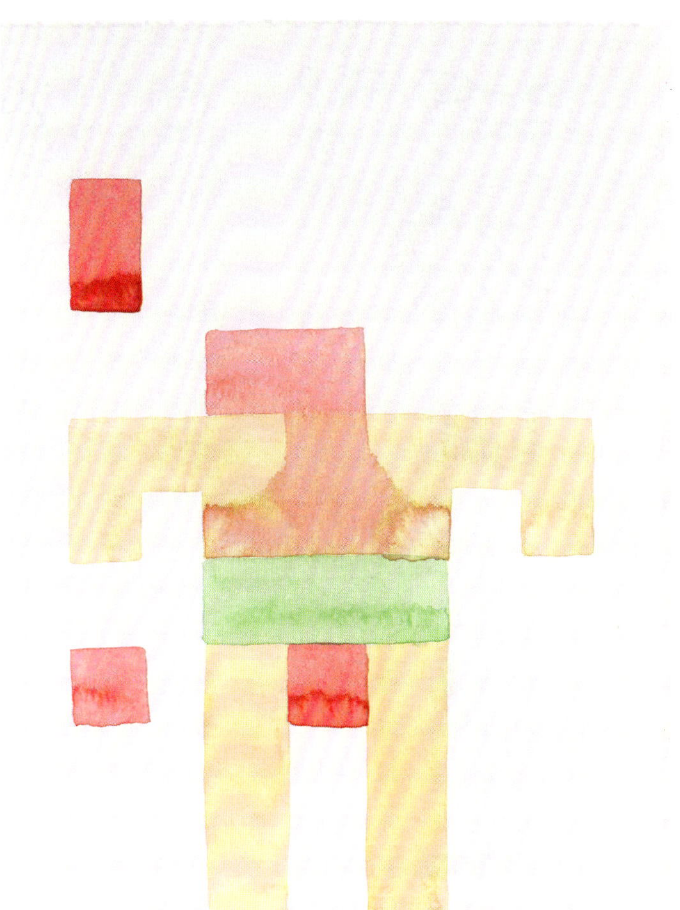

Why don't you say something?, **2017**, watercolor and ink on paper, **35 × 70** cm

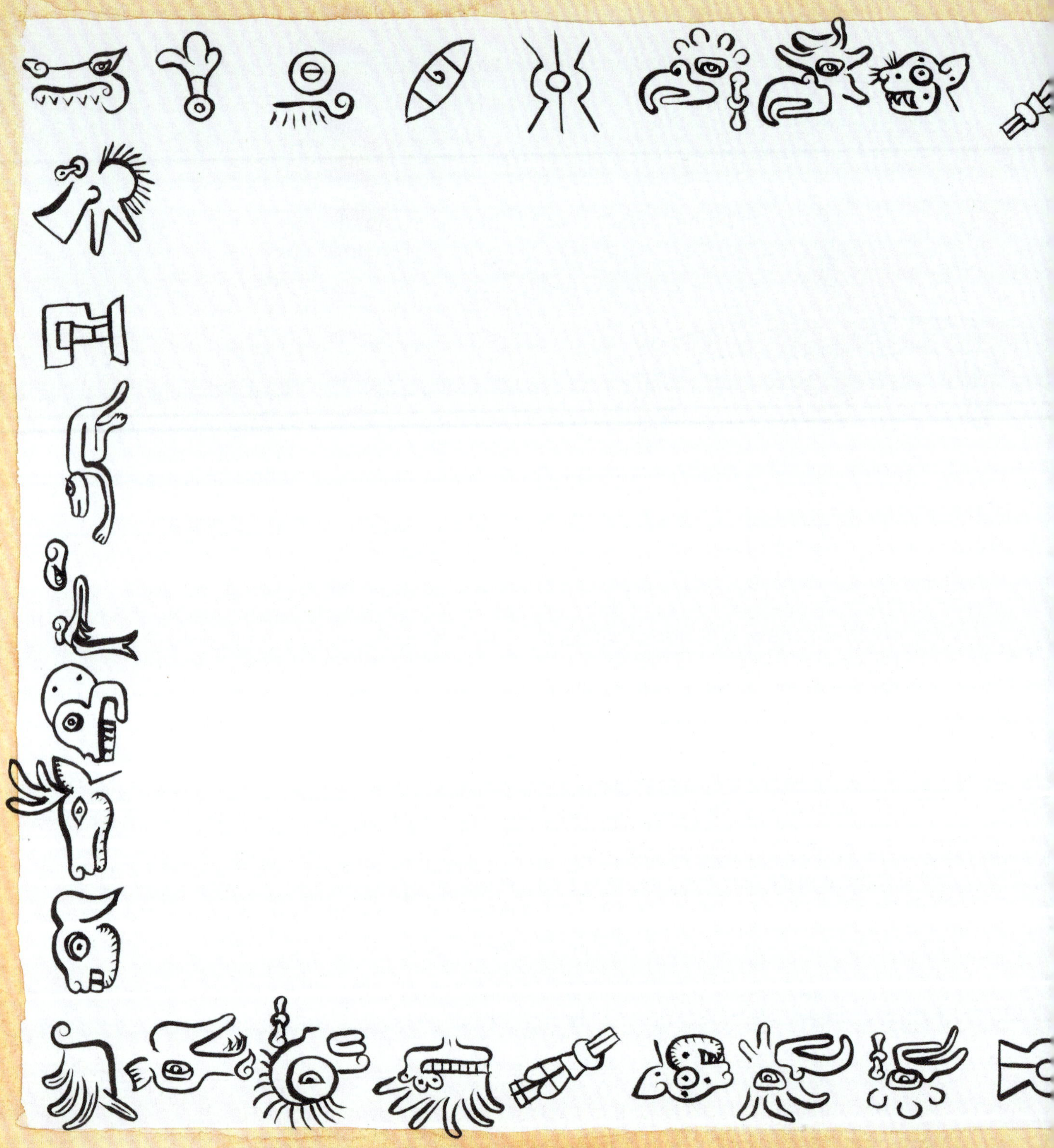

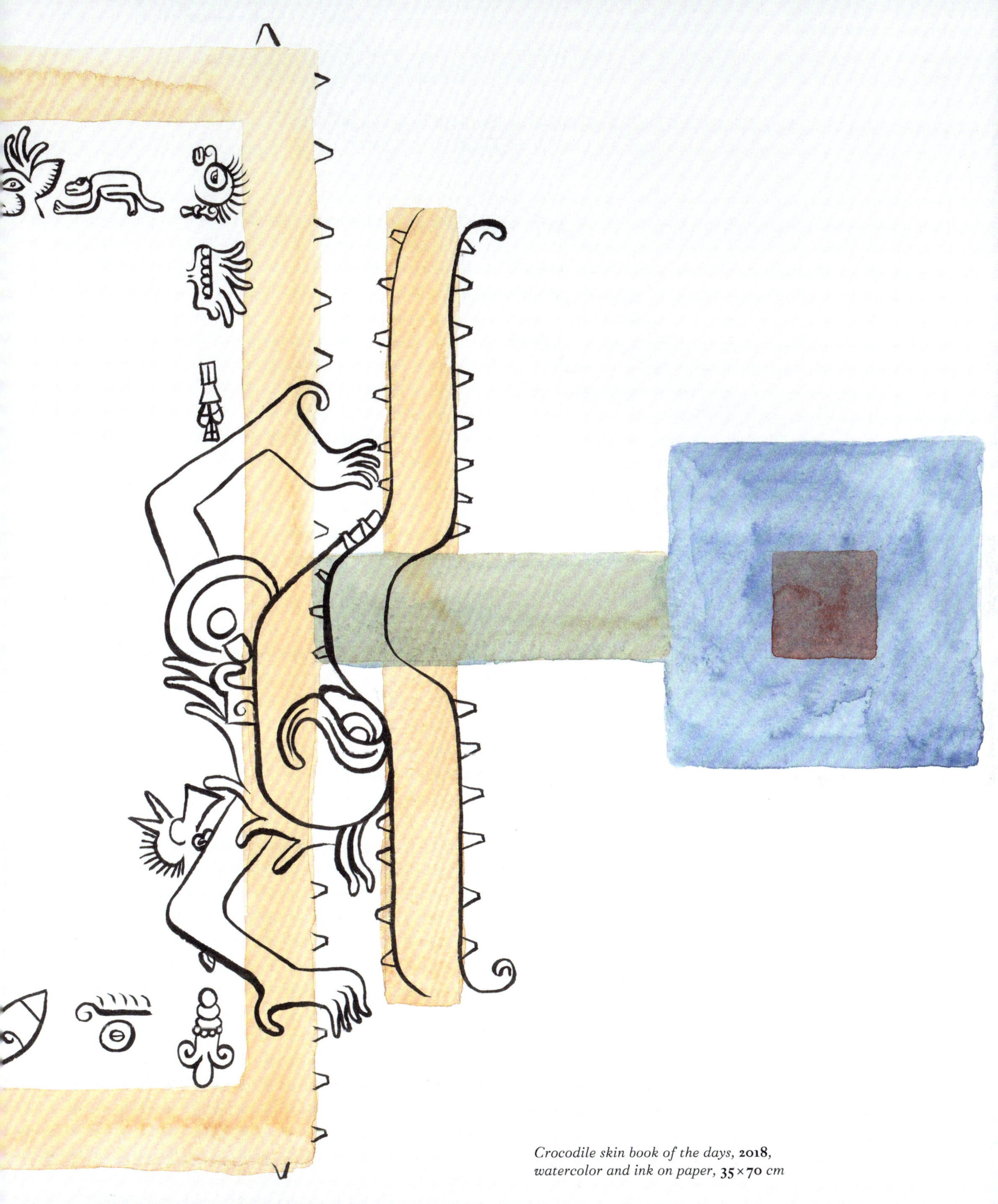

Crocodile skin book of the days, 2018, *watercolor and ink on paper*, 35 × 70 *cm*

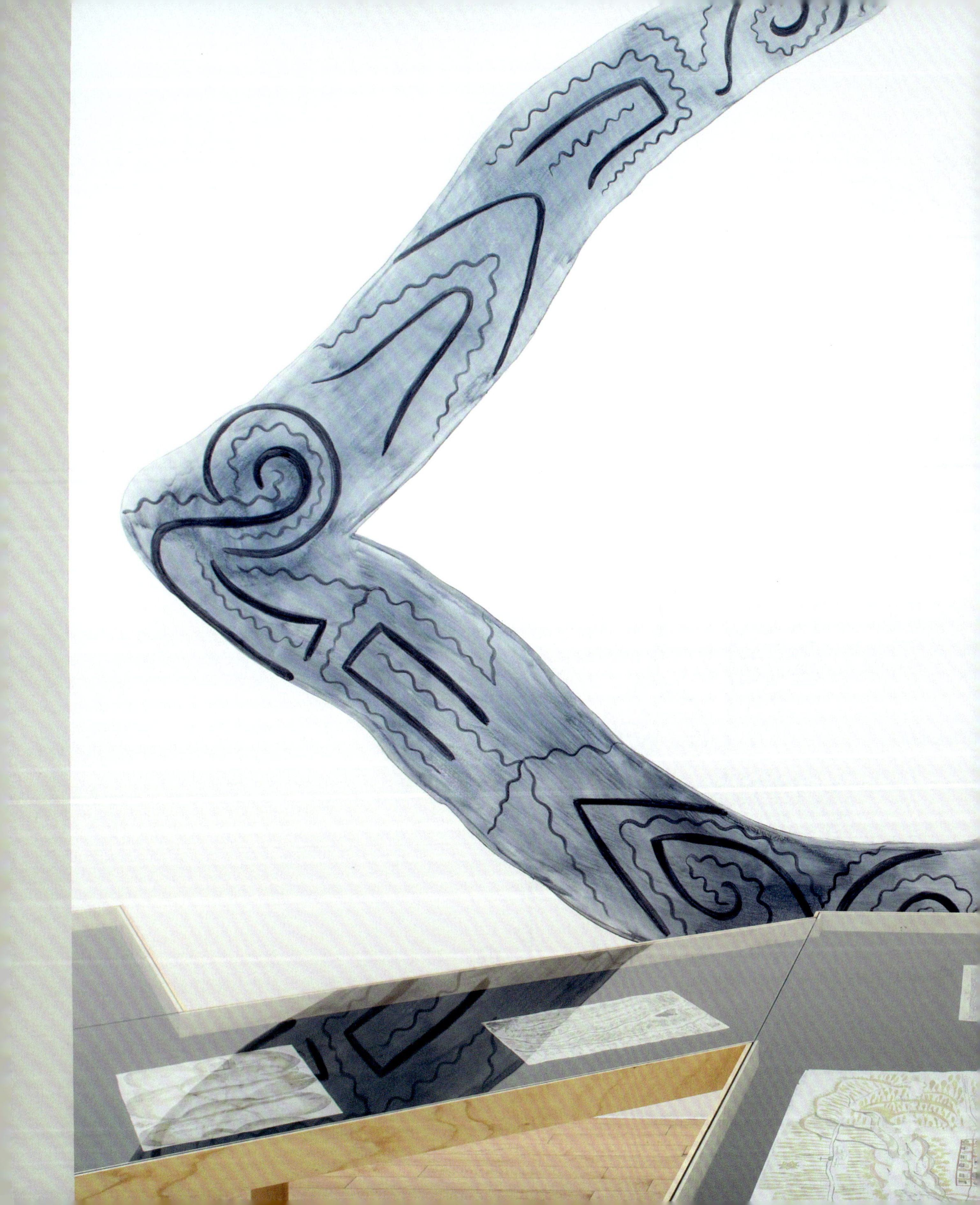

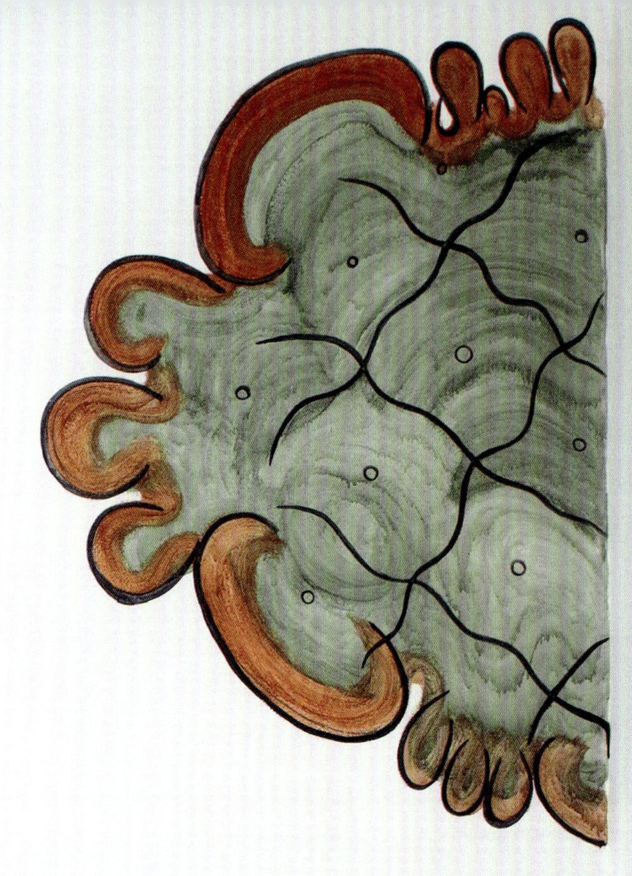

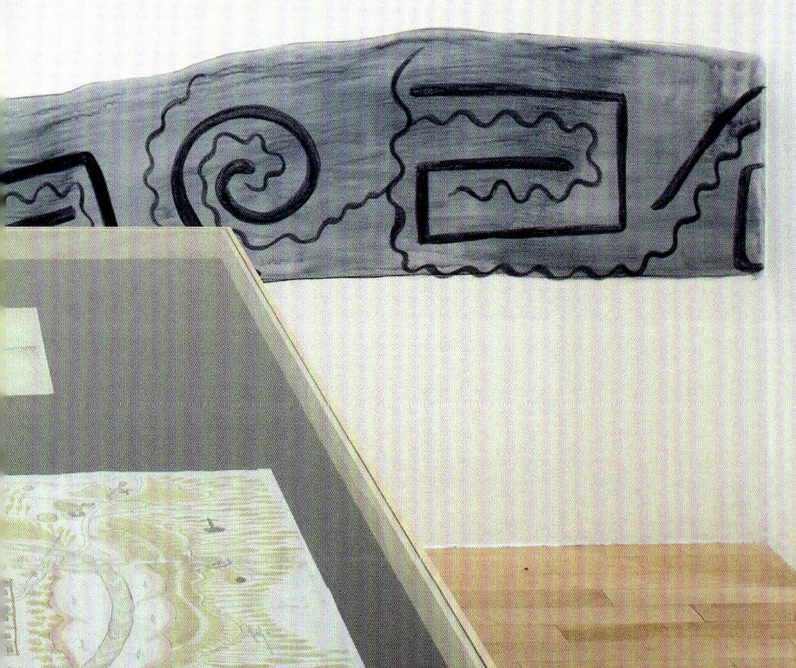

Altepetl, **2018**, egg tempera on wall with natural dyes,
In Tlilli in Tlapalli, **2018**, Museo Amparo, Puebla Mexico

THE IDENTITY OF IMAGES PAST AND PRESENT

DIANA MAGALONI

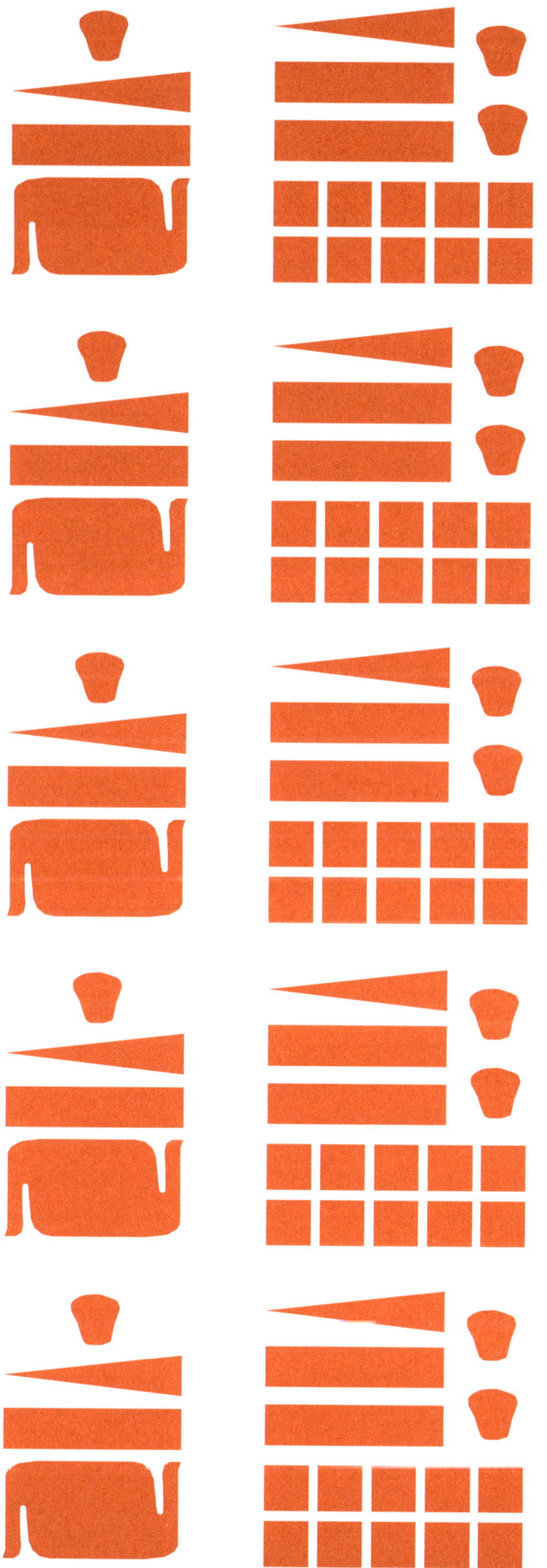

This paper was presented on April 29, 2021, in the context of the exhibition *Amarantus* by Mariana Castillo Deball at MGKSiegen, Germany.

There is a Kogi myth, from the Elder Brothers of the Sierra Nevada de Santa Marta, Colombia, that reads:

First, there was the sea; everything was dark,
There was no sun, no moon.
There were no people,
There were no animals, no plants.
Only the sea extended everywhere.
The sea was the Mother. She was not people,
She was not a thing.
Mother is the spirit of light that will be.
Mother was Thought and Memory.[1]

The Mesoamerican people—as in this Kogi myth—imagined the Earth as a Mother, a living being. For the ancient Mesoamerican peoples the Earth was imagined as a fantastic reptile floating in the waters of the ocean. Art translates the myths of creation as visual stories that become metaphors and symbols, and Mariana Castillo Deball works with these images to create new approaches and new stories. An example of how the story of creation takes physical form and an aesthetic can be seen in an Olmec jade tablet, with incised symbols, from Ahuelican Guerrero, which today resides in the Dallas Museum of Art's collection. The tablet depicts the story of creation as early as 900–500 BCE. At the bottom of the central incised drawing, there are three circles that represent the three stones of the first hearth, where the gods lit the first fire and where the first *comal* (griddle) was placed to heat tortillas. Over these stones, there is a complex of natural and man-made mountains (with the pyramidal structure covering the

1 Written in the entrance to Museo del Oro, Bogotá, Colombia.

original mountain of creation), signaling the community, the people from the mountain, the earth as a sacred First mountain. In Nahuatl, the mountain of creation, as a symbol of a community of people and a territory, is called *altepetl*. The mountain has a cave opening in the bottom, the path to the world of the dead, the ancestral underworld. Over the stepped pyramid, there is a the first maize plant, which is the Olmec Cosmic Tree at the center of four other elements that signal the four pillars or trees that sustain the heavens. Both the first mountain and tree are in the midst of the creative waters, represented by the jade surface in itself. The perimeter of the plaque is incised with the markings that represent the four cardinal directions and, in the corners, the solstices in both the eastern (upward) and western (downward) horizons. The unity of these eight partitions symbolizes both space (represented by east, north, west, and south), and time represented by the solstices, or the points in time that signal the movement of the sun through the horizon on the days that mark the arrival of winter and summer. These same elements appear once again in the image of the foundation of Mexico-Tenochtitlan in the Codex Tovar in the sixteenth-century, which is the symbol that we still recognize in our Mexican flag. An eagle (the sun), perches on a nopal (the Mexica cosmic tree), and the nopal grows from a rock (the Earth) in the midst of Lake Texcoco—a metaphor for the primeval creative waters. The image found in the Olmec tablet has been redone through the centuries, from 500 BCE to the sixteenth century CE, when the already-conquered Nahua people painted their myths of creation for the Spaniards. Just as these symbols recreate and retell the myth of creation so that we are reminded that we partake of the forces that govern the cosmos because we occupy space and are beings of time, Mariana Castillo Deball makes these concepts reenter history in her art. She creates opportunities and circumstances that allow us to feel the past in the present; in a way her art is like a conceptual threshold. In this brief essay, I will try to describe our collaborative work and to illuminate Mariana's work through the lenses of key indigenous concepts, to reveal how these concepts materialize in a different moment in history.

IN TLILLI IN TLAPALLI

Mariana and I began collaborating through a suggestion made by Ramiro Martínez, director of the Museo Amparo in Puebla, that we work on an exhibition together. The exhibition was titled *In Tlilli in Tlapalli: Imágenes de la nueva tierra: identidad indígena despúes de la conquista*, and was shown from June to September of 2018 at Museo Amparo in Puebla.

In 2006, I was able to study the original twelve volumes of the Florentine Codex (originally titled the *Historia general de las cosas de Nueva España*). The colors in the original Florentine Codex can be divided optically into two opposite groups: the translucent dyes, which are luminous because they allow the white of the paper to be seen, and the opaque, granular colors that cover up the substrate. The analytical study we made of the pigments showed that the transparent colors were for the most part organic in nature, and very different from those made in any European tradition of painting. The opaque pigments were natural minerals along with artificial compounds such as Maya blue and Maya green. We also identified the use of the red color minium, which is the only European pigment.

Both organic dyes and mineral pigments were central to the *in tlilli in tlapalli* manuscript painting tradition. Painted books were understood to be the foundation of knowledge. The *in tlilli in tlapalli*—that is, the concept of knowledge—thus, is conceptually the actual stuff of painting: the black lines with which drawings were made and the colors that filled them up. Our work revealed compellingly how these artists drew on this tradition of *in tlilli in tlapalli*. Their conscious selection of materials and techniques, no less important in their eyes than the choice of words and images, adds yet another layer of symbolic and historic meaning to the Florentine Codex.

In her work, Mariana has explored the world-forming power of colors derived from the concept of *in tlilli in tlapalli*. As I have proposed, the Nahua *tlacuiloque* of the Florentine Codex used pigments not only to paint but also to convene, to make present the cosmic forces that are at the base of creation. All of the pigments created with flowers have the energetic living quality of the sun, and daylight, while the mineral pigments obtained from the entrails of the earth are characterized by the terrestrial, underworld energy of the earth and the night. Together they bring forward the world. Images in the Florentine Codex become *ixiptla*, living presences of what they represent. In that way, Mariana created a garden in the shape of the Mesoamerican space-time unity, an abstraction of how the cosmos works and of its cycles, where she and Tatiana Falcón planted the flowers and vegetables mentioned in the Florentine Codex as the sources for making colorants. They also created spaces in the garden where the minerals were placed. The structured-colored garden then became a world in itself.

The structure of the cosmos, and its cycles as presented in Mariana's garden, are based on the first page of the Codex Fejérváry-Mayer, so-called for the man who collected it. There is a sun at the very top of the image, which designates the East, along with a tree that sustains that part of the cosmos and two gods that flank the tree. The left side of the image represents the North; the bottom, the West; and the right, the South. The dots and symbols that are placed in the perimeters of the four corners of the world formed the *tonalpohualli*, or the divinatory calendar of **260** days. The four loops between the trapezoid shapes each have a circle on top where the symbol of the year-bearer is placed: *Acatl* (reed), to the east, *Tecpatl* (flint) to the north, *Calli* (house) to the west, and *Tochtli* (rabbit) to the south. These four loops multiplied by thirteen dots creates a year cycle made of **365** days per year. The **365** days in the year are counted with the solstices, so this space-time unity has the **260**-day divinatory, solar calendar and a yearly calendar. If one were to pull the drawing from the center, this design would become a pyramid. This is an image of vertical and horizontal time and space, the image of the cosmos. Mariana uses the concept of the *tonalpohualli* as the interwoven space and time in her drawings *Petalcoatl I, II & III* (**2018**). In *Petlacoatl I*, the surface of the Earth is woven or ordered to represent a specific day. You can see how the gradient of the watercolor she uses for these works resembles the language of pigments made from flowers, and as I mentioned before, flowers have a particular *tonalli*, or energy from the sun. In *The woven earth and the tangled underworld* (**2018**), Mariana brings all of this knowledge together through simplicity and abstraction, depicting the ordered and the potential, in an intuitive and contemporary fashion.

The *tonalpohualli* was painted on special sacred books called *tonalamatl*, which have a structure like an accordion and can have many folding patterns and thus different ways to read them other than in a linear fashion. Again, this document represents thought and memory and one can use it to interpret the present. Mariana reinterprets these concepts in several works. In *Tonalamatl IV* (2018), she depicts the four colors of the four corners of the world in a configuration of space and time that is particular to that day. It depicts a destiny, but just like the *tonalamatl*, you can shape it. *Tonalamatl III* (2018) includes both the signs and the thirteen numerals. It also denotes the chance configuration of a particular day. In *Crocodile Skin of Days* (2018), Mariana depicts a reptilian monster in a square shape "eating" time. In the belly of the beast, she depicts the divinatory signs, which in the potentiality of the underworld are recycled and transformed. *Devouring Time* (2018) depicts the mouth of this being. Her drawings *Scorpion time I & II* (2018), represent a collection of days and constellations of energies. Just like the *tonalamatl*, it is up to the reader to interpret them and to bring a story to them in order to own them. These drawings are in the spirit of the continuation of oral histories. On a different scale, Mariana also reinterprets the *tonalpohualli* for the exhibition *Amarantus,* at the MGKSiegen, through aluminum structures that wrap around the exhibition gallery. At the exhibition *In Tlilli in Tlapalli*, she made these circles in scagliola and installed them directly on the walls.

A previous work by Mariana that takes a deeper look into the *tonalamatl* is the drawing and film *El "donde estoy" va desapareciendo* (2011). Mariana starts this work from the moment of the sacred ritual of killing a deer for its pelt, and transforms its skin as a support for the codices. The deer was considered a solar deity for many Mesoamerican people. The film begins with a poem in many languages that speaks of this act of transformation. The sequence also depicts an image of the moment in the conquest when the resolution is taken to burn the sacred books to deprive people of this knowledge. Those that survived were dispersed, mostly to libraries in Europe, and the memory and thought of the peoples who created them were sequestered. Mariana's work also speaks of the moment in which these two worlds, the Amerindian and the European, depicted as a drawing with one body and two faces, come together through study and scholarship. The memory and thought kept in them has been transmitted in several languages, including English, German, and Italian, depending on where the original codices are stored. Mariana incorporates into her work the story of colonialism, but also of the codices' lives in foreign libraries and their study, so her nuanced work is never easy to categorize, but is a continuation of the influx of the Amerindian knowledge into the contemporary world.

A central topic of Mariana's work is the Nahua concept of *ixiptla*, an important concept that cannot be easily translated because it touches upon a different reality. *Ixiptla* derives from the verb *xip[ehua]* which means to peel a skin, such as a fruit, or as was customary after the war, to flay the skin of the defeated warrior so that the victorious would wear it, thus acquiring the opponent's bravery and power. In doing so, one becomes that other person and owns their attributes. Another translation that is still disputed is that this word also derives from *[ix]tli*, meaning eye or face, and conceptually refers to a conscious being. This concept is the same as the Mayan concept of *B'aahil a'n*. Paintings are not representations, but rather are conscious beings, or presences, because of their wrapping or skin and because of their having eyes. Alfredo López Austin, further explains that *ixiptla* is related to the notion of *nahualli*, which relates to the capacity of powerful individuals to transform themselves into the identity of others. For instance, if you are a powerful doctor or shaman and you want to fight a sickness, you can become that sickness so that you know it so well that you can fight it. There are ancient Mesoamerican ceramic sculptures that appear as figures that combine human and animal attributes. For example, a sculpture that has the attributes of *Tlaloc*, the deity that governs storms and rain, may be considered as an *ixiptla* of this entity. The skin of this figure transforms it into that being, not as a disguise, but as a ritual process of transformation. More recently, the Brazilian anthropologist Eduardo Viveros de Castro, who studies Amazonian thought and language, says that there is an underlying concept in the Amerindian world, that everything is imbued with life, from a tree to the stars, so that the body and the clothing become the only way to have identities and become an individual. Power in this context means the ability to become the other.

Putting together the idea of colors as meaningful through their materiality and the concept of *ixiptla*, we begin to understand a new facet of the work of the Mesoamerican painters. They were painting *ixiptla*. This important conceptual underpinning is true for paintings created in the sixteenth century by indigenous artists. The images in the Florentine Codex are a good example. Their style, considered European, is actually a way of capturing the power of the other, the power of the Europeans, and not an act of submission. *Ixiptla* can help us think through these difficult human tragedies because these artists were asserting their worldviews despite their circumstances. We can think of the colors on the images of the Florentine Codex, or any other Mesoamerican work of art, as the skin of painting, the way to transform them into image-*ixiptla*, so that the materiality of these colors becomes meaningful and important. An *ixiptla* is made through a process of creation akin to a ritual. Each part of the work becomes a means of incarnating the forces they represent, imbued with life and death. In *Ixiptla I & II* (2017), Mariana captures the power of color and creates an *ixptla* depicting a bundle of things where a human being is being transformed into something other. Mariana also explores this idea in her works *What's the matter with you* (2017) and *Water walk* (2018), as well as in her study of the *Xipe Totec* in both the Art Institute of Chicago and Museum Fur Volkerkunde, Basel.

Mariana explores archaeological work through the *ixiptla*-skin concept. For instance, she uses the molds of monuments of the Maya area created in the 1800s by the researcher Alfred Maudslay, and transformed them into the flayed skins of an *ixiptla*. In this regard, the Ethnological Museum in Berlin, which owns these paper molds, becomes the bearer of the skins of monuments, like the Mexica warriors who flayed the skins of their prisoners. Mariana reproduces Maudslay's paper mold technique in her piece *You have time to show yourself before other eyes* (2014). Another way in which Mariana has used this technique is to wrap trees in what she calls "paper traps," a project she proposed for the 2014 Berlin Biennale. In one installation, she displayed gessos, the tree paper traps, and archival photographs alongside one another. She brings together these *ixiptla* and questions how these two worlds collide and the complexity of it all.

The questions "whose past?" and "whose history?" are very much in Mariana's mind. One of her projects, *Who will measure the space, who will measure the time?* (2015) is composed of a series of columns in which she merges the formal elements of Brancusi's *Endless Column* (1938) with a ballplayer's mask from western Mexico from around 500 BCE. Intuitively, she merges two distinct worlds and times through their formal qualities, a process akin to the images of the Florentine Codex. The process of creating the columns is a communal one, Mariana worked with the ceramic workshop Taller Coatlicue in Atzompa, Oaxaca. In this manner, time and space are created by the group of artists and by the viewer of these columns, merging worlds and multiplying connections.

Xipe Totec, Art Institute of Chicago II, 2018, watercolor and ink on paper, 35.5 × 21.5 cm

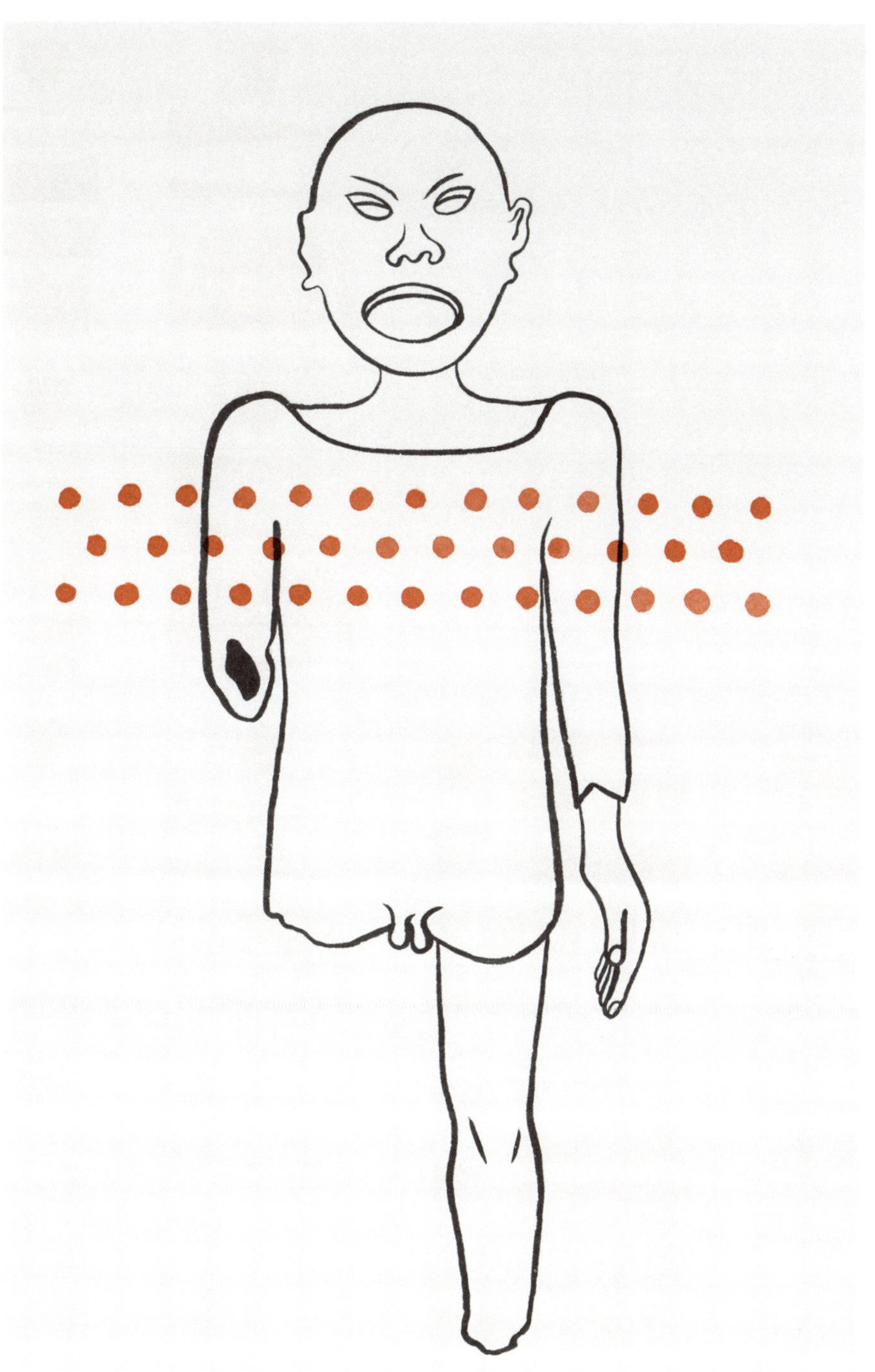

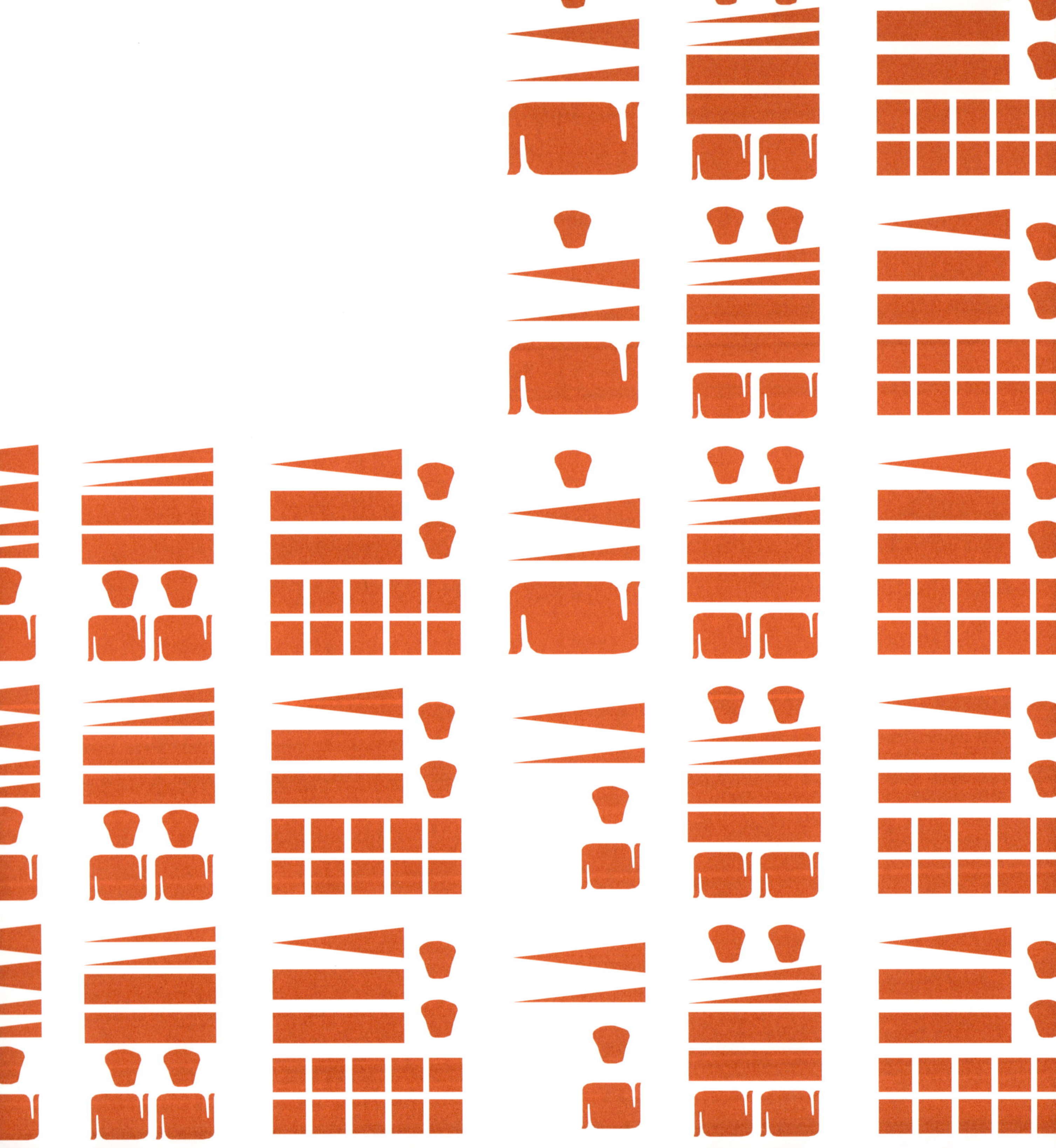

MBO XTÁ RÍDÀ SKIN PEOPLE

HUBERT MATIÚWÀA

For my mother, Valentina Calleja, who told me the countless tales of the *mbo Xtá rídà*. When I was a child, she called me *adà Xtá rídà* (skin child), she transformed the terror of these stories to create a new world, and she wrapped my fear in the skin of her words.

Numa lá' nànà Xtá rídà.

When the priests arrived to evangelize our culture, they dedicated themselves to hunting the *mbo Xtá rídà*,[1] who spoke an older variation of *mè'phàà* and held the gift of stretching their skin. They told countless stories of terror of the *mbo Xtá rídà*: for example, that they sought lodging in homes, and that upon sleeping they stretched one ear to make their bed, and they stretched the other to make their blanket. During the night, they arose to steal the children and eat them.

The *mè'phàà* villages who did not convert to Christianity were called demons, cannibals, skin people, or people who skin, and for this reason they were exterminated. Owing to their sustained resistance, a narrative of hate was drawn up around them. The priests fostered this terror to prevent the alliance of the different *mè'phàà* communities.

Every narration of oral memory is a testament of a time. There was a place called Yopitzingo, the village of the *yopes*, a name attributed to the *mè'phàà*. Distinguished by their resistance and defense of their territory, they were known for their rituals related to the skin. Their primary center for

1 Skin people, gentilic of those who, they say, were the ancestors of the present day *mè'phàà* people. *Mbo* means "people," *xtá* means "skin," and *rídà* or *rídaá* means "hanging," "intertwined," or "opposite." This can be translated as "people of intertwined skin" or "people with hanging skin."

ceremony was Tehuacalco,[2] which means "house of sacred water," the place where they performed their rituals to *Xtóaya'* (Skin of Water), one of the most important deities of their culture; it was she who raised *Àkha'* (Sun) and *Gòn'* (Moon), who, in turn, created the movement that made life possible.

In the present, *Xtóaya'* symbolizes fertility and abundance, and the rituals associated with her are related to the changes of the skin of the earth, seasons of drought and rain. The drought season is represented by the deity *Àkùùn ewe* (Famine), who in a ritual of expulsion is drowned in a river, in the mouth of *Xtóaya'*.

With respect to the *yopes*, who from oral memory we call *mbo Xtá rídà* (skin people), the journalist Fray Bernardino de Sahagún notes:

> "The word yopeuhtli, or the thing that has been peeled off, derives from the Nahua verb yopehua, which means to peel something off, synonym of xipehua, which translates as to skin, to remove the skin. Yopitzingo is the prehispanic name of the place where the yopes lived."[3]

In current Nahuatl, the words referenced here have the same meaning. For example: *xipehua* (to peel or to skin), *yopehua* (to peel something off), *yopeuhtli* (peeled off). According to this etymology, a relationship is drawn between Yopitzingo and the skinning ceremonies.

The oral narratives have a cause and a purpose: to transform memory into action. The hate toward the *yopes* was nourished, satanizing the rituals in which they skinned their rivals in combat. The wearing of the skin gave birth to multiple stories of terror. The purpose of this narrative was to colonize the collective imagination against the survivors of Yopitzingo so that they would be persecuted and assassinated by their own congenators.

Through the language of poetry, the book *Mbo Xtá rídà*, or *Skin People*,[4] recreates a new imagination and presents these characters as fantastic beings who helped to create the world: through their tears the sea was salted, they created the hills and the clothing of each animal, they spoke in the language of dreams and they bestowed upon us the capacity to interpret it, and they stretched their skin and wrapped us in her so that we might feel the world.

The word *xtá* (skin) is very important in *mè'phàà* culture: it is the ethical principle. The verbs *estar/vivir* in Spanish—to be/to live—has the same root as *xtá* in its daily use. The word *xtá* is the foundation for naming and indicating the characteristics of the personality, and it aligns being with acting: *Phú xtátsíska tàtá tsúkuè* (That man is a piece of lazy skin/That man is very lazy).

The purpose of skin is to cover and care for that of which it forms a part, like the relationship between flesh and skin. The root of the word *xtá* is related to the words *xtáyaa* (stalk of a tree), *xtíya* (honeycomb/the clothing of water), *xtá ga'un* (womb/skin that nourishes). All of these words relate to care: the stalk of the tree protects it from the open sky, the honeycomb protects the honey, the womb protects and nourishes the fetus. We, the *mè'phàà*, are the *mbo Xtá rídà* (skin people). This means we must care for the place where we live—we are the skin of the *numbaa* (earth-world).

2 Currently, this is one of the most important archeological zones in the state of Guerrero.

3 De Sahagún, F. B., *Historia general de las cosas de la Nueva España*, Tomo III (México: Imprenta del ciudadano Alejandro Valdés, 1830).

4 Hubert Matiúwàa, *Mbo Xtá rídà, Gente Piel, Skin People* (Chilpancingo de los Bravo, Guerrero: Gusanos de la memoria, Ícaro Ediciones, 2020)

In the Mountain of Guerrero, Mexico and in Sutiaba, Nicaragua, the *mè'phàà* defend this conception of life, first in the face of Nahuatl expansion, then in the face of Spanish colonization, and currently in the face of extraction by mining companies and territorial control by the criminal groups of the illegal drug trade.

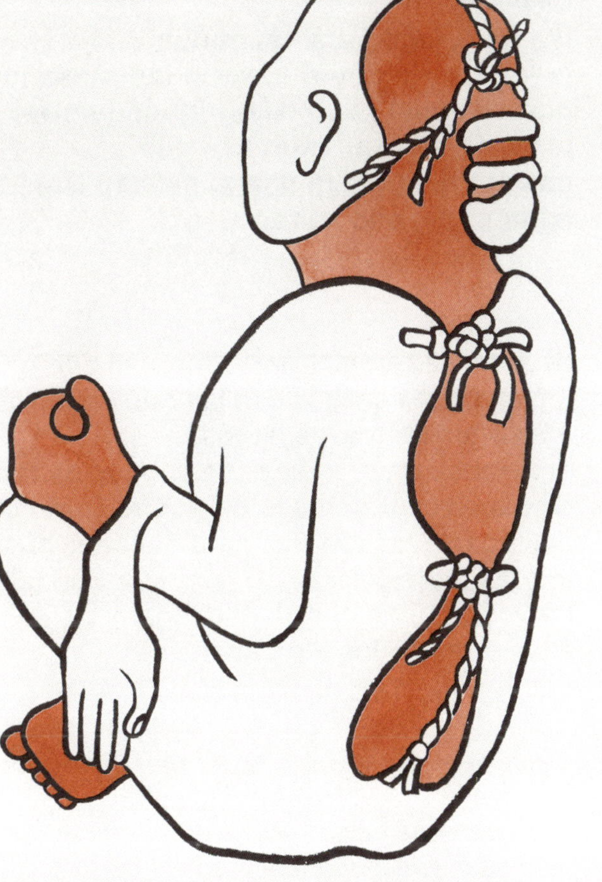

Xipe Totec, Basel I, **2018**, watercolor and ink on paper, **35.5×21.5** cm

Ná wí'ñuu ngrigùún' awúun júbà,
nguáná witsuùn nguáná gùwìin,
paska xtá ña'wuùn rí numbrá'a mijnéè,
mbijuìin' jamí mbijuà'
ñawúùn,
tsa'tsiìn, jagò jùbà' tsùdùùun,
judeè ixè xkùdùú rí nàjmuu ídò nutsáñuùn,
nuríwìí amùù xàbò tsí ngrigùún jambàà.
Ídò na'ne wakhíí mbo Xtá rídà
nawáthan nùtsínjmu jamí na'wan iya,
ikhín natiin enè xàbò.

Se les veía caminar por la montaña en grupos de cinco o diez,
tenían orejas anchas con las que se envolvían,
eran altos de brazos largos,
no usaban ropa, a veces se cubrían de lodo,
cargaban instrumentos de guerra como lanzas,
atacaban a los viajeros para quitarles sus alimentos.
Por las tardes,
los mbo Xtá rídà bajaban a jugar y a tomar agua en los pozos,
allí era donde los atrapaban.

You used to see them walking in the mountains in groups of five or ten,
they had wide ears in which they blanketed themselves,
they were tall and long-armed,
they did not use clothing, sometimes they covered themselves in mud,
they carried instruments of war, like spears,
they attacked travelers to steal their food.
In the evenings,
the *mbó Xtá rídà* came down to play and to drink water from the wells,
this was where they caught them.

Ná xujiun xnu'daa niguwéè
rí mònè majnWdáa
wáji tsinuu ajngáa
rí rígà inuu numbaa,
gàjmàá a'wóo gíñá
ni'nìì mbro'on
ná nigùmaa iduu à'gùán
tsí netsè numbaa e'ne,
nìgrígùùn gajmììn àbò'
tsí nìrìyàà' iya inuu numbaa,
tsí nènè júbà
jamí nènè májáàn jùbà' ná mujuwa ló'.

Vinieron del sueño
para encarnar
la piel de nuestro mundo,
con la lengua del aire pintaron la noche,
antes que riera la primera estrella
se arrastraron con las serpientes,
dieron cauce a los ríos
y escamaron los cerros.

They came from the dream
to give flesh to
the skin of our world,
with air's tongue
they painted the night,
before the first star could laugh
they crawled with the snakes,
they gave bed to the rivers
and scaled the hills.

Mbi'íí itsí rí tra'à ña'wuùn,
txùùn idxùun,
nambita'a nè
xó bìtú tsí ngrigùún' awúun xàxè.
Ajngáa rí nutheèn,
ñajuun mè'phàà Xtá rídà
ikhaa rí naxkaxiì numbaa
jamí xáwii ngrigòò xó àñà'.

Tienen brillantes
incrustados en las orejas,
el cabello,
atado de luciérnagas,
es huella
en la cobija del monte.
Su lengua de piel
despierta y anda ligera
con los pasos del venado.

They have diamonds
embedded in their ears,
their hair,
tied up with fireflies,
a footprint
on the hill's quilt.
Their tongue of skin,
awakens and treads lightly
with the footsteps of the deer.

Nixmíí xtíñuù
mbámbá xùkú:
nixná mògò'
tsí mà'nè dxíyoò dùùn,
xkuni xtíin rí nixudaa inuu xùkú gòn',
ikhajngó marma'àn àkuììn
rí xó agu gòn' ñajun iduu rí mbro'on,
nixnáa xtíñuù gíñá ñò'òn,
rí magòò ma'gè inuu mikuíí
ná ma'ne ríyà'
jambàà rí kuíjè inuu numbaa.

Bordan
la ropa de cada animal:
al borrego
le dan algodón
para ser hermano de las nubes,
al tejón lo llaman gòn'
y con el antifaz
le recuerdan que sus ojos
son luna de noche,
al pájaro visten con la ropa del aire
para dibujar en el cielo
las raíces de la tierra.

They embroider
the clothing of every animal:
to the sheep
they give cotton
so it may be cloud's brother,
for the racoon, the name *gòn'*
and with the mask
they remind it that its eyes
are night's moon,
the bird, they dress with the clothing of air
so it may paint in the sky
the roots of the earth.

Gàjmàa iya iduu ixè ninìì àdo,
nitháàn:
–Ikháán' manbi'yaa' ña'wun daan,
matagéwaàn jambòo numbaa,
mataxnáxíí tsinuu mbámbá ajngáa,
rú'khuè ma'ne jùmàa'.
Ikajngó àdo ña'wun daan
ñajun tsí jaya jumuu xuajian ló'.

Con lágrimas del árbol
amasaron al gusano,
le dicen:
—Te llamarás Oreja de Olla,
mide el mundo,
tráenos la cicatriz de su palabra,
será tu memoria.
Desde entonces,
el gusano medidor
guarda la historia de nuestro pueblo.

With tears from the tree
they kneaded the caterpillar,
they tell it:
"You will be called the Ear of the Pot,
measure the world
bring us the scar of its word,
that will be your memory."
Since then,
the caterpillar who measures
holds the history of our people.

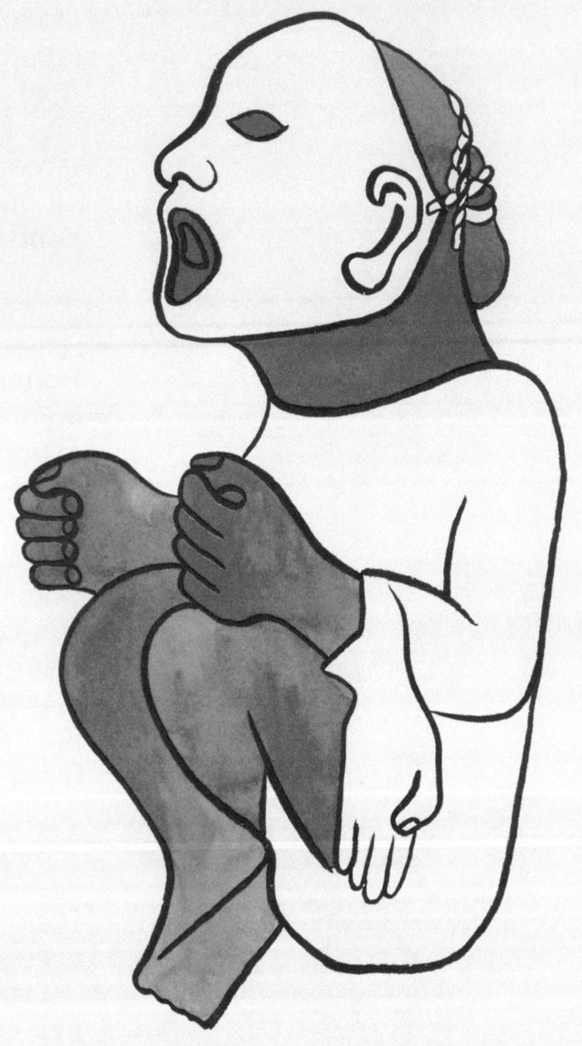

Xipe Totec, Basel II, 2018, watercolor and ink on paper, 35.5 × 21.5 cm

Tsú'tsú' tsú', tsú' tsú' tsú',
na'duu àkuìin tsú'tsún,
nusian xùkú,
nakixíín, nùnì xingàá
rí majne gúkú ajngúùn.
Mbo Xtá rídà
nithaa xòwè:
–¡Phú jínà riga gù'wá ló',
xó jiná awúun daan janíí ná juwá ló'!
Nìkhá xòwè ná jùwá' a'gùán,
nixsgráxii mijnè,
nè'nè nduwèe rí nijañun,
ikajngó nigoo nè'nè kuwèè
xtá ri'yuu agùún à'gùán
xkua'nii nikuxíí agù rí nà'nè mbita'à
mikuíí.

Tsú'tsú' tsú', tsú' tsú' tsú',
toca el tambor de su corazón,
los animales bailan,
brincan y dan vueltas
para que madure su palabra.
Los Xtá rídà
dijeron al Tlacuache:
–¡Qué oscura está la casa,
parece estómago de olla!
Él fue a las estrellas,
se hizo el muerto,
les robó la piel
y levantó la noche celeste.

Tsú 'tsú' tsú', tsú' tsú' tsú',
sounds the drum of their heart
the animals dance,
skip and spin
to ripen their word.
The *Xtá rídà*
said to the Opossum,
"How dark the house is,
like the belly of a pot!"
He went to the stars,
played dead,
stole their skin
and raised up the celestial night.

Xó tambá'thoo ida ló',
tsáà xàbò nindxá ló',
kuatuùn gòn' rùmìa ló',
mbo Xtá rídà
nènè makíí ìtsá ló',
nixnaa xtá xuwia ló'
asndo rí nirakààn ló'
gàjmàá xnún'daa inuu numbaa.

Los xàbò
aún no abríamos los ojos,
la luna tenía amarrado
nuestro ombligo,
los Xtá rídà
maduraron nuestros huesos,
nos envolvieron con su piel
y caímos
en racimos con los sueños.

We xàbò
still had not opened our eyes,
our navel
tied up by the moon,
the *Xtá rídà*
ripened our bones,
they cloaked us in their skin
and we fell
in clusters with dreams.

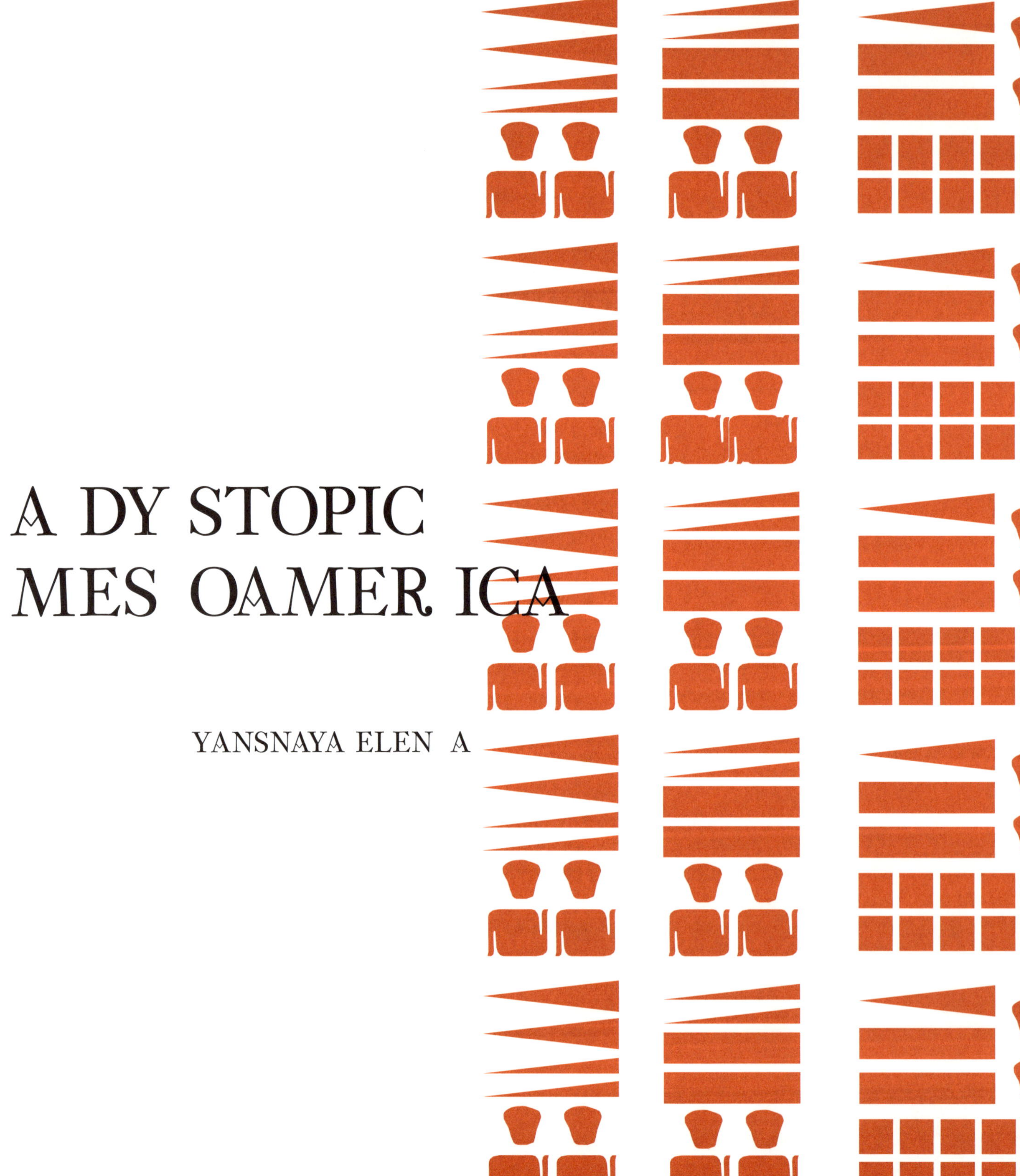

A DYSTOPIC MESOAMERICA

YANSNAYA ELENA

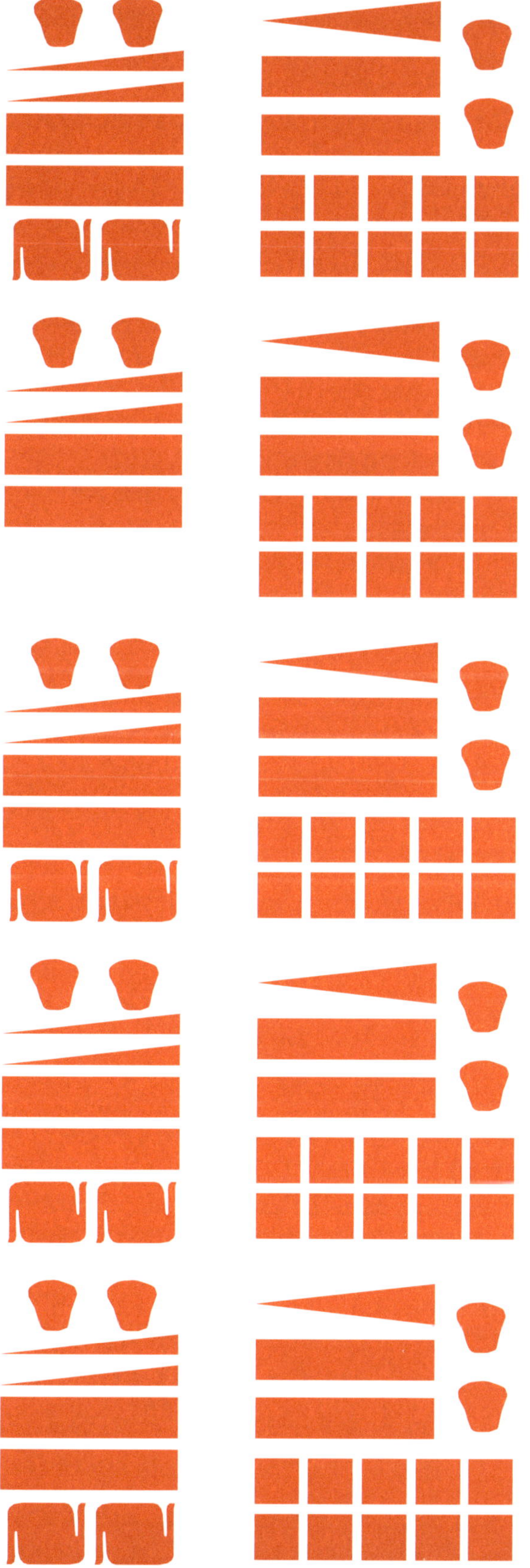

To imagine a world without capitalism, colonialism, or patriarchy. An exercise of this sort seems to fly in the face of the very notion of Mesoamerica, because any universe to be built in the future gets hijacked by the same systems that oppress us in the present.

THE FUTURE AS SPACE

Time is such an abstract concept that in order to be able to refer to it, we have to use metaphors of space. I don't know what time is if I don't think of it in terms of a line—the timeline—the transit of the hands of the clock on the bell tower, the calendar, the little boxes all through my daily planner. During one period, I was obsessed with the attempt to understand how the passage of a year was traced in people's minds. In the imaginary drawing I carry in my mind, the year is an irregular four-sided polygon: December and January make up one side; February, March, April, May, and June constitute the right side; July and August form the base of the polygon; and September, October, and November close the figure along the left side.

The world's languages make it clear that we need metaphors of space to account for time. The very conjugation of Spanish clearly reveals the way we move through a particular space when we use the word *ir*, "to go," in the formation of the future tense: we're going to read a book, I'm going to a concert, you're going to work tomorrow. The future is a universe created out of an act of enunciation: all that will occur once it is enunciated. If something occurs on the final day of January of 1945, the future includes all that happens from that day forward; but if it happens on the final day of January of 2019, that future is cut off from the decades that the 1945 date effectively includes. Thus we might say that the future is being unstoppably phagocytized by that mouth called the present that digests it and offers it up again in the form of the past.

While in languages like Spanish metaphors of time privilege the image of the horizontal line where the future is up ahead and the past remains behind, in languages like Aymara—which is currently spoken in Bolivia, Peru, Argentina, and Chile—the metaphors utilize the idea of a horizontal line, but the future remains behind us, at our backs, because given that it is not cognizable, it is impossible to look at it; the past is located, in contrast, ahead of us, because we have already experienced it and it is therefore known and can be scanned within our sights. Other languages, like my mother tongue, Mixe, which is spoken in the state of Oaxaca in the south of Mexico, also utilize a linear metaphor, except that it is vertical, and the future falls down upon us, moving across the body and bathing us in time: *menp këtäkp*. The possibilities offered to us by the language or languages we by chance happen to speak provide us with the initial metaphors to be able to speak of the future.

But these complex narrations are constituted out of distinct spaces of enunciation that create a universe of disputed narrative interweavings. The future, that vast space with infinite possibilities, folds up before the rigidity of events as they occur. And what occurs is a territory where a range of diverse narratives takes place and the power of some narrating voices might choke out the future of others.

The current systems that generate structures of oppression project against the narratives of the future from inside hegemonic constructions: within many fictive creations, capitalism continues to exist in those territories, represented by mega-corporations that control even the most minute details of sociopolitical organization: the patriarchy, for its part, secures its place in the future by taking absolute control over women's bodies and their reproductive capacities, while colonialism continues to reproduce racial categories as well as the dynamics between metropolis and periphery. These futures exist, of course, within a handful of languages and audiovisual narratives—the hegemonic ones. In general, it seems to me that dystopias are reinforced versions of the current situation; in them, the present colonizes the territories of the future and perhaps their greatest significance is located in their function as warnings.

On the other hand, there are enthusiastic narratives that propose scenarios of the future in which technology has resolved the problems of the present, without taking into consideration that present-day technological development is constructed via environmental exploitation that is leading us to an unprecedented climate crisis. A future that involves extraordinary technological development would have to account for the nature of the materials that comprise it: where they come from, on which bodies and territories they are built. How would a world without capitalism, colonialism, or patriarchy function? Does imagination suffice to posit and furnish such a world in detail? Because it's true that a significant part of future universes is held hostage to present systems of oppression and it seems logical that even their future negation should be shaped in contrast to their current reality.

Other possibilities, however, inhabit that narrative universe we call the future, and are being articulated from within other sites of enunciation, the spaces that historically have neither had a future nor been considered bearers of any avant-garde whatsoever. The movement known as

"Afrofuturism" is situated among those voices that seek a place in discussions about the future; based in Afrodescendance, Afrofuturism proposes possibilities and aesthetics that aim to create a future in which the current racial system is called into question and other possibilities seemingly cut off by the past might take up space. In these creations, the possibility of a different future is proposed as an emancipatory horizon for the Afrodescendant population. Those who take part in this movement underscore that Afrofuturism does not just involve the creation of alternative futures distinct from present-day reality, but also that it further entails a questioning of the past, because to narrate a future that disarticulates colonialism or posits a future without it requires an examination of past systems and occurrences that have determined the existence of current oppression. In "Mexafuturismo,"[1] published in *Literal Magazine*, the Mexican writer Alberto Chimal posits the possibility of building narratives that contemplate other realities for the peoples who have been structurally oppressed in this country.

These futures made from emancipatory imagination might be constructed outside of the hegemonic spaces of literature and audiovisual production, given that it's not just a matter of including populations that have been historically oppressed within hegemonic narratives as a condescending act to cleanse a historical guilt.

TOWARD A MESOAMERICAN FUTURISM

If Indigenous peoples have been narrated as peoples anchored to tradition, and if we've been singled out for the absurd adherence we feel toward the past and to customs as the elements responsible for our poverty and precarity, to create a Mesoamerican futurist movement that disarticulates the narrations of oppression might make visible the mechanisms that in the present and the past have cut off our voice.

What are the possibilities for exploring that futurism? In the following lines I hope to sketch out a framework that might later permit us, together with and from a range of voices, to detail, revise, and inhabit that future universe.

The category of Indigenous encompasses a diverse range of peoples and nations that experience a historical condition of oppression that has been actualized as institutional racism, impoverishment, and the plunder of their assets and territories. In Mexico, there are currently sixty-eight Indigenous groups to which eleven million people belong, representing close to 10 percent of the total population. When the Mexican State was created, Indigenous peoples represented approximately 70 percent of the population.

Before the establishment of the colonial order, this continent was inhabited by a heterogeneous and radically diverse mixture of cultures and languages; for example, the Inuit population, which inhabits the Arctic regions in the north of this continent, followed a historical path that was completely different from that of the Mixe-Zoquean population, which began to populate the warm lands of what is currently the Mexican Isthmus. The great differences between the linguistic systems of those peoples, like the differences among their cultural expressions and geographic surroundings, were erased once the colonial system subsumed them

1 Alberto Chimal, "Mexafuturismo", in *Literal Magazine*, 2019. https://literalmagazine.com/mexafuturismo/

into the category of "Indio," and later, into the category of "Indigenous."

A futurist narrative universe would necessarily have to break this category, and disarticulate the historical condition that provides its foundation. Conversely, other possible categories could emerge, in which Indigenous peoples might be able to build multiple futures. In one of those, Mesoamerica could emerge once more, with another name, as a cultural region united by the cultivation of maize and yuca, by a set of narrations that explain the world, by the flourishing of a certain kind of writing, and by a set of cultural features that could be argued and polemicized, but that transfer the core of the discussion away from the category of "Indigenous." Mesoamerica, that cultural region created through an analysis of the past from archeological studies, could be a newly resuscitated category in the future, whether or not it might correspond to the boundaries that archeologists and historians have assigned it in the past.

A future Mesoamerica will have the flexibility to reinvent itself as a multilingual cultural universe with a past that is different from the one currently ascribed to it. Future Mesoamerica will knock out the current borders that have fractured its nation-states and reduced it to a historical region of the past without present-day content. In contrast with the technological optimism of the green capitalism that seeks to combat climate crisis with greater technological development—and hence greater cost in natural raw materials—Future Mesoamerica might posit a solution to climate crisis based in the current moment, broadening the intensely reduced concept of technology that arises from the Industrial Revolution. In Future Mesoamerica, the technologies that harmonize humanity with nature and return it to the ecosystems as one element of many will reach great heights as processes of post-capitalist resilience. Future Mesoamerica will be like the networks of mushrooms that establish communication systems among trees: a network of minuscule sociopolitical organizations with significant local agency that will establish networks for resolving common problems when needed, without centralizing their coordination. The technologies we conceive of today as archaic will once again be valued for their effectiveness in putting the brakes on the climate crisis: in opposition to the foolish behavior of agro-industry and the monocultures of the past, it will be the response offered by systems of complex, organic, and diverse cultivation like the *milpa*, the cornfield. Diversity as a technology, as a tool for intervening in territories, will posit organic possibilities that are different from the capitalist technology whose hegemony is based on consumption of the natural environment. In this scenario, barely outlined here, all that current hegemonic structures consider archaic will emerge as sensible technological responses to put the brakes on the illogical and insane race humanity is undertaking toward its own destruction. These structures of the past, like the *milpa*, continue to be contemporary for many of the peoples who are subsumed and hidden behind the category of "Indigenous."

This approach, which must be imagined in detail as the narrative universe of a possible future, has deep roots in the past. After the wars of conquest, between battles, famines, epidemics, and forced labor, more than three-quarters of Mexico's native population died. The sociopolitical structures had collapsed and the world that had been known up to that point ceased to exist any longer. Under these circumstances, it must have seemed quite implausible that all the way in the twenty-first century so-called Indigenous peoples would continue to exist, speaking our languages and recreating our own forms of organization. Against all odds, our structures have made it here, to this future, with the lessons learned from the past and transformed into our contemporary ways of living.

Our existence in small-scale community organizations cleared the way for the possibility of life. That wager for a future, despite a context that provided us with so much death, makes me think that in the face of the climate catastrophe that draws ever nearer, the response, in the form of our new futurist narratives, should be anchored in the lessons forged in that past. We've learned responses from within the catastrophe we have survived and we can, from that place, write futures in multiple and diverse spatial metaphors. That is a wager: the possibility of conjugating our world in the future.

THE INTERMEDIARIES IN BETWEEN: ALFRED MAUDSLAY AND MARIANA CASTILLO DEBAL ON ZOOMORPH P

JENNIFER
REYNOLDS-KAYE

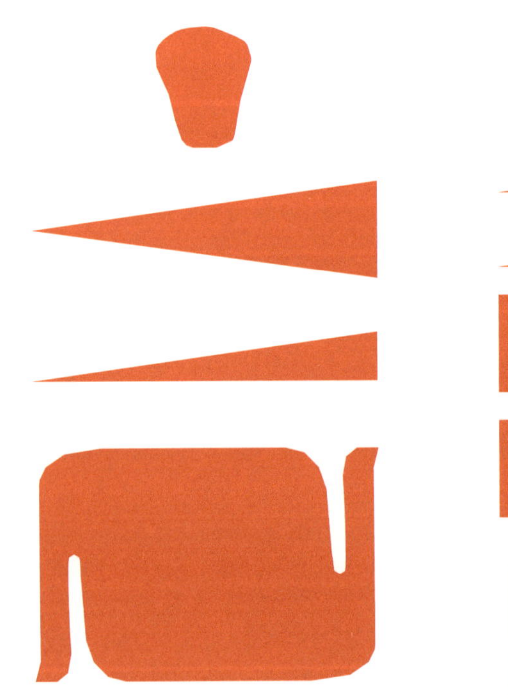

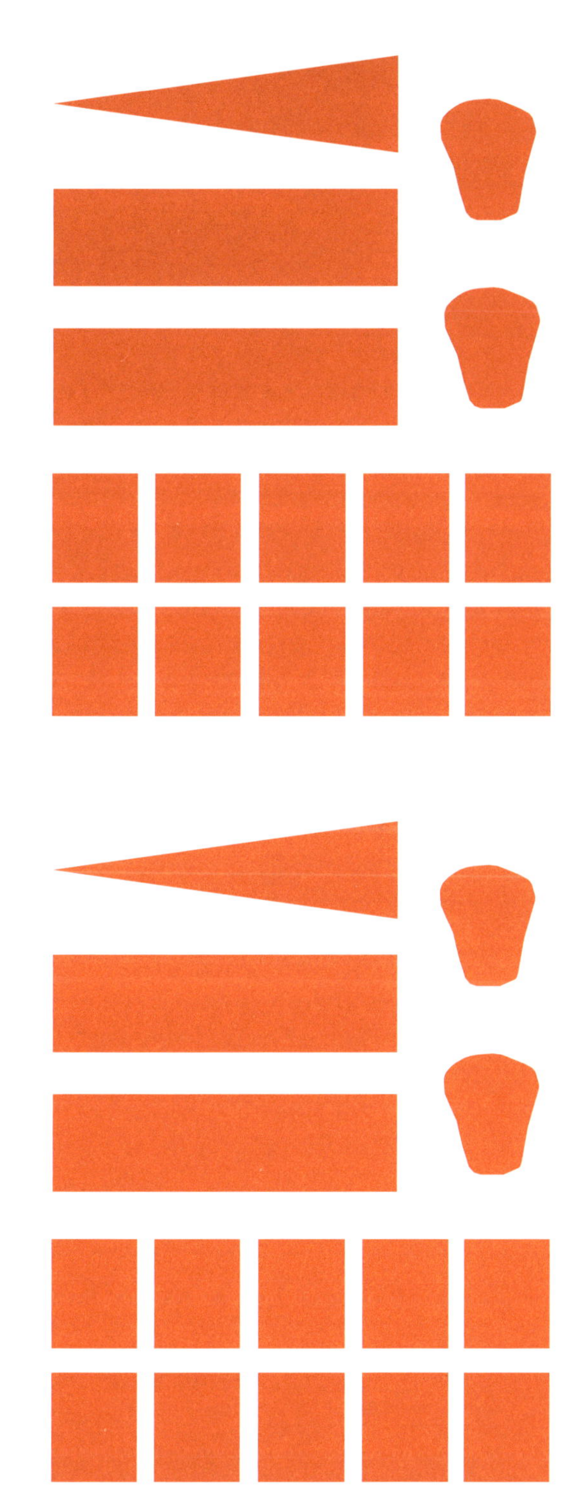

As a contemporary artist, Mariana Castillo Deball has developed a strong practice of analyzing the field of archaeology as it evolved over the course of the nineteenth-century, both in the field and in the post-excavation site of the museum. She experiments with the materials, technologies, and methodologies of archaeology to gain an embodied understanding of their logics. Her primary focus has been on pre-Columbian sculptures, codices, and iconography, though her work also expands to encompass art of the Americas at large.[1] Epistemological and ontological questions about pre-Columbian objects are crystallized into her artistic practice, which ranges from printmaking and sculpture to the written word. Her artwork results in deep and nuanced distillations of major issues such as excavation, circulation, reproduction, repatriation, and knowledge production through accessible artworks and texts. Some of the guiding questions for her practice include: How do you extract meaning from extraction? How do you unpack the baggage of archaeology? How do you use the materials and practice of archaeology to reveal its inherently colonial and troubled past? How do you recover the lost narrative of plunder and despair against the victories of discovery and collection formation?

By investigating the materials and methods of archaeology through a hands-on approach, Castillo Deball gains physical knowledge both of the pre-Columbian artisans, sculptors, and painter-scribes (*Tlacuilo*) and the scholars who crafted the artwork's afterlives, often after entering Western institutions. Castillo Deball develops a

1 San Francisco Art Institute, "Mariana Castillo Deball: Feathered Changes, Serpent Disappearances," March 14, 2016, https://sfai.edu/press-releases/mariana-castillo-deball-feathered-changes-serpent-disappearances.

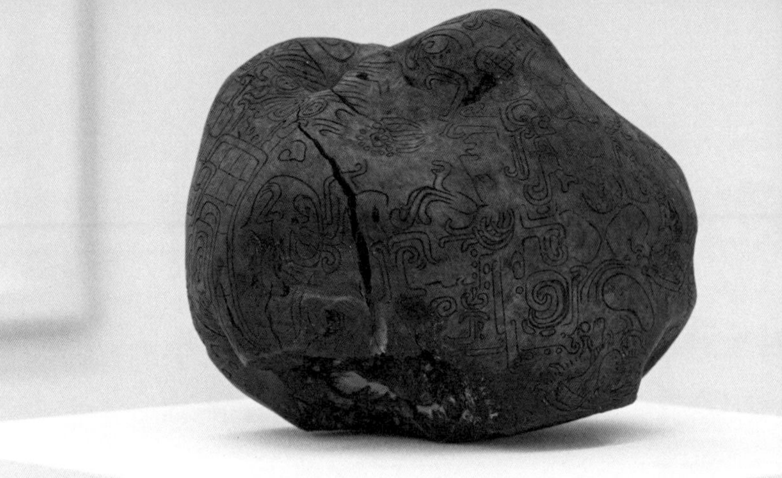

Zoomorph P, 2013. Miniature version of the monumental sculpture Zoomorph P, 746–805 CE, carved briar-wood root, 35 × 35 × 35 cm, at the Maya site of Quiriguá Guatemala

"composite biography" within her artwork that opens onto considerations of the artwork's importance for the source community and its later role in knowledge production and collection formation.[2] Each artwork is an additional chapter of that piece's biography that becomes accessible to a broader public by display in an art museum or gallery. Through her thoughtful and layered interventions, Castillo Deball encourages audiences to "discover" the challenges of archaeology, while simultaneously troubling that notion of "discovery" to acknowledge the winners and losers of the historically colonial enterprise.[3]

This integration of the past and the present comes to light in the carved briarwood root sculpture, *Zoomorph P* (2013), and the six black-and-white prints that were created from the piece. Castillo Deball's sculpture is a miniaturized version of an eponymous Classic period Maya sculpture from the site of Quiriguá in Guatemala. Working from a briar root purchased from a purveyor of discarded wood in Berlin,[4] Castillo Deball incised the undulating and irregular shape with a reduced iconographic program on the original monument. She retains some of the most important imagery of the original Zoomorph P, including the primary figure of the ruler Sky Xul on the north side of the Zoomorph and a large creature on its south face. This experimentation with scale and transformation of materials is a common practice in Castillo Deball's work. For example, in the exhibition at the New Museum, *Mariana Castillo Deball: Finding Oneself Outside*,[5] she was commissioned to create an inlaid wood floor installation based on the Mapa de Teozacoalco, a sixteenth-century Mixtec map from Oaxaca, Mexico originally comprised of twenty-three sheets of European paper pasted together. The Mapa de Teozacoalco records the dynastic lineage of the rulers of Teozacoalco from the tenth through sixteenth centuries, and currently resides in the Benson Library at the University of Texas at Austin.[6] This dissemination of indigenous knowledge and history beyond the source community is part of the legacy of colonialism in Mexico and Central America more broadly, and one that Castillo Deball reckons with in her work.

Given Castillo Deball's commitment to material transformation and explorations of the archaeological enterprise and its colonial entanglements, this essay offers a few reflections and possible inroads to understanding *Zoomorph P* and the six prints produced from the piece. First, the essay considers the importance of the original

2 For more on a composite biography, see Sally M. Foster and Siân Jones, *My Life as a Replica: St John's Cross, Iona* (Barnsley: Windgather Press, 2020).

3 Walter Mignolo, *The Idea of Latin America* (Oxford: Blackwell Pub, 2005).

4 Jennifer Reynolds-Kaye in discussion with Mariana Castillo Deball, Zoom, April 15, 2021.

5 "Mariana Castillo Deball: Finding Oneself Outside," http://www.newmuseum.org/exhibitions/view/mariana-castillo-deball.

6 Barbara E Mundy, Elizabeth Hill Boone, and Mary Elizabeth Smith, "At Home in the World: Mixtec Elites and the Teozacoalco Map-Genealogy," in *Painted Books and Indigenous Knowledge in Mesoamerica: Manuscript Studies in Honor of Mary Elizabeth Smith* (New Orleans: Middle American Research Institute, 2005), 36–81.

sandstone monument at Quiriguá, as well as affiliated pre-Columbian technologies like clay stamps and codices. Castillo Deball makes these connections evident in her miniature sculptural recreation that serves as a stamp that she draws out in her prints and through curatorial juxtaposition. Following this is a brief summary of the late-nineteenth-century "discoveries" of the Zoomorph P and the circulation of its imagery through publications and plaster cast replicas. One of the central protagonists at this time was the English explorer, Alfred Percival Maudslay, whose photographs, paper squeezes, and plaster casts are a primary influence for Castillo Deball in creating not only *Zoomorph P* but other artworks and installations as well.[7] Finally, we conclude with the six prints produced by inking and rolling *Zoomorph P* as it relates to the archaeological processes capturing data, including its inverse connection to paper squeezes and line drawings.

Zoomorph P is a monumental sculpture carved out of a sandstone boulder and located on the site of Quiriguá in Guatemala. Quiriguá was a Classic Period Maya (250–900 CE) site that was founded around 400 CE and which fell into decline around 900 CE. Its location in between the two major sites of Tikal and Copan lead scholars to think of Quiriguá as a "way station" in between these two sites.[8] Quiriguá consists of an impressive architectural program centered around a Great Plaza.[9] Additional structures radiate from the Great Plaza, Ceremonial Plaza, and Plaza of the Temple, and throughout the site are an array of stone monuments, including Zoomorph P and its accompanying Altar P.

Zoomorph P is a very large sculpture, measuring 3 m long by 3.5 m wide by 2.2 m high. The location and iconography of Zoomorph P had led scholars to argue that the monument is a water accession throne dedicated by the fifteenth ruler of Quiriguá, Sky Xul. A team of artisans, likely led by one master craftsman,[10] incised Sky Xul's portrait into the stone on the north side of the monument. He maintains an upright and regal position, with his legs crossed, arms extended to display objects in his hands, and head donning a highly ornamented headdress. He sits within the jaw of a large crocodile whose teeth and mouth wrap around his body. On the south side of the sculpture, the sculptors carved a large face of a creature with furrowed eyebrows, narrowed eyes, and a shell in its mouth. The top of the boulder is carved to resemble the Maya creation mountain, linking the accession of Sky Xul to the throne with the coming of a new cycle. This connection between a founding story and the accession of a ruler is a common strategy to legitimize the event as part of the cosmic order.[11]

In transforming the monumental stone sculpture into a handheld briar-root version, Castillo Deball performs a similar operation as the original creators in carving away at a natural material. She maps out, digs into, and removes sections of organic matter piece by piece to achieve the desired outcome. While her tools may be smaller and

7 For example, *What we caught we threw away, what we didn't catch we kept* (2013).

8 Matthew George Looper, *Quiriguá: A Guide to an Ancient Maya City* (Guatemala City: Editorial Antigua, 2007), 30.

9 UNESCO World Heritage Site Centre, "Archaeological Park and Ruins of Quirigua," https://whc.unesco.org/en/list/149/.

10 Matthew G. Looper, "Quirigua Zoomorph P: A Water Throne and Mountain of Creation," in *Heart of Creation: The Mesoamerican World and the Legacy of Linda Schele*, ed. Andrea Joyce Stone (Tuscaloosa: University of Alabama Press, 2002), 186.

11 Looper, 195.

the iconographic program more compressed, her technique of producing the carved sculpture aligns with and perhaps mirrors the Maya artisans. In a related vein, Castillo Deball also echoes the pre-Columbian technology of creating and using stamps as a way to imprint patterns and text onto a surface.[12] Castillo Deball makes this connection between *Zoomorph P* as a stamp that connects to pre-Columbian stamps explicit in her exhibition *You have time to show yourself before other eyes*, for the Berlin Biennale in 2014. In this display, she juxtaposes Zoomorph P and a selection of prints with a display of pre-Columbian clay stamps from the Berlin Ethnological Museum.

Additionally, when Castillo Deball inks and rolls out *Zoomorph P* onto the horizontal white surface of paper, she creates a visual analogue to pre-Columbian codices. While formats vary, one method was to join long strips of animal hide or paper and then either roll the document or fold it like an accordion. Similar to the Mapa de Teozacoalco, these documents recorded important information, such as dynastic lineages, origin stories, important historical dates and events, and were even used to arbitrate land claims or for divination.[13] Castillo Deball has carefully studied many types of codices in her extensive research into pre-Columbian iconography, and often copied them to better grasp their visual vocabulary and conceptual logic. For example, in her piece, *El donde estoy va desapareciendo / The "Where I am" is vanishing* (2011), Castillo Deball creates an ink-and-cotton paper drawing and video installation to tell the story of the *Codex Borgia,* from the skinning of the deer to make the hide, to its significance in its source community, to its circulation within Europe.[14] Partial renditions of sections of the original codex float across the page in a similar manner to the images of Sky Xul in the print created by inking and rolling *Zoomorph P.* In both artworks, the blank spaces surrounding the figures lend a sense of missed, forgotten, or erased information resulting in incomplete knowledge about the past. What has been

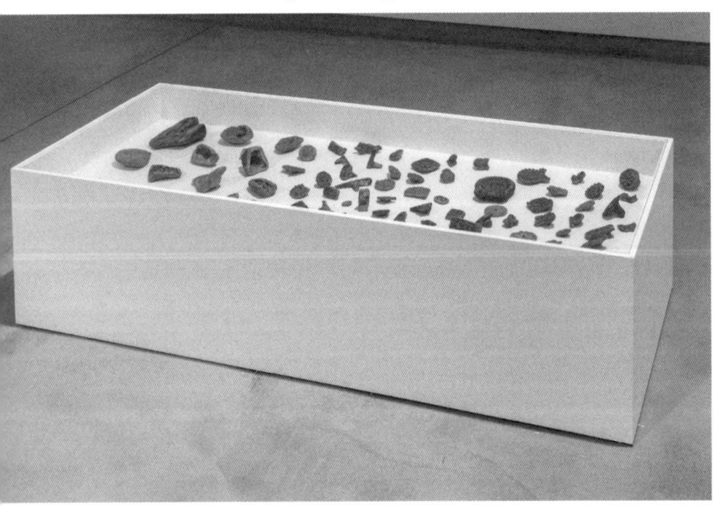

You have time to show yourself before other eyes, 2014, installation view including pre-Columbian stamps from Berlin Ethnological Museum, Berlin

12 Castillo Deball mentioned that she experimented with carving uncommon materials such as cabbage into stamps while in art school. Reynolds-Kaye and Castillo Deball, interview. See also Mallory E. Matsumoto, "Copying in Clay: Maya Hieroglyphs and Changing Modes of Scribal Practice," in *Res: Anthropology and Aesthetics* 71–72 (January 1, 2019): 52–63, https://doi.org/10.1086/704762.

13 Elizabeth Hill Boone, *Cycles of Time and Meaning in the Mexican Books of Fate*, 1st ed (Austin: University of Texas Press, 2007); Bruce E. Byland, *In the Realm of 8 Deer: The Archaeology of the Mixtec Codices* (Norman: University of Oklahoma Press, 1994); Mary Elizabeth Smith and Elizabeth Hill Boone, *Painted Books and Indigenous Knowledge in Mesoamerica: Manuscript Studies in Honor of Mary Elizabeth Smith* (New Orleans: Middle American Research Institute, 2005); Elizabeth Hill Boone and Walter Mignolo, *Writing Without Words: Alternative Literacies in Mesoamerica and the Andes* (Durham: Duke University Press, 1994).

14 Rita Gonzalez, "New Acquisition: Works by Mariana Castillo Deball | Unframed," https://unframed.lacma.org/2017/05/03/new-acquisition-works-mariana-castillo-deball.

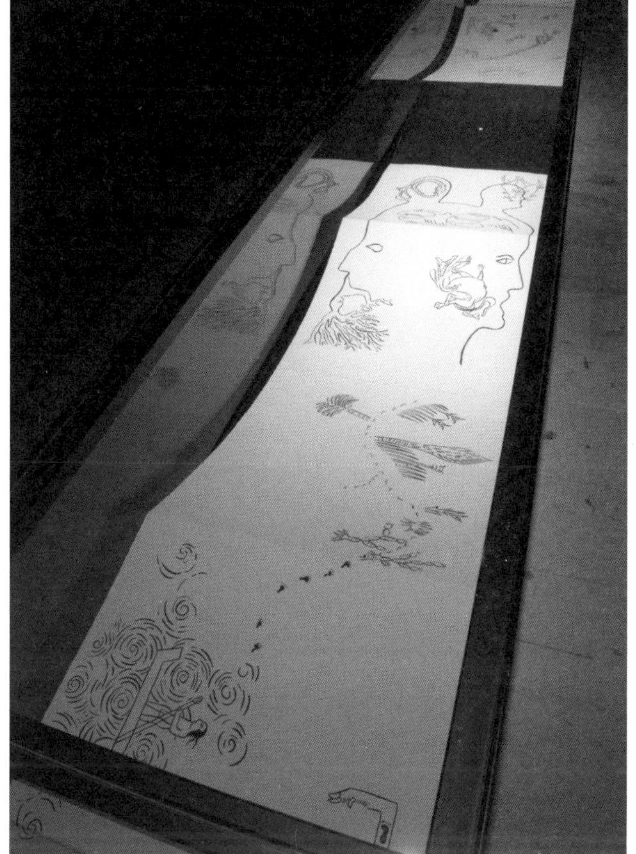

The "Where I am" is vanishing, 2011, ink on cotton paper, 100 × 40 cm, 2011, 54th Venice Biennale, ILLUMinations

lost in the process of archaeological recovery, and who has shaped the fragmentary nature of the past? How can we fill in the gaps and erasures in a culturally responsive and ethical way? In the empty fields, Castillo Deball acknowledges the indeterminable nature of uncovering and restoring the pre-Columbian visual and material archive.

The site of Quiriguá entered the Western visual imagination with illustrations by English artist Frederick Catherwood for the publication *Incidents of Travel in Central America, Chiapas, and Yucatan.*[15] The images and descriptions published in this book inspired English archaeologist[16] Alfred Maudslay to visit Mexico and Central America seven times between 1881 and 1895 with the goal of expanding British and European knowledge of the pre-Columbian world. Using a combination of photography, paper squeezes, drawings, and plaster casts, Maudslay embarked on one of the most extensive recording exercises of pre-Columbian artworks in the nineteenth century. According to photographic historian Duncan Shields, "By employing the most advanced techniques of the day for archaeological work, including photography, plaster casts, and exploratory trenches, some for the first time in a Central American archaeological site, Maudslay made the first empirically detailed study of the ruins of the Maya."[17] His work has culminated in the collection of over eight hundred photographs,[18] and over four hundred plaster casts in museums such as the Victoria and Albert Museum (V&A), the British Museum, and the Museum of Archaeology and Anthropology at Cambridge University. He published the majority of his findings in his eight-volume (four volumes of texts and four volumes of plates) *Biologia Centrali-americana: Or, Contributions to the Knowledge of the Fauna and Flora of Mexico and Central America Archaeology.*[19] Maudslay's importance has recently come to the fore, as perhaps best exemplified by a collaboration between the

15 Looper, 2.

16 Although Maudslay dismisses Catherwood's drawings as "rough sketches of two of the monoliths," it must have been enough to whet his appetite. Alfred Percival Maudslay, *Biologia Centrali-Americana: Or, Contributions to the Knowledge of the Fauna and Flora of Mexico and Central America Archaeology*, ed. F. Ducane Godman and Osbert Salvin, vol. 2 (London: R. H. Porter and Dulau & Co., 1889), 1.

17 Duncan Shields, "Multiple Collections and Fluid Meanings: Alfred Maudslay's Archaeological Photographs at the British Museum," in *Photographs, Museums, Collections: Between Art and Information*, ed. Elizabeth Edwards and Christopher Morton (New York: Bloomsbury, 2015), 33–34.

18 Shields, 28.

19 Alfred Percival Maudslay, *Biologia Centrali-Americana: Or, Contributions to the Knowledge of the Fauna and Flora of Mexico and Central America Archaeology*, ed. F. Duncane Godman and Osbert Salvin, 4 vols. (London: R. H. Porter and Dulau & Co., 1889).

British Museum and Google Arts and Culture that made possible the 3D digitization of his casts and paper squeezes.[20]

According to Maudslay's entry on Quiriguá in Volume II of *Biologia Centrali-Americana*, this Maya site was the first that he had ever visited, and it "induced [him] to take a permanent interest in Central-American Archaeology, and a journey which was undertaken merely to escape the rigours [sic] of an English winter has been followed by seven expeditions from England for the purpose of further exploration and archaeological research."[21] He returned in 1882 to complete a photographic study of the site, and in 1883, he embarked on his most ambitious project at Quiriguá. This included a topographical survey of the site by Charles Blockley, and creating plaster casts of the important monuments by Lorenzo Giuntini, one of the foremost cast-makers in England. According to Maudslay's account, Giuntini's rendition of Zoomorph P, then known as "the Great Turtle," required over two tons of plaster to create six hundred molds.[22] These molds would have had to dry, be carefully packed and carried back to the port of Yzabal, before being loaded onto a ship and hauled back to England. Maudslay describes how "The work of packing and transporting the moulds to the port was one of even greater difficulty than bringing the material, for there were over a thousand pieces of plaster moulding of all shapes and sizes with delicate points and edges which had to be protected from the slightest jar, and large paper moulds, some of which measured nearly five feet square."[23]

The plaster molds from the 1883 expedition arrived safely in England (unlike the unfortunate paper molds from the following year),[24] and Giuntini reassembled the six-hundred-piece molds to create multiple copies of the Zoomorph P.[25] In 1884, one of the plaster versions was presented to the newly opened Museum of Archaeology and Anthropology (MAA) at Cambridge, from which Maudslay had graduated in 1872. A second plaster cast of Zoomorph P was on

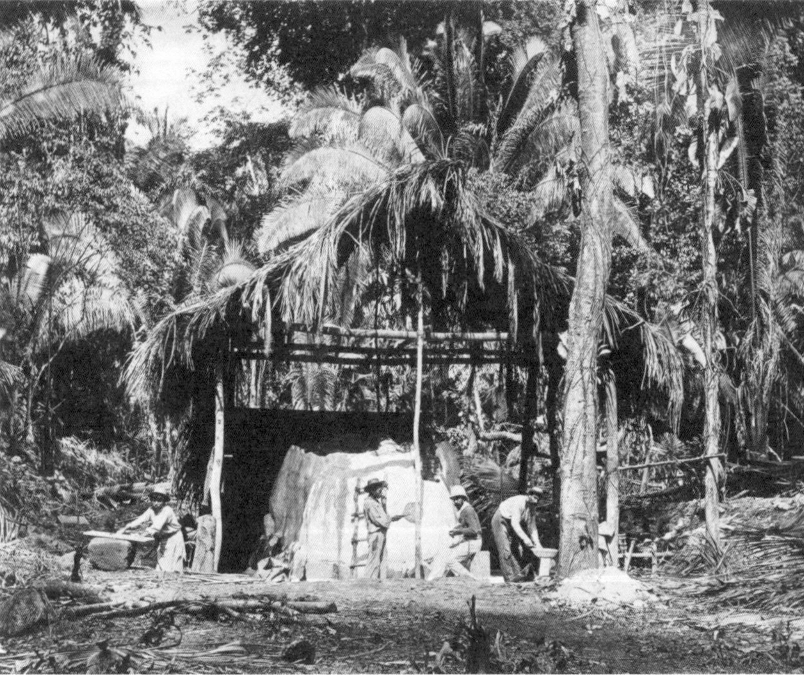

Alfred Percival Maudslay and assistants making a cast of Earth Monster under a thatched shelter, Quiriguá, Guatemala, 1883. Black-and-white photograph, 20.5×25.5 cm

20 Chance Coughenour and Jago Cooper, "The British Museum and Google Arts & Culture: Decoding the Secrets of the Ancient Maya," Google, November 29, 2017, https://blog.google/outreach-initiatives/arts-culture/british-museum-and-google-arts-culture-decoding-secrets-ancient-maya/.

21 Maudslay, *Biologia Centrali-Americana*, 1889, 2:2.

22 Maudslay, 2:3.

23 Anne Cary Morris Maudslay and Alfred Percival Maudslay, *A Glimpse at Guatemala, and Some Notes on the Ancient Monuments of Central America* (Detroit: B. Ethridge-Books, 1979), 150.

24 Maudslay, *Biologia Centrali-Americana*, 1889, 2:4.

25 Jody Joy and Mark Elliott, "Cast aside or Cast in a New Light? The Maudslay Replica Maya Casts at the Museum of Archaeology and Anthropology, Cambridge," in *Authenticity and Cultural Heritage in the Age of 3D Digital Reproductions*, ed. Paola Di Giuseppantonio Di Franco, Fabrizio Galeazzi, and Valentina Vassallo (McDonald Institute, 2018), 14, https://doi.org/10.17863/CAM.27029.

display at South Kensington Museum (later known as the V&A) by **1894**.[26] A comparison of the installation of the plaster-cast replicas of Zoomorph P reveal the range of meanings and importance depending on the institution. At the MAA at Cambridge, the plaster cast was warmly received and considered a centerpiece of the museum's installation from the beginning. The importance of the cast became even more evident in the architectural plans for the new museum at Downing Street. Opened in **1913**, the entire layout was designed with the cast of Zoomorph P at the center of the first floor and an open railing on the second floor that permitted that "the enormous zoomorphic sculptured rock could be seen from every angle from the mezzanine above."[27] Meanwhile, Maudslay proposed a bequest to the South Kensington Museum of all the plaster casts and paper molds in **1885**,[28] only to have them temporarily displayed, sent to storage, and then transferred less than ten years later to the British Museum, as "the British Museum [was] the more appropriate place for the Collection, and it was [his] intention, in the first instance, to have offered the Collection for acceptance of the Trustees of the British Museum,"[29] but Maudslay refused because they required that the casts remain in the basement.

26 Sarah McGowan, "Alfred Percival Maudslay and the V&A," *V&A Blog* (blog), July **6**, **2015**, https://www.vam.ac.uk/blog/caring-for-our-collections/alfred-percival-maudslay-and-the-va.

27 Joy and Elliott, **15**.

28 Cecil Smith, "Minute Paper: Maudslay Collection. Question of Housing for British Museum Collections of Casts of Central American Sculptures," August **31**, **1885**, MA/1/M**1294**/s; Maudslay, A.P. (Bequest); Part **2**: **1902**–**1922**, BM/V&A Archives.

29 Alfred P. Maudslay, "Letter to Edward Maunde Thompson, Director of the South Kensington Museum, Science and Art Department," September **12**, **1893**, MA/1/M**1294**/1; Maudslay, A.P. (Bequest); Part **1**: **1885**–**1897**), Victoria & Albert Museum Archives.

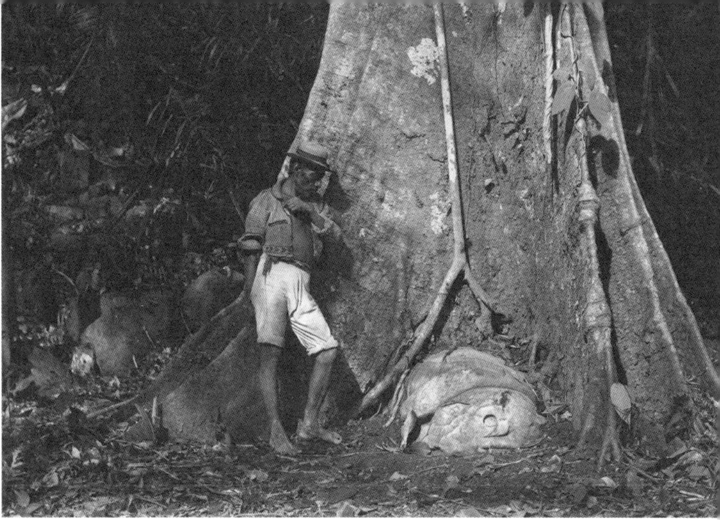

Alfred Percival Maudslay, at Monument N, near the eastern border of the Great Plaza, Quiriguá, Guatemala, **1894**. Black-and-white photograph, **15**×**21** cm.

Though there is much back-and-forth in the archive over the transfer of the collection, it nevertheless becomes clear that neither institution valued the collection as highly as Maudslay had anticipated.

At both the MAA at Cambridge and the British Museum, Maudslay did receive the honor of having halls or rooms named after him. While Maudslay's impact on the history of Maya epigraphy and archaeology is undeniable, he certainly did not accomplish the work on his own. Too often, the indigenous and mestizo workers who executed most of the work of the plaster casts remain unacknowledged or unknown. The work was challenging from the beginning, as Maudslay himself acknowledges, in that "All provisions and all materials for the work, including such things as photographic dry-plates, moulding-paper, lime, oil, and nearly four tons of plaster, had to be carried in small quantities, sometimes on mules, but more usually on men's backs, from the port of Yzabal, about **24** miles distant, over a range of hills, along a track which proved almost impassable in bad weather."[30] After hauling in the materials, the laborers had to clear

30 Maudslay and Maudslay, **150**.

the dense foliage; set-up, clean, and maintain the camp; and facilitate the paper squeeze and cast production, including building scaffolds, keeping fires, and preparing materials. Workers often suffered from illnesses or ran away to their homes, and Maudslay even describes the experience of managing the laborers as "pure slave-driving."[31] While they remain nameless in Maudslay's written accounts, these men appear in many of his photographs, for Maudslay was unique at the time for capturing an excavation site as part of his documentation.[32] While Maudslay often complains of these workers and berates them in his accounts, how can scholars and artists today use these indications of men in written word and photographic evidence to tell their story? What are ways of recuperating these lives and shedding light on the dark underbelly of archaeology as a colonial and unfortunately exploitative enterprise? One way is by reading these images and texts against the grain and by creating artwork that encourages a deep provocation of archaeology as a field. Castillo Deball's repertoire is an important contribution to this process of opening up and unpacking the baggage of the archaeological project.

One of Maudslay's trusted friends who does appear named in text and image is Gorgonio Lopez, who would eventually become an important intermediary and ally for Maudslay. It was typically Gorgonio who Maudslay sent to scout potential areas and sites, create the paper squeezes, retrieve original sculptures from Yaxchilan in 1886,[33] and recruit and oversee the laborers. Though Lopez often remains overlooked in later scholarship on Maudslay, from the archival records, it is clear that he was an astute negotiator, able navigator, and skilled craftsman. In his acknowledgement section in *A Glimpse of Guatemala*, Maudslay writes, "In conclusion, I am glad to express my acknowledgement for the good services rendered to me by the companions in my travels, the men of the Lopez family, and especially my friend Gorgonio, whose gentle manners and sweet disposition helped to smooth over many a bad half-hour during my earlier expeditions, and whose ceaseless vigilance over the welfare of my wife during our last journey did so much to lessen for her the discomforts of camp-life."[34] Maudslay invited Lopez to England in 1891,[35] and in 1892, encouraged the special commissioner to Guatemala, Federico Arthes, to hire Lopez to make casts of Seibal for the Guatemalan exhibit at the Chicago World's Fair.[36] While Maudslay pays tribute to Lopez and connects him to a broader world of opportunity, he does not extend this collegiality to the majority of the workers who help him achieve his own success.

As a contemporary artist deeply committed to the history of archaeology, particularly in Mexico and Central America, Castillo Deball has done extensive research on Maudslay's work. In the summer of 2012, she traveled to the British Museum to view the paper squeezes and plaster casts,[37] and that visit inspired the display conventions of the triangulated metal racks that later

31 Ian Graham, *Alfred Maudslay and the Maya: A Biography* (Norman: University of Oklahoma Press, 2002), 115.

32 Shields, 34.

33 Carolyn E. Tate, *Yaxchilan: The Design of a Maya Ceremonial City* (Austin University of Texas Press, 2013), 167.

34 Maudslay and Maudslay, xi.

35 Graham, 234.

36 "Corpus of Maya Hieroglyphic Inscriptions," https://www.peabody.harvard.edu/cmhi/site.php?site=Seibal; Graham, 195–96.

37 Castillo Deball, *What we caught we threw away, what we didn't catch we kept.*

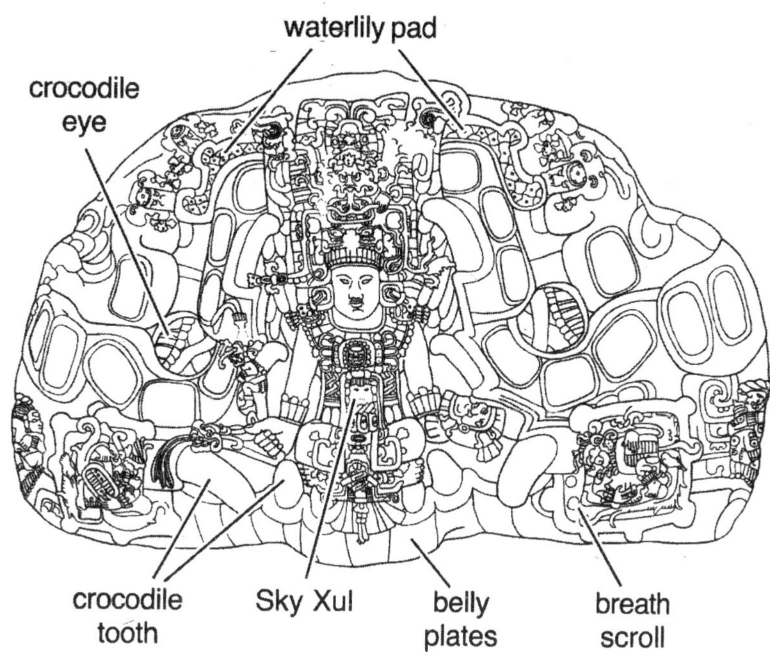

Matthew Looper, Line Drawing of Zoomorph P north, © FAMSI, 2001

appear in her installations, including *You have time to show yourself before other eyes* (2014). Castillo Deball incorporated photographs of Maudslay himself and some taken by him in the exhibition *What we caught we threw away, what we didn't we kept* (2013).[38] In addition to the shape of *Zoomorph P* deriving from Giuntini's six hundred-piece mould, Castillo Deball was also inspired to carve a piece of wood because of a photograph where you see a sculpture "trapped below the roots of a tree"[39]. In both form and material, she created *Zoomorph P* as a response to impressions and images guided by Maudslay's vision.

When *Zoomorph P* is inked and rolled across a horizontal sheet of paper, the sculpture becomes a stamp and the print becomes almost an inverse line drawing. In thinking about the range of archaeological tools and visual practices, the line drawing is one of the most prevalent strategies for translating the complex iconography of an uneven three-dimensional surface into a two-dimensional plane. A line drawing flattens the curvatures, brings clarity to sections hidden in shadow, and tentatively repairs broken sections. Its monochromatic palette and simple tools lend an accessibility and legibility, and it is easily reproducible across all types of publications. Castillo Deball relied upon line drawings of the Zoomorph P, including those published by Matthew Looper in *Quiriguá: A Guide to an Ancient Maya City*.[40] Though she could not carve the entire iconograph program of the monumental sculpture, she used Looper's line drawings to reproduce the most salient aspects, as mentioned before. By coating *Zoomorph P* with black ink and moving it across the white paper, Castillo Deball creates an artwork where the black lines become white absences, and in turn, the blank paper becomes coated in black. Though this is common practice and expectation in printmaking, when placed within

38 For an exhibition checklist that includes details on which photographs were included, see the: "Mariana Castillo Deball at Chisenhale 24 May–14 July 2013," Exhibition Handout, 2013, https://chisenhale.org.uk/wp-content/uploads/Mariana-Castillo-Deball_Exhibition-Handout.pdf.

39 Reynolds-Kaye and Castillo Deball, discussion.

40 Looper, *Quiriguá*.

the context of the archaeological line drawing, the tonal reversal feels like a gentle questioning to this tried-and-true method of capturing visual information. The fragmentary nature of the carved imagery also lends itself to a sense of both a making and an unmaking, or perhaps a transference of knowledge that is always already partial.

Throughout her work, Castillo Deball is perpetually experimenting with the materials and methodologies of archaeology in new and complex ways. In this one investigation into the history of the Zoomorph P at Quiriguá, she opens onto the original purpose of the objects, its iconographic program, and its nineteenth-century reinterpretations. The legacy of Alfred Maudslay, Lorenzo Giuntini, Gorgonio Lopez, and the dozens of once-known laborers is felt through the hands-on nature of the sculpted briar root and its rolled out manifestations on paper. Similarly, Castillo Deball's connection to clay stamps, codices, and sculptural ingenuity links her practice to the Classic Maya and other pre-Columbian civilizations who drew upon these technologies. And while the visual archive and material record remains forever incomplete, the artistic interventions by Castillo Deball invite subtle provocations of the relationship between the past, present, and the intermediaries in between.

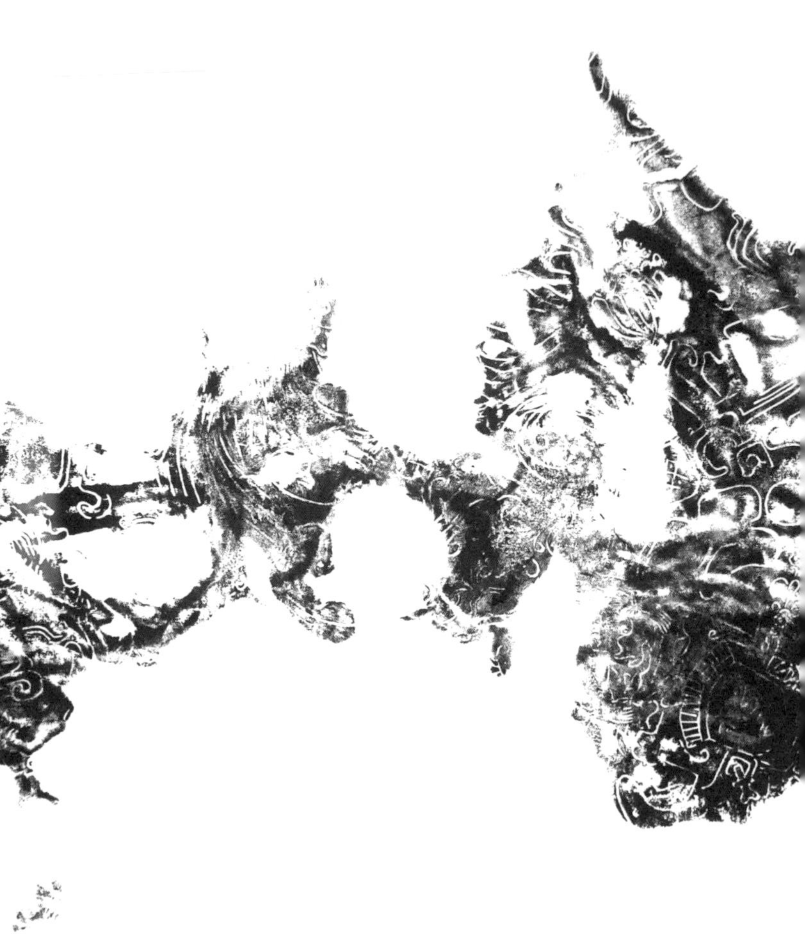

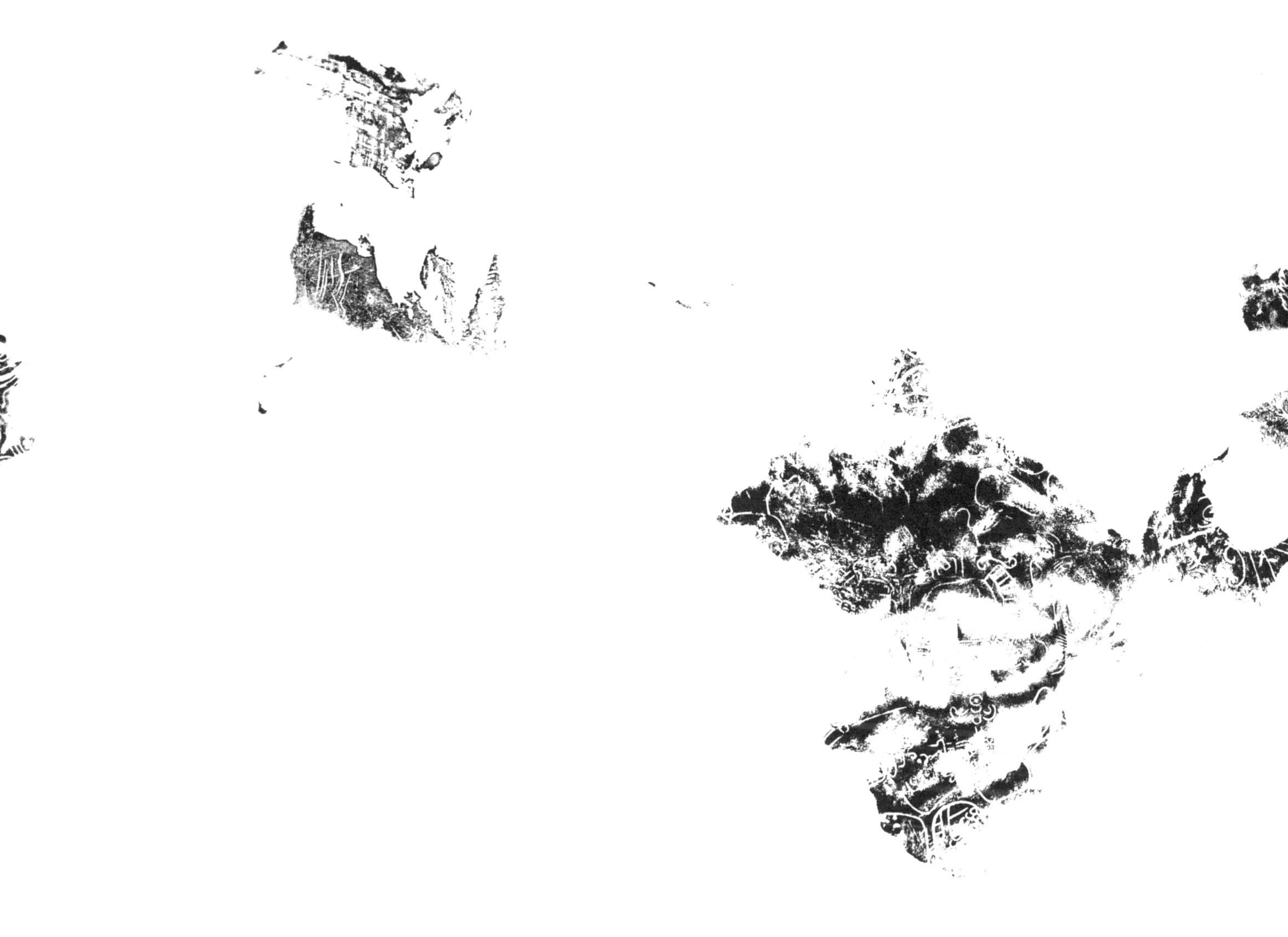

Imprint Zoomorph P, **2013**, woodcut print on cotton paper, **240×55** cm

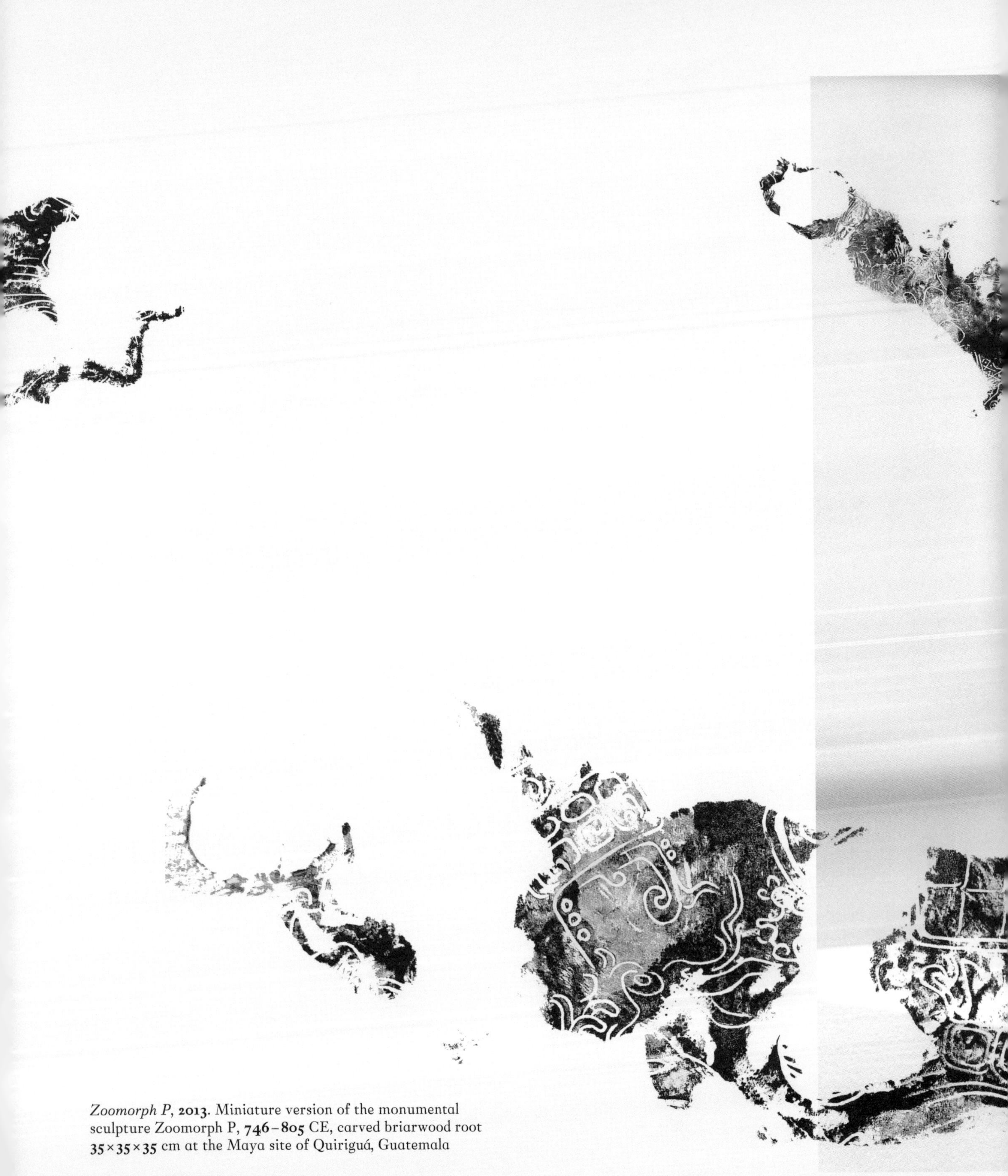

Zoomorph P, **2013**. Miniature version of the monumental sculpture Zoomorph P, **746–805** CE, carved briarwood root **35×35×35** cm at the Maya site of Quiriguá, Guatemala

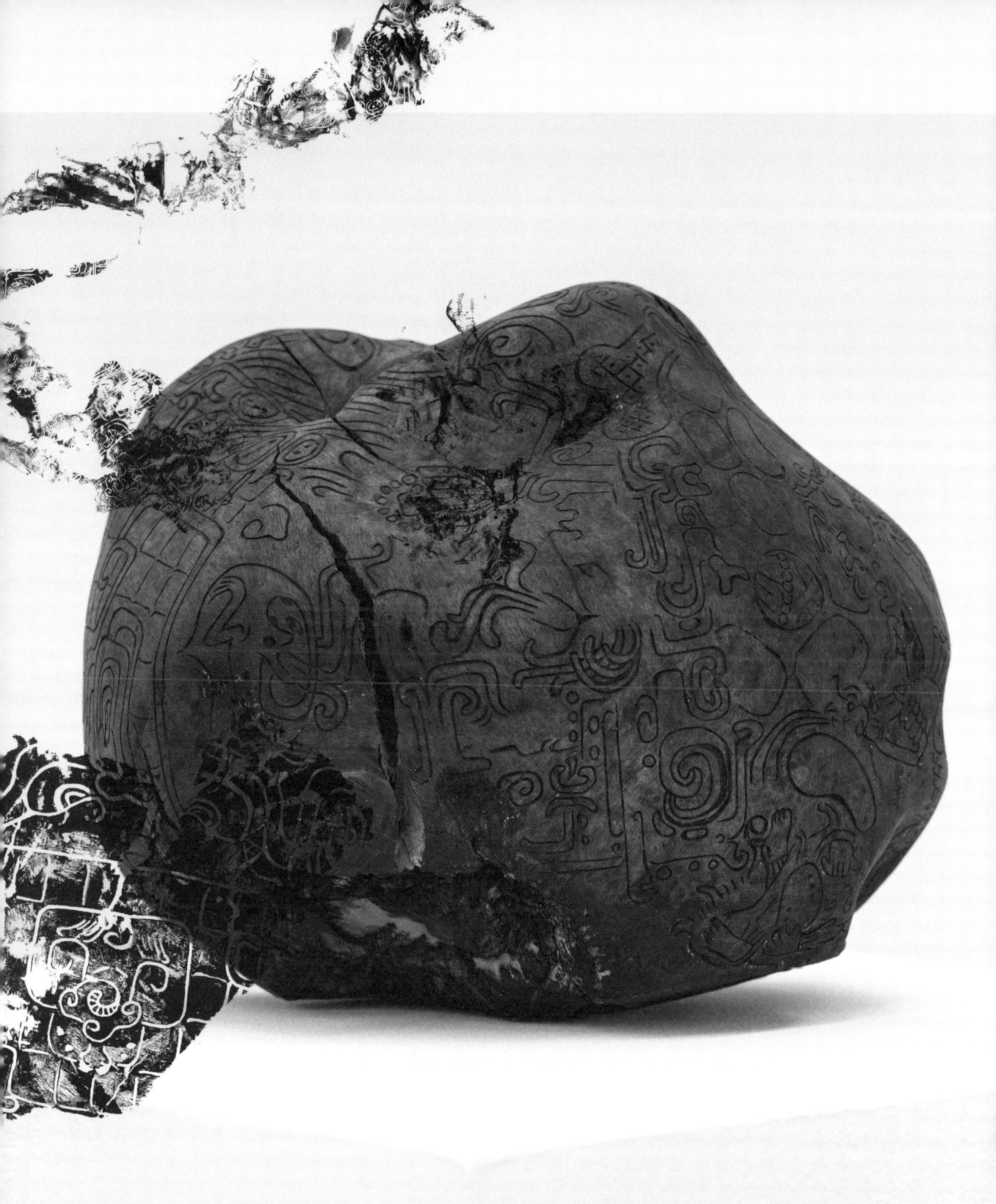